THE DIRECTOR AS ARTIST
Play Direction Today

THE DIRECTOR AS ARTIST
Play Direction Today

R.H. O'Neill
Loyola University, New Orleans

and
N.M. Boretz

HOLT, RINEHART AND WINSTON
New York   Chicago   San Francisco   Philadelphia
Montreal   Toronto   London   Sydney
Tokyo   Mexico City   Rio de Janeiro   Madrid

This book is dedicated to

Richard Patrick O'Neill
Rosary and Stephen Hartel
Sarah and Joseph Messinger

and my children

Rachelle, Barret,
Rory, and Dale

Cover photograph:
The late director Alan Schneider
directing at Stanford University, CA.

Library of Congress Cataloging-in-Publication Data

O'Neill, R. H.
  The director as artist.

  Bibliography: p.
  Includes index.
  1. Theater—Production and direction. I. Boretz,
N. M. II. Title.
PN2053.044   1987   792'.0233   86-33520

ISBN 0-03-064146-2

Holt, Rinehart and Winston
The Dryden Press
Saunders College Publishing

Preface

Directing is a relatively recent phenomenon. There is no set, time-honored tradition dissecting and standardizing the art of directing, or the teaching of directing, as there is for, say, dramatic literature. The oral tradition has been handed down through the centuries; the written tradition is only several decades old. To formalize the actual "hands-on" process and problems of directing is, therefore, a fairly unique occurrence in the world of print—and this is just what *The Director as Artist* starts out to do. This text offers a problem-solving, actor-centered approach to the art of directing. It is organized around the myriad responsibilities and problems facing the contemporary director, who must oversee the entire theater production. Through an exploration of the depth and breadth of the director's education as an artist, the book isolates, identifies, and tests options to resolve dilemmas the director actually confronts in the range of roles he or she performs as actor, coach, manager, interpreter, historian, designer, administrator, critic, and analyst. Supported by interviews with over seventy-five professional directors, it synthesizes valuable information that effective directors have implemented in their productions, clarifying instinctual principles these directors employ so that they can then be applied to the work of the novice director.

Few directors work in ideal situations. Inexperienced directors frequently believe that 1) learning to direct is a reasonably logical process; 2) that they will always have a supporting staff of technical professionals and acquiescent assistants to handle all practical matters outside the rehearsal hall; 3) and that director, cast, and crew will be full-time, paid professionals who are available for extensive rehearsal and production schedules. *The Director as Artist* attempts to dispel such common misapprehensions and to shed light on the actual directing process and on the role contemporary directors play.

Most directors today will eventually work in colleges, universities, theater organizations affiliated with academic institutions; possibly regional, semi-professional, or volunteer community-arts groups; or public and private secondary schools. Few will direct on Broadway—not for lack of talent, but because the focus of theater in the United States has decentralized to many other areas. Resumés of even the most commercially successful directors today list teaching or visiting-artist positions in universities with resident companies, and prestigious college degrees in theater arts.

The Director as Artist introduces essential principles and procedures for excelling in today's directing world. Each of the book's eleven chapters suggests methods for putting theoretical resources into action. Chapter 1 provides an overview of the theory and mechanics of the director's work as stager and serves as a foundation for examining the artistic functions of the director. No matter how brilliant the direction, if the director cannot assist others to execute it, all insight is wasted. Chapters 2–11 examine the other significant roles of the director as critic, analyst, interpreter, historian, designer, actor, coach, manager, audience, and administrator, and include countless details often taken for granted, the small blocks from which a solid production is built. The sequencing of these chapters follows the plan of action many directors take. Three of these chapters (7–9) are devoted to the most significant and potentially difficult task of directing: working with actors. They concentrate on problems in rehearsal and suggest ways of working alongside actors to maximize their performance.

Each chapter includes exercises; and several problem/solution features, set apart from the text, deal with typical dilemmas directors might encounter in each specific role. At the end of each chapter are several longer or final projects that augment theory with practical assignments. The text concludes with a glossary of technical terms and a bibliography of sources for further study.

The Director as Artist provides fundamental theory and specific techniques for application in both classroom and production situations. It will be of particular use to the many young directors involved in nonprofit or college theater, where extensive work in many disciplines is required. It will help them 1) value their roles as critic, analyst, and interpreter in examining the play on several aesthetic levels; 2) understand their roles as historian and designer so they can grasp not only how plot and character elements explain an action, but its visual context within a historical time

and place; 3) acquire the artistic objectivity to respond to their own production as if they themselves were the audience; and 4) develop their skills as administrator since creativity and artistic concerns can be severely damaged by organizational inefficiency. Primarily intended for use in an initial undergraduate course in directing, *The Director as Artist* will, it is hoped, provide a continuing resource for staging challenging productions when novice directors begin to operate completely on their own.

Acknowledgments

No project that consumes five years of one's life can be completed without the assistance of numerous individuals. Though the list that follows is by no means complete, it is indicative of the many people who helped bring the book to fruition.

Hundreds of hours of interviews were conducted with many directors and other theater professionals throughout the country. Though not all sources are quoted in the book itself, all interviews provided background for its direction. Heartfelt thanks are extended to the following, who contributed enormously through their comments:

JULES AARON   Director, California Institute of the Arts, Valencia

SHELDON APTEKAR   Professor of Theater, Kingsborough Community College, New York.

CLIFF BAKER   Artistic Director, Arkansas Rep., Little Rock

PAUL BAKER   Stage director, Dallas, TX

ALBERT BERMEL   Professor of Theater, Herbert H. Lehman College of the City University of New York.

JOHN BETTENBENDER   Dean, Mason

Gross School of the Arts, Rutgers University, NJ

NED BOBKOFF Director of Theater, Dowling College, Oakdale, NY

UMBERTO BONSIGNORI Film director, theatrical and television films, New York

STORER BOONE Director, Beverly Dinner Theatre, New Orleans

DONALD BORCHARDT Professor, Rutgers University, Newark, NJ

ROB BUNDY Staff Repertory Director, The Acting Company, NY

JOSEPH CHAIKIN Professional director, NY

WAYNE CHAPMAN Director, University of Arkansas, Little Rock

KELSEY COLLIE Director, Howard University, Washington, DC

PAUL ANTOINE DISTLER Director, Division of Performing Arts, Virginia Polytechnic, Blacksburg

CHERYL DOWNEY Film director, Los Angeles

MARTIN ESSLIN Professor of Drama, Stanford University, CA, and Andrew Mellon Professor at Tulane University, New Orleans

ZELDA FICHANDLER Producing Director, Arena Theatre, Washington, D.C.; and Director/Professional Actor Training Program, New York University

ALLEN FLETCHER Artistic Director, Denver Theatre Center

BILL FLYNN Director of Theater, Mercer County Community College, NJ

ROGER FOX British American Theatre Institute, Santa Fe, NM

COLEMAN FREEMAN Director, University of Oklahoma, Norman

MICHAEL GERLECH Director, Texas Tech University, Lubbock

PATTI GILLESPIE Chairman, Department of Communication Arts and Theater, University of Maryland, College Park

EARL GISTER Associate Dean, Yale School of Drama

KENT GRAVITT Professional director, Los Angeles

RON GURAL Chairman, Tulane University, Drama Department, New Orleans

CLIFF HAISLIP Director, University of Arkansas, Little Rock

JAMES HARBOR Director, Goodman Theater, Chicago

TED HERSTAND Chairman, Theater Department, University of Oklahoma, Norman

TED HOFFMAN Chairman, Theater Department, New York University

PAUL HOSTETLER Director, University of Washington, Seattle

JANICE HUTCHINS Director, American Conservatory Theater, San Francisco

LEON KATZ Cochairman, Department of Drama and Dramatic Criticism, Yale School of Drama

ERIC KREBS Managing director, George Street Playhouse, New Brunswick, NJ

JEROME LAWRENCE Playwright, director, and teacher, Los Angeles

PETER LAYTON Professional director and founder of the Drama Studio, London, England, and Berkeley, California

EUGENE LEE Actor, Negro Ensemble Company

JAMES LEE Chairman, Theater Department, Connecticut College, New London

JIM LEVERT Director, actor, and producer, Los Angeles

MONROE LIPPMAN Professor Emeritus, University of California, Riverside

RUTH LYONS Director, Southern Illinois University, Carbondale

Tom Markus   Director, Yale University

Marshall W. Mason   Artistic director, Circle Rep., NY

Jack McCullough   Director, Trenton State University, NJ

Pat Miller   Producing director, Chocolate Bayou Theatre Company, Houston

Pamela Nice   Director, Gustavus Adolphus College, Minneapolis

James Nicholson   Director, Boston University

Natasha Ogoi   Director, Moscow, USSR

Ron O'Leary   Associate professor and director, University of Maryland, College Park

Vicky Ooi   Professor, University of Hong Kong.

Arthur Penn   Film and stage director, NY

Peter Robinson   Professional director, Los Angeles.

Richard Schechner   Professional director and professor, New York University

Alan Schneider   Professional director, NY, and Head, Graduate Director, Training Program, University of California, San Diego

Rolf Stahl   Director, Berlin, Germany

Ted Swindley   Artistic director, Stages, Houston

Megan Terry   Playwright and director, Omaha Magic Theatre, NE

Frederick Tollini S.J.   Chairman, Department of Theater Arts, University of Santa Clara, CA

Joe Totaro   Associate professor and head of the acting program, University of Maryland, College Park

Arthur Wagner   Head, Graduate Actor Training Program, University of California, San Diego

Ronald Wainscott   Director, Towson State College, Baltimore

Stan Wojewodski   Artistic director, Center Stage, Baltimore

Bryna Wortman   Director, Circle Rep., NY

Garland Wright   Director, Guthrie Theatre, Minneapolis

In addition, many colleagues reviewed the manuscript along the way, providing valuable suggestions and thorough advice: Lee Adey, University of Minnesota—Twin Cities; Edward Amor, University of Wisconsin—Madison; Vincent Angotti, University of Evansville; Milly Barranger, University of North Carolina; Linda Burson, University of Kentucky (most recently of Beloit College); Walter Esselinck, University of Michigan; Arthur C. Greene Jr., University of Virginia; John Herr, University of Connecticut; Theodore Herstand, University of Oklahoma; Stanley Longman, University of Georgia; Richard Palmer, College of William and Mary; and Norman Welch, University of California—Los Angeles. Special thanks are extended to William Raffeld, University of Illinois at Chicago, for his thorough, detailed, insightful criticism and comments provided over an extended period of time.

Thanks are also due Ernest Ferlita, S.J., Chairman of Loyola University's (New Orleans) Drama and Speech Department, as well as Don Brady, Bob Fleshman, Herb Sayas, Alex Gonzales, and Larry Warner. Dean William W. Eidson, Vice President George Lundy, and former Vice President for Academic Affairs Robert Preston provided the assistance necessary for the mounting of this complex project.

This book was supported, in part, by the

Academic Grant Fund of Loyola University, New Orleans.

In addition to her contribution as writer, Professor Boretz was responsible for researching the book's many photographs, which create an organic connection between text and image. This interweaving of text and illustrations coincided with the writing of the text over a period of years.

Grateful acknowledgment is made to those who contributed charts and illustrations: Ronald Wainscott, Paul Hostetler, and the Society of Stage Directors and Choreographers.

Holt, Rinehart and Winston provided a steadying hand during the preparation of the final manuscript: Karen Dubno and Anne Boynton-Trigg gave valuable advice throughout the developmental process. Kathleen Nevils, Herman Makler, and Jon Blake provided expert assistance.

Other important individuals include Mary Ann Morrison, whose consistently intelligent critical contributions expanded the clarity and progressiveness of the book, and Elaine Partnow. Also, many people assisted in the typing of the manuscript: the staff at Kinko's on Carrollton Avenue, Patrick Shannon, and Maureen Mitchell.

Fundamentally, the director functions as a leader, and these acknowledgments would not be complete without mentioning several influential leaders, including Monroe Lippman, Arthur, Wagner, and Werner Erhard.

Contents

Chapter 9
The Director as Manager
Coordinating the Ensemble 243

Chapter 10
The Director as Audience
Evaluating the Production
Objectively 278

Chapter 11
The Director as
Administrator
Organizing the Production 295

Table of Problem/Solutions

Chapter **8**

The Director as Coach

Chapter **9**

The Director as Manager

Chapter **10**
The Director as Audience

Chapter **11**
The Director as Administrator

Chapter **1**

The Director as Stager
Understanding Staging Techniques

This green plot shall be our stage, this hawthornbrake our tiring-house.
A Midsummer Night's Dream (Act III; scene i)

The role of the director, of one who guides, orders, and manages every aspect of a theater production, begins with the mastery of certain fundamentals. There are two aspects to directing. One is the capacity for vision of the experience and the second is the craft for achieving it. How to enhance the first aspect, the director's capacity for vision, will be covered in chapters 2 through 11 of this book. This chapter contains the rudimentary, "nuts-and-bolts" information needed to serve as the basic groundwork. We will first examine the techniques of directing as a mechanical operation, and then follow with accounts of the multiple functions of the director as artist, critic, analyst, interpreter, historian, designer, actor, coach, manager, audience, and administrator.

This chapter explores techniques for manipulating the stage and its components. It begins with a short history of the escalating importance of staging in the art of direction, and then analyzes the two chief components of any staging: composition and picturization. Suggestions for handling problem sequences, like crowds or violent scenes, conclude the chapter.

EVOLUTION OF STAGING TECHNIQUES AND DIRECTING

The role of the director as stager is a contemporary phenomenon, developing only within the past 100 years. Prior to the mid-nineteenth century, productions were staged haphazardly. Though many artists (often actors) functioned as managers, no one held the central position, separate and apart from the company, as director. Claiming center stage, lead actors performed their roles according to their whims regardless

1

of where or with whom they played. Lesser actors withdrew to the back of the stage at a distance from the leads. The audience went to see a star's performance, not a director's conception of a production. Costumes and sets that were chosen were often anachronistic. Actors dressed to make themselves appear their most attractive; and standard stock scenery (outdoor, indoor, marketplace sets, and the like) was randomly used. So plays as diverse as Shakespeare's *Macbeth* and Alexandre Dumas's *Camille* could employ the same settings and costumes at very different performances. The audience, hungry to see a thrilling interpretation by a specific star, could care less about any such breach in verisimilitude. Visual continuity in the production was not valued, and most plays were staged in just a few days time.

Then, in 1866, a change occurred. The Duke of Saxe-Meiningen, perhaps our first director, dedicating his troupe to theatrical art, began to *direct* his players. Meiningen paid close attention to the movement actors made within the stage space. For example, he would work for hours with each member of a crowd scene, developing the conception of each participant. He committed himself to shaping the authenticity of the entire production. Influenced by Saxe-Meiningen, Konstantin Stanislavski expanded the function of the director and raised his structuring of a playscript to the level of art. The Russian director's rehearsals would sometimes span a year or more, during which time he would painstakingly work on each detail of a production, creating the most meaningful staging and service to the play at hand.

In the twentieth century, the emphasis on detail initiated by Stanislavski and spurred on by the births of film and television has increased the importance of the role of the director as coordinator. Contemporary directors function as the unifying element of productions. They are responsible not only for the artistic interpretation of the ensemble but for the impact of the many highly technical elements in stagecraft, sound, and special effects. Rarely do productions *not* have a director.

COMPOSITION AND PICTURIZATION

Directing a play requires a mastery of staging techniques which will influence the stage/audience relationship by developing within a director an ability to compose and give meaning to significant groupings onstage. *Composition* is the physical arrangement of actors with, or to, each other within a stage space. *Picturization* is the meaning that is being suggested through that arrangement. Picturization grows out of the organic life of the scene. (Note the picturization of a broken universe suggested here in this production shot of *Antigone*.) Of course, the director moves the characters or objects around to create new arrangements, and consequently, new meanings. Normally called "leading the eye," strong and aesthetically pleasing compositions will take the audience's eye from picture to picture.

Picturization: the meaning *suggested* by scenic design and the arrangement of figures: a broken universe.

Antigone by Jean Anouilh. Department of Theater, Loyola Marymount University. Director: Judith Royer, C.S.J. Designer: Howard Reed. Photo: Howard Reed.

Transforming a script into a series of three-dimensional groupings requires the skill to envision the impact of certain choices in composition and picturization as you plan and *mount* a production.

> I find as a director, I can't resist certain kinds of visual images to do with the actor. If there's any play I want to do very much, a visual counterpart exists in me that imagines the figures of the characters at particular moments. To dream the play in terms of imagery is a necessary activity of mind I have to both guide the actor to and avoid the actor from simply embodying my images.
>
> (Joseph Chaikin, director)

A script must be transformed into living actors—in costume, under lights, on specific parts of the stage.

A knowledge of composition and picturization facilitates the work of directors much like a knowledge of anatomy facilitates that of doctors. Understanding the anatomy of composition and picturization is prerequisite to heathfully serving the "body" (theater production).

Unfortunately, composition and picturization are often given either an undue importance, as if they were the only aspect of directing (whole texts have been devoted exclusively to composition) or no importance at all (some books on theater criticism disregard the tangible nature of the stage). Beginning directors sometimes underestimate the value of the techniques of composition and picturization, particularly if these directors have previously worked with a masterful director who "appears" to have ignored these techniques. In reality, such experts more than likely function intuitively from an already acquired command of techniques.

Although the entire production tells the story, good directors must realize that composition and picturization serve to *seamlessly* support its unfolding. As storytellers, directors shape the presentation of the events within a play, planning and implementing their artistic choices—their major contribution being the way each artist, because of experience, sees, interprets, relates, and communicates the sequence of happenings in the play. "But each for the joy of working, and each in his separate star, shall draw the thing as he sees it, for the God of things as they are" (Rudyard Kipling, *When Earth's Last Picture Is Painted,* 1892).

Each element the performers interact with: the space, time, event, and/or silence, elucidates one aspect of the story and is enhanced or diminished by composition and picturization. As directors, you work with a moving arrangement of actors relating to each other and to all fixed and changing facets in the production. Your goal is clarification, because ". . . the great artist is the simplifier" (H.F. Amiel, November 25, 1861). To do this, you must know the principles of composition, including: the types of stages, kinds of emphasis, ways of achieving emphasis, types of focus, and kinds of aesthetic elements. The excitement comes in putting these nuts-and-bolts data on "automatic," and operating from that sensitivity to design onstage.

PRINCIPLES OF STAGE COMPOSITION

Types of Stages

The stage is the canvas on which you mount the composition. Any arrangement of actors on a stage must take into account the size, location, and nature of the theater space. You compose differently on the various stages and each type necessitates certain differing procedures.

A *proscenium stage* is the easiest to assess for composition. The theater is composed of an arch that acts as a frame separating the audience from the stage. Since the audience is located on one side of the action, you have a great deal of control over the stage picture. Proscenium theaters provide opportunities for realistic and for stylistic productions. The distance between audience and stage allows for the creation of greater illusion, especially through scenery, lighting, and special effects.

Whereas on a proscenium stage you "paint" the picture, on an *arena stage,* a structure surrounded by the audience, you sculpt the figures. An arena stage emphasizes the actors and eliminates most solid scenery over two feet high, since it blocks the vision of the audience. Because you are creating a series of images for multiple views, composition is largely enhanced through costuming and lights.

The curved approach, the rise, and flexible furniture strengthen multifaceted compositions. Since an actor in one corner who starts to cross will automatically make a dynamic movement for half the arena but a weak one for the other half, the curved approach will keep actors in open view of the audience longer. Similarly, the rising movement in composition is experienced by the entire arena as strong, especially when done center stage where the actor can be seen by most, if not all, of the audience.

Arena stagings require flexible furniture that can be rolled in and out and located before entrances, where the actors' movements are open to more members of the audience, or placed at the outer edges of the stage. A door or window must be visualized inventively by placement at the head of an aisle, by using a thin outline or a half door or window, or by rolling onstage a window bench with a thin frame over it. The arena floor, a strong area of the composition, should be incorporated into the arrangement without contrasting too drastically from the set.

Problem:

You are having visibility problems grouping actors on your arena stage.

Solution:

Grouping actors in an arena partially covers each for part of the audience. 1) Minimize covering by encouraging actors to change positions; to adjust their bodies in the areas they are using; or to sit down when silent. 2) Direct different actors to avoid facing the same way and to keep a good playing space between them. 3) Combine or eliminate minor characters to reduce the number onstage. Aid visibility by arranging them on the floor, side areas, or aisles to avoid blocking the principals.

On a *thrust stage*, a round, square, or trapezoid space, with spectators on three sides, you sculpt *and* paint. A thrust stage emphasizes the silhouettes of the performers rather than the scenery. Scenery is limited to occasional scenic pieces, backdrops, or upstage platform units. Arrangements of actors should encourage the use of sculptured lighting, costumes, and background effects.

A thrust stage combines some of the best features of the proscenium and arena stages. The audience surrounds most of the action so spectators have different perspectives on the actors. However, opportunities for vivid tableaux with tall scenic devices and effects exist because of the rear wall. Actor groupings have close proximity to the audience since actors perform on a platform thrust out into their midst. But all actors can claim distance if "pictured" near the rear wall. The size of the platform of the thrust stage varies significantly from a shallow crescent to a deep horseshoe shape.

While the proscenium, arena, and thrust stages are the major types built, *environmental theaters,* found natural or architectural spaces, may use various combinations of the three. Huge open-air spaces, inexpensively seating great numbers of patrons in the tens of thousands may necessitate scene changes and magical illusions to maintain audience interest. Found stages could include spaces outside a restaurant, at the shopping mall, in the basement of a church, on the field in a park, among countless others. The type and size of stage space affects all compositional choices.

Emphasis

Along with understanding the types of stages, your work in composition requires a mastery of *emphasis*. Above all, the stage composition is tied together and focused around a point of emphasis because the director literally guides the audience's eyes.

Single Emphasis: focus is directed to one actor.
Act without Words I by Samuel Beckett. McCarter Theatre/Stage Two. Director: Robert Lanchester. With Nat Warren-White. Photo: Cliff Moore.

Emphasis—"leading the eye," a forcefulness of expression—places special importance on a specific point in a composition and tells the audience where to look, at what to look, and when to look. Onstage it should be given to the dominant actor or actors in a scene, usually the active ones who initiate action and speak the most lines. Five ways to emphasize actors exist: single emphasis, duoemphasis, secondary, diversified, and offstage emphases.

Single Emphasis

The simplest, *single emphasis,* focuses on *one* actor or group at a time. When "giving" the scene to another, an actor takes a body position of less prominence, perhaps turning away from the audience, so that the other actor is emphasized. Single emphasis directs the eye to one point of attention.

"Giving" the Scene to Another: one actor turns away so that other actors are emphasized.
Ah, Wilderness! by Eugene O'Neill. Loyola University Theatre. Director: R.H. O'Neill. Design: Herb Sayas. Lighting: Daniel Zimmer. With David Greenan. Photo: Loyola University Theatre.

Duoemphasis

Duoemphasis has two points of attention. A shared emphasis, it ar-
ranges the stage picture so that the attention goes to two actors or groups
of equal importance in a scene. Use duoemphasis when the scene is
carried by two characters. Frequently duoemphasis directs actors to share
the stage by taking similar positions, such as a quarter of full-fledged
position facing one another. An object may be placed between them or
figures behind or to the side to emphasize the two actors. Duoemphasis
highlights equally important characters.

Secondary Emphasis

Secondary emphasis employs two foci of attention, but one is subordinate
to the dominant one. Use this emphasis to draw attention to a secondary
character, who is being talked about, or to offset certain individuals in

Diversified Emphasis: several areas of attention are equally dominant
emphasizing more than one actor.

Ah, Wilderness! by Eugene O'Neill. Loyola University Theatre. Director: R.H. O'Neill. Design: Herb
Sayas. Lighting: Daniel Zimmer. With David Greenan. Photo: Loyola University Theatre.

a crowd. For example, in the courtroom scene of Bertolt Brecht's *The Caucasian Chalk Circle*, two mothers are fighting for the right to keep a child. The child should be the secondary emphasis for it is the object of the conflict, while the mothers are the major emphatic figures. Secondary emphasis also means the next strongest of three, four, or more elements.

Diversified Emphasis

Rather than ranking emphasis, a *diversified* (or multiple) *emphasis* alternates among a variety of points of attention with three or more equally dominant areas. Spread three, four, five, six, or more single characters or groups in positions of equal strength in the stage space. Characters should be arranged so that the audience's attention can comfortably pass from one to the other, as each claims focus in the scene. Many groups naturally form a diversified emphasis unless one or more members are singled out.

Offstage Emphasis

This final form of emphasis does not stress any point of attention onstage. In *offstage emphasis*, actors turn away from the stage and concentrate on the auditorium or backstage areas. Actors sometimes focus on an exterior pending event: the threat of a robber, a storm, or a flood, for example.

Ways of Achieving Emphasis

A knowledge of the kinds of emphasis leads us to the question of how to implement emphasis in a composition. Achieving this emphasis involves a number of variables, principally the use of balance; stage areas—planes and levels; and body positions. All of these ingredients need to be arranged to bring emphasis to the appropriate spot. Who and what is emphasized and the order of that emphasis clarify and picture the story of the play.

Balance

Balance—the weight, number, or proportion in a composition—is a way of obtaining emphasis. It is largely influenced by the amount of space between objects and their placement. Equal or unequal proportions on either side of the stage create emphasis. The dominance in any composition is shaped by the balance in the arrangement of elements. In theater this means that an element of balance must exist in the fixed elements onstage: setting and furniture, although adjustable elements throughout a production, can create balance. Various lighting intensities produce different weights onstage; different costumes shift focus by changes in sheer mass; additional props can add weight to a gesture or figure.

Symmetrical Balance: figures are grouped equally on either side of the center line.
Moby Dick Rehearsed by Orson Welles. McCarter Theater. Director: William Woodman. Photo: Cliff Moore.

Two types of balance, symmetrical and asymmetrical, should shape the fixed elements of all compositions because lopsided arrangements confuse audiences. Both types of balance deal with the same weight of all parts of the stage on either side of the center line, but symmetrical balance also contains the same groupings.

In *symmetrical balance* objects and items on either side correspond in proportion. Symmetrical balance is employed less in the theater because its regularity and formality appear artificial. Consequently compositions that are totally symmetrical may be nondramatic or static; the more dynamic relationship being slightly offcenter.

Although symmetrical balance may seem forced, sometimes its use is desirable: 1) in plays with artificial, symmetrical dialogue; for example, in the scene from Rogers and Hammerstein's *The King and I* where Anna is teaching the King of Siam's children English and they keep bowing to her, a symmetrical classroom might underscore how regimented the children are; 2) in works set in time periods such as the Greek, Roman, seventeenth or eighteenth century when such order was characteristic of the art and architecture of the time; for instance, in *A Funny Thing Happened on the Way to the Forum,* a musical based on Plautus's comedy, the chaotic behavior might be offset by a formalized Roman pavillion with perfectly spaced archways and columns; 3) in scenes of great formality such as occasions of state, courtroom and military scenes; for example, in George Bernard Shaw's *Pygmalion,* a symmetrical ballroom set might suit the scene when Eliza Doolittle is formally presented to British society.

What makes a regiment of soldiers a more noble object than the same mass
of mob? Their arms, their dresses, their banners, and the art and artificial
symmetry of their position and movements.

(Byron: *Letter to John Murray*, February 7, 1821)

In *asymmetrical balance* groupings of equal weight are incapable of
division into similar halves on each side of the stage set. More members
stand on one side of the stage and their relative locations on opposite
sides of the dividing line vary. Although either side of a plane divided
by half might be different, when combined together the weights and
effects of both sides become equal. In asymmetrical balance, the stage
functions like a scale: on one side a character placed farther from the
center line balances, on the other side, two or more closer to the ful-
crum.

Distance from the center line determines how balance is created, so
that three characters close to the center line could balance one character
far away from it. Asymmetrical balance onstage differs from a scale in
that the addition of levels or of more figures to a stage group of four
may not change its weight against the other side.

Asymmetrical Balance: two figures balance one figure farther from the
center line.
Long Day's Journey into Night by Eugene O'Neill. Hong Kong Repertory Theatre. Director: Vicki Ooi.
Set: Weng Cheong.

A knowledge of balance helps to achieve emphasis in the fluid, moment-by-moment actor groupings you create. Emphasis and balance are implemented by choosing stage areas and body positions for actors. Certain conventions for stage areas and body positions have prevailed throughout the history of the theater, because they strengthen the visibility of actors and the effectiveness of compositions. Understanding these conventions will sharpen your ability to compose.

Stage Areas

Stage areas, the various acting locations onstage, are composed of planes and levels, A *plane* is the series of imaginary lines parallel to and facing the audience from the edge of the stage to the rear. A *level* is the measurement of the differences in height from the stage floor. To achieve emphasis you must make sound decisions about planes and levels. Effective compositions use planes and levels to highlight dominant actors.

Planes. The term *plane* comes from vaudeville where acts were located by indicating whether they were being played in Plane or Drop One, Plane or Drop Two, and so forth. In placing actors, remember *the closer a plane is to the audience and the center line, the stronger the actor's location.* In the two diagrams shown here of a proscenium stage, note its geography; its axis and curtain line. The proscenium plane's major parts, viewed from the actor's perspective to these features, can be abbreviated as follows: 1) UR—up right (to the rear on *actor's* right); 2) UC—up center; 3) UL—up left (again, *actor's* left); 4) RC—right center; 5) C—center; 6) LC—left center; 7) DR—down right; 8) DC—down center; and 9) DL—down left.

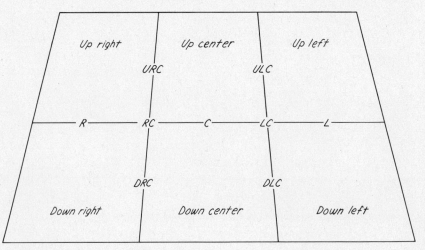

Proscenium Stage Geography: "Right" and "Left" refer to the *actor's* view facing the audience.

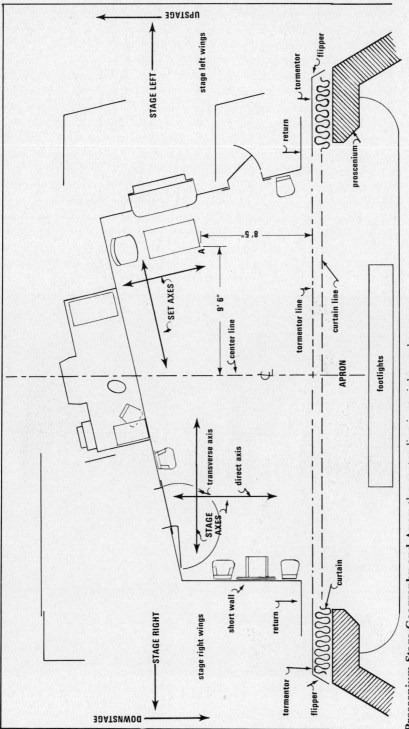

Proscenium Stage Geography and Axes: the center line is at right angles to the tormentor line. These lines fix the stage areas.
From Henning Nelms, *Scene Design.* Dover Publications, 1975.

Other factors being equal, the emphasis of various areas descends from: DC (strongest), C, UC, DR, DL, R, L, UR, to UL (weakest). Stage right is stronger than stage left because the habitual eye movement of Western audiences follows that path (SR to SL).

Planes affect mood. Play the scenes of strong emotional experience closest to the audience. The down center position, powerful and bold, can fire combats and climactic sequences. In complicated scenes, use a strong downstage figure to command focus. Intimate and informal, the down right position highlights narratives and private scenes. Up right and up left are rarely effective for important scenes unless other elements of composition strengthen them.

On an arena stage, the planes viewed differ for various spectators. When you guide actors on an arena stage, visualize the floor as the face of a clock and point out where the numbers on it would lie. Direct actors to advance toward or away from those numbers, for example, from the one o'clock to the three o'clock location. You may prefer to give instructions by using stage furniture on the arena for reference points, such

Plane—Close to Audience: the strongest emotional scene played downstage center.

Doctor Faustus Lights the Lights by Gertrude Stein. Bates College Theatre. Director: Paul Kuritz. Photo: Rick Dennison.

Plane—Downstage Strength: even in a complex scene the downstage figure commands focus.
Threepenny Opera by Bertolt Brecht and Kurt Weill. Williamstown Theatre Festival. Director: Peter Hunt. Design: John Conklin. With Raul Julia. Photo: Steven Nils Boyd.

as, cross to the arm chair; or by establishing one side of the arena as the imaginary proscenium, opening and determining the stage floor from that perspective. Each location operates as a *sphere* rather than as a plane because, at some point in every scene, the actors' faces should be seen by some part of the arena audience.

Levels. Along with planes and spheres, directors enhance emphasis by the use of levels. The nature of the composition, its balance and emphasis are shaped by the altitude of the actor above the stage floor. Generally, other factors being equal, the attention of the audience is drawn to the highest person in the line of vision among all onstage.

Plane: down right position for intimate scenes highlights narratives.
A Streetcar Named Desire (or *Un Tranvia Llamado Deseo*) by Tennessee Williams. Teatro de las Americas, produced by Centro Cultural Paraguayo Americano. Director: Alexis Gonzales. Design: Michael Burt. Lighting: Naco Rabito. Photo: Jose Maria Blanch, S.J.

All theaters provide opportunities for horizontal relationships; directors should consider vertical ones by introducing traps, windows, entrance ways, and ledges. Levels expand possibilities for emphasis by allowing simultaneous viewing of various objects and persons while directing the eye to the highest one. Besides using platforms for entrances, exits, or climbing, you can diversify a stage with graduated heights: levels of window sills, furniture, pillows, staircases, and ladders. Consider variety in body levels including lying or sitting on the floor or standing on furniture; resting on the arm or back of a chair; leaning or bending over an object; standing flatfoot or on tiptoe; standing on or striding a step; hanging from an overhead object.

Besides variety, levels generate energy. Even though too many levels sometimes breaks up the dynamics of movement, the movement of ac-

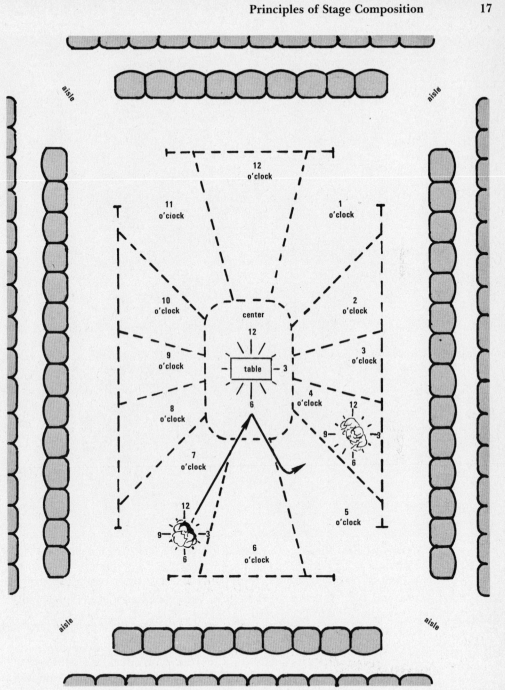

Arena Geography: directions are designated like the hands on a clock; each performer has a separate clock.
From Henning Nelms, *Scene Design*. Dover Publications, 1975.

Arena—Vertical View: the arena audience sees actors from numerous viewpoints.

The Pittsburgh Public Theater. Audience and stage space conceived and designed by Peter Wexler. Photo: Adam Weinhold.

tors on different levels generates a more dynamic feeling than on a flat plane. Depending on the height of the actor and the stage opening, movement from a lower to a higher level usually looks strong, and the reverse, weak. Besides indicating the emotional state of a character (that is, a peasant groveling on a low level, with a king acknowledging a salute on a higher one), movement on levels projects the progression of the action (the ascent or descent of the protagonist). However, always evaluate behavior on levels in connection with planes. For example, a movement on a level up center would be much more powerful than on the same level up left. The effectiveness of any level is also conditioned by the body position of the actors.

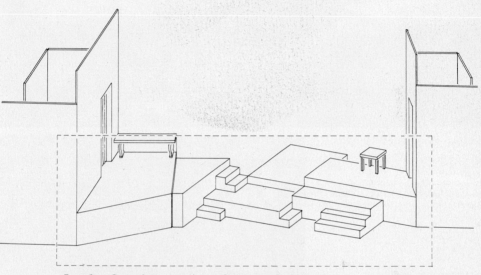

Levels—Complex: a variety of steps and platforms expands possibilities for emphasis.
From Henning Nelms, *Scene Design*. Dover Publications, 1975.

Levels—Simple: even a few steps in a simple set add possibilities for variety.
From Henning Nelms, *Scene Design*. Dover Publications, 1975.

Levels—Graduated Heights:
platform and steps are subtly
placed for visual variety.

I Remember Mama by John Van Druten.
University of Santa Clara, Louis B.
Mayer Theatre. Director: Frederick J.
Tollini, S.J. Scene design: Gary Daines.
Costumes: Barbara Murray. Lighting:
Albert L. Gibson. Photo: Glenn
Matsamura.

Levels—Body Levels:
individual actors may be
placed on different levels to
emphasize important actions.

Long Day's Journey into Night by Eugene
O'Neill. Hong Kong Repertory
Theater. Director: Vicki Ooi. Set:
Weng Cheong.

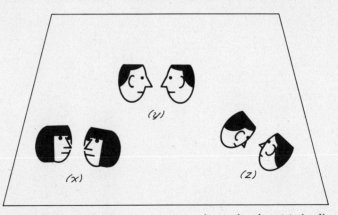

(y)

(x)   *(z)*

Body Positions—Shared Scene: actors—opposite each other (x); in direct profile (y); in "given" position (z).

Body Positions

To create emphasis, directors arrange groups of actors in specific *body positions*—facings and postures—on certain levels and planes. These body positions may be evaluated in relation to the audience, to other actors, and to the visual landscape.

To encourage variety, directors use different combinations of body positions. They refer to the actor's *body in relation to the audience* because *the more fully the actor faces the audience, the stronger the position.* An actor with a strong body position normally claims focus regardless of the area of the stage in use. Certain principles influence the strength of the body position. Standing erect is stronger than leaning. Sitting erect is stronger than slouching. Slouching is stronger than lying down. Body positions can be strengthened or weakened by the direction in which the head is turned.

Within the constraints of a given scene, the bodies of the actors, whether stationary or moving, should face the audience as fully as possible. Gestures done with the upstage hand (farthest-from the audience) will less likely hide the actor's body. To strengthen visibility, keep any stage stance open, for example, have kneeling actors put their weight on the downstage knee, the one closest to the audience.

Expansive stances dominate space by employing the entire body of the actor. For example, a kneeling actor possesses less emphasis than the standing actor who claims more of the stage. Large, open gestures of characters with arms extended and palms facing the ceiling draw greater focus than small, closed gestures indicating withdrawal, passivity, and weakness. Finally, since the stage is three-dimensional, consider depth when creating dominant body positions. Generally, triangular patterns make a larger impact than one-dimensional linear ones because they make use of the stage depth and look more lifelike and interesting.

Body Positions—Combinations: a variety of body positions employed to emphasize the nature of the scene: comedy or drama?

Keystone by Lance Mulcahy, John McKellar, Dion McGregor. McCarter Theatre. Director: Nagle Jackson. Design: Desmond Heeley. Photo: Cliff Moore.

Moby Dick Rehearsed by Orson Welles. McCarter Theatre. Director: William Woodman. Photo: Cliff Moore.

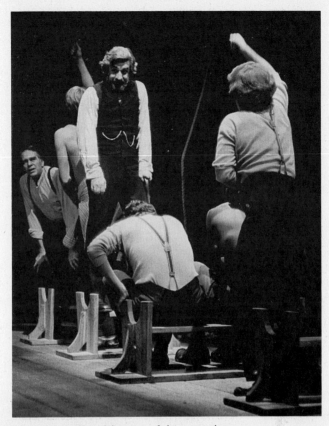

Body Positions—Standing Figures: claim attention.
Moby Dick Rehearsed by Orson Welles. McCarter Theatre. Director: William Woodman. Photo: Cliff Moore.

Since the strongest position of the actor is facing the audience, the hierarchy of positions descends from: 1) *full front,* in which body and head directly face the audience; 2) *quarter position,* in which body and head are at a 45° angle away from the audience; 3) *profile,* with the actor at a 90° angle away from the audience; 4) *full back position,* with the back of the actor directly facing the audience; and 5) *three-quarters,* with the actor between profile and full back away from the audience. Full back demands more focus than a three-quarter turn, probably because of the larger body mass and the tension created by not being able to see the actor's face. In actual production, a variety of these body positions adds interest to a scene.

Besides body positions in relation to the audience, *body positions in relation to others* must be considered. Throughout a production, actors participate with others onstage. Generally, the more a scene is shared, the more similar the characters' body positions. Contrasting the characters' body positions balances them as well. Different body positions,

Body Positions—Proscenium Stage: full front, quarter, three-quarters, back, profile (facing audience).

Background: both background set design and stillness of actors emphasize the importance of one performer.
Threepenny Opera by Bertolt Brecht and Kurt Weill. Guthrie Theater. Director: Liviu Ciulei. Set: Liviu Ciulei. Costumes: Corrie Robbins. Photo: Joe Giannetti.

Body Positions—Arena Set: in an arena the actors face the audience from various areas.

The Toy Cart by King Shudraka. Bates College Theatre. Director: Paul Kuritz. Photo: R. Dennison.

generate the composition's shape, which stimulates the feeling aroused in the spectator. Emphasizing actors follows three patterns: 1) two or more actors may either share the spotlight in the scene; 2) one may "give" the scene to the other; or 3) they may focus offstage. While variations of these options exist (see the five types of emphasis), emphasis in composition is frequently achieved through the actors' relation to others.

Audiences see *actors in relationship to their background* as well as to each other. The effect of any body position includes its placement against the landscape. The same body position is strengthened or diminished by different landscapes. For example, if two actors have profile positions onstage, the one in front of, and framed by, a huge fountain will have more dominance than the other standing before a curtain. Along with objects behind actors, colors can either enhance or weaken their positions. For example, an actor placed in front of a black curtain wearing a black suit will stand out less than an actor sporting a white suit. An

Body Positions—Proscenium Set: a proscenium stage suggests strong use of full-front positions for emphasis.

Lysistrata by Aristophanes. Florida State University School of Theatre. Director: Charles Olsen. Photo: John Nalon.

effective background intensifies body positions, for instance, the stillness of people in the background offsets the movements of a lively actor. Spatial design integrates body position within a visual plane.

The shape of any composition results from the union of body position and stage area in the spatial design of a particular theater such as an arena or proscenium. You compose intuitively from a knowledge of the actors, the theater, and the play. You use emphasis to direct attention to a specific area and balance to please the viewer by equalizing opposite parts of a composition.

EXERCISES

1. Bring in copies (reproductions) of paintings which illustrate the five kinds of emphasis. Pictures may be found in art books at the library, in postcards/books at museums, or in books/pictures in school art departments. Demonstrate each position in class and evaluate its effect on the audience.
2. Choose a famous painting or sculpture of a human being, then create and direct a scene around the body position in the art work. At some point in the performance, the action of the scene should

lead the actor to momentarily assume that pose. Your purpose is to show how body position grows out of scene action.

3. Create five specific compositions with different techniques of plane, level, and body position. Indicate emphasis, single, duoemphasis, secondary, diversified, or offstage; and type of balance, symmetrical or asymmetrical.

Focus

Along with achieving emphasis through balance, stage area, and body position, some compositions employ *focus,* the use of line to strengthen emphasis. Focus channels the eye path of the viewer by setting up lines within the arrangement that direct the vision. While all compositions require emphasis, because a "picture" without it confuses spectators, only some compositions use focus. For example, a composition with duoemphasis—two actors in profile sharing the stage—might not use actual lines to sharpen emphasis.

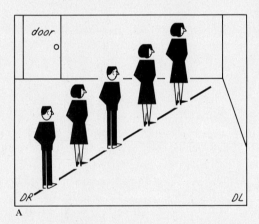

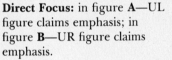

Direct Focus: in figure **A**—UL figure claims emphasis; in figure **B**—UR figure claims emphasis.

A

B

Direct Focus

Focus can be direct, counter, or indirect. *Direct focus* emphasizes a figure by the use of an actual line. When looking at a line, our eyes follow to the end. Direct focus engages a series of figures in a diagonal line so that the spectators' vision follows from one figure to the next until it rests on the focal one. When several figures are in a diagonal line, the one at the upstage end, whether upleft or upright, claims emphasis. When they are on levels, the diagonal line runs from the lowest to the highest figure's head and gives the topmost figure the focus. The costumes of the actors and placement of their arms and legs can all direct attention to the emphatic figure. You can create a throughline by arranging objects and people within a pattern. The focus lies at the apex of the point toward which all lines lead. Any line is intensified by the use of eye direction. Visual line focus with all figures looking at the next or central figure strengthens the latter's emphasis!

Direct Focus: visual-line focus with all figures looking at most important figure.

Voices by J. Janda. University of Santa Clara. Director: Frederick Tollini, S.J. Set design: Kelly Abella. Costumes: James O. Crino. Photo: Gary Daines.

A   B

Direct Focus—Apex: (**A**) triangle with apex at side of stage; (**B**) triangle with apex down center.

Direct Focus—Apex: the most important figure placed at the apex of a triangle in open body position.

Hello, Dolly! by Michael Stewart (book) and Jerry Herman (music and lyrics). Plays-in-the-Park. Director: R.H. O'Neill. Design: Vern Smith. Photo: Sanford Greenberg.

The best geometrical arrangement that direct focus often uses is the *triangle*. The figure standing at the apex of a triangle attracts attention by the use of two diagonal lines extending from the left and the right of the figure. These lines draw the audiences' eyes down either side of the triangle to its apex. Emphasis can be expanded by the use of an open-body position by the figure at the apex and more closed-body positions by side figures.

Counterfocus

Differing from direct focus which proceeds from one point to another without interruption, *counterfocus* opposes a point of attention. A small portion of a group turns away from the central area of emphasis thus offsetting it through contrast. Note how counterfocus upright increases variety in composition in the scene from *Equus* depicted here. Despite the subordinate emphasis, the composition retains sufficient focus because of the emphasis of the dominant figure, down left.

Counter Focus: the downstage figures claim emphasis; upstage figures are subordinate.

Equus by Peter Shaffer. Beloit College Theatre. Director: Linda Burson.

Counterfocus involves contrasting one figure's body position to the line of the others. For example, if all of the figures but one stand profile facing the door, while that one is entering through a window, the counterfocus attracts attention momentarily to the window.

Counterfocus also develops from contrast in the eye direction. If all figures except one gaze in a direction, the odd figure strengthens the visual line. Counterfocus is sometimes used at the fringes of the composition, where a character faces away from and offsets the central emphasis. Counterfocus sometimes visualizes one character's different reaction to an event.

Indirect Focus

Unlike direct focus and counterfocus, *indirect focus* uses a roundabout effect to eventually give dominance to one actor. Some actors face one direction while others regard different points. Indirect focus creates

Indirect Focus: audience attention is subtly directed to the dominant figure in a complex scene with many figures.

Joseph and the Amazing Technicolor Dreamcoat by Andrew Lloyd Webber and Tim Price. University of Texas at Austin. Director: Kathleen Conlin. Set design: Craig Edelblut. Costumes: Judy Dearing. Photo: Alan Smith.

unity through subtly guiding the attention of the spectator to a point.
A director can channel the eye path of the audience along a circuitous
route to the correct area.

Aesthetic Elements

Direct, counter-, and indirect focus all use the element of *line* to direct
the attention of the audience to an emphatic area. In addition to sometimes directing the focus, *where all the visual areas converge to a point,* line
always structures the composition. Line is one of four aesthetic or beau-
tifying elements that make up any composition. All four ingredients
should be investigated—for each to a differing degree influences em-

Composition: drama evolves through a dancelike composition.
Dr. Faustus Lights the Lights by Gertrude Stein. Bates College Theatre. Director: Paul Kuritz. Photo:
Rick Dennison.

phasis. The combination of line, mass, form, and color—in the guise of costumed actors (body positions) on the set (stage areas)—produces the arrangement.

Any stage production challenges the director to create ever-evolving compositions, much like a series of moving paintings and sculptures, or dance. In each frame, certain features of line, mass, form, or color are emphasized and balanced. For example, a gesture might stress line, the gesture's linear arrangement from one place to another; mass, its weight and bulk; or form, its shape or structure.

Line

Line, the real or imaginary direction, prevails as the force which most shapes emphasis and balance in any arrangement. Onstage every group is composed of a series of lines, the dominant of which may be its course of direction. For example, a large group of people lying down or resting on low furniture, evenly spaced across the stage, creates a horizontal line.

Composition: space around a figure strengthens an expansive stance.
On the Road to Edo by Maureen O'Toole. Arizona State University Theatre for Youth. Director: Rosemarie Willenbrink. Set design: Susan Johnson. Costumes: Donna Barts. Photo: Johnny Saldana.

Repetition: three figures in repetitive poses strengthen existing emphasis.

Form

Along with line, the audience's eyes are influenced by *form,* the uniqueness and beauty of the silhouettes in a composition. For example, while a chandelier hanging above a ballroom set might draw focus and create interest, a ragged remnant of curtain could distract audiences.

You can strengthen emphasis through form by using five elements: space, repetition, reinforcement, sequence, and contrast. Greater *space* around a figure distinguishes it and establishes dominance through isolation. Space creates emphasis and balance through form. Note how space strengthens the expansive stance in a composition.

Repetition and reinforcement strengthen an existing emphasis. *Repetition* adds support through form. For example, several courtiers bowing to a king enhance his authority. Scenic *reinforcement,* such as framing an actor under a doorway or window, or relating an actor to a massive column or throne, increases importance. Remember if an arch is placed in the center of the back wall of the setting, that area will equal or surpass the downstage in dominance, because the arch will frame any-

Reinforcement: figure framed by window claims attention.

Sequence: (**A**) semicircular; (**B**) straight line. A rhythm of distance between figures creates pleasing compositions.

A

B

one standing in front of it. Highlight actors by having them stand where a strong, scenic line terminates.

Sequence is defined as a regular recurrence of proportional space. Pleasing stage compositions contain a rhythm of distance between the figures and/or groups of figures. Aesthetic compositions often possess intrinsic elements of sequence.

Contrast in forms, such as the placement of differing outlines against one another, creates emphasis patterns. In vigorous scenes, involving fast-moving capes or scarves tossed in the air, costumes evolve into progressive forms as different shapes dominate space. Finally, the figure in strongest contrast to the rest claims attention. For example, three figures similarly dressed give dominance to a fourth figure in distinct attire.

Mass

Besides form, the weight or *mass* of the figures shapes the structure of the composition. Large masses project a feeling of strength; small masses, of tension; diffuse masses, of confusion. The largest bulk in a

Contrast: figures down left claim attention through contrast in costuming.
Othello by William Shakespeare. Bates College Theatre. Director: Paul Kuritz. Photo: Rick Dennison.

given section draws the most attention. For example, a heavily costumed figure takes focus from a simply dressed one.

Along with the weight of figures, consider the *stability* or force of gravity on the total composition. Stability ties down the picture to the stage and satisfies the audience's need for coordination of the entire picture through the force of gravity. Stability is reached by using the weight of characters on the down left and down right areas of the stage. The number of stabilizing elements needed to tie down the stage varies depending upon the numbers in the entire picture. The more mass upstage, the more weight needed for stability at the down right and down left portions. Masses onstage must be coordinated into the total frame of the composition to evoke appropriate emphasis and balance. Note that instability creates dramatic tension and may be very useful to directors.

Color

Finally, manipulation of *color,* the strength of an object's field of attraction, greatly influences the composition. The stage palette includes fixed colors of permanent objects and movable colors of lighting projections. Obviously, brightly lit actors attract more attention than softly lit ones; but other forms of lighting, such as colors reflecting off of costumes and props and the movement of actors in and out of lighted areas, affect emphasis. Color can transform stage compositions as mod-

Mass: Strength is projected by a large mass; tension is projected by a small clustered mass.

A Christmas Carol. by Charles Dickens. Adapted by Nagle Jackson. McCarter Theatre. Director: Francis X. Kuhn. Costumes: Elizabeth Covey. Photo: Cliff Moore.

A Raisin in the Sun by Lorraine Hansberry. Northwestern University Theatre. Director: Leslie A. Hinderyckx. Photo: Thomas Lascher.

Stability: (**A**) unstabilized composition needs figures added down left and down right; (**B**) stabilized composition with added figures for balance.

ern lighting systems make possible instantaneous changes in the intensity, direction, and tone of light.

Color can assist you in enlivening, distinguishing, and changing characters. *Enliven the characters, rather than the decor,* by putting color on figures rather than on objects. Costumes on people are more readily changed than sets. A heavily decorated, colorful, but fixed set can overwhelm a production and work against the action onstage. In a one-set show, the set's colors must not fight with other colors expressing the development of the characters. Distinguish characters through color by individualizing them from the group. For example, the good figure is sometimes dressed in white, the bad one in black, and the mob in gray.

Use lighting to *change the dominant color* of a figure to a weak one or vice versa. Employ a progression of colors to develop emphasis; for example, intensifying tones in costumes or lighting as harshness in the environment accelerates.

Color, mass, form, and line can be combined to create vital visual arrangements. Although a painter may use these elements directly, di-

Color/Lighting: lighting intensifies the somber, harsh quality of the scene.
Peer Gynt by Henrik Ibsen. Guthrie Theater. Director: Liviu Ciulei. Design: Santo Loquasto.
Lighting: Jennifer Tipton. Photo: Joe Giannetti.

rectors must deal with them indirectly, by arranging living human beings
on a three-dimensional stage platform. Furthermore, stage compositions
must project specific meanings tied to the text. Each scene is a part of
the greater composition—the play. The body position, plane, and level
of the actors in each grouping must visualize their emotional relationships from moment to moment. Apart from their aesthetic value, compositions must progressively picture the play's emotional content. An
understanding of picturization can assist you in transforming compositions into mood pictures.

EXERCISES

1. Make ten different triangle arrangements with actors and furniture. Then, structure a direct, counter-, and indirect focus composition. Create the same focus without triangles as well.
2. Direct several actors to wear jeans, two poster boards hinged at the
   shoulders, and bags over their heads. Put the differently colored
   actors in various positions and areas onstage. Explore each kind of
   emphasis by creating five compositions, without regard to compositional techniques. Challenge your ability to instinctually perceive
   the process.

TECHNIQUES OF PICTURIZATION

Picturization creates the meaning of the composition; it is composition *plus* meaning. How characters sit, kneel, relate, or stand next to each other creates a "picture" evolving out of the situation and the dialogue. You do not create free-form compositions, but those tied to the emotional content of a text. Moment by moment, you create a picture sequence of *character relationships* evolving from actions.

When placing characters together, you imply their relationship through body positions and stage areas used. Note the differing relationships implied by the tightly grouped people in these two arrangements captioned "Picturization."

Compositions that do not support characters' relationships and actions undermine the play. Evaluate the interpretation conveyed by the on-stage grouping and identify arrangements that visualize the meaning of the scene.

Classification of Scenes

Every play is composed of different scene types. While some are unique to specific authors, certain overall classifications exist. Each scene should be assessed for type to help you picture its emotional content.

Exposition Scenes

Some crucial scenes are expositional, that is, they provide the background necessary for following the story of the play. Such scenes often open the play. For example, Niccolo Machiavelli's *Mandrake* begins with the young Callimacho's recounting to his servant Siro the circumstances surrounding his love for Lucrezia. The subsequent plot deals with his pursuit of her. Because exposition scenes give so much information, lead characters must be clearly visible and audible. They may need to physically enact some of the previous events. The meaningful narration of the protagonist dominates picturization.

Environmental Scenes

In these scenes the surroundings of the protagonist pervade the action. For example, in Lanford Wilson's *The Rimers of Eldritch* when the trees (enacted by actors) start to move and become alive, the scene takes on an atmospheric focus. Maintaining emphasis on the protagonist within a mood environment may challenge your talents. Lighting effects, such as a color wash to strengthen diversified emphasis could blur the protagonist into the environment.

Climax Scenes

Difficult to picture, climax scenes depicting the summit of the action frequently involve much physical action. For example, the climax of

Picturization—Character Relationships: tragic elements are implied by body positions of tightly grouped figures.

Macbeth by William Shakespeare. Virginia Museum Theatre. Text prepared and directed by Tom Markus and Terry Burgher. Set design: Joseph A. Varga. Costumes: Bronwyn Caldwell. With Tom Markus, Nan Wary, Majlis Jalkio, Jane Moore. Photo: Virginia Museum.

Picturization—Character Relationships: comedic elements are implied by body positions and facial expressions.

A Christmas Gift by McCarter Theater. Director: Robert Lanchester. With Penelope Reed, Greg Thornton, Cynthia Martells. Photo: Cliff Moore.

many Shakespearean plays occurs on the battlefield or during a sword fight. Often the actors begin the scene at some distance. As hurdles are overcome, they increasingly threaten each other with their physical proximity.

Beginning and Ending Scenes

Like climax scenes, beginning and ending scenes offer much opportunity for striking arrangements especially before and after the dialogue starts and stops. Opening and closing scenes often visualize the changed motivations of the protagonist and the development of the play (see section on Scenic Movement, pp. 49–51).

For example, Charles Dickens's *A Christmas Carol* opens on Christmas Eve with Scrooge, bent over his books in his office, scowling at anyone who tries to celebrate. The closing scene reveals Scrooge, the benefactor, showering gifts on all his friends and enemies to get them to join him in celebrating Christmas Day.

Encounter Scenes

Occurring throughout plays, an encounter scene focuses on the emotional status of or conflict in a relationship. Typical examples include the reunion scene between Blanche and Stella in Tennessee Williams's *A Streetcar Named Desire*, or between Biff and Happy in Arthur Miller's *Death of a Salesman*. Often the play's development reveals a shift from the characters' original intimacy or reticence.

Event Scenes

Conversely, the event scene focuses on a specific occurrence: a funeral, birth, wedding, murder, trial, voyage, and so on. When picturing such situations remember to include the location as a meaningful part of the composition. Also explore the details connected with the time and place.

Privacy Scene

The opposite of a public event, this scene emphasizes seclusion. The solitary individual has an interior focus. Emotional content is strengthened through picturing the protagonist's private thoughts. Hamlet's "To be or not to be" sequence is a classic example of a privacy scene.

Scene Tags

While different features of a scene can effect its classification, the decisive one is its content; specifically its action. Many directors clarify scene type even further by giving each scene a phrase identifying the action: confession, farewell, confrontation, mourning, love, fight, and so on.

Mood

The mood of a particular scene can be developed from identifying its tag, then making those circumstances vivid for the actors. For example, an opening scene of William Shakespeare's *Hamlet* finds Hamlet calling out to the ghost of his dead father. You must picture the extremity of those graveyard circumstances for the actor and audience. If effectively done, a mood of terror should erupt.

Mood is developed through the series of evocative picturizations. These result from the dynamic use of body positions and stage areas appropriate to the action. To vividly picture, you need a solid knowledge of the sequence of character action. You must understand how to implement this with actors on the groundplan and in movement (see *The Director as Coach*).

The groundplan and movement allow for the sequencing of images and for the development of action. Because of their crucial significance to picturization, the final section of this chapter examines them in detail.

Reading and Doing a Groundplan

The *groundplan* or floor plan—a scaled drawing of the walls and objects that occupy the floor of a setting—indicates the amount of space, the location of objects, and the areas existing between objects. Evolving out of a thorough understanding of the play, an effective groundplan functions as the map upon which the action develops. Although it does not establish the details of individual blocking—of who goes to the window and says what lines—the groundplan sets the pattern of movement according to the requirements of the play's action. As you begin sensing the pattern of movement from the relationships in the play you can particularize ideas for the groundplan.

Reading

You must understand how to read a professional groundplan accurately. If not, you can mistake the location of set pieces and provoke severe traffic problems, once the final set and props are in place. The real floor plan of a set may obstruct and jeopardize actors' movements by putting objects or furniture in unanticipated areas. Misreading a groundplan may necessitate the complete restaging of a play shortly before opening.

You should know how to do a groundplan which enables a character to go from point A to point B in the most dramatic way. Otherwise, you may spend too much rehearsal time rearranging furniture when you could have identified the options in floor patterns in advance.

To read and do a groundplan, evaluate the following criteria: 1) the scale of the groundplan; 2) the type of scenic arrangement; 3) the placement of furniture and objects; 4) the function of scenic devices; and

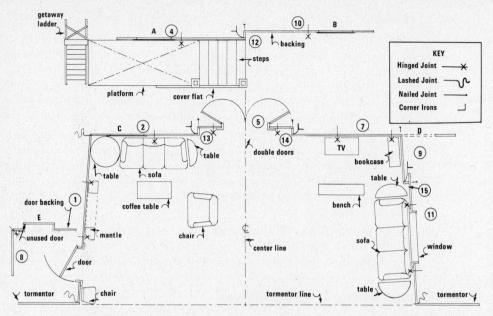

Groundplan—Professional: drawn to scale by designer with details for technician.

From Henning Nelms, *Scene Design.* Dover Publications, 1975.

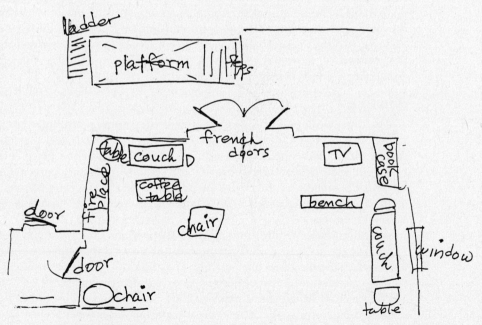

Groundplan—Director's: the professional plan drawn freehand by director for own use.

5) the flexibility of this arrangement. Initially, you must understand the scale of the groundplan and how it affects the action.

Scale

To create a composition with emotional content you must correctly interpret the *scale* of the groundplan and indicate the nature of the space available. Otherwise, you may fantasize meaningful groupings in your head that cannot be executed on the stage floor.

An accurate interpretation of the amount, kind, and arrangement of space on the groundplan is a prerequisite for picturization. First, visualize the layout of the floor plan. Assess the number of characters that will fit on a platform; the height of a staircase; the space between furniture. Remember that the average person is at least a foot and a half wide and will need at least two feet to move between areas. Examine the size of the group and the physical action required in restricted areas such as on a ramp, platform, or step. Evaluate the maximum usage of space without overcrowding and the minimum shifting of set pieces of furniture. Interpreting the scale should help you determine the balance, if sufficient mass exists on both sides of the stage. When one area weighs too much, you constantly have to compensate for that overload.

If you have difficulty reading the scale, tape out the placement of furniture and objects on the stage floor. Taping should clarify the location of objects and any problems with the given specifications. For example, you may discover that the width of the steps is too narrow for an actress in a hoop skirt or that their location differs from the one used in rehearsal. If you must draw your own groundplan, begin by sketching it as part of a larger context with exits leading to specific areas. For example, lay out the entire floor plan of a building of which a particular room is a part to remind you where the doors and windows lead. In a simply drawn plan, you can place furniture and make some decisions about staging; or, obtain a copy of the theater's floor plan with precise dimensions (depth, width, height) of the stage floor and wing area. Using a ruler and a measurement key (for example, $\frac{1}{2}'' = 1'$), draw a floor plan of the stage opening. Find its center and decide upon the desirable opening for your setting (this may not be the same size as that of the theater). Determine the depth of the set then draw in the set line. Establish the length and angle of the side walls and pencil in those lines. Lay out entrances, windows, staircases, fireplaces, and other features. Finally, cut out different pieces of furniture, drawn to scale on pieces of cardboard, and juggle these around on the floor plan until an ideal arrangement is reached.

Scenic Arrangement

Once you have studied the scale of the groundplan, evaluate it for type of scenic arrangement and set changes. When assessing groundplans, you must assess the pros and cons of different types of scenic arrangements and changes including: 1) A *box set:* a setting in which the walls are completed on three sides with flats and overhung with a frame ceiling. Set changes result from unlashing the flats and removing them, lifting the set into the flies, or turning the flats over. 2) A *multiple setting:* a variety of sets within one simultaneous setting. Several locations co-exist on the same stage and the action moves from one part of the stage to the next. 3) A *revolving stage:* a turntable or circular disk which pivots at the center. Settings may be placed on this turntable to create quick changes of scenery. 4) A *unit setting:* an architectural arrangement which does not change throughout the play in spite of any changes in locale indicated by the play. 5) A *wing and drop setting:* an arrangement composed of a backdrop and side flats leading up to it; several wing and drop settings can be placed behind the initial one.

Examine which type of scenic arrangement works best for your groundplan. For example, a multiple setting may suit a large thrust stage housing a medieval pageant with numerous set changes. The capacity for development is a key to picturization. Study how much variety your groundplan provides.

Scenic arrangement can be augmented by other adjustments, including: 1) shifting stage locations through lighting changes; 2) employing side areas outside the proscenium arch for short scenes; 3) making changes in a unit set by closing and opening a window, a door, a drape, or an arch; 4) flying in scenery (a small three-fold, box set can be lowered in and then opened up onstage); 5) wheeling in a *wagon stage,* a low platform with all props and furniture preset; 6) projecting scenery when realism is not demanded (sufficient distance between the cyclorama and the projector is necessary and correction for distortion of the picture may have to be made); 7) alternating use of the forestage and of the inner stage by dividing the stage halfway up with a curtain. Scenes can be played on the forward part of the stage while scenery is changed behind the curtain; 8) shifting the set in view of the audience as part of the action; and 9) unlashing the scenery, folding it in sections, and carrying it offstage during intermission while the new scenery and furniture are put into place.

Furniture Placement

Along with the scenic arrangement, you will need to check the groundplan for the placement of furniture and objects. The accessibility of furniture and objects affects picturization by establishing a believable space and shaping the movement of the actors. For instance, informal furniture may encourage more relaxed behavior as characters gather around it. Once objects and furniture have been set in place, the pattern the actors develop from them is somewhat predictable. Furniture should enhance the action of the play, especially in moments of strong emotion. For instance, a heavy table could be used in a confrontation sequence to divide two opponents.

Furniture should be checked for *grouping, location,* and *flexibility.* A furniture or object group usually comprises two units—a sofa and table; a rock and a tree. A functional stage set contains at least three groupings of furniture or objects and two clear areas. These spaces should allow for characters sitting in one area to converse with those in another.

Vary the location of furniture. Place furniture and objects in more than one plane and area. At least one grouping of furniture should be put downstage, left or right, to give actors a reason for crossing there.

Flexible furniture creates more possibilities for picturization. Look for furniture to be walked to and circled; for chairs to swivel; for stools and telephones (with long cords) to be moved around.

Scenic Devices

The accessibility of furniture should be augmented by the effectiveness of scenic devices: entrances, windows, fireplaces, stoves, thrones, and staircases. When a groundplan calls for a variety of furniture and scenic devices, patterns on the stage floor are formed by them. For example, when one character is seated downstage on the stage apron, the presence of a window to the rear allows another to eavesdrop. Like furniture, the accessibility of scenic devices should advance opportunities for compositions with meaning. For example, spacing scenic devices across the stage and not localizing them in one area expands the actor groupings possible.

Entrances and *exits* are two of the most important scenic devices because so many climactic moments revolve around them. Entrances and exits project the beginnings and endings of major encounters and/or punctuate certain statements. When directors know where the characters are coming from and going to, more possibilities for picturization can occur.

Emotional entrances and exits underscore a play's meaning. For example, Madame Ranevsky's return home (entrance) to the cherry orchard estate and her farewell (exit) from it before its demolition unify *The Cherry Orchard* by Anton Chekov, a play about the end of the Russian aristocracy.

Because the arriving and departing character normally claims focus, entrances and exits create ongoing opportunities for picturization. Outlets should be placed on more than one wall for variety. When entrances and exits have stairs leading up to or down from them into a trap, even more visual possibilities exist. Emphatic entrances use an opening on the back wall so the actor faces the audience, whereas strong exits employ an outlet on the side so the profile can be seen for the longest time. If only one or two entrances exist, congestion may develop around them. However, since few rooms contain over three doors, beware of using more of them than would logically exist. Some farces and comedies, which depend upon unexpected entrances and exits, require the ingenious placement of doors.

After doorways, *windows* provide the next most accessible scenic device. Their placement depends on several factors related to their function in the play. Windows work well along side walls when characters have to look outside and react to what is seen. Side windows do not necessitate the use of exterior sets behind them. A window in the back wall is demanded when the audience must see people through it. Remember you may have to position another character down right or down left to give the character looking out the rear window a reason to turn downstage and be seen.

Besides doorways and windows, *staircases,* the most emphatic scenic device, create many visual opportunities. Staircases provide variety by adding levels to raise one character over another. However, staircases are bulky pieces devouring space since the tread on which a character stands is usually one-foot deep. Based on this, the amount of lost playing space should be calculated. A popular arrangement places the staircase far upstage so that it does not materially affect or stop the action. Side staircases, superior for entrances because the arriving character is in full view of the audience, are inferior for an exit because the characters leaving have their fronts turned offstage. Exits up a side staircase are best handled by having the character run up a few steps turn back to speak and then exit.

Other useful scenic devices include: *fireplaces, mantlepieces,* and *stoves.* Place them along side walls to allow actors to warm themselves and still be seen in profile. People generally remove their coats when arriving, so fireplaces and stoves set next to entrances present clutter, congestion, and illogical hazards. A fireplace along the side wall counteracts the tendency of characters to cluster center stage. It both stimulates a number of crosses and provides an area for individual reflection while others carry on the action. The usefulness of a fireplace depends on its location—a downstage side fireplace is close enough to the center of the action for characters turning to it to be seen.

Like fireplaces, *thrones, podiums,* or *jury boxes* demand emphasis and are advantageous on the right and left walls. Throne scenes involve a gathering of people with a head of importance. When placed up center, a throne so dominates the stage that it becomes almost impossible to emphasize the people facing it whose backs are to the audience. Remember side choices, while not reducing strong spots, encourage open and varied picturization.

Flexibility of Groundplan

Scenic devices promote emphasis and balance. Like furniture, they support the action of the play. A study of scenic devices, furniture, scenic arrangement, and scale should lead you to an assessment of the flexibility of your groundplan.

Exciting picturization for any play evolves from a groundplan with sufficient elasticity to augment the range of action in a play. An effective groundplan generates picturization by establishing a believable space and shaping the action of the play. Develop groundplans that provoke dynamic movements, *forcing* the action to become interesting, building the critical peaks of the play. Use angles because nothing dulls the stage like a physical setting built lateral to the proscenium line. Putting objects on a groundplan into some sort of angle automatically creates a dynamic flow from one position to another.

Movable groundplans increase interest. For example, some directors prefer furniture and sets on wheels that adjust easily to fill or empty the space. Beware of elaborate stagings, forcing the audience repeatedly to look at the same arrangement. Rather look for groundplans that promote organic interaction with objects and set pieces, that avoid the cliché use of the environment.

> It's always valuable to stay away from what is first of all conventional, such as the conventional western street. If you can't stay away from it, try with a high degree of specificity to put materials into that street that create an organic interaction between the environment and the actors functioning in it. For instance, we were required to shoot the scene in *Little Big Man* where Dustin Hoffman is a drunk in the street at Metro on a plain old back lot with store fronts. And my designer said, "Why don't we put some railroad cars for dealing in buffalo robes down the middle of the street. And suppose all of this occurs in a downpour and the dirt streets of the West were just seas of mud." Well that triggered a whole response in me which made us shift the scene into that milieu. We just swamped that street and everyone in it with water so it looked as if it had just rained and the labor was going on. When Dusty had to walk down the street to get to the barber shop he had to pull his feet out of the mud. All of this became real sensual material for the actor, the director, and the designer to work from (Arthur Penn, director).

EXERCISES

1. Pick a scene from a play and create a strong storytelling picture for each beat. Give each beat a label so the title conveys the meaning of the beat and helps picturization.
2. Using the actual dimensions of a specific theater, draw a groundplan for a play.
3. Balance the weight of five figures using body position, and area. See how many types of focus can be created by your composition.
4. Picturize the following greetings: husband and wife meeting after an absence of ten years; son and father meeting after a return from war; daughter and mother meeting before girl's going to college; student and counselor meeting before summer camp; two strangers meeting in an empty alley.

Movement

Along with a knowledge of groundplans, picturization depends on an understanding of stage movement. The stage picture is alive-in-action

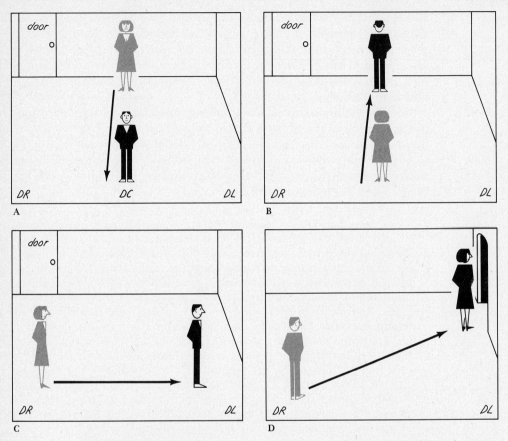

Movement Strength: (**A**) strongest—full front to down center; (**B**) weakest—back to audience; (**C**) strong—parallel, following audience eyepath from left to right;

as opposed to motionless. Meaningful compositions evolve from movements—through the sequence of body positions and stage areas used.

Movement dominates the stage. *A moving actor claims focus over a stationary one.* Drawing attention away from nearly everything including speech, movement not only creates the arrangement patterns, it fuels the audience's emotional reaction to the composition.

The amount of movement affects the audience's response to a composition. Onstage actors move more than they do in real life to enhance interest and to establish focus. Short, quick movements evoke a bright mood whereas slow intense ones suggest a sad mood. In general, large numbers of movements imply energy, excitement, and violence. Little or no movement creates quiet depression, emotional tension, or serenity. If all movements are short and fast, tension may develop. Conversely, long graceful crosses may indicate harmony and grace. Conserving movement until the end of a scene can increase suspense, contain energy, and offset emphasis and balance.

Direction

Direction in movement—the approach to or from a point of interest, shifts in body position and stage area—is always related to another person or object. Actors engage predominantly in forward movement since people rarely back up or sidestep toward something. A confining space can restrict creativity in composition and result in repetitive movement. Proximity to and visibility by the audience strengthens the weight of a movement. Generally, bold body movement approaches the audience, and weak body movement recedes from the audience. Standing up in full view is a firm movement, in contrast to slouching, a weaker positioning. Often becoming faster or slower, strong movement may draw actors progressively nearer to each other's location to strengthen the emotional position. Simply moving actors apart diminishes the intensity between them.

Timing

Three possibilities exist when timing movement with dialogue: movement before, after, and on the line. Movement *before* the line emphasizes the line; movement *after* the line stresses the movement; movement *on* the line strengthens both line and movement. For example, if Tom dashes to the door then says, "She's sick," the words are emphasized. If he says, "She's sick," then dashes to the door, his running is stressed. If he dashes to the door while saying, "She's sick," her sickness and his exiting are simultaneously underscored. The same principle applies for pauses. Pausing before the line, "He failed," emphasizes the line; pausing after it stresses the pause/response. Halting while saying, "He failed," emphasizes both.

Movement on the lines can add meaning to them. Moving toward someone or retreating from them while saying, "Go away," implies different things as do rising or sitting on a line.

Since dialogue is seldom held for movement, unless a specific cue is called for, normally movement comes on the words. For example, a good arrival remark like "Anybody home?" sometimes describes the entrance. Picturization here would result from movement on the line, supported by feelings generated by it. Beside the timing of movement, you must develop a movement vocabulary.

Shorthand Movement Terms

When moving actors, using shorthand terminology saves time and encourages precision in picturization. Give movement instructions to actors from *their* perspective. As we have stated before, *stage right* refers to the part of the stage on the actor's right; *stage left* to the actor's left. Many directors shorten this to "cross left" or "cross right." The term *above* implies behind or nearer to the back, while *below* means in front of. For example, the direction to move above the chair means to go behind it. *Downstage* indicates the area nearest the audience, *upstage* means the opposite.

These terms originated in the Italian theater of the sixteenth century when the stage floor was slanted or *raked* higher in the back than in the front. The practices of the early sixteenth century are summarized in Sebastiano Serlio's (1475–1554) *Architettura* (1545). The front part of the stage floor is level since it is to be used by actors. The back part slopes upward at a sharp angle or rake to increase the illusion of distance. All scenery was originally on this raked portion. Directors referred to the slant toward the back as *up*stage and the descent toward the audience as *down*stage. The word "upstaging" (a derogatory term) implies one actor unfairly gaining focus over another by moving upstage, thus forcing the partner to turn away from the audience. Encourage scene sharing rather than upstaging.

Scene-sharing Terms

Some scene-sharing terms directors use to sustain picturization are: dress, steal, ease, cheat, drop, and cover. To *dress stage* means to spread out or balance the stage. When an actor changes position, the partner adjusts to and balances the new position. To *steal, ease, cheat,* or *drop,* the actor makes an inconspicuous movement into a different position or area. If done when s(he) does not have the attention, the movement may not distract from the focal person. To *cover* means to go downstage of other actors or objects to hide them from the audience. To *counter* implies shifting the body in the opposite direction to give the passing actor space and focus.

Stage Turns

Besides scene sharing, turns are an intrinsic part of picturization. When turning, actors expand or contract their visibility to the audience. Accordingly, directors use the terms: "open up" or "turn out," "turn in," and "blend." To *open up* or *turn out* means to turn more of the body toward the audience. To *turn in* or *close in* calls for the opposite, to turn in or away from the audience. To *blend in* means to move further into the group (less visibility).

Words for actors' turns—the *quarter, half, three-quarter,* and *full* turns, depend upon how broad the turn is away from the audience. A quarter turn is on a clock, a quarter away from the audience; a half turn is turning to face the opposite direction; a three-quarter turn is pivoting in a three-quarter circle away from the audience; a full turn is pivoting all the way around back to the original position. The basic convention underlying all turns is: Turns should usually be made *toward* the audience and the larger (the more visible) the turn, the stronger.

Stage Crosses

Like turns, crosses change picturization and claim authority according to actor visibility. *Since the moving actor seizes and claims attention,* actors should cross in front of stationary actors to keep the focus. The strongest approach, the *direct cross* invites the actor to walk the shortest line between one spot and another, as in a direct exit, when the actor heads toward the exit. Unless otherwise specified, the actor crosses directly to a position immediately opposite the person addressed so that they share equal weight onstage.

The *indirect cross* is sometimes used to avoid awkward moves in front of or behind furniture and people. The actor takes a random pass to the point of arrival, going either in a circular path around the furniture or in a diagonal line. An indirect cross consumes more time and space. If a scene is about the crossing, you can use the indirect diagonal to make the actor appear to cover considerable territory before exiting. The curved cross keeps the front of the actor visible longer than the direct cross. In either one, when two actors are walking together, the upstage actor can keep in sight by moving a step before and glancing toward the other.

Crosses: a moving figure claims attention as the performer moves in front of stationary actors.

You Can't Take It With You by George Kaufman and Moss Hart. Boston University School of Theatre Arts.

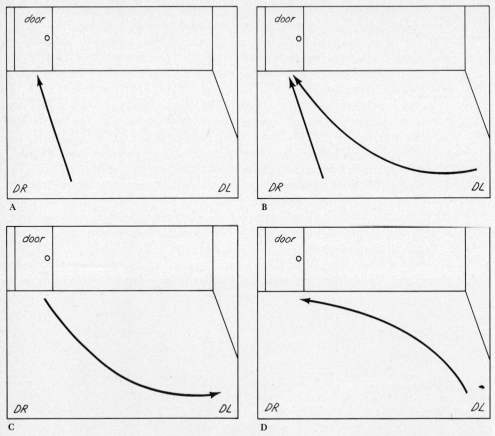

Crosses: (**A**) direct approach to upstage; (**B**) direct and curved approaches for two performers respectively; (**C**) curved approach to downstage; (**D**) curved approach to upstage.

The following conventions hold true for most crosses: 1) A *cross downstage,* toward the audience, claims emphasis over a horizontal cross. 2) A *horizontal cross* is strongest from right to left, when the actor faces the audience, since we are accustomed to follow that direction when reading. 3) A *diagonal cross* is less strong than a horizontal cross, in which the actor's profile is seen. Actors crossing diagonally to the rear or upstage must move with their backs to the audience. 4) A *cross upstage,* toward stage rear, is the weakest of all and is used in sequences implying utter defeat, confusion, departure, and farewell.

Entrances and Exits

Generally, entrances and exits arrest the most attention as crosses. Entrances through a major central doorway have more impact than through a side or less dominant doorway. Similarly, the addition of height and mass impacts the power of the movement. Use entrances down a circular stairway or exits up an incline to generate suspense. Create an ominous effect by having one actor unnoticed by another but seen by the audience, enter from above, come down a staircase, or approach from the rear. Any extraordinary entrance automatically arrests focus. The simplest unusual entrance is slipping through a window. Others include sliding down banisters, falling through an entrance, coming up a trap door, appearing behind a hidden panel, entering backward, dancing and turning while entering, or flying in from overhead.

One of the most dramatic exits is the *double turn exit*. The actor walks toward the door, turns, says a line, walks a little further, turns, says another line, then walks to the door again, saying a final line, and exits! Through this interrupted exit the actor increases audience interest and punctuates the importance of the final line. Conversely, an anticlimactic exit involves re-entry, when the actor exits and then returns onstage to say a line. Re-entry can be used to create a comic or confused effect.

Entrances, exits, crosses, turns, scene sharings move the composition and create meaning. They are intrinsically tied to the tempo and rhythm of the play.

Tempo and Rhythm

No study of movement can commence without an examination of tempo, the speed and rhythm, the pattern of the action. Determining the movement for picturization demands an understanding of a play's velocity and its accents. These sustain the infinitesimal movements that develop the play. Tempo and rhythm are shaped by the groundplan. Both should be evaluated prior to its finalization. On reading, for example, a Tennessee Williams play, you may sense the slow lyrical movements of the heroine. You will need a setting that provides furniture to recline on and a spatial arrangement that supports such languid body positions. Wooden boxes on a cluttered multi-level set would hinder the tempo and rhythm of this play.

The tempo and rhythm of a particular play result from a variety of factors, including the congestion and the stresses affecting people's lives. Each play has a fundamental tempo and rhythm, largely determined by its nature; its place, characters, and above all, its action.

Tempo onstage does not just mean fast or slow speed. It stimulates and sustains the illusion of the play and is an intricate part of its make-up. Stage time and actual time differ. For example, when Richard is waiting for Muriel on the beach in Eugene O'Neill's *Ah, Wilderness!*, stage time seems interminable, but the actual time of the monologue is less than ten minutes.

The tempo of specific scenes may be influenced by *place*. A hot, sweaty beach in Florida evokes different movement than a moonlit beach in Alaska. The time of day, the season, the year, the weather create a specific atmosphere that generates a certain velocity in the movement. The placement of stage objects also affects the alacrity with which action is accomplished. Some floor patterns speed the action, while others retard it by placing hurdles—furniture, levels, winding steps—in the path of the actor.

Besides the speed of action, its *rhythm* influences movement for picturization. Rhythm results from the dynamics built into individual units of the play. Each play has its own series of moments which contribute to the build of its beats, sections, scenes, and acts. The progression of happenings generates the pattern of the play.

At every level, the characters create the sense of flow through their words and actions. The type of protagonist and other characters affects the kind of movement and dialogue. For example, a brash character may act and speak in an aggressive fashion.

Play rhythm results from the patterns of words and silences between characters. You can gauge a play's rhythm by simply scanning to determine which characters have the most lines, what their natures are like, and how the dialogue is arranged, such as short sentences between a variety of characters or long monologues interspersed over a short period of time. Knowing the playwright can indicate what rhythms to look for in a play. Some authors like Tennessee Williams lean toward lyrical patterns, while others like Samuel Beckett favor more staccato, vaudevillian, or abrupt exchanges. The rhythm of the play is also influenced by whether characters speak only to each other or also address the audience to generate a three-fold communication.

When creating picturization, set some rhythm at the outset and enhance it throughout the play. The initial use of music, lighting effects, and/or a preset predisposes audiences to the play's rhythm.

Problem

The tempo and rhythm of your production is too slow.

Solution

To increase the tempo, decrease the time between new impressions: 1) by facilitating scene changes, or beat changes in scenes; 2) by emphasizing variety in movement; 3) by deleting some physical action; or 4) by intensifying the urgency behind actions. Encourage actors to pick up cues and to relate to fewer people onstage. These choices should be rooted in the actors' heightened inner life. Some ways to intensify the rhythm in the scene include increasing the size of sounds, the amount or the contrasts in the movements; and using stronger areas, levels, or body positions; or creating sudden changes in speed.

Understanding tempo and rhythm helps you develop meaningful movements for picturization. Tempo and rhythm influence all stage movement including its two principal forms: *business*—the smaller activities that do not carry an actor through, but confine the actor to, space— and, *blocking*—the changing location of the actor.

Stage Business

Business differs from movement (which can include any motion on-stage) by referring specifically to physical chores occurring in smaller spaces. Stage business involves all those tangible activities, like putting on make-up, eating, polishing shoes, that characters do with props to fulfill specific needs. Stationary physical tasks visualize the characters' circumstances and frustrations. They clarify character and "picture" conflict. Stage business should also be distinguished from character behavior such as twitching, hunching, scratching the neck. These are mannerisms related to and part of the characterization while stage business deals with external tasks.

Some business is called for by the playwright and directly written in the script. For example, Richard reads a love letter in Eugene O'Neill's *Ah, Wilderness!*, the three witches stir a cauldron in *Macbeth*. Other stage tasks might be added to strengthen the emotional and visual meaning of a scene. For example, Hamlet might sharpen his blade in the "To be or not to be" sequence in *Hamlet.*

An important way to identify business is to ask yourself, "What are the characters doing besides talking?" Physical tasks root the actor and audience in the circumstances of the scene. Nothing relaxes actors more than giving them physical tasks appropriate to their action.

Physical tasks visualize the concerns and needs of the individual characters. Business can picturize their routines (eating, writing, studying) or activate them (discovering an object, telling one's fortune). Costumes (removing a coat or straightening a shirt collar) offer readymade opportunities for activities that reveal character.

Remember business should advance the action of the scene by picturing who the character is. In fact, a character is defined sometimes by an activity, such as the fifty-year-old Gaev in *The Cherry Orchard* who constantly pops gum balls, indicating his childlike attitude.

Sometimes business is used for technical purposes, to disguise an action. For example, one character might be warming by the fire to distract the audience from something happening across the stage. To intensify business so that it can be seen from the back of a house, enlarge the size of the movement surrounding the business, the focus of other characters on and their reaction to the business, and the vigor of the action. Remember, all business must be large enough to be seen by the audience and must augment the focal point of the blocking.

Blocking

All business is part of the larger movement pattern of characters, the *blocking*. Business must be evaluated in conjunction with meaningful blocking. The procedure having the most comprehensive effect on all aspects of picturization is blocking. Blocking determines the body positions and stage areas used. On the most basic level, it implies the specific logistics directors give actors to go from point A to point B or to avoid bumping into one another. Blocking's fullest interpretation, incorporating both the text and characters, includes the whole array of motivational choices in picturization.

Blocking is intrinsically connected to the *desires of the characters and action*. It is motivated by the precise needs of characters at certain moments. Body movement in life and blocking differ. When blocking, a director selects motivated movement, to reveal special relationships between characters (in costumes and under lights) and their environment.

Any time characters move onstage, they do so for a reason. They are either approaching toward or withdrawing from someone or something; or going to get something, for example, a character might cross to the door to get someone else to leave. Blocking visualizes these motivations. It translates the text into purposeful physical action which is selected and trimmed. This physicalization should reinforce the logic of the text and fit particular characters.

In Tennessee Williams's *A Streetcar Named Desire,* the delicate Blanche might stroll from the bathroom and daintily powder herself as she prepares for her date with Mitch (her motivation: to get a proposal). The brutish Stanley might kick the refrigerator door closed and bite off a beer cap with his teeth (his motivation: to terrorize Blanche). Both actions are logical and appropriate to the characters.

Preblocking

While blocking may be discovered in rehearsal, some of the director's imaginative work may involve *preblocking*. You can preblock by testing general patterns of character movement on your groundplan. There is no single, uniform, correct way to do any blocking. Most directors develop individual methods based on experience and their own approaches to staging. One method might be: 1) draw or obtain a groundplan of the stage areas/furniture; 2) compare this groundplan with each page of the script so that the stage picture is always under consideration; 3) make pencil notations in the text margin for the movement of performers; 4) if possible, use a photocopy of the groundplan so you can notate major changes in each scene—this will give you a clear record of your place; 5) keep these plans in your prompt book, and make changes as desired in rehearsal or for technical requirements.

Another preblocking procedure involves using a miniature model of the set built to scale by the designer and moving toy figures around on it. A three dimensional construction like a doll house provides an effective way for testing the use of space.

Preblocking frequently involves preliminary blocking, determining where major entrances and exits, given scenes, and certain movement patterns take place. Afterward, actors can discover more specific choices in rehearsal. Pinpoint two or three boundaries (like a kitchen table, a sink, and a door) where a scene begins and ends emotionally and physically, then experiment with movement between those points of tension. Important preliminary work lies at high points and beginnings and endings of scenes when certain impressions can be underlined visually for the audience.

Predetermining where scenes will occur prevents important areas from being overused before these scenes occur. Areas can function imaginatively in successive scenes by shifting furniture and objects, as an area may be determined more by its parts than by its location. For example, in one area an actor can lean against a huge tree, sit in or swing from it, and peer out through its branches. Finally, invent unconventional performance spaces, such as parts of the auditorium. Generally speaking, a convention, such as using the aisles as acting areas, should be established from the play's beginning so that the audience knows what to expect. However, exceptions from the rule work when strategically planned.

Preblocking develops from logical character action. Every movement must have a reason according to a character. For instance, serving from a tea tray gives a character reason to cross from table to table. Scenes

Movement—Fixed Location: actor, confined by location, can claim attention through gesture.

The Rimers of Eldritch by Lanford Wilson. Rider College Theatre. Director: R.H. O'Neill. Designer: Robert W. Scheeler.

largely develop through movement between specific objects or places onstage. For example, in Tom Jones and Harvey Schmidt's *Celebration,* the garden, the house, and the garden wall exit could be used as the bases for the secretive love scene. The disguised orphan must successfully climb the garden wall into the garden and enter the house without being identified. Angel protects him by listening for Rich's approach.

Other movement patterns, fixed in location, comprise changes in body position. In Lanford Wilson's *The Rimers of Eldritch,* a scene with a judge confined to "the bench" develops through the size and the energy of gestures.

Preblocking should allow actors the spontaneity to find the impulse for the appropriate character movement. When actors feel the need to move as an expression of their characters' drives, imaginative patterns evolve. If the groundplan works and the actors connect to the characters' circumstances, general movements will, like a net, begin to contain specific actions in rehearsals. Be sure to record these adjustments in your prompt book.

Blocking Notations

Blocking notations can be descriptive (that is, you can make written notations) or diagrammatic (most efficient). Always use a pencil. Notations can be simple, performer by performer or fitted into the stage area considering a variety of movements. Examine the blocking notations in the illustration at the bottom of page 62 (including light plot) used for a production of *The Rimers of Eldritch.* Note the necessity of sixteen light areas to augment the intricate blocking.

You may prefer descriptive blocking, done right near the text itself and written out in word form. Draw a line from the precise point in the script where the blocking is to occur to the margin and write there a description of what has happened. Some conventional symbols include: "X" for the cross, "EN" for entrances, "EX" for exits, and capital initials for each character (A, B). The final location of the character may be designated by either the appropriate area or by the player's relationship to a particular piece of furniture, for example, Tom crosses down right of chair could be "T. X DR chair."

When diagrammed on the floor plan, blocking can be entered into the prompt book as follows. The left hand page (the back of the previous page) contains a photocopy ¼" scale drawing of the set floor plan. The drawing should be an accurate scale or the blocking will be incorrect. Paste the script page in the prompt book on a sheet on the right so the diagram directly faces it. If the movement is complicated, place two diagrams of the stage floor opposite a given page of text. It is better to insert more copies of the floor plan and to have the action be briefer but clearer on each diagram. The upper groundplan can correspond to the upper half of the script's dialogue and the lower diagram to the bottom half. When annotating blocking, give each character a symbol and place it on the diagram at the character's location at the end of the previous page. Indicate the direction of the character's subsequent movements by a line. A symbol such as a circle with a hat on top of it or a head with a nose can be used to show which way a character is

facing. Again, diagram blocking in pencil so corrections can be made easily. Simple notations can be quickly interpreted. Use capital letters to

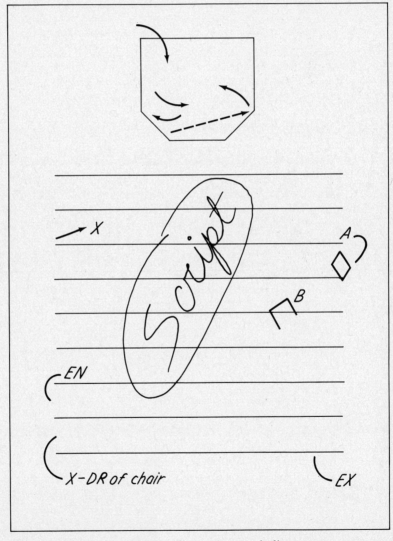

Blocking Notations—Descriptive: director's notes indicate movements on script pages with symbols and/or words. (Suggestion: draw groundplan on each page of script to indicate positions.)

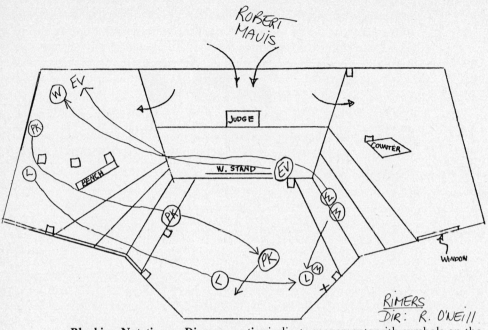

Blocking Notations—Diagrammatic: indicate movements with symbols on the groundplan.

The Rimers of Eldritch by Lanford Wilson. Rider College Theatre. Director: R.H. O'Neill. Designer: Robert W. Scheeler.

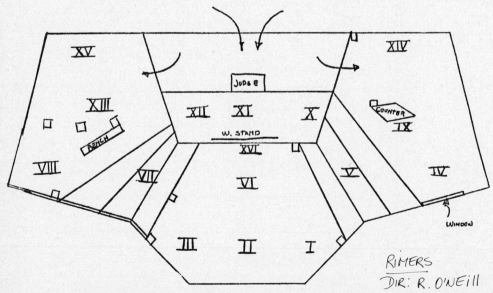

Blocking Notations—Diagrammatic: indicate lighting areas with symbols on the groundplan.

The Rimers of Eldritch by Lanford Wilson. Rider College Theatre. Director: R.H. O'Neill. Designer: Robert W. Scheeler.

indicate the character and then number the successive locations of characters, like 1, 2, 3, 4, and 5. Write the number next to the dialogue where a change of location occurs.

Whatever blocking method is used, two essential principles apply. One deals with movement: an *audience normally focuses its attention on whoever is moving* and, in the absence of movement, on the upstage character within a group. The second principle deals with character. The *protagonist should be visible throughout the scene,* and the antagonist should create a strong counter emphasis.

Inventive Blocking

Inventive blocking can transform the visualization of a production. Besides being effective, it excites the imagination. Inventive blocking captures the meaning of a scene in a graphic and sometimes startling way and is the antithesis of what New York critic, Albert Bermel, decries as directing mechanically:

> Certain directors don't pay sufficient attention to visual variety in a performance, except in a mechanical way, which was already dated six generations ago when the Duke of Saxe-Meiningen decreed that there must not be symmetry onstage. These directors may not offer direct symmetry in the arrangement of a group of actors and their setting. They'll arrange the setting at a slight angle. But they'll have an actor parading first on the right side of the stage, then on the left, and then in the center. They'll seat one actor on a sofa and another standing behind it, then the two of them will exchange places. This is mechanical blocking, not visually mechanical at any moment, but dynamically static over a period of time. It doesn't exploit inventive, unexpected use of the stage's resources.

Good directors appreciate dynamic blocking. They explore the stage span: edges, center, back, sides, downstage, furnishings, the entire animate and inanimate space for possible character action. They value ingenious use of space, surprising tasks, little shocks of truth that arouse audience interest. For example, a character balancing on the edge of the apron as if it is a tightrope, while contemplating suicide creates excitement because the movement represents a "surprising" use of the edge of the space, and projects the central conflict inside the character.

Inventive blocking largely evolves from "picturing" the conflict in a scene. Ask yourself "What is the central focus of the characters? Is it how they relate to themselves, to others, or to an outside force?" Analyze the play in terms of physical focus, where the actor's energy literally goes. The focus may be *interior* (inside of the characters, for example, in Shakespeare's *Hamlet*), *relational* (between characters, as in Shakespeare's *Romeo and Juliet*), or *situational* (around the characters in their physical surroundings, as in Thornton Wilder's *The Skin of Our Teeth*): These are the three places actors can look onstage (Ted Swindley, artistic director, *Stages,* Houston, Texas). Use each character's focus to discover blocking.

Inventive blocking can also result from strenghening the development of the obstacle(s) from a scene's beginning to its end. Try physical obstacles—a broken leg; or psychological obstacles—loneliness. Use obstacles to get the characters to adjust their behavior so that relationships at the end of the scene differ from those at the beginning. As they become increasingly thwarted by obstacles, the characters should vary the shape and location of their movements.

You can intensify conflict (one character opposing someone or thing) through picturing contrasts (different items placed together). Contrasts in the visual representation of characters and space mean juxtaposing diverse images against one another. For example, opposite movements can heighten the value of each. A crowd going off in defeat downstage could contrast with a victorious leader exiting upstage. Powerful arrangements can be developed through contrast, particularly at high points, beginnings, and finales of scenes.

Contrast at the high point was used recently in *Macbeth,* produced by college students from Wellesley and MIT at Princeton University, in the scene where Macduff's wife and babies are killed by ruffians. The two ruffians arrived with Lady Macduff onstage rocking her infant, with her small son beside her, playing with a toy sword. The more attractive assailant, smiling and giggling rather than immediately killing them—a traditional staging which the audience anticipates—engaged the child in a make-believe sword fight and began allowing the child to win. The mother, who had been seized by another assailant, watched the scene with relief. Then, snuggling the boy in his lap and rocking him back and forth, the ruffian jabbed a knife over and over into the boy's back. The picturization of the assailant stabbing the boy contrasted with that of the child at play with a toy sword. Two diverse pictures captured the violation (emotional significance) of the scene. Showing the fun of the make-believe war game maximized the brutality of the child's slaughter.

Special Blocking Problems

Inventive blocking sometimes results from handling special blocking problems. Besides violent and emotional sequences, problem scenes include crowd and table scenes. All three types require extra skill in blocking.

Crowd Scenes

Remember the composition of a crowd depends on individuals. The more varied the people who gather in the crowd, the more excitement conveyed by their actions. However, to get a mass reaction, the crowd must be blended into a single entity. Avoid extremes in stature, in animation, and in other differentiating characteristics so characters blend as a group.

Motivate the crowd by breaking up into small clusters of two or three, so each group can react individually and as a mass. Sometimes putting one, two, or three people downstage, nearer to the audience, will allow them to turn away from the leader and talk together, yet still be seen by the audience. Have several strong members meander in and out of all the groups to create a cohesion and flow for the crowd.

A big problem of the crowd sequence is visibility. The audience should not see the outer limits of the crowd. To avoid this, several actors can be squeezed into each of the exits so that the audience gets the impression of many more people outside. Direct characters to lean into the set from doorways and windows and use shadows and sound effects. The crowd can be grouped on one side of the stage and use a single entrance. Place more space between individual members or have the group straggle offstage to the right and left. Or space the crowd so that it is never more than two or three actors deep. Knots of people staggered in depth create a sense of size. Finally, use high intensity lighting at the central area and more diffuse lighting toward the edges to suggest numbers. Energy affects the impression of size, especially violent activity combined with poor visibility and lots of background sound.

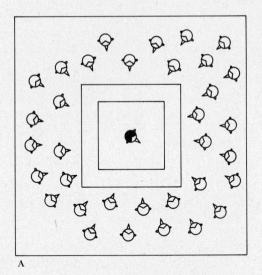

A

B

Blocking—Crowd Scenes: (**A**) arena stage—a higher level for important figures is most effective. (**B**) proscenium stage—emphasis on space between leader and crowd can be effective.

You may have difficulty giving the leader focus when expanding a band of characters to appear as a large crowd. Some solutions include: pinpointing your focus by placing the leader on a higher level than the rest of the group or by spacing the leader to the left or right of the group.

Table Scenes

Table scenes also present visibility problems. The difficulty with a *table scene* is arranging the players at the table so that the illusion of reality is maintained while all the players are seen. To overcome the dilemma, you might consider the following: 1) Have some characters sit close to the table and some sit farther away. 2) Choose a round table or a card table placed on the diagonal so actors can cheat toward each other in their placement. 3) Put higher stools on the upstage side of the table

Blocking—Table Scenes: a round table enables actors to place or move themselves for visibility.

Ah, Wilderness! by Eugene O'Neill. Loyola University Theatre. Director: R.H. O'Neill. Design: Herb Sayas. Lighting: Daniel Zimmer. With David Greenan. Photo: Loyola University Theatre.

than on its downstage side so upstage actors can be seen. 4) Place smaller people or those who leave the table early, on the downstage side of the table. 5) Plan for characters to use toasts or stand up when they say important information. 6) For royalty scenes, follow the convention of having no characters on the downstage side of the table. Place kings and queens up center, important leaders to their left and right, and lesser characters flanking each side of the table.

Emotional and Violent Scenes

Some of the most difficult scenes to stage are emotional and/or violent scenes. In these scenes, *the dominant principle involves hiding any fake action from the audience and emphasizing the response of the recipient.* The recipient, not the assailant, controls the audience reaction and creates the force of emotional expression for the audience. Often the actor being kissed or hit stands with the back three-quarters to the audience, covering much of the embrace or strike from view but engaging interest through powerful response to the event.

The traditional pose for a kiss places the girl, standing or sitting, tilting her head upstage, and the boy with his head downstage. The kiss is covered by the boy turning the girl's head toward him, upstage, and placing his own head below hers. Heighten suspense by beginning a love scene with actors somewhat apart and allowing the movement within the scene to draw the actors closer and closer together in a progressive visualization, culminating in the embrace.

Choreograph attacks by professional fight directors, so that actors are not harmed while body positions are being impacted. Some violent behavior can be partially enacted, but no actor should ever be in danger of being bruised. The execution of stage falls must be practiced a great deal. As the player falls, the shock must be absorbed in several places, the usual sequence being the side of the leg, the hip, shoulder, and hand progressively hitting the floor. Implement any real fight as a noncontinuous activity. A sharp attack is often followed by several moments of inactivity in which the fighters reorganize their efforts. Hide the blow from the audience, because, if it is unseen and the recipient responds with violent action, the audience will imagine a devastating assault.

Various techniques of illusion can transform a mild blow into a severe one for the audience. For example, a slap given with a cupped hand placed against the lower flesh of a cheek will hurt less; and, if the victim turns the head away at the moment of contact and then moans, the slap will appear fierce. For brutal slaps, direct the victim to put a hand against the hidden upstage cheek, and the assailant to slap that hand instead of the cheek, or redirect the audience's eyes and have the victim create the slap. This kind of staging needs rehearsal with a fight director to disguise fakeness and evoke the proper rhythm and sounds. Time and practice the recipient's recoiling and gasping. Moaning needs to be sourced in the area violated, such as from the head, chest, or stomach.

Scenes of shooting and stabbing sometimes require much covering of body positions. If a gun must go off during a fight, the actors can get into each other's arms and then one can shoot at the floor because even fake bullets can have damaging emissions. When an actor must shoot from a distance, place the victim at stage rear to prevent the gun from being pointed toward the audience. Direct the assailant to aim the pistol slightly below the victim to avoid random mishaps from blank cartridges. If a gun is to be fired off-stage, and usually this is the best course of action, the gun held onstage by the assailant can be hidden at the instant of firing. Distract the attention of the audience by having the victim yell a fraction of a second before the shot goes off.

You can hide the action of a stab from the audience by placing the victim above the assailant. Since a dagger goes into a body more swiftly than it is removed, have the assailant "withdraw" the knife with difficulty. The body requires several seconds to respond to a blow, so the victim should not recoil immediately. It normally takes time to die, even to die quickly. Audiences may laugh in a death scene when the victim collapses too suddenly. Timing is important.

The final body position of a corpse can cover the wound, with the head closest to the audience and the feet more upstage (a more pleasing posture than the reverse). Hide the actual execution or death of a character by using a covered location; for instance, having the body fall behind furniture, an object, or other people who partially conceal the "corpse" from the audience. Remove dead bodies as soon as possible from the stage. Since the audience knows that the player isn't dead, the corpse can easily become a distraction. Direct actors, when carrying a body offstage, to keep the head of the victim higher than the feet and to make sure someone is on the downstage side, covering the body from the audience. These are but a few of the possibilities you can explore. Since violent or emotional scenes often culminate the play's action, they require thorough planning and rehearsal for *meaning, safety,* and the *appearance of effortless spontaneity*.

Violent scenes are perhaps the hardest to block. Accurate notations of these sequences should be kept in your prompt book.

EXERCISES

1. Preblock the opening scene of a Shakespeare play for an arena production and then for an open-air proscenium production. Stage both versions in class.
2. Observe the movement of people in real life at a specific event: waiting in a hotel lobby, cheering at a game, complaining at rush hour. Then direct the sequence two ways—as it occurred in reality and in a selected stage version.

The Prompt Book and Scene Breakdown

No study of picturization is complete without an examination of the prompt book, where the director keeps all preparation work for a play. The prompt book contains impressions, blocking, research, character analyses, and scene breakdowns. Although some prefer a standard 9″ × 12″ binder, there are many other perfectly appropriate kinds of notebooks. Often the script is glued in this book to facilitate note taking in the margins around each page of text. Once in rehearsal, final blocking and technical cues are recorded in the book.

Some directors include the scene breakdown, a production plan of the various ingredients onstage, on a page opposite each page of script. Often this blank page contains columns for specific areas to be evaluated in each scene; such as ones for the action, objective, and scenic movement. Since there may not be enough space in the columns to put down all your observations, you can jot down other notes on the text itself.

Note the character analysis on Richard from *Ah, Wilderness!*. Such random notes are filtered throughout a prompt book. Taking notes on a play when reading is hectic and not necessarily organized—immediate impressions immediately recorded.

Besides character analyses, many directors do scene breakdowns. In the following breakdown for the opening scene of *Ah, Wilderness!*, the characters, action, and mise-en-scene for the initial moments of the scene are delineated.

The most important element of the breakdown is scene action. Note under the "action" column, the action of the protagonist or most active character(s). Actions may be physical and/or verbal. While most directors do not do line-by-line or sentence breakdowns for the character's actions, they may note major actions in each scene. Beware of presetting line-by-line actions which prompt you into insisting on character interpretations that your cast is not prepared to play.

In the third column, note the scenic movement and what technical effects might be needed. Notations concerning the production's physical life—lighting, tempo, offstage sound, music—may be placed here. Because of its complexity, scenic movement for a musical may require its own page of columns for sets and lights, characters, costumes and props.

Like preblocking, the scene breakdown is just a guide and not normally filled in completely before rehearsal. Aside from pivotal moments, much of the scene-by-scene production plan may be adjusted once you begin working with the tangible realities of living human beings, such as actors and technicians.

Plotting the production plan steers you into evaluating the script. It is impossible to work on staging techniques (composition, picturization) without assessing the text. Chapter 2 extends our study by examining how to successfully choose a script.

Character Analysis of <u>Ah, Wilderness!</u>
director : R.H. O'Neill

Act I

Richard - light brown hair, grey eyes, prep-school
reflection of college style Arthur--just out of high school.
Medium built, average height. Age : 16. Extreme sensitiveness,
restless, apprehensive, shy, dreamy, self conscious,
intelligent. Plain simple boy, posey actor solemnly
playing a role, grins sheepishly -- all boy, reluctantly
called back to Earth from another world, scornfully superior,
blushing bashfully, frowning, portentously with dignity.
Hurt and mad, so mad he can't find words unflattering,
astonishment, abashed, guilty, crushed, he bristles defensively,
enthusiastically shaken but putting on a brave front,
righteous indignation, embarrased but not ashamed, humiliated
and wronged anger, blurts to himself, masochistic, satisfaction
in his own sorrow, especially in the concern it arouses in
the family circle, with disdain, tragic sneer, proud, cruel
smile, pessimist, indignant, with contempt and disdain,
righteously aloof and disdainful, bitter, humiliated,
wronged, rebellious.

Act II

Physical - trouser's knees dirty - one torn, lurches in
violently, eyes are glossed and wild. He is trying for dignity,
drunkenly, glorying in the sensation he's creating. Recites
with heroic, dramatic emphasis, laughs dramatically
with double eyed sardonicism, leers, quotes with ponderous
mockery. His pallor takes on a greenish, sea-sick tinge;
his eyes seem to be turned inward uneasily -- he realizes
he is home - looks about, sees his mother; calls to her,
appealingly like a sick little boy.

Prompt Book—Notes: director's notes for character analysis include all
aspects of individual character's role—physical appearance, behavioral traits,
director's interpretation of personality.

BLOCKING	* CHARACTERS *	PROPS/SOUND
	Protagonist : mother (voice) [Tommy enters...] Antagonist : miller (voice)	

		SECTION I ACTION sound cue #1 overture cap (tossed) ball (on string) 2 boards for fireworks
ⓣx.'s from → u.l. runs around table, stops d.r. bouncing ball in the air	**l2** AH, WILDERNESS! ACT I 1 VOICES *are heard in a conversational tone from the dining-room beyond the back parlor, where the family are just finishing breakfast. Then* MRS. MILLER'S *voice, raised commandingly:* "Tommy! Come back here and finish your milk!" *At the same moment,* TOMMY *appears in the doorway from the back parlor—a chubby, sun-burnt boy of eleven with dark eyes, blond hair wetted and plastered down in a part, and a shiny, good-natured face, a rim of milk visible about his lips. Bursting with bottled-up energy on the Fourth, he nevertheless has hesitated obediently at his mother's call.* (WARN Crackers.) B E A T TOMMY. (*Calls back pleadingly as he wipes milk from his upper lip*) Aw, I'm full, Ma. And I said "excuse me" and you said "all right." (*Reaches door up* L *His father's voice is heard speaking to his mother.* MILLER—"Oh, let him run about." *Then she*	lemonade pitcher, hankerchiefs in sewing basket, news- paper, dominoes, watering can, onstage offstage table noises

Prompt Book—Script Notations: scene breakdowns occur page by page, with actions and props described in detail on the script page itself.

Ah, Wilderness! by Eugene O'Neill, p. 12. Copyright 1933; copyright renewed 1960 by Oona and Shane O'Neill. Reprinted with the permission of Charles Scribner's Sons.

SAMPLE SCORE: AH, WILDERNESS!, dir R.H. O'Neill

"AH WILDERNESS" SECT. 1	ACT ONE / SCENE ONE	DIRECTOR: Rosary O'Neill
CHARACTERS	* ACTION *	MISE · EN · SCENE
1 Protagonist: Mother Antagonist: Tommy Arthur Lily Mildred	SCENE TAG · _Leaving the Table_ TO PLAN THE HOLIDAY to control to escape to conceal to excuse to pry	* SCORCHING: 7:30: 4th ① overture ② crackers ③ crackers (3 small) ④ Song _Oh Waltz Me_ slow dawn rising on cyc.; distant nostalgic sounds PROPS: fan, parasol, watering can, kerchiefs, lemonade / pitchers
2 Protagonist: Miller Sid Antagonist: M. Miller ⎫ Lily ⎬ Mildred ⎪ Arthur ⎭	SCENE TAG · _Rallying Forces_ to celebrate at the picnic to confirm _other_ plans	sun coming up louder bang from fireworks pipe and pouch for Arthur; dominoes, newspaper, toys for Tommy; specs sewing box, kerchiefs
3 Protagonist: Mother * ⎫ (Arthur) ⎬ (Mildred) ⎭ Antagonist: Father ⎫ Sid ⎬ Lily ⎭	SCENE TAG · _The Complaint_ to squelch Richard's reading to rescue him	bright sun book, glass (for toast) reactions to increased heat, fan, glasses for lemonade

SPINE OF PLAY : TO CELEBRATE 4th OF JULY
⟹ OBSTACLES CREATE BLOCKS TO THAT CELEBRATION & CAUSE FRUSTRATION

Prompt Book—Breakdown: each scene is analyzed in an outline opposite the text.

72

FINAL PROJECTS

1. Challenging nuts-and-bolts assignment: Design a proscenium floor plan for a specific scene (or Act) from a serious realistic play. Analyze the compositional values for all major moments in the scene. After determining all the kinds of emphasis in the scene, demonstrate how you would achieve emphasis in each case. Label or title the scene's units and the areas each will employ on the floor plan. Finally, create the movement (blocking and stage business) pattern for the scene.

2. Analyze a one-act play in terms of physical focus, where the actors' physical energy literally goes. Use three color pens: one color for character, one color for relationship, one color for situation. Decide what each line of text is saying and its focus (or color). Then add up the colors and see which color (focus) predominates in the play (Ted Swindley, artistic director, *Stages*, Houston, Texas). Draw a groundplan and do preliminary diagrammatic blocking for the play.

3. Make three unrelated lists of ten characters, ten physical places or sets, and ten relationships you know. Randomly choose two characters, one situation, and one relationship. Rehearse in the real place, if possible, then on the make-believe set. Create a scene by totally engaging those three dynamics (Ted Swindley). Block the scene for class in three different ways by shifting the focus from an emphasis on character, to relationship, to physical surroundings. Hand in descriptive blocking of all three scenes.

Chapter **2**

The Director
as Critic
Choosing a Script

Theatre is a place people should confront ideas and emotions. Theatre should not give answers necessarily, but the more brilliant theatre asks questions. It presents significant questions for the audience to deal with and answer for themselves. As a director, what I'm looking for is "What kinds of questions am I asking the audience?"

Ted Swindley
artistic director, Stages
Houston, Texas

A command of staging techniques should prepare you for your role as critic. This chapter focuses on the initial task of choosing scripts. Criteria for evaluating scripts for performances are delineated in detail. The goal is to help you to avoid pitfalls in this crucial preliminary area. To quote critic Martin Esslin: "The first principle I tell directors is, 'Choose the right play.' In other words, to be a good judge of plays is the major qualification of the director."

Any solid assessment requires a fertile period of study. You must evaluate scripts, identify the demands of the playwright, and spend a lot of time imagining your future work with actors and designers in generating the realization of the play chosen. Your task will largely involve "mind" and "book" work. While little of this may be "technical" or "rehearsal" oriented, this reading, research, and study will be the foundation for *all* later work in production. You will have to imagine, when alone, the *possibilities* which each play presents! Remember, "Nothing is ever accomplished by a reasonable man" (George Bernard Shaw).

Choosing a play to direct will challenge all your critical abilities. Do not overlook the *personal, literary, historical,* and *practical* criteria. Using these with experience, you will get a *feel* for a particular script before weighing the practicality of doing it.

With new works, try to assess if the play has literary, long-lasting merit. Be less concerned with the *mise en scène* than with the play's writing. Is it first-rate? Look for excellence of idea and expression; search for plays that reach for something. Beware that many new plays don't stretch any further than everything else that is available. It's not that they are bad plays, they just don't express anything new.

Spend time reading, reassessing, and seeking counsel about any weaknesses in the play, until you acquire sufficient expertise for a general response. Lack of knowledge in one domain, for example, in literature or history, encourages you to overlook a play's demands there. Ignorance can trap you into a fatal script selection. The following criteria will help you in choosing and then evaluating the strengths and weaknesses of your chosen play.

PERSONAL EVALUATION

When assessing a script you must first "turn yourself on" to wanting to do it. Ideally, you should respond so strongly to initial readings that you feel destined to do the play. Whether it is a costumed period piece or

Evaluation: when reading the play, the director may see it as a costumed period piece.

A Flea in Her Ear by Georges Feydeau. Boston University School of Theatre Arts.

Evaluation: when reading a new play, the director may be attracted by contemporary ideas and issues.
The Old Flag (world premiere) by Vincent Canby. George Street Playhouse. Director: John Schwab. Set design: David Mitchell. With Paul Austin, Afemo, Bill Pullman. Photo: Suzanne Karp Krebs.

a new work by a living playwright, when you sense: "If only I had the talent to write plays, this is the play I would write, then that's the play to direct" (Marshall W. Mason).

Problem

How can you learn to like a play you are required to direct?

Solution

Try to analyze *why* you don't like the play at a first reading. 1) If it's a superficial spectacle, focus on that fantasy world, engage colleagues (visual artists, musicians, and others) to help you in capitalizing on the magical nature of the event. Fantasy compels the world of theater, and Disneyland-type events need little content to entice audiences. 2) If you lack enough competent actors, stage only selections from the play or scenes from different works by the same author (for example, various love scenes from Shakespearean plays are

easier to direct than an entire production of *Romeo and Juliet*. 3) If the play's message alienates you, see if you can relate to a character or situation in it. Work from that experience
of truth to a fuller interpretation. 4) Consider relocating the play to an environment that
inspires you. "Stretching" the text might rescue the evening not only for you but for the
audience as well. 5) If you find nothing at all of value, then refuse the assignment. You
have outgrown this directing situation, and your integrity as an artist would be at stake.

LITERARY EVALUATION

After personal response, evaluate a play for its excellence as literature.
The ancient Greek, Aristotle (circa 355–323 B.C.), has provided us with
six elements to assess in a drama. In the *Poetics*, the first systematic
treatise ever written on drama, he states that every drama has six parts:
plot, character, thought, diction, music, and spectacle. The first four
often provide the director with the major keys for analyzing a play.

Plot

Plot is the mechanics of unfolding a dramatic story. It determines the
structural development of the play's action. "Plot includes both outer
actions (such as Romeo stabbing Tybalt) and inner ones (such as Romeo
falling in love with Juliet); the sequence and arrangement of these actions in a series of scenes and acts is one of the most difficult tests of a
playwright's skill" (Robert Cohen, *Theatre*, p. 25).

Read plays just for plot, because a play with a strong construction will
carry itself. Do not be deluded into believing a thin play will metamor-
phose onstage. Martin Esslin says:

> One of the things that shows up in a good script is that the same type of
> action, pace, volume, tonality must never go on for too long. The basic prin-
> ciple of dramatic structure is that it is happening in time, and its beats, their
> subsections, must always be working by contrast. If you have a slow section,
> it must be followed by a fast section, if you have a loud section, by
> a soft one. Study where the climactic points are, so that you are working
> up towards climaxes. Very often one should evaluate a play not from begin-
> ning to end, but from the climactic scene, working downward and upward
> from it.

When examining a script for nothing but its plot, ignore the characters and the set, and look for the central track unifying the play from
its beginning to its end. See if the moments along it solidify, and logical
action develops from scene to scene. For example, the central track in
Shakespeare's *Hamlet* is to avenge the ghost of his father; in Tennessee
Williams's *A Streetcar Named Desire*, it's to find Blanche a home; in Anton
Chekhov's *The Cherry Orchard*, it's to save the estate.

Choose solid plays that possess competence for an evening worthy of an audience and for company members to spend weeks working on. For example, Johann Wolfgang von Goethe's *Faust* which is composed of myriad characters, fragmented scenes, and a running time of over eight hours is brilliant as literature but precarious as theater.

Some plays grow through formal plot structures, while others mature through informal ones: adjustments in mood, developments in information, or shifts in events. Learn how to identify a play's plot *and* how to ascertain if no plot exists. To do this, study at least one method of ordering events. Start with Aristotle!

Aristotelian Plot

Cause-to-effect or *Aristotelian plot* is a mounting sequence of incidents created by a *single* action. Dramatic theory has long taken for granted this arrangement as the only pattern. In the opening background scene (exposition), the protagonist is confined in both space and time and subject to overwhelming circumstances. Then an inciting incident occurs where one character poses a conflict to the self or someone else. As the action progresses, the person's range of choice increasingly reduces. The character is compressed into a turning point, where an extreme change of fortune (reversal) and a shocking realization (recognition) are experienced. The turning point produces the play's climax when the warring forces are brought to their limit. The climax stimulates a purging experience (catharsis) in the audience and the play's denouement where the protagonist comes to some understanding of the events.

The Three Unities

Any study of cause-to-effect sequencing should examine the effect of the so-called *three unities* of *time*, *place*, and *action* on the play's structure. Aristotle's disciples in the seventeenth century elevated some of his loose observations into ironclad rules and insisted a play was supposed to have a single action, which must be conceived to take place in a single locale and within a single day's time. According to historian Peter Arnott, "In Greek plays the first two had been only loosely adhered to, and time and place were manipulated according to need . . . Even the unity of action hardly existed for Euripides, who was quite capable of juxtaposing two different stories to make a thematic point" (Peter Arnott, *The Theatre in Its Time*, p. 234).

However, Arnott insists:

Aristotle stressed the compactness of the action. In Greek tragedy dramatic time is, for the most part, approximately equal to real time, or at least seems to be. In *Oedipus, the King* the immediate dramatic action occupies an hour or so of Oedipus's life, which is also the length of the play. Again, though this is often true, it is not always true . . . The plot of a play can usually be expressed in one short, simple, declarative sentence. Oedipus seeks the cause of the plague that has fallen on Thebes and discovers that it is himself (Arnott, *The Theatre in Its Time*, p. 85).

Aristotelian plot contains uniform segments produced by specific causes. The number of *dramatis personae* is limited and shifts of locale and differentiation between actual time is minimized. The theatrical force comes from adding one part to another in a cumulative sequence (Bernard Beckerman, *Dynamics of Drama*, pp. 189, 192–196). *Logic and suspense* should condition the sequencing of events. A suspenseful play starts with a methodical pace, that intensifies with increasing urgency.

Character

Besides a script's plot, its characters must be evaluated. Character depth and complexity are key to a good play because most plays live or die in the onstage creation of individuals. To develop strong interest, a play must make the audience care about the characters from the outset. Since a finite number of plots exist (some say as few as seven!), what distinguishes one plot from another is its individuals, their words and their behavior. The audience's concern about the characters motivates their interest in the plot. Martin Esslin claims that even the most violent action remains basically uninteresting if the audience does not know, does not like, and is therefore not sufficiently interested in the characters. He says that, "A character who never says a line which is arresting, witty, amusing, or interesting will have great difficulty in capturing the audience's sympathy or, conversely, loathing. Then however ingenious the twists of plot he is involved in, the audience will care little for them" (Martin Esslin, *Anatomy of Drama*, p. 49).

Vulnerability

When evaluating plays, look for intriguing characters. Traits like vulnerability and uniqueness fascinate audiences. The vulnerable character endears audiences by totally exposing the character to attack. In comedy, vulnerability comes from naiveté or vanity and is connected to physical manifestations. The pretentiousness of the infamous Malvolio in Shakespeare's *Twelfth Night* makes him vulnerable to assault.

In *Twelfth Night* (Act II; scene iii), the riotous Sir Toby Belch celebrates throughout the wee hours and mocks the straight-laced, vain steward, Malvolio:

Sir Toby: Out o' tune, sir? ye lie. Art any more than a steward? Dost thou think, because thou art virtuous, there shall be no more cakes and ale?
Clown: Yes, by Saint Anne, and ginger shall be hot i' th' mouth too.
Sir Toby: Th'art i' th' right. Go, sir, rub your chain [a steward's badge of office] with crumbs. A stoup of wine, Maria!

In drama, vulnerability results from inner vision, from the characters "seeing like the poet" into spiritual meanings. The character who sees more than others lives on many levels. S(he) is more vulnerable to a range of wounds and can be assaulted by many things. Sometimes this character is seen by others as slightly insane because this spiritual plane of existence is lacking in many lives. How many of us, for example, hear voices in ringing bells as Joan describes in scene v of George Bernard Shaw's *Saint Joan*?

Uniqueness

Like vulnerability, the uniqueness of a character fascinates audiences. Examine the distinctiveness of a play's cast. Look for roles that are *not* interchangeable. For example, Blanche and Stella in Williams's *A Streetcar Named Desire* differ widely as women and as sisters, but the three "angels" in the television series, *Charlie's Angels*, appear to be cut from the same cloth.

Many things make a character unique including ambiguity and high stakes. Uniqueness sometimes relates to some uncertainty of meaning which keeps the audience in suspense and allows the character to have fewer commonplace responses to a situation.

Martin Esslin states:

Any great character in literature contains a complexity, a contradiction which is made absolutely clear through the fascinating events happening in the play. Take a character like Bertolt Brecht's Galileo. Usually one thinks a great scientist is all spirit, and Brecht says, the other way around. The more sensual you are, the better scientist you will be. He makes Galileo say that the greatest pleasure in life, even better than good eating and sex, is making a discovery. And so, he links Galileo's scientific eminence with what is usually regarded as being the opposite of intellectual achievement, namely lechery and gluttony. Brecht has designed a character which explodes a usual cliché about scientists and shows the opposite to be true. Through a series of fascinating scenes and actions, the audience is taught, through contradiction, what it is like to be the discoverer of the moons of Jupiter."

Through contradictions, ambiguity can keep an audience in suspense. *Ambiguity* in a central character is especially intriguing. Richard III as an evil king might not have survived an act without the charm of his engaging appeal. Fierce alienation from Richard occurs because audiences initially sympathize with him and are surprised (J.L. Styan, *Drama, Stage, and Audience*, pp. 228–229). As Roger Fox puts it: "When you're talking about surprising an audience, that is all down to the truth of the character, because if characters are built truthfully then the audience is allowed through the play to see them a bit at a time. When you first meet someone, you see a bit of them. You've known someone for six days, six months, six years, and suddenly you see another side to them."

Besides the duality of a character, strong aspirations signal uniqueness. Characters with high stakes—Medea in Euripides's *Medea*, Lady Macbeth in Shakespeare's *Macbeth*, Tartuffe in Molière's *Tartuffe*—engage us by the extremities of their choice. How extreme a choice, for instance, is it for Medea to murder her children when Jason chooses to remarry? Characters with outrageous aspirations create theater that rides the razor's edge of human experience.

Organization

Besides evaluating the strength of the characters, you should assess their impact on the play's organization. When character rather than plot unifies a play, incidents are organized around people rather than around cause-to-effect events. While there may still be a plot, the play focuses on the development of an understanding of the characters' actions and motivations.

Anton Chekhov writes plays that are organized around character development:

> Chekhov's technique is to create deeply complex relationships among his characters, and to develop his plots and themes more or less between the lines. Every Chekhovian character is filled with secrets, none of which are every fully revealed by the dialogue. There are ten major characters in *The Three Sisters* and no one of them can be regarded as the principal character. The play focuses on the network of relations among these characters—and to a lesser extent, on their interactions with the four minor characters. . . . At the end of the play every life has been touched by every other (Cohen, *Theatre*, pp. 213–214).

Chekhov "fingers" the balance in each character's circumstances. He brings several strands of action onstage simultaneously, and by juggling them, shifts the equilibrium of the relationships.

Plays may also be organized around the experiences of only one character. In Arthur Miller's *After the Fall*, Quentin narrates and participates in a series of flashbacks about his life as he comes to terms with his conscience. In Samuel Beckett's *Krapp's Last Tape*, the only conflict occurs within the "dialogue" of but one character's mind.

Thought (Idea)

Besides plot and characters, every play should have something to say that seems pertinent to its audience. *Thought* is the meaning behind the play's statement. The insight that a play expresses about humanity represents its greatest literary value. Look in particular for a play's message or philosophy. Stanislavsky said, "Never forget that what keeps the theatre alive is not the brilliant lights, nor the splendor of sets and costumes, nor the effectiveness of the *mise en scenes*, but the idea of the playwright. Nothing will hide the weakness of the idea of the play. There is no theatrical pencil that can do it" (Nikolai M. Gorchakov, *Stanislavski Directs*, p. 390). The play's truth should infect the soul, so that when the audience leaves they will have gained something. Italian director Umberto Bonsignori says: "Productions enrich the soul in two ways: 1) the audience relives an experience that they went through, gets insight into it, or confirms their thoughts about it or 2) the audience is enlightened, advanced a bit, or made to consider something they hadn't thought of before because of the play."

Aesthetic Expression

The idea of the play generates the audience's aesthetic experience. Playwright Jerome Lawerence claims:

An anesthetic is the exact opposite of this aesthetic experience an audience demands. What does an *an*esthetic do? It deadens you, it turns you off, it makes you a vegetable. When an anesthetic is administered to you, you experience absence of pain, but also absence of pleasure, of intellect, of inspiration. And so, the aesthetic experience must be the exact opposite: what will make us "God-like," taller human beings, "turn us on" rather than turn us off. We go to a play, demanding something. We want to wake up the next morning and say, "I am augmented, I am lifted up. Something happened to me in the theatre which shook me up, which sandpapered my soul."

Superior plays present various levels of thought and feeling for spectators to respond to; some might experience one thing while others might perceive another and still others something else. Can not Arthur Miller's *Death of a Salesman* be seen as one man's life; as the story of all salesmen; as a myth about the American culture; or as a problem play dealing with being a failure in any society?

Organization

Plays can be organized around ideas. The opposite of linear cause-to-effect, this *organization* pivots around an idea, theme, or context having a weak or no plot. This *idea* structure relies upon multiplicity and juxtaposition of parts—one scene parallels or contrasts with others rather than develops causally from the one before. Instead of one line of action pointing toward a resolution, an explosive incident provokes a chain reaction mounting in intensity (Beckerman, *Dynamics of Drama*, pp. 197; 244).

A strong example of this organization is August Strindberg's *A Dream Play* which distorts reality and follows the chaotic order of a nightmare. Myriad characters and locations are freely introduced and haphazard problems abound.

Note that the play only appears to have the disorderly, haphazard quality of dream life. The dramatist does not abandon control. In reality, *A Dream Play* is carefully structured. The juxtaposition of incidents is formulated to produce certain resonances so that, although a point may not be specifically made, the audience is left with an impression, an association of ideas (Arnott, *The Theatre in Its Time*, p. 394).

Often the broad scope of the action or reaction cannot be physically reproduced onstage, so the play's setting must be abstract (*Dynamics of Drama*, pp. 197; 244). Sometimes the set does not represent any locale but serves as an emblem of the universe.

In the play [*A Dream Play*] the idea of a cyclic universe, passing through periods of suffering to ultimate regeneration, is expressed in a striking visual image that dominates the stage: a castle, which we see at the beginning rooted in dung and which gradually grows until at the end it bursts into a glorious flower. The idea of unity and diversity is expressed in characters who are, at the same time, many and one, different aspects of the same personality (Arnott, *The Theatre in Its Time*, p. 394).

Diction

After idea, seek plays that have a heightened or transcendent quality in their language. *Diction* relates not only to the pronunciation of spoken dialogue, but to the word choice and select literary character of a play's text, including its tone, imagery, cadence, and articulation, as well as its use of literary forms and figures. A play's diction is a creation of *both* the playwright *and* the spoken voice of the actor. New York director Marshall W. Mason says:

> Although they may base their work in real people and situations, directors should be discontent unless the reality that's being depicted is translated, transformed, or transfigured into a shimmering experience through the elevation of language. Stanislavski says that all art is attempting to become music. In theatre, there is an element of musical composition, of rhythm and structure. The more beautifully expressed the ideas are, the more articulate the diction of a play, the more it should attract directors.

Various kinds of diction place different stresses on direction. More demanding than prose, poetic drama requires a heightened apprehension of reality from both artists and audience. Since poetry condenses action, actors take an intense journey into their souls. The visualization executed by designers conveys a heightened, more spiritual reality. Directors and designers often begin rather than end with the abstraction of an idea culminating in the reality of a graphic set or costume.

Poetic diction often places sturdy demands on actors' voices. For years many actors' vocal skills were considered primary because of the difficulty of mastering superb diction.

Evaluate the diction of the following passages and the requirements they place on the actors' emotions and voices:

Macbeth: She should have died hereafter;
>   There would have been a time for such a word.
>   To-morrow, and to-morrow and to-morrow,
>   Creeps in this petty pace from day to day,
>   To the last syllable of recorded time;
>   And all our yesterdays have lighted fools
>   The way to dusty death. Out, out, brief candle!
>   Life's but a walking shadow, a poor player,
>   That struts and frets his hour upon the stage,
>   And then is heard no more. It is a tale
>   Told by an idiot, full of sound and fury,
>   Signifying nothing.

(*Macbeth*, Act V; scene v)

Juliet: Wilt thou be gone? It is not yet near day.
    It was the nightingale, and not the lark,
    That pierc'd the fearful hollow of thine ear;
    Nightly she sings on yon pomegranate tree.
    Believe me, love, it was the nightingale.
Romeo: It was the lark, the herald of the morn,
    No nightingale. Look, love, what envious streaks
    Do lace the severing clouds in yonder east.
    Night's candles are burnt out, and jocund day
    Stands tiptoe on the misty mountain tops.
    I must be gone and live or stay and die.
Juliet: Yon light is not day-light, I know it, I:
    It is some meteor. . . .
    O now be gone, more light and light it grows.
Romeo: More light and light, more dark and dark
    our woes.

                    (*Romeo and Juliet*, Act III; scene v)

Hecuba: Rise, stricken head, from the dust;
    lift up the throat. This is Troy, but Troy
    and we, Troy's kings, are perished.
    Stoop to the changing fortune.
    Steer for the crossing and the death-god,
    hold not life's prow on the course against
    wave beat and accident.
    Ah me,
    what need I further for tear's occasion,
    state perished, my son, and my husband?
    O massive pride that my fathers heaped
    to magnificence, you meant nothing.
    Must I be hushed?

                          (*The Trojan Women*)[1]

Mirabel: (unlocking the door and surprising her in the salon) Do you lock yourself
    up from me to make my search more curious? Or is this pretty artifice con-
    trived to signify that here the chase must end and my pursuit be crowned,
    for you can fly no further?
Mistress Millimant: (points at him with her closed fan) Vanity! (pirouettes playfully
    and turns from him, opening her fan to shield her face) No, I'll fly and be
    followed to the last moment. Though I am upon the very verge of matrimony,
    I expect you should solicit me as much as if I were wavering at the gate of a
    monastery, with one foot over the threshold. I'll be solicited to the very last,
    nay, and afterwards!
Mirabel: (raising her eyebrows) What, after the last?

---

[1]From *The Trojan Women* by Euripides. Translated by Richmond Lattimore, in
The Greek Tragedies (Vol. 2), © 1958 by the University of Chicago.

Mistress Millimant: (assuredly) Oh, I should think I was poor and had nothing to bestow if I were reduced to an inglorious ease and freed from the agreeable fatigues of solicitation. (walks away from him)

(William Congreve, *The Way of the World*, Act IV; scene i)

Yank: (changing a count as he shovels without effort) One—two—tree—(His voice rising exultantly in the joy of battle) Dat's de stuff! Let her have it! All to-gedder now! Sling it into her! Let her ride! Shoot de piece now! Call de toin on her! Drive her into it! Feel her move. Watch her smoke! Speed, dat's her middle name! Give her coal, youse guys! Coal, dat's her booze! Drink it up, baby! Let yuh sprint! Dig in and gain a lap! Dere she go-oes. (This last in the chanting formula of the galley gods at the six-day bike race. He slams his furnace door shut. The others do likewise with as much unison as their wearied bodies will permit. The effect is one of one firey eye after another being blotted out with a series of accompanying bangs.)

(*The Hairy Ape*, scene iii)[2]

Tusenbach: What are you thinking of? (pause) You are twenty, I am not yet thirty. How many years have we got before us, a long, long, chain of days full of my love for you—

Irina: Nikolai Lvovich, don't talk to me of love—

Tusenbach: (not listening) I have a passionate craving for life, for struggle, for work, and that craving is mingled in my soul with love for you, Irina, and just because you are beautiful it seems to me that life too is beautiful! What are you thinking of?

Irina: You say life is beautiful—yes, but what if it only seems so. Life for us three sisters has not been beautiful yet, we have been stifled by it as plants are choked by weeds. I am shedding tears—I mustn't do that (wipes her eyes and smiles). I must work, I must work. The reason we are depressed and take such a gloomy view of life is that we know nothing of work.

(*The Three Sisters*, Act I)[3]

Cocklebury-Smythe: May I be the first to welcome you to Room 3B. You will find the working conditions primitive, the hours antisocial, the amenities non-existent and the catering beneath contempt. On top of that the people are for the most part very boring, with interests either so generalized as to mimic wholesale ignorance or so particular as to be lunatic obsessions. Their level of conversations would pass without comment in the lavatory of a mixed comprehensive and the lavatories, by the way, are few and far between. . . .

(*Dirty Linen*)[4]

[2]From *The Hairy Ape* by Eugene O'Neill, p. 216. Copyright 1922; renewed 1950 by Eugene O'Neill. Reprinted by permission of Random House, Inc.

[3]From *The Three Sisters* by Anton Chekhov. Translated by Robert Cohen, in *Theatre* (Mayfield Publishing Co., Palo Alto, Ca.) 1981.

[4]From *Dirty Linen* by Tom Stoppard, © 1976. All rights reserved. Reprinted by permission of Grove Press, Inc.

Jerry: Well . . .
Emma: How are you?
Jerry: All right.
Emma: You look well.
Jerry: Well, I'm not all that well, really.
Emma: Why? What's the matter?
Jerry: Hangover.
(He raises his glass.)
Cheers.

(*Betrayal*, scene i)[5]

Music and Spectacle

Besides diction, Aristotle referred to two more ingredients, *music* and *spectacle*, that were part of good plays. While less important to a play's worth than plot, characters, thought, and diction, music and spectacle powerfully influence an audience's response to a play. Music differs from diction (spoken *words*) in that it is a cacophony of *sounds*. Every play should be assessed for its aural component. In doing so we should remember that Greek plays were chanted and sung. Nevertheless, all plays contain an orchestration of sounds. Music can include songs, footsteps, muffled talking, telephones, calls, nocturnal sounds, and so on. In musical comedy, operetta, and opera, music is the primary component.

Some plays, such as musical reviews, are organized around musical numbers. Their dialogue simply serves as a bridge between songs. Some scenes develop from the orchestration of sounds. "Catastrophe," the first scene of Arthur Kopit's play *Wings* illustrates this technique.

IMAGES	SOUNDS OUTSIDE HERSELF (SOUNDS live or on tape, altered or unadorned) Of wind.	MRS. TILSON'S VOICE (VOICE live or on tape, altered or unadorned)
Mostly, it is whiteness. Dazzling, blinding	Of someone breathing with effort, unevenly.	Oh My God oh my god oh my god—
Occasionally, there are brief rhombs of color, the color red being dominant.	Of something flapping, the sound suggestive of an old screen door perhaps, or a sheet	trees clouds houses mostly planes flashing past, images without words, utter disarray disbe-

[5]From *Betrayal* by Harold Pinter, © 1978 by Harold Pinter, Ltd. Reprinted by permission of Grove Press, Inc.

| | or sail in the wind. It is a rapid fibrillation. And it is used mostly to mark transitions. Of an airplane coming closer, thundering overhead, then zooming off into silence. | lief, never seen this kind of thing before! Where am I? How'd I get here? |
| Utter isolation. In this vast whiteness, like apparitions, partial glimpses of doctors and nurses can be seen. They appear and disappear like a pulse. They are never in one place for long. The mirrors multiply their incomprehensibility.[6] | Of random crowd noises, the crowd greatly agitated. In the crowd, people can be heard calling for help, a doctor, an ambulance. But all the sounds are garbled. Of people whispering. | Yes, feels cool . . . nice . . . Yes, this is the life all right! My plane! What has happened to my plane? Help. . . . |

Kopit achieves this "scrambled" effect through a brilliant dramaturgical design whereby the information conveyed on stage assumes the form it would take in the perceptions of the stroke victim herself; in other words, by his fashioning of the dramatic dialogue and imagery, Kopit gives his audience the opportunity not merely to observe a stroke, but to experience it (Cohen, *Theatre*, p. 281). You should examine the range of sounds in a play and look for ways to strengthen it through sound effects and music during the intermission and the production itself.

Besides its aural features, you must evaluate the visual aspects of a play. Spectacle encompasses the scenery, costumes, lighting, make-up, properties, visual arrangements, and the general look of the theater and stage. Effective visualizations can be both elaborate and subtle.

Along with spectacular settings and effects, the climax of the play often chills audiences with its visualizations: Oedipus pulling his eyes out in Sophocles's *Oedipus, the King*, Agave brandishing her son's head on a pole in Euripides's *The Bacchae*, Lear howling in the storm like a mad animal in Shakespeare's *King Lear*, Alan experiencing ecstasy on a god-like horse in Peter Shaffer's *Equus*, Mother Courage emitting a si-

[6]From *Wings* by Arthur Kopit, © 1978. Reprinted by permission of Hill & Wang, a division of Farrar, Straus, & Giroux.

lent scream upon hearing about her third child's death in Bertolt Brecht's *Mother Courage*.

The visual component of theater, while ranked last by Aristotle, should never be underestimated, especially in modern theater with its new technologies intriguing the appetites of any director. Some plays like *The Magic Show* have run for years on Broadway solely because of the visual effects onstage.

> Is not stage decor a continual description, which can be much more exact and much more powerful than a novelist's one? After the settings so powerful in their depth, and so astonishing in their verisimilitude, that we have recently seen in our theatre, we can no longer deny the possibility of evoking the reality of a milieu on the stage. It is up to the dramatists to make use of this reality. Let them provide the characters and the action; the designers, working from their directions, will provide the descriptions, as exactly as found necessary.
>
> (Emile Zola, 1867)[7]

Genre

Having evaluated a play for its components, its *genre* or type of drama must be assessed. Knowing the type of play and its period helps us appreciate the purpose and scope of its action. For example, Greek tragedy was written for audiences of over twenty thousand, for choruses doing broad dancelike movements on an arena backed by several masked actors performing on a raised stage. Now critics recognize a number of genres besides the original tragedy and comedy which are often more rigidly defined today than in Aristotle's time.

Robert Cohen defines *tragedy* as "a serious play (although not necessarily devoid of humorous episodes) with a topic of universal human import as its theme, in which the central character or characters confront suffering decline, and often death. Traditionally, tragedy involves the downfall of a character of elevated stature." Tragedy evokes pity and terror in the audience, resulting in a catharsis, or a "purging of the emotions" (Cohen, *Theatre*, p. 25).

Like tragedy, *melodrama* deals with serious events but it has a simplified theme. The protagonists are nice rather than elevated, the villains obsessively mean. Melodrama achieved great popularity in the nineteenth century by combining music (*melos*) with a simplified plot (*drama*). Historian Peter Arnott says, "In melodrama, good was always good and evil always evil. A string of exciting, though often implausibly contrived, situations placed the hero or heroine in predicaments from which they were able to extricate themselves only at the last moment by strength, superior moral qualities, or sheer luck. It was axiomatic that virtue should be triumphant, and mass audiences thrilled to fights, escapes, and natural disasters, staged with increasing scenic artifice as the century wore on" (Arnott, *Theatre in Its Time*, pp. 334–335).

[7]From *Theatre in Its Time* by Peter Arnott (Little, Brown, & Co., 1981), p. 362.

Both tragedy and melodrama treat great loss, but in tragedy the protagonist is responsible while in melodrama the loss results from external, uncontrollable forces. Romeo and Juliet cause each other's deaths.

> For never was a story of more woe
> than that of Juliet and her Romeo.
> (*Romeo and Juliet*, Act V; scene iii)

In W.H. Smith's *The Drunkard*, a nationally successful melodrama of the nineteenth century, drunkenness causes a family's woes. A temperance lecture in play form, *The Drunkard* is occasionally performed now as a comedy. The soap opera ("Dallas," "General Hospital") is the popular melodramatic form today. Bad melodrama, at its extreme, can be humorous.

> When some one peculiar quality
> Doth so possess a man that it doth draw
> All his effects, his spirits and his powers.
> In their confluctions all to run one way
> This may truly be said to be a humour . . .
> (Ben Jonson, *Man Out of His Humour*, 1599)

While tragedy and melodrama should evoke serious feelings, *comedy* and *farce* engage our sense of humor. Robert Cohen's definitions pinpoint their distinctions:

> A comedy is a humorous play with an *important* theme, in which characters confront themselves and each other with amusing results. Comedy can be intense, passionate, insightful, and moving, but its organization of the dramatic experience avoids sustained pity or terror and elicits more laughter than shock. A farce is a humorous play—and it had better be *wildly* humorous—on a *trivial* theme, usually one that is thoroughly familiar to theatre goers.
> Mistaken identify, illicit romance, elaborate misunderstandings—these are staples of farce. Identical twins, lovers in closets or under tables, full stage chases, switched potions, switched costumes (often involving men in women's costumes or women in men's clothes) mis-heard instructions, and various disrobings, discoveries, and disappearances characterize this age-old and perennially durable form" (Cohen, *Theatre*, p. 26).

The difference between comedy and farce can be further clarified by examining *The Bourgeois Gentleman* by Molière, a comedy and *A Flea in Her Ear*, a Georges Feydeau farce. *The Bourgeois Gentleman* is a comedy of character that deals with the social climber. The central character is a middle-class merchant who attempts to improve his status by increasingly ridiculous choices. He sacrifices family objections, common sense, and his own welfare in pursuit of his goal (Cohen, *Theatre*, p. 179). *A Flea in Her Ear* is a farce about infidelity; it involves mistaken identities, full-stage chases, hiding lovers, partial disrobings, outrageous discoveries, and the eventual chaotic disruption of an entire household.

Although comedy and farce are age-old genres, *tragicomedy* which combines tragedy and comedy is a twentieth-century phenomenon.

Tragicomedy intersperses moments of humor with those of rage and despair and concludes without the violent catharsis which the audience is led to expect. This form has audiences laughing one moment and thoughtful the next. Often the humor in tragicomedy is irreverent, such as in Joe Orton's *Loot* which satirizes our obsession with death and funerals, or Peter Nichol's *Joe Egg* which treats mental retardation humorously.

Problem

When evaluating a play you are baffled about, how to stage a sequence like this scene from *Suddenly Last Summer*:

Catharine: You don't have to hold onto me. I can't run away.
    Doctor: Miss Catharine?
Catharine: What?
    Doctor: Your aunt is a very sick woman. She had a stroke last Spring?
Catharine: Yes, she did, but she'll never admit it.
    Doctor: You have to understand why.[8]

[8]From *Suddenly Last Summer* by Tennessee Williams, © 1958 by Tennessee Williams. Reprinted by permission of New Directions Publishing Corp.

Evaluation—Solution: the actors quietly struggle with a painful communication; the director chooses a "serious" approach.
Suddenly, Last Summer by Tennessee Williams. Rider College Theatre. Director: R. H. O'Neill. Design: Thomas J. P. Sarr. Costumes: Marie Miller.

Solution

This sequence can be directed many ways, depending on its genre. If you choose comedy, you might direct Catharine to run wildly and have the Doctor stop her on the line, "You have to understand why." Should you choose to be serious, you could direct the actors to quietly struggle with the painful communication. Knowing the performance style of the playwright—in this case, Tennessee Williams—is your starting point. Examine the nature of twentieth-century Southern drama and Williams's place within that context *before* approaching the staging of the play.

The two final genres of plays are the *history play* and *musical comedy*. The history genre deals with events in a serious manner, such as medieval plays on religious history, like *Abraham and Isaac* or the playlets in the York Cycle including the *Creation*, the *Fall of Lucifer*, and the *Crucifixion*. While performances might contain some humor, the respectful approach this genre assumes is indicated in Shakespeare's *Henry V* by the character called "Chorus" who begins the prologue by asking the audience's indulgence for the humble presentation of great events:

Chorus: O for a Muse of fire, that would ascend
    The brightest heaven of invention!
    A kingdom for a stage, princes to act,
    And monarchs to behold the swelling scene!
    Then would the warlike Harry, like himself,
    Assume the port of Mars, and at his heels
    (Leash'd in, like hounds) should famine, sword and fire
    Crouch for employment. But pardon, gentles all,
    The flat unraised spirits that hath dar'd
    On this unworthy scaffold to bring forth
    So great an object. Can this cockpit hold
    The vasty fields of France? Or may we cram
    Within this wooden O the very casques
    That did affright the air at Agincourt?

Whereas the history genre emphasizes noteworthy figures and real events, the musical genre often stresses flights of fancy or fantasy. Defined by its reliance on music, especially on songs, this genre frequently combines with another: musical comedy (music plus comedy), grand opera (music plus tragedy) or operetta (music plus farce). You should note that the music genre expands the director's responsibilities (see Chapter 10: Managing a Musical).

Assessing genre and the components of a play can indicate the strengths and weaknesses of a script. Literary analysis of a play, be it a musical or a tragedy, is one of the most crucial tasks for the director. Ideally, any literary evaluation should be coupled with and followed by a historical one.

Problem

You need to choose a well-constructed play and are considering Henrik Ibsen's *A Doll's House*.

Solution

Evaluate the components and genre of the play for today's audience. *A Doll's House* is an extremely well-made and stageworthy play. Your analysis leads you to believe that the play has a strong plot and clear development of *characters*. While Torvald appears a bit one-dimensional, Nora is unique and has many contradictory sides: dishonest, sturdy, playful, decisive, and vulnerable. The *idea* of the play (woman's subordinate place in society) is still timely, unfortunately. Its diction while heavy handed at times, especially in translation, has some rich and vibrant passages—particularly in the Nora/Torvald scenes. Incidental *music* and singing could be used because of the Christmas holiday setting and children playing offstage. The Tarantella scene (Nora dancing with a tambourine) has exciting possibilities. *Spectacle*: the setting—one turn-of-the-century, comfortably, but not expensively, furnished room could limit visual appeal. Variety would have to be searched for in the staging. The genre, largely domestic *tragedy* (with vast social implications), deals with discussion rather than violent action. Conclusion: based on literary merits, it is a strong choice.

HISTORICAL EVALUATION

Along with its literary merits, you must evaluate the historical time frame of the play's action (see Chapter 5 for expanded discussion). Martin Esslin says: "I am always greatly put off by all the foreign names being pronounced wrongly in a play. The director hasn't even bothered to find out how those names are pronounced, let alone, let us say, the difference between the female and the male family name in Russian. In English plays, American directors make the most ghastly mistakes because they don't understand the culture so everything is misunderstood. I always advise students to study history and languages."

When assessing the historical play, examine the outlook of the people in its time and place and what significance the play could have for your specific audience. Inappropriate script choices result from misassumptions about the type of material to which an audience will relate.

Directors need to consider two opposite approaches, both valid, though in one they may lose part of the play and in the other they may lose part of the audience. The first approach involves altering or contracting the play's world to fit within the dimensions of our own, accommodating its concerns and its cultural ambience to those we're familiar with by "updating," so to speak, its reality. In principle, this approach makes plays from distant times more available to contemporary audiences, though in fact it runs the risk of losing the particularity of the plays themselves. Directors might mistakenly consider directing a thoroughly foreign play as if it were American when the logic of its plot, characters, behavioral patterns, and rhythms might be totally French, German, Russian or British, etc.

The second approach involves the determination to woo contemporary audiences to expand the limits of their familiar cultural locale to accommodate the plays. This approach has the undeniable virtue of preserving the integrity of the play and the play's world, and also of providing significant educational service to contemporary audiences, but in fact the gratitude of audiences for this service tends to evaporate along with its patience. Humankind, to paraphrase T.S. Eliot, cannot bear too much familiarity. Both approaches have their own kind of integrity and their own pitfalls.

(Leon Katz, dramaturg, Yale Drama School).

PRACTICAL EVALUATION

Along with your historical assessment, practical considerations should influence a script's choice. Whenever you evaluate scripts, you imagine them in a set of circumstances. The closer that vision is to reality, the likelier the play's success will be in production. Assess scripts for a particular time, for the type of space, the company, and the budget.

Time and Place

Marshall W. Mason, artistic director of Circle Rep. states:

Theatre is very much of the moment and so finding the right moment to do a play is important. There is a time to do a script, whether it be a classic or a new play. But it's possible for a new play to come along and for you to decide, "This is last year's news." A year or so ago every play was about cancer. I did choose to do Patrick Meyer's *Glorious Morning* in spite of the fact that it was the tenth play about cancer in New York City that year. I said, "The relevance is a little too late but let's do it anyway because it's such a beautiful and truthful play." The critics didn't go for it because they'd seen too many plays that year on the same subject.

Besides the right time, a play needs the right space. Your facility should enhance the play. For example, a highly verbal play requires superb acoustics and an "intimate" place that encourages active listening.

Company

Also examine whether a play suits your specific group. For instance, a fluffy 1940s revue is inappropriate for a theater committed to new work. Mounting Charles Dickens's *A Christmas Carol* will demand more staff than doing Tennessee Williams's *The Glass Menagerie*.

Scrutinize casting requirements. Remember, inexperienced actors work best in plays with physical action as in William Gibson's *The Miracle Worker*, where Annie must repeatedly force Helen to feed, dress, and care for herself. Complex roles require experience and technique. In educational theaters, look for plays with challenging roles for many young adults, for scripts that don't depend totally upon one or two stellar performances. Conversely, because of budgetary considerations, professional theater often requires plays calling for consummate performances of a few accomplished actors. On the other hand, in some community theaters, you may have to locate plays with several moderately demanding roles for mature women.

Budget

After the talent, budget also influences performance evaluation because directors deal with tangible items costing money. Besides the cost of doing a play you may need to consider a script's commercial appeal, which is sometimes ranked in the following order of audience interest: musical, mystery, comedy, drama.

Many directors choose plays in terms of seasons. Ask yourself: What else is being shown at this time, in this class, at this institution? How does my play augment those choices? Some theaters may engage you in seasonal planning, balancing a season with a variety of plays. This lengthy process may begin with conversations about what issues in the world and what kinds of theatrical experiences need addressing. Eventually, logistic reality such as the second show needing a smaller set due to less building time limits selections.

Some theaters effect a compromise with budgetary restrictions. They focus half the season on plays of the finest quality with which audiences are comfortable and the other half on innovative plays that could lose money, although the theater is nurtured by including them. Choosing a script is one of your most critical assignments as a director and cannot be approached too carefully.

> Choose an author as you choose a friend.
> (Wentworth Dillon, Earl of Roscommon, 1633–1685, "Essay on Translated Verse")

FINAL PROJECTS

1. Evaluate which play from each group would be more difficult to do at your theater based on the script's plot, character, thought, and diction; and on its genre:
   a. Shakespeare's *Hamlet* or Chekhov's *The Seagull*
   b. Goethe's *Faust* or Sophocles's *Oedipus*
   c. Oscar Wilde's *The Importance of Being Earnest* or Brandon Thomas's *Charley's Aunt.*
2. Allowing for diversity and range, propose a three play summer series with 14 actor slots (that averages out to about 4.5 actors per show) for a college theater. Justify why you have chosen these scripts for this theater based on practical criteria of time and space, company, and budget.

3. Stage a one-act play or a scene from the following list of plays
    (supplied by Ronald Wainscott) for final scenes. Justify your selec-
    tion based on personal, literary, and historical criteria:

1. *Ah, Wilderness!*, Eugene
    O'Neill
2. *The Iceman Cometh*, Eugene
    O'Neill
3. *Anna Christie*, Eugene O'Neill
4. *Moon for the Misbegotten*, Eu-
    gene O'Neill
5. *End of Summer*, S.N. Behr-
    man
6. *Biography*, S.N. Behrman
7. *Holiday*, Philip Barry
8. *The Philadelphia Story*, Philip
    Barry
9. *The Glass Menagerie*, Tennes-
    see Williams
10. *Cat on a Hot Tin Roof*, Ten-
    nessee Williams
11. *Night of the Iguana*, Tennes-
    see Williams
12. *A Streetcar Named Desire*, Ten-
    nessee Williams
13. *Summer and Smoke*, Tennessee
    Williams
14. *Streamers*, David Rabe
15. *In the Boom Boom Room*, David
    Rabe
16. *Hurly Burly*, David Rabe
17. *The Wager*, Mark Medoff
18. *When Ya Comin' Back Red Ry-
    der?*, Mark Medoff
19. *Gemini*, Albert Innaurato
20. *Come Back, Little Sheba*, Wil-
    liam Inge
21. *Picnic*, William Inge
22. *The Children's Hour*, Lillian
    Hellman
23. *The Autumn Garden*, Lillian
    Hellman
24. *A Raisin in the Sun*, Lorraine
    Hansberry
25. *A Delicate Balance*, Edward
    Albee

26. *Look Homeward Angel*, Ketti
    Frings
27. *The Subject Was Roses*, Frank
    Gilroy
28. *The Show-off*, George Kelly
29. *A Thousand Clowns*, Herb
    Gardner
30. *The Member of the Wedding*,
    Carson McCullers
31. *All My Sons*, Arthur Miller
32. *A View from the Bridge*, Arthur
    Miller
33. *Of Mice and Men*, Arthur
    Miller
34. *The Mound Builders*, Lanford
    Wilson
35. *5th of July*, Lanford Wilson
36. *Balm in Gilead*, Lanford Wil-
    son
37. *The Time of Your Life*, William
    Saroyan
38. *Golden Boy*, Clifford Odets
39. *Awake and Sing*, Clifford
    Odets
40. *That Championship Season*, Ja-
    son Miller
41. *American Buffalo*, David Ma-
    met
42. *Glengarry Glen Ross*, David
    Mamet
43. *Petrified Forest*, Robert Sher-
    wood
44. *Born Yesterday*, Garson Kanin
45. *The Boys in the Band*, Mart
    Crowley
46. *Ceremonies in Dark Old Men*,
    Lonnie Elder III
47. *A Hatful of Rain*, Michael
    Gazzo
48. *The Royal Family*, George S.
    Kaufman and Edna Ferber

49. *You Can't Take It With You,* George S. Kaufman and Moss Hart
50. *True West,* Sam Shepard
51. *Buried Child,* Sam Shepard
52. *Curse of the Starving Class,* Sam Shepard
53. *Crimes of the Heart,* Beth Henley
54. *In the Wine Time,* Ed Bullins
55. *Wedding Band,* Alice Childress
56. *Lu Ann Hampton Laverty Oberlander,* Preston Jones
57. *Painting Churches,* Tina Howe

Chapter 3

The Director as Analyst
Examining the Text

Action creates character and character creates action. A good play will have just that action, which will make the character interesting, and the interesting character so designed, that out of the character will come the action. It's a double connection. Remember, the characters are created by the author. The actor just fills them in.

Martin Esslin

Much of your work as critic depends on an in-depth understanding of the playwright and of the script. The breaking down of various acts, scenes, sections, and beats discussed in Chapter 2 must be based on a firm grasp of the content of the play. This chapter will deal with analyzing the script. Apart from any interpretation you may place upon it, a script and author must be evaluated in and of themselves.

One of the dangers of play analysis is overindulgence that causes us to leap into action, doing unwarranted things to and with a script. Most times this results in a production concept that is diametrically opposed to what is happening in the text. At a cursory glance, the play's wording can sometimes obscure the undercurrent of a scene that should be its dominant action. Allow time to experience a script—both its meaning and its literary devices, even if and especially when you are unclear about what to do in production. Script analysis deals with your journey with the playwright. You get to know the author, his or her works, and a particular series of events that (s)he has created.

As detailed as your interpretive breakdowns may be you should leave room before and throughout rehearsals to stimulate your imagination to fly and unite with the soaring vision of the playwright. Jot down any impressions you may have throughout your study of the play and its playwright, for these fleeting ideas may prove useful at the most unexpected times.

This chapter will deal with the philosophy and psychology of the writer behind the play. It will help you identify the features of play construction, which you need to understand in order to convey the playwright's intended message to your audience. This chapter addresses two major directing concerns: getting the *key* to the author, and identifying the *notes* of each play.

GET THE KEY TO THE AUTHOR

Read the Other Works

Most of us know that we need to understand the playwright and to read the author's other works. The question perplexing us is what specifically to look for. For example, one could read forever books on Shakespeare and his plays. Obviously the more brilliant the playwright, the more difficult the reading assignment. But remember play analysis is for the director's enhancement. You don't *necessarily* have to do anything with your research. Your goal is to understand the philosophy of the playwright. This outlook, like a multifaceted key, may unlock your particular play.

Identify Underlying Themes

Open the door to the author by reading the body of work, or as much of it as possible. (Directing Shakespeare does require extensive preparatory reading.) See if you can imagine the underlying theme running throughout.

For instance, Tennessee Williams is continually pointing out how individuals are trapped by the society they live in. The crippled Laura of *The Glass Menagerie*, unable to cope in the outside world, is imprisoned by her brother's final abandonment.

Blanche DuBois, ostracized by small-town gossip which she can't even escape in the big city, is taken off to an insane asylum in *A Streetcar Named Desire*. Brick at 25, a victim of society's loathing of inversion, resigns himself to the prison of alcoholism in *A Cat on a Hot Tin Roof*. This alienation, this sense that "I'm not part of you" is an underlying theme predominating in Williams's work.

Find the Characters Appearing in Every Play

Look at what characters appear in every play. They are often clues to the playwright's outlook. For example, Arthur Miller is very concerned with the relationship between father and son. Witness the breach between Willy Loman and Biff in *Death of a Salesman*, Eddie and his future son-in-law, Rodolpho, in *A View from the Bridge*, Joe and his son Chris in *All My Sons*. Chris describes this alienation from his father's world to his girlfriend, Ann:

> . . . and then I came home [from the war] and it was incredible. I—there was no meaning in it here; the whole thing to them was a kind of a—bus accident.

I went to work with Dad, and that rat-race again. I felt—what you said—ashamed somehow. Because nobody was changed at all. It seemed to make suckers out of a lot of guys. I felt wrong to be alive, to open the bank-book, to drive the new car, to see the new refrigerator. (*All My Sons*, Act I)[1]

If the idealistic son alienates himself from his materialistic father, can these two extreme codes of ethics ever be reconciled? Question: Can the son's idealism survive in the father's realistic "dog-eat-dog" world?

Besides plays, reading works of an author can include other types of literature: novels, sonnets, short stories, epistles. George Bernard Shaw's literary analysis of Ibsen, *The Quintessence of Ibsenism*, reveals as much about Shaw's philosophy on playwriting as Ibsen's. Like Shaw, many playwrights including Bertolt Brecht, Luigi Pirandello, Jean-Paul Sartre, Eugene Ionesco, and Edward Albee have also written many valuable prefaces to their own works. The key in auxiliary readings is not "what am I going to do with this" but "how does this reveal to me the mindset of the playwright? What issues was this author concerned with and why?"

Review articles describing the background and philosophy of the author and critiques of productions. Hearing authors talk about their plays in an interview is sometimes inspiring. There are tapes of Lorraine Hansberry, the first black playwright to be produced on Broadway, in which she defends the philosophy behind *A Raisin in the Sun*. (She was attacked by both blacks and whites for her philosophy.) Listening to these tapes would be particularly valuable if directing Hansberry's *To Be Young, Gifted, and Black*, which contains a scene where a journalist harangues the playwright.

Seeing photographs of the playwright or productions also draws you into the author's world. For example, pictures of Arthur Miller and his ex-wife Marilyn Monroe (whom he wrote about in *After the Fall*), and photos of the McCarthy trials (another subject of the play) would reveal different sides of Miller.

Study the History of the Period

Along with reading the other works, study the history of the period during which the playwright lived and wrote. Any playwright is always reacting to and interpreting what is going on at a given moment.

Family Relationships

Your study should begin with an examination of family relationships, the core unit at the heart of most playwrights' lives. It has been claimed that Eugene O'Neill's mastery as a writer was sourced in the fact that

[1]From *All My Sons* by Arthur Miller. In *Arthur Miller's Collected Plays*, copyright 1947; copyright renewed 1975 by Arthur Miller. Reprinted by permission of Viking Penguin, Inc.

he could write with such accuracy and abandon about his immediate family (mother, father, two brothers), because they had all died by the time he reached thirty-five. Many plays have strong biographical strains. O'Neill was said to be so anguished when writing *A Long Day's Journey into Night* that he would emerge, stricken with grief, from his daily sessions of writing (Gelb, *O'Neill*, p. 534). Similarly, Shakespeare's masterpiece *Hamlet* was written after the death of the poet's only son, eleven-year-old Hammet. Tennessee Williams grieved throughout his lifetime for his sister, Rose, who like Blanche in *Streetcar* and Catherine in *Suddenly Last Summer* was institutionalized.

Explore the playwright's view toward family life. Who were the family members who created the most enduring impressions? Where were the tensions; what were the concerns? For example, alcoholism and drugs were issues infiltrating the O'Neill home (both O'Neill's mother and brother were addicts). Who was the parent or sibling, like Williams's Rose, who was most cherished; who was feared? While not all plays have biographical overtones, most playwrights (except, perhaps, Genet and a few others) were influenced by family relationships.

What was the larger family circle of the playwright? For the Florentine playwright/politician Machiavelli, it was the world of the 16th century Italian court. For Molière, it was his company of actors including his illicit "daughter," Armande, whom he later married, and his 17th-century patron King Louis XIV of France. Any study of the circle of friends of the writer also conditions our understanding of the artist.

Social Conditions

Every playwright comes from a culture. We must perceive how to relate these social facts, if pertinent, to the play. The circumstances in *Death of a Salesman* reveal a collapse of morality in the American culture, an anxiety in personal issues, a fear of loss of self-esteem, and the dissolution of family life. All these social conditions prevailed in the post-World War II America of the author. You have to understand what was going on in the playwright's thoughts and feelings and its relationship to the social moment.

First identify the broadest social issues. Learn what the social conditions were: segregation (*A Raisin in the Sun* by Lorraine Hansberry), women's liberation (*A Doll's House* by Henrik Ibsen), death of an aristocracy (*The Cherry Orchard* by Anton Chekhov), and so on.

Ask yourself, "How was the world changing in this period? What particular issues were influencing the lives of families and countries?" The social conditions affect how the playwright's characters act toward each other and toward society, and why the playwright created these characters in the first place.

Even in Greek plays, chanted rituals in huge theaters, the characters reflect a social context. In Aristophanes's anti-war comedy *Lysistrata*, Greek women strike for peace by practicing celibacy—and the war stops.

When the aristocrat Aristophanes wrote the play, he was calling for an end to strife against Sparta.

Studying the social conditions of the period should reveal to you the values by which people lived. Often playwrights address how change affects the characters. In *Hamlet*, the hero's predicament results from his uncle marrying his mother and seizing the throne. Many plays are structured on sweeping societal changes such as the death or overthrow of a king (Euripides's *Agamemnon*; Sophocles's *Oedipus*; Shakespeare's *Macbeth, Hamlet, King Lear*; Calderon's *Life Is a Dream;* Racine's *Phaedre*, to name but a few).

IDENTIFY THE NOTES IN EACH PLAY

Along with an examination of how the world around playwrights shaped their philosophy, you will need to examine certain features or notes in each play, including action, characters, place, and theme. Every play, like every piece of music, has a different melody.

Action

Reading the words should instill you with a sense of the action of a play. Try to read the play for its momentum, to feel the rhythm of the action. Action is *direct* when the words convey the action and *indirect* when the words are a "coverup" for the true meaning. The words are set aginst what a character thinks and feels. Read the play and allow yourself to be swept into the thoughts and dreams of the characters.

Martin Esslin finds the rhythm of the action one of the most salient features of a play. He defines *rhythm* as follows:

> Rhythm in drama is formed by the succession of sound and words, which is equivalent to the sound pattern in music. Whether those intervals are sharp, short, or long, you must have ups and downs, and variety. You have a separate theme and variations of the theme; you can't go by the same melody for too long; and you have to have counterpoints, and things that are surrounding different faces. One of the physiological rules of human nature, is if you talk at the same pace and the same rhythm for too long, people actually fall asleep. So the main task of the director, is to set up a constant alternation of pace and intensity and decibels, which will never allow anybody to feel the play is going on exactly the same all the time. That is why you have to work up to climaxes, where suddenly the action becomes different.

To understand the rhythm of a play, you must explore how the action is structured to create a specific emotional and intellectual response in the audience (see Chapter 2 for literary evaluation and Chapter 4 for scene breakdowns). Here we will look at how the characters and situations are developed to reveal the mounting action of the playwright. You should examine the peaks of the play; to what moments you need to build and why; and what kind of characters you are dealing with in that build.

Any examination of the peaks in a play should explore the *reversals* that occur to the characters. A reversal comes when a character is thwarted by the truth of the situation, whether from the circumstances, the environment, an antagonist, or simply from a revelation of information.

Problem

You are having difficulty identifying the reversals in a *Hamlet* sequence.

Solution

Identify all the lines where surprising information is given. Then identify the major reversal creating this adjustment:

Ophelia: Good my lord, how does your honor for this many a day?

Hamlet: I humbly thank you; well, well, well.

Ophelia: My lord, I have remembrances of yours, that I have longed to re-deliver; I pray you now, receive them.

Hamlet: No, not I. I never gave you aught. [*reversal*]

Ophelia: My honor'd lord, you know right well you did; And, with them, words of so sweet breath compos'd as made the things more rich. Their perfume lost, take these things again, for to the noble mind rich gifts wax poor when givers prove unkind. There, my lord.

Hamlet: Ha, ha! Are you honest? [*reversal*]

Ophelia: My lord!

Hamlet: Are you fair? [*reversal*]

Ophelia: What means your lordship?

Hamlet: That if you be honest and fair, your honesty should admit no discourse to your beauty.

Ophelia: Could beauty, my lord, have better commerce than with honesty?

Hamlet: Ay, truly; for the power of beauty will sooner transform honesty from what it is to a bawd than the force of honesty can translate beauty into his likeness. This was sometime a paradox, but now the time gives it proof. I did love you once.

Ophelia: Indeed, my lord, you made me believe so.

Hamlet: You should not have believed me [*reversal*], for virtue cannot so inoculate our old stock but we shall relish of it. I loved you not. [*reversal*].

Ophelia: I was the more deceived.

Hamlet: Get thee to a nunnery [*reversal*]. Why wouldst thou be a breeder of sinners?

(*Hamlet*, Act III; scene i)

In a reversal, the character will either be cleansed, enlightened, uplifted or discouraged, heartbroken and disenchanted, as Ophelia is in the above scene. Identify these points for yourself so that later in your discussions with the actors it will be clear to everyone where the changes for the characters occur.

Mark off in your script crucial transition points in the plays, the acts, and each scene. This study should be augmented by your in-depth scene breakdowns (see Chapter 4).

Characters

No study of the action of a play can be understood without a profound understanding of the *characters* who generate the action. You will need to examine the characters for their background, dreams, and symbolic value.

Background

Knowing the background of the characters helps you understand their actions. For example where a character was born and raised influences where s(he) wants to be and what s(he) wants to do. Coming from the Belle Reve plantation in Tennessee Williams's *A Streetcar Named Desire*, Blanche is likely to be miserable at Stanley Kowalski's tiny slum apartment on the fringe of the French Quarter.

Note Williams's opening description of the two characters:

> Stanley is about twenty-eight-years old, roughly dressed in his denim work clothes. He carries a bowling jacket and a red-stained package from the butcher's. He stops at the foot of the steps to his apartment, hollers for his wife, heaves the package at her, then starts back around the corner . . .
>
> Blanche comes around the corner, carrying a valise. Her appearance is incongruous in this setting . . . She is daintily dressed in a white suit with a fluffly bodice, necklace and earrings of pearl, white gloves and hat, looking as if she were arriving at a summer tea or cocktail party in the garden district. She is about 30. Her delicate beauty must avoid a strong light. There is something about her uncertain manner, as well as her white clothes, that suggests a moth (*A Streetcar Named Desire*, scene i).[2]

These two descriptions reveal Blanche and Stanley as opposites. Remember: the characters create the conflict or opposing actions.

Thoroughly explore the characters' background so you can identify their actions. While actors must formulate background in detail themselves, later during rehearsal you might ask them questions—if you feel it appropriate or necessary—to help them focus in on their characters' actions. Also, the actors will come to you as a resource when they encounter any dilemmas or inconsistencies (see Chapter 8: The Director as Coach).

The background of the characters consists of material that supports the characters' actions in the script. This material, while fully imagined

[2]From *A Streetcar Named Desire* by Tennessee Williams, © 1947 by Tennessee Williams. Reprinted by permission of New Directions Publishing Corp.

by the actors based on their personal experience, must be created within the reference points the author gives you. As mentioned in Chapter 2, you need to evaluate each line of dialogue for specific points of information. For example, if a character says, "I went to bed early last night," that is a point of information. You might need to calculate exactly when she goes to bed—say 10 P.M.—and her nightly routine. The actress might go into even more detail to capture the experience behind the line that influences her current stage moment. Note the information in Blanche's opening scene in *Streetcar*. Points of information are *italicized*:

Eunice: I think she said *you taught school*.
Blanche: Yes.
Eunice: And *you're from Mississippi*, huh?
Blanche: Yes.
Eunice: She showed me a picture of your home place, *the plantation*.
Blanche: Belle Reve?
Eunice: *A great big place with white columns*.
Blanche: Yes . . .
Eunice: A place like that must be awful hard to keep up.
Blanche: If you will excuse me, I'm just *about to drop*.
Eunice: Sure, honey. Why don't you set down?
Blanche: What I meant was *I'd like to be left alone*.
Eunice: (offended) Aw. I'll make myself scarce, in that case.
Blanche: I didn't mean *to be rude*, but—
Eunice: I'll drop by the bowling alley an' hustle her up. (She goes out the door.)
(*A Streetcar Named Desire*, Act I; scene i)[3]

This technique of identifying information *in* the lines will help you read *between* the lines to other information leading to your discovery of the meaning of the play. For example, Blanche's description of her miserable journey to her sister's not only exposes her urgent circumstances, it echoes the action of the individual trapped by society. The scene reveals the desperation, sensitivity, and idealism of the misfit; and how idealism can lead into a fearful, unreal world. For Blanche that is to the insane asylum at the climax of the play. You get the peaks of the play through looking at the character's background and behavior: turmoil (a strange sordid apartment), the inner agitation (Blanche's increasing need to drink).

As director, you are seeking to merge with the playwright's view. You are imagining how to reveal that churning experience to the audience in the fullest way. But the play and the actors are totally subjective in a detailed universe of action so the ideas must be revealed through the specificity and significance of what they do.

Use your intuition to understand the characters from the inside. Then

[3]See note 2 above.

test your intuition by examining certain background information about them:

1. where they live
2. whether they are married
3. whether they have children
4. whether they behave themselves
5. whether they are underpaid
6. whether they are disciplined
7. whether they are organized or disorganized
8. whether they are meticulous or messy
9. whether they are bold or aggressive
10. whether they are critical or accepting

When you collect any traits (items 5–10), think about how do-able they are. How do these traits show up in the action of the text? Do they lead you to identify the protagonist (Blanche) or the antagonist (Stanley) and the battle developing out of who they are?

EXERCISES

1. Read several works by a playwright and describe the underlying theme.
2. Identify traits 1–10 above for the two leading characters in a play.

Class Struggle

The struggle between individuals is often augmented by a larger class struggle within the play. For example, Blanche is from the upper and Stanley from the lower class. George Bernard Shaw's *Pygmalion* deals with a lower class flower girl being schooled to enter the upper class. Any staging of that play would necessitate a study of the inherent conflict between the British social classes. In the first act, at Higgins's laboratory on Wimpole Street, class lines are delineated:

Liza: (overwhelmed) Ah-ah-ow-oo!
Higgins: There! That's all you'll get out of Eliza. Ah-ah-ow-oo! No use explaining. As a military man you ought to know that. Give her her orders: that's what she wants. Eliza: you are to live here for the next six months, learning how to speak beautifully, like a lady in a florist's shop. If you're good and do whatever you're told, you shall sleep in a proper bedroom, and have lots to eat, and money to buy chocolates and take rides in taxis. If you're naughty and idle you will sleep in the back kitchen among the black beetles, and be walloped by Mrs. Pearce with a broomstick. At the end of six months you will go to Buckingham Palace in a carriage, beautifully dressed. If the King finds out you're not a lady, you will be taken by the police to the Tower of

London, where your head will be cut off as a warning to other presumptuous flower girls.[4]

Some plays address the clash between nations. Shakespeare's plays address the overthrow of regimes. *The Trojan Women*, by Euripides, is about the fall of Hecuba and also the fall of Troy.

Dream of the Characters

Characters should be seen in their largest aspect. In major works, millions of other people can readily relate to the character's dilemma. You will need to explore the vision of the character in its fullest sense.

In many plays, the characters escape from the reality of the situation into a dream life or into a contemplative experience. The playwright has put the character realistically into circumstances which s(he) cannot face. For example, in Shakespeare's *Hamlet* the most famous monologue results from such a crisis. Hamlet cannot accept his newly married uncle as his father and king.

Problem

Determine the details of Hamlet's crisis.

Solution

1. Identify what Hamlet is considering doing and the background behind each word *italicized* in the following monologue. (Obviously, you could emphasize other words as well.)

Hamlet: To be, or not to be, that is the *question*:
       Whether 'tis nobler in the *mind* to suffer
       The slings and arrows of *outrageous fortune*,
       Or to take *arms against a sea of troubles*
       And by *opposing, end them*. To die: to *sleep*,
       No more; and by a sleep to say we end
       The *heart-ache* and the *thousand natural shocks*
       That flesh is heir to: 'tis a *consummation*
       Devoutly to be wish'd. To die: to sleep,
       To sleep? perchance to *dream*, there's the rub;
       For in that sleep of death *what dreams may come*,
       When we have *shuffled off* this mortal coil,
       Must give us *pause*!

(*Hamlet*, Act III; scene i)

2. List the actions that *Hamlet* is contemplating, then examine how they might affect a) his personal life with Ophelia, his mother, his friends; b) his societal place as a scholar and as the Prince of Denmark; c) his international position with other countries. Your research should strengthen your understanding of the complexity of Hamlet's dilemma.

[4]From *Pygmalion* by George Bernard Shaw. Reprinted by permission of the Society of Authors on behalf of the Bernard Shaw estate.

When characters start running from their circumstances as do Hamlet, Laura (the sister in *The Glass Menagerie*), and Macbeth, they may go deeper and deeper into unreality or a "dream" life. All of these characters, for example, have been considered "mad" by some scholars. Blanche, in particular, exemplifies escapism. Drowning her sexuality in fancy coverups, she uses affectation to hide her belief that what others say about her is true.

Problem

What does the following dialogue reveal about Blanche's escapism? What artificial likenesses does Blanche use to hide from the world?

Blanche: I received a telegram from an old admirer of mine.
Stanley: Anything good?
Blanche: I think so. An invitation.
Stanley: What to? A fireman's ball?
Blanche: (throwing back her head) A cruise of the Caribbean on a yacht!
Stanley: Well, well. What do you know?
Blanche: I have never been so surprised in my life.
Stanley: I guess not.
Blanche: It came like a bolt from the blue!
Stanley: Who did you say it was from?
Blanche: An old beau of mine.
Stanley: The one that give you the white fox-pieces?
Blanche: Mr. Shep Huntleigh. I wore his ATO pin my last year at college. I hadn't seen him again until last Christmas. I ran into him on Biscayne Boulevard. Then—just now—this wire—inviting me on a cruise of the Caribbean! The problem is clothes. I tore into my trunk to see what I have that's suitable for the tropics!
Stanley: And come up with that—gorgeous—diamond—tiara?
Blanche: This old relic? Ha-ha! It's only rhinestones.
Stanley: Gosh. I thought it was Tiffany diamonds. (He unbuttons his shirt)
Blanche: Well, anyhow, I shall be entertained in style.
Stanley: Uh-huh. It goes to show, you never know what is coming.
Blanche: Just when I thought my luck had begun to fail me—
Stanley: Into the picture pops this Miami millionaire.
Blanche: This man is not from Miami. This man is from Dallas.
Stanley: This man is from Dallas?
Blanche: Yes, this man is from Dallas where gold spouts out of the ground!
Stanley: Well, just so he's from somewhere! (He starts removing his shirt)
Blanche: Close the curtains before you undress any further.
Stanley: (amiably) This is all I'm going to undress right now. (He rips the sack off a quart beer-bottle) Seen a bottle-opener? (She moves slowly toward the dresser, where she stands with her hands knotted together) I used

to have a cousin who could open a beer-bottle with his teeth. (Pounding the bottle cap on the corner of table)

(*A Streetcar Named Desire*, scene x)[5]

Solution

Identify how Stanley sees the behavior of Blanche and all that alienates him. Stanley is the "brute" from whom Blanche is running.

Symbolic Value

Characters must also be investigated for what they symbolize. This is a dangerous, but critical task. It is *dangerous* because actors cannot play literary symbols, and *critical* because important characters often have broad social meaning (for example, in Arthur Miller's *Death of a Salesman*, Willy Loman is an individual and also a symbol of the failed salesman).

> Charley (stopping Happy's movement and reply. To Biff): Nobody dast blame this man. You don't understand: Willy was a salesman, and for a salesman there is no rock bottom to the life. He don't put a bolt to a nut, he don't tell you the law or give you medicine. He's a man way out there in the blue, riding on a smile and a shoeshine. And when they start not smiling back—that's an earthquake. And then you get yourself a couple of spots on your hat, and you're finished. Nobody dast blame this man. A salesman is got to dream, boy. It comes with the territory.
>
> (*Death of a Salesman*, Act II; "Requiem")[6]

Every character must be understood for what s(he) symbolizes such as the father, the mother, the maid, the doctor. You will have to find actors who can play these characters as individuals; who can relate to their unique destinies, goals, and idiosyncracies. But, you will also have to explore what it means to be a salesman in *Death of a Salesman*, a doctor in Anton Chekhov's *Uncle Vanya*, a fool in Shakespeare's *Twelfth Night*, a maid in Jean Genet's *The Maids* or Wendy Kesselman's *My Sister in This House*, a seaman in the adaptation of Herman Melville's *Moby Dick*.

Place

Along with developing an understanding of the characters, you should study the place or setting of the play. Establishing the place onstage is the foundation of the play's reality. Know where the action takes place at every point in the script. Is it in the country surrounded by woods and lakes, as in *The Seagull* by Anton Chekhov, or in the city, with sirens and subway noises as in *The Prisoner of Second Avenue* by Neil Simon?

[5]See note 2 above.

[6]From *Death of a Salesman* by Arthur Miller. Copyright 1949; copyright renewed 1977 by Arthur Miller. Reprinted by permission of Viking Penguin, Inc.

Appropriately, in both these plays, the protagonists long for the opposite surroundings, the excitement of the city and the relaxation of the country, respectively.

The Meaning of the Place

Imagine how the place influences the outlook of the characters. Did the playwright live in such a place; if so, what were its frustrations and delights? Spend time looking up pictures of the setting of the play as well as perspectives of artists on the setting. (Consider the many ways New York City has been filmed, described, and pictured by its different inhabitants, interpreters, and admirers.)

Imagine yourself living in that place. Try to experience while reading the play and researching it how the environment of the play influenced its writing. How, for example, has living in St. Louis affected the motivations and subsequent actions of Laura and Tom in *The Glass Menagerie*? What influence has the deep South had on their overbearing mother, Amanda Wingfield, and her present predicament in the midwest?

Everyday Circumstances of the Play

Besides the meaning of the place you will need to explore the immediate circumstances of the play. What is the season of the year? How does the weather influence the coldness or warmness of the scene's mood? If it's cold and snowy, windy and gray outside, that affects the mood of the entire scene. Whatever the characters are doing and feeling will be conditioned by the gray mood. Shakespeare is often preoccupied with weather and nature as symptomatic of the larger upset in the universe. The first witches scene in Shakespeare's *Macbeth* creates the mood of foreboding for Macbeth by calling the day both fair and foul.

1 Witch: When shall we three meet again?
    In thunder, lightning, or in rain?
2 Witch: When the hurlyburly's done,
    When the battle's lost and won.
3 Witch: That will be ere the set of the sun.
1 Witch: Where the place?
2 Witch: Upon the heath.
3 Witch: There to meet with Macbeth.
1 Witch: I come, Graymalkin!
2 Witch: Paddock calls.
3 Witch: Anon!
All: Fair is foul, and foul is fair:
    Hover through the fog and filthy air.

                                (*Macbeth*, Act I; scene i)

Both Chekhov's *The Three Sisters* and Williams's *Streetcar* open on a May day; but, the former is a wonderful spring day in Russia, and the latter, a warm, humid day in New Orleans.

Besides weather, note the time of day of each scene. People feel different at breakfast when they get up, fresh to start the day, than they do at the end of a long, and perhaps trying day, full of difficulties. Toward dinnertime, you might find the characters preoccupied with the problems and events of the day and less communicative; or, just the opposite—ready to forget the day's troubles and have a good time. Many Plautine comedies, like the musical adaptation *A Funny Thing Happened on the Way to the Forum*, for instance, are based on a holiday spirit. Ground rules are broken and the rules are backwards from normal, conservative Roman routine.

Theme

Besides the action, characters, and setting, any study of a play must ultimately focus on its theme or message. Usually, as directors, we want to identify this focal point immediately since it underpins so much of the characters' actions. However, understanding the theme of the play evolves from a thorough exploration of its words.

Repetition

Examine how certain words are used throughout the script. Often when a word is used several times, its significance is assured (most playwrights carefully pick their words). To illustrate, let us look at Chekhov's *The Three Sisters*: the sisters' dream of "going to Moscow" is repeated throughout the play. Moscow, like Never Never Land, where the lost boys go in Philip Barry's *Peter Pan*, is the symbol for the haven where all problems subside. In the opening of the play Olga says:

> Father was given his brigade and came here with us from Moscow eleven years ago and I remember distinctly that in Moscow at this time, at the beginning of May, everything was already in flower; it was warm and everything was bathed in sunshine. It's eleven years ago and yet I remember it as though we had left it yesterday.

Later the middle-aged and handsome Colonel Vershinin arrives on the scene from Moscow.

Tusenbach: Alexander Vershinin has come from Moscow.
Irina: From Moscow? You have come from Moscow?
Vershinin: Yes, your father was in command of a battery there, and I was an officer in the same brigade. (to Masha) Your face, now, I seem to remember.
Masha: I don't remember you.
Vershinin: So you are Olga, the eldest—and you are Masha—and you are Irina, the youngest—
Olga: You come from Moscow?
Vershinin: Yes, I studied in Moscow . . . I used to visit you in Moscow.

(Act I)[7]

---

[7]From *The Three Sisters* by Anton Chekhov. Translated by Robert Cohen in *Theatre* (Mayfield Publishing Co., Palo Alto, Ca.), 1981, pp. 3–22.

The repetition of words and their use throughout the script is a clue to the overall idea of the scene and play. In the above scene the word "Moscow" is repeated to such an extent that the significance of the place as a wish-fulfillment becomes obvious.

Although some plays' words will not bear up under detailed scrutiny, others continually haunt you with their deeper layers of meaning. For example, as soon as you discover the Moscow theme in *The Three Sisters*, you might begin noticing a subtle strain of unexpressed sexuality and love, as underscored by the end of the play:

Olga: Here she comes!
    (Masha comes in)
Vershinin: I have come to say goodbye—
Masha: (looking into his face) Goodbye—(a prolonged kiss)
Olga: (Who has moved away to leave them free) Come, come—
    (Masha sobs violently)
Vershinin: Write to me—Don't forget me! Let me go!—Time is up! Olga, take her, I must—go—I am late.
    (Much moved, he kisses Olga's hands, then again embraces Masha and quickly goes off)
Olga: Come, Masha! Leave off, darling—
    (Enter Kulygin, Masha's husband)
Kulygin: (embarrassed) Never mind, let her cry—let her—my good Masha. My dear Masha!—You are my wife, and I am happy, anyway—I don't complain; I don't say a word of blame—Here, Olga is my witness—we'll begin the old life again, and I won't say one word, not a hint—

(The Three Sisters, Act IV)[8]

Again a study of repressed love might lead us to the question "What are the characters hiding from each other?" Kulygin will not say a word. What is happening in the pauses and silences? What anguish is beneath the unspoken communications?

An analysis of the words, their repetitions and meanings leads to the tensions beneath them. Since drama is based on conflict, finding the *difficulties* of the characters will give us more clues to the theme. In *The Three Sisters* each of the heroines (Olga—a spinster schoolteacher, Masha—a bored wife, and Irina—a depressed youth) are frustrated by their lives. Each longs for Moscow and some fulfillment.

Names and Titles

Along with the repetition of words, phrases or silences, names of the title and characters of the play should be examined. Often these are vital clues to the theme. For example, Harold Pinter's *Betrayal* is a play about the betrayal of adultery. Calderon's Spanish classic *Life Is a Dream* is about living a dream, Molière's *The Imaginary Invalid* is about a hypochondriac and *The Bourgeois Gentleman* is about a social climber.

[8]See note 7 above.

Shakespeare's *Tempest* is about a fantastical storm. Study what the title means. Sometimes that meaning is concretely expressed in the play itself: Maggie (Margaret) from Williams's *Cat on a Hot Tin Roof* explains why she is a "cat." (Note added emphasis of *cat*.)

Mae: Why are you so *catty*?

Margaret: Cause I'm a *cat*! But why can't *you* take a joke, Sister Woman?

Mae: Nothin' pleases me more than a joke that's funny. You know the real names of our kiddies. Buster's real name is Robert. Sonny's real name is Saunders. Trixie's real name is Marlene and Dixie's— (Gooper downstains calls for her. "Hey, Mae! Sister Woman, intermission is over!"—she rushes to door, saying.) Intermission is over! See ya later!

Margaret: I wonder what Dixie's real name is?

Brick: Maggie, being *catty* doesn't help things any . . .

Margaret: I know! Why!—Am I so *catty*?—'Cause I'm consumed with envy an' eaten up with longing?—Brick, I'm going to lay out your beautiful Shantung silk suit from Rome and one of your monogrammed silk shirts. I'll put your cuff links in, those lovely star sapphires I get you to wear so rarely . . .

Brick: I can't get trousers on over this plaster cast.

Margaret: Yes, you can, I'll help you.

Brick: I'm not going to get dressed, Maggie.

Margaret: Will you just put on a pair of white silk pajamas?

Brick: Yes, I'll do that, Maggie.

Margaret: *Thank* you, thank you so *much*!

Brick: Don't mention it.

Margaret: *Oh, Brick*! How long does it have t'go on? This punishment? Haven't I done time enough, haven't I served my term, can't I apply for a—pardon?

Brick: Maggie, you're spoiling my liquor. Lately your voice always sounds like you'd been running upstairs to warn somebody that the house was on fire!

Margaret: Well, no wonder, no wonder. Y'know what I feel like, Brick? *I feel all the time like a cat on a hot tin roof*!

Brick: Then jump off the roof, jump off it, *cats* can jump off roofs and land on their four feet uninjured!

Margaret: Oh, yes!

Brick: Do it!—fo' God's sake, do it . . .

Margaret: Do what?

Brick: Take a lover!

Margaret: I can't see a man but you!

(*Cat on a Hot Tin Roof*, Act I)[9]

Richard in Eugene O'Neill's nostalgic romance, *Ah, Wilderness!* quotes the *Rubaiyat* of Omar Khayyám:

A Book of Verses underneath the Bough, A Jug of Wine, A Loaf of Bread— and Thou Beside me singing in the Wilderness—

[9]From *Cat on a Hot Tin Roof* by Tennessee Williams, © 1975. Reprinted by permission of New Directions Publishing Corp.

After the title, examine the meaning of each character's name. Names suggest the meaning of the theme. Study the sound, tones, and rhythm of a name. In *Streetcar*, Blanche DuBois (French for "white woods") is a supposed-poetic virgin who comes from Belle Reve ("beautiful dream") plantation to her sister Stella's (stationary "star"). In an opening scene, Blanche actually refers to her sister as "Stella, Stella for star." By marrying Stanley Kowalski (listen to the sound of *that* name), a Polish dock worker, Stella has become Stella Kowalski (no longer "star of the woods" but "star of Kowalski"). This kind of examination could go on and on into oblivion.

While a study of names may not show up directly in the action onstage, each character does operate from and is colored by a specific name which s(he) is given at birth. How s(he) accepts or rejects that name is a part of the character's identity.

In less realistic plays, the name of the character is sometimes a symbol for the theme of the play. *Everyman* the medieval allegory is about the journey of Everyman toward death and the opponents, named Fellowship, Beauty, Goods, and so, he confronts along the way.

Study the opposing forces that the characters' names might indicate. For example, in Miller's *Death of a Salesman* the names of the parents, "Willy" and "Linda" have a slower, more downbeat sound than the uplifting names of the sons "Happy" and "Biff." "Willy" and "Linda" are ordinary names as opposed to the more unusual "Happy" and "Biff." (Question: Why do you think these names were chosen?) What were the parents expecting of their sons? And how did they disappoint them? In a materialistic world like the Loman's, the children represent the only key to immortality. Do the names express this wish-fulfillment of the parents? Finding the contrasts in the names sometimes enlightens you about the conflict in the play.

Some great playwrights, like Shakespeare, use names to underpin the conflict. Juliet is forbidden to marry Romeo.

Juliet: O Romeo, Romeo, wherefore art thou Romeo?
Deny thy father and refuse thy name;
Or if thou wilt not, be but sworn my love
And I'll no longer be a Capulet.

(*Romeo and Juliet*, Act II; scene i)

Viola begs Olivia to heed Count Orsino's desperate love:

Viola: If I did love you in my master's flame,
With such a suff'ring such a deadly life,
In your denial I would find no sense;
I would not understand it.
Olivia: Why, what would you?
Viola: Make me a willow cabin at your gate
And call upon my soul within the house;

Write royal cantons of condemned love
And sing them loud even in the dead of night;
Hallow *your name* to the reverberate hills
And make the babbling gossip of the air
Cry out '*Olivia.*' O, you should not rest
Between the elements of air and earth
But you should pity me.

(*Twelfth Night*, Act I; scene v)

Besides augmenting the conflict, names reveal the background and social settings of the characters, as in "Count Orsino" and "Olivia" (upper class) as opposed to the aforementioned "Stanley Kowalski" (lower class).

Conclusion

The characters and place are the keys to the action. The more you know about them and the playwright the more the theme of the play will reveal itself. A strong play, like a chameleon, presents two truths or sides to any idea. Some scripts present endless philosophical perspectives on a theme.

The illumination of the play and the journey with the playwright is never ended. In this chapter we have explored some stops along the way. Each will differ for various writers and plays. A number of issues may pose more questions. The critical thing is to address the *questions* of the play.

The illumination of the moment-to-moment experience of the play comes from life: the playwright's, the play's, and yours. Life is not a plot and a scenario. It intervenes, it reveals itself from the inside. If you keep your senses attuned to the rhythm of the playwright and direct the work in that rhythm, not just yours, you will experience the illumination needed to project the play. The next chapter explores how your interpretive work of breaking down the script furthers text analysis.

FINAL PROJECTS

1. Consider the aspects of play analysis discussed in this chapter (action, characters, place, and theme) and describe them in Chekhov's *The Three Sisters*. Determine in particular why there is so much excitement at Tchebutykin's gift of the samovar.
2. Study the life of George Bernard Shaw and the social conditions in England during his lifetime. Apply this information to *Pygmalion*. Discuss in essay form its relevance to the plot.
3. Discuss the madness of Blanche DuBois in Williams's *A Streetcar Named Desire* in comparison to Ophelia's in Shakespeare's *Hamlet*. Explain the distinctions to an actress who has been cast in both roles.

4. This is an ideal major project to be completed over the length of the course. Choose a one-act play or a scene from one of the full-length plays listed on pages 95–96 for analysis and prepare a production book. Using the following Guidelines for Play Analysis and Scene Analysis (adapted from Ronald Wainscott), examine the significant features of the piece you have chosen in anticipation of staging the work.

Guidelines for Play Analysis for a Production Book

Your analysis must include the following items. Although a work-in-progress, all items must be present. Number the sections for easy location. You may include additional information if you wish.

1. Play title, date of edition, publisher, editor if applicable.
2. Describe your initial, intuitive response to the play. If this is impossible due to a previous encounter with the play, describe your feelings about the play before beginning detailed study and research.
3. Identify the significant, given circumstances of the play.
4. Discuss the structure of the play. Describe the basic conflict. Give special attention to inciting incident and climax if appropriate for your play. This section should be a description and evaluation of the period of conflict and its most important shifts and peaks. Be sure to include discussion of secondary climactic moments or events. Discuss the playwright's focus in terms of dramatized, reported, and omitted action. Remember that this is not a retelling of the story of a play.
5. Describe the period and society which the play represents. In what ways is this important to your interpretation of the play?
6. Evaluate all characters of the play. Describe their physical, social, psychological, and moral characteristics. Give special attention to social characteristics. What does each character want in the play and in pivotal scenes? What is each character willing to do or risk to get it? Identify character strengths and weaknesses. How does each character function structurally in the play? That is, if each character is examined objectively, not as a person, but as a device or object manipulated by the playwright, how is each functioning in the play?
7. Describe the mood and tempo of the play.
8. Briefly describe any ideas for design. Present ideas which you might communicate to designers when beginning work with them on the play. If you have specific design plans you may include them as well.
9. Make an annotated bibliography of research materials. The annotation should briefly note important discoveries which helped your understanding of the period, production problems, setting, playwright, interpretation of the play, and so on.

Guidelines for Preparing a Scene Analysis for a Production Book

1. Identify your scene selection and explain why you chose it. Explain how the scene fits into the play. What did you try to accomplish with the scene?
2. Evaluate in detail the characters in this scene. Explain the character struggles, conflicts, problems, and so forth, which are specific to this scene. Is one character the driving force in this scene? Where is the focus in terms of character?
3. Describe the structure of this scene.
4. Describe in detail the previous action for this scene. What has just happened to everyone involved? Where have they been? Why are they here now? If the play does not provide this information what did you and the actors create?
5. Carefully describe the mood and tempo for this scene. Pinpoint any major mood or tempo shifts, especially emotional builds or significant silence.
6. Make an accurate groundplan for your scene.
7. Make a prompt book for the pages of your scene. Include the page preceding and following your cut scene.
8. Divide the scene into beats or dramatic units.
9. Include all blocking and notes from the production.
10. Evaluate your results with the scene. How did the produced scene measure up to your expectations? List your successes and failures with the space, acting problems, rehearsal methods, and so on.

Chapter 4

The Director
as Interpreter
Breaking Down
the Script

Egad. I think the interpreter is the hardest to be understood of the two.
R.B. Sheridan, The Critic, *1779*

An interpreter, translating the playwright's message, brings to realization—through performance—the meaning of a play. Sometimes this translation's individualized point of view far removes the particular director's interpretation from other more standard productions. For example, at The Performance Garage, Richard Schechner directed an updated, *nude* version of Euripides's *Bacchae* entitled *Dionysus 1969*. More recently, at Yale, JoAnne Akalaitis set Samuel Beckett's *Endgame* in a *subway* station—infuriating the playwright. The truth of an interpretation, however, must stem from the support it can garner from the text—playwright's approval or no.

In Tennessee Williams's *A Streetcar Named Desire*, one director might emphasize the harsh inhumanity, poetry, and tragedy of the play—pointing up all those moments where "poor" Blanche plays victim to society. Another director will choose to stress the play's humor, as one production at the Guthrie Theatre did several years ago, emphasizing the bitchery with which Blanche tries to manipulate the world around her. And *both* interpretations are valid—so long as the script clearly supports what the director cleverly envisions.

The times in which a play is produced may bear heavily on where a director places his emphasis. Two successful interpretations of Shakespeare's *A Midsummer Night's Dream* in *their* times include Max Reinhardt's monumental, 1930s movie version, which clearly emphasized the fantasy and romance so prevalent in the escapist films of the Great Depression; while in the topsy-turvy world of the 1960s, Peter Brook's farcical interpretation, with trapezes and a bare, white set, stressed the dream's heavy psychological meaning. An astonishing interpretation captures the best way to translate the script's meaning onto the stage—each in its own time.

Once the script has been chosen and analyzed, directors do a particular type of script breakdown to prepare for the transformation of words on the written page into stage action. This involves dissecting the play into the ingredients of action, and interpreting stage action.

At first, you may consider the scene breakdown or production plan a mechanical and passionless chore. The technique is derived from using analytical skill to feed the emotional soul of your work. Do not give up before you reach that point. The late Alan Schneider, an inspired Broadway and international director, meticulously approached analytical work:

> I grew up during the Group Theatre and Kazan was the major director. And I studied Kazan's notebooks very carefully; and his actions and beats were my teachers. I break the script up, into beats, which means sections or paragraphs, or elements, or pieces. To me a beat is something happening. So I'm looking for changes of relationship between the characters, between a character and his environment, between one element and another. I break up the script into something happening, and then something else happening, and then something else happening. I then identify, or tag, or describe, or illuminate, or struggle with these beats as much as I can over a period of time. I take, for example, the first scene of *Godot*, and I spend two weeks on two pages, trying to figure out what's happening. Anything to give the performance some sense of structure or form or sequence, that's what you want.

THE SCENE-BY-SCENE PRODUCTION PLAN

The scene-by-scene *production plan* or breakdown describes the production's structure in performance terminology. In a typical breakdown, notations might be placed opposite each page of the script in your prompt book and include some of the following: the spine of the scene and of each character (including costumes, entrances, and exits), and beats. For each beat, the protagonist's action, objective, obstacle, and scenic movement (props, sets, sounds, lights) might also be indicated. Note the technical emphasis on the breakdown of *Suddenly Last Summer* in Table 4.1.

Breaking down a scene fuels the creative process. You identify questions about certain moments as you start imagining their potential physical expression. If you do insufficient or no scoring, you set yourself up to approve predictable acting choices in rehearsal and schedule too little time for creating visual and aural effects to maximize expressiveness. The scene-by-scene production plan forces you to confront detailed issues about a production prior to meetings with designers, administrators, technical assistants, and actors; it examines and inspires every aspect of staging a play; it begins and ends your interpretive work.

As a guide, the scene-by-scene production plan should be flexible so as to allow you, in the course of rehearsing a play, to really discover

Table 4.1: R.H. O'Neill's Production Plan for *Suddenly Last Summer*

Act & scene	Lights	Props	Costumes	Cast on stage	Sound	Backstage
Preset	house full, stage half.	tags on plants, leaf UR, sherry carafe, 6 glasses & tray, 3 ashtrays, functional lighter with adjustable flame, bookstand with poetry volume and two photos, cigarette box.	none	none	spring	ready for start
change to Act I scene i	house out, stage out, during storm melody.	same	none	none	thunder melody	Ven. & Dr. ready
scene i sec. 1	stage up to swamp, blue silhouette (mood of gloom) to realistic 4:30, hot damp after rain. All before actors enter.	cane handker-chief (Ven.), reticule with contents, doctor's bag with alcohol, cotton, syringe, pad and pencil, handker-chief (Dr.).	jewelry (Ven.); watch, hat (Dr.)	2	#1 swamp fade-in with birds over.	Fox. ready
addendum	mood focus on Ven. during monologue				#2 summer with cockatoo and vultures.	
sec. 2	same	water glass with brown liquid, handker-	purse, hat, gloves, rings, earrings,	5	none	Fox. ready for 2nd entrance; Geo. and

Table 4.1 (*continued*)

Act & scene	Lights	Props	Costumes	Cast on stage	Sound	Backstage
		chief, fan (Holly), tennis racket and cover (Geo.).	necklace (Holly); watch, ring, hat (Geo.).			Holly ready for entrance
sec. 3	same	same	same	2	#1 thunder #2 sweet bird #3 sweet bird	Fox. Cath. & Sister ready
sec. 4	at 5:00 P.M. hot and sticky	wheelchair off, prayer book (Sis)	none	5	#1 swamp fades in	none
scene ii	same	same	pocketwatch & rosary beads (Sister).	2	#1 swamp fades out #2 blender	Holly & Geo. ready
scene iii sec. 1	5:15	same	same as scene i, sec. 2.	4	none	none
sec. 2	same	same	same	3	none	Fox., Ven. & Sister ready
sec. 3	at end, blue silhouette during freeze of actors, then blackout	wheelchair, cane, pillow, reticule & contents.	same	6	thunder into spring	none
Intermission	house up to full, stage half.	same	same	none	spring	All ready (but Dr.)
Act II scene i sec. 1	5:45 house out, preset out, blue silhouette up when actors freeze into position, fade up to realistic lighting.	daiquiri, portfolio containing several folders with papers & notebook, hat and bag (Dr.) remain.	same	6	spring into #1 thunder melody	Dr. ready for entrance

Table 4.1 (*continued*)

Act & scene	Lights	Props	Costumes	Cast on stage	Sound	Backstage
sec. 2	6:00 same	same	same	7	swamp into vultures, to dusk in swamp, dusk fade out	none
sec. 3	6:15 same	hat & racket (Geo.) on, chair off, cane off, reticule off.	same	5	same	none
sec. 4	6:30 same	same	same	2	none	Geo., Fox., Ven., Holly ready for entrance
sec. 5	6:45 same	same, chair on, cane on, reticule on.	same	7	#1 swamp #2 bird singing twice	Fox. ready 2nd entrance
sec. 6	7:00 (p. 37) change to mood focus on Catherine	same	same	6	#1 summer #2 fade-in snatches of steel band	Fox. ready 3rd entrance
sec. 7	7:30 general lighting to blue silhouette, to blackout with lag fade on Doctor.	same	same	7	spring	All ready for finale.
Finale	up full for bows, dim as actors take places, than blue silhouette as they leave in character. Blackout then house up to full.	same, actors remove personal props.	same	7	spring into steel band for bows, then fade into spring	none

what the story is about. Update the breakdown throughout rehearsals to incorporate rehearsal discoveries into preproduction planning.

Do your production plan before rehearsals. Too much informality in your approach encourages laziness and generality onstage. Once in rehearsal little time remains for research and evaluation. A thorough understanding of the play frees you to make intuitive and exciting choices that clarify the text.

Gestation Period: Rereading the Script

The rest of this chapter describes the steps to be followed to develop a scene-by-scene production plan. The insight needed to break down a script stems from a *gestation* period, the nurturing space between productions. This reading, research, and analysis cannot be generated in a few days or weeks.

During your gestation period, reread the script to discover how the action matures, how the relationships develop, how scenes blend and contrast with each other. When rereading, make notes but *avoid* cementing your approach. (There is a distinction between a thoroughly developed interpretation that is cement and one that is pliable. You want to communicate with actors and an audience, not stone them. You want to provide a map, not a prison.) Remember: recording information doesn't necessarily mean that you have solved the problem or that you're bound to your notations.

Problem

You feel rereading a play more than once is a waste of time.

Solution

1. Reread the play one time for each specific item: for props, entrances and exits, clothing, lighting, and so forth. Challenging yourself with specific problems may renew your interest.
2. Reread the play for plot structure, for rehearsal beats, for each character's throughline. Jot down your ideas:

> Every composer knows the anguish and despair occasioned by forgetting ideas which one has not time to write down.
>
> (Victor Hugo)

Researching the Script

Researching—the interpretation, revision, and application of facts—supports you in assessing and manifesting the physical nature of a play. You can do many types of research: historical, sociological, environmental, biographical, psychological, and theatrical (including the history of the play and its production). Some directors examine specific issues from their own pasts to experience the character's predicaments, others visit places (biographical) or attend events similar to those in the script. Most research the play/playwright relationship and its historical environment. (This analysis is covered in depth in Chapters 3 and 5.)

Research should inspire you to enrich the life of the text. Sometimes a *dramaturg*—a critic trained to express an informed opinion on the art or technique of dramatic composition—can assist in your textual research. A third eye between you and the playwright, (s)he does extensive research and then observes rehearsals periodically, perhaps weekly. When a dramaturg, rather than an impartial observer, reviews rehearsals, (s)he provides informed feedback rather than cold impressions.

A dramaturg who is educated, has volumes of information at command, and who has developed an amazing visual sensibility, can be a boon. However, don't let a dramaturg soften you into neglecting your own historical research so that you withdraw from decision making.

Editing, Revising, Rewriting

A dramaturg can assist in editing, revising, or rewriting. Occasionally you may be called upon to enrich the play by adding layers of meaning to a dated work by cutting, rearranging, amending, or updating the script. A word of caution is needed about copyright laws and obligations to the script which may prohibit tampering. Whether revising alone or collaboratively, do not count on fixing the script while in rehearsal; then rehearsals become sessions for redoing rather than directing the play. Allow time before rehearsals begin for revisions. Additions and re-arrangements require creativity, planning, and time. Edited dialogue necessitates additions in action, technical effects, or narration to provide missing information. Deletions and additions can change the order of material and oblige you to re-establish the sequence in which the audience learns the facts. Although facts presented in improper sequence produce no emotional effect, the same information, arranged suspensefully, arouses interest. Notice how the provocatively arranged information in the first column falls flat with the sequencing in the second:

1. John and Mary have been married for ten years with no children.
2. John falls in love with Mary's sister.
3. Mary learns she's pregnant.

1. John falls in love with Mary's sister.
2. Mary learns she's pregnant.
3. John and Mary have been married for ten years with no children.

FUNCTIONAL ANALYSIS

Once directors have studied and prepared the script, production analysis begins. Although individual directors break down texts differently, most approaches involve functional criticism.

Functional analysis addresses how the play's component parts create specific responses in the audience—how the spectator experiences the play as a whole. Differing little from good directorial analysis, functional criticism simply specifies the precise use of language in directing. A mastery of functional analysis should enable you to predict what reactions will occur in the audience from moment to moment. It should enlighten you as to how a theatrical performance is working, how cast and crew operate, and how much or little needs to be done with each element in a production. To do this analysis you need the ability to dissect a play, and discover how it builds to a conclusion.

> Functional analysis, like performance theory, regards a play's text as a resource among many in theatrical communication. It focuses on the precise strategies of conveying sequences of information to the spectator concerning the play's story, its world, its texture and its meanings. And it classifies the strategies variously as the vocabulary, the grammar and the rhetoric of theatrical communication. The spectator "recovers" the wholeness of a play and responds to it through a controlled sequence of perceptions, the control in the last analysis governed by the ultimate synthesizer of the telling of a tale—the directors. For the temporal sequence the control is made up of all the elements of theatrical performance at their disposal—text, actors, scenery, and so on. A precise understanding of the interplay of functions of all these elements is the practical aim of functional analysis. There is little doubt that gifted and experienced directors can know, without the paraphernalia of functional analysis, which of their choices work and which do not, but the training of directors can be advanced considerably by an analytic vocabulary that can pinpoint why certain things seen and heard in certain combinations in certain sequences produce certain effects.
>
> (Leon Katz, drama critic, Yale University)

Informational Impact

As functional analysts, you must examine *two* causes for the effects Leon Katz refers to above: the *informational* and the *emotional* conflict of each moment. Identify what points in the production give information and the sequence in which it comes. The audience needs to know how to piece the events together. At the beginning, the information quickly gathers in their heads, unfolding not just from the exposition but from a multitude of sources.

> The director "tells" the play on many levels and with multiple resources: scenery, costumes, lighting, etc., and it's obvious that each element collaborates in the telling. But a significant point is that the "telling" expands through these resources into a "telling" of an environment of meanings—cultural,

intellectual, psychological, ethical, etc.—and it does so sequentially by evoking bits of information from all these resources and ordering them in a temporal sequence. *The ordering of information is the ultimate basis of theatrical effect.*

(Leon Katz)

Emotional Impact

Besides the information level, you need to identify what is creating the *emotional* impact of a scene. Sometimes a subtle shift in a character's behavior creates a jarring effect. For example, in Chekhov an incidental action in the stage direction may contrast with a focused action in the story. The technique relies on these actions, countering each other, having the opposite emotional effect. For example, in *The Cherry Orchard*, the bourgeois Lopahin revels in his purchase of the estate and clumsily hits a table. The minor blunder reveals a major change in the order of power at the orchard.

Lopahin: What's happened? Musicians, play so I can hear you! Let everything be as I want it! (Ironically bumps into the little table, almost upsetting the candelabrum) I can pay for everything! (Goes out with Pischick) (Act IV)[1]

In other scenes, Chekhov offsets and suspends many different points of focus to evoke nostalgia. For example, at the end of *The Cherry Orchard* the following actions balance each other: the sound of doors being locked; carriages driving away; the dull thud of an ax on a tree; footsteps and then the old ill servant, Firs, mumbling to himself; the sound of a snapped string mournfully dying away.

EXERCISES

1. Study the end of Chekhov's play, *The Three Sisters*, and identify the five simultaneous actions creating the emotional impact of the play.
2. Analyze *The Room* by Harold Pinter from the informational point of view, from what the play will be about when staged. (Remember: Pinter's "simple" stories only begin to suggest the play's meanings.)
3. Arrange the following information in the order of most suspense:
   a. The lights are out.
   b. Tides are spilling over the roadways.
   c. The telephone goes dead.
   d. The door swings open.
   e. Mother telephones to warn her.
   f. Kathy bars all windows.
   g. The door swings open.

[1]From *The Cherry Orchard* by Anton Chekhov. In *Chekhov: The Major Plays*, a new translation by Ann Dunnigan. © 1964 by Ann Dunnigan. Reprinted by arrangement with New American Library, N.Y.

    h. John telephones to alert her.
    i. Kathy bars all doors.
    j. A next door neighbor starts to drive to town.
    k. The car stalls.
    l. A hurricane alert blasts on the radio.
    m. Eerie screams get louder and louder.
    n. Kathy is writing a book on hurricanes.
    o. The electric typewriter stops.

Spine Analysis

Since the ordering of events rides on the spine of the play, functional analysis begins with identifying it. The *spine* is the main action expressing the meaning of the play and propelling its entire movement. Defining where the central idea begins helps you locate the spine. For example, in *Hamlet*, the appearance of King Hamlet's ghost might be the starting point for the central idea: vengeance for a king's murder. Once the idea is located, you must logically develop the action from scene to scene based on the strengthening of the idea until its culmination.

The character's desires either propel or impede the main action. For example, Hamlet's desire to avenge his father's murder (*advancing* the action) leads him to hunt down and to convict his uncle, the new king. His love for his mother, remarried to his uncle, (*impeding* the action) makes him hesitate. After identifying the spine, analyze how the words develop it by clarifying the characters' desires.

Problem

You can't identify the spine of the play.

Solution

1. Find the *obstacles* to what the characters want to help you pinpoint the spine.
2. Study the final moments of the play for the meaning or "idea" of the action. Go backwards from that ending. Note how the action of each scene leads up to that meaning.
3. Evaluate the final moments of the play to see what has been won or lost. Frequently the spine contrasts with the outcome of the characters. For example the spine of Tennessee Williams's *The Glass Menagerie* is to save Laura through marriage, although at the end she is alone.

Character Analysis

Once you find the spine, locate what each character does to implement it by doing character analyses prior to casting. Read through the script for descriptions of each character's behavior, jot down and then collate notations for review. Observe what times of the day—morning, twilight, evening—and which activities give characters energy. Determine which pieces of the character are operating in which parts of the scene. Like a puzzle, a character is only complete at the end of the play. Assess which character traits and actions are operating in each scene (see Chapter 8, for a more-detailed analysis).

Scene Breakdown: Rundown Sheet

Having evaluated the play's spine and its roles, many directors examine how each scene advances the spine of the play. Some directors begin by making a *rundown sheet*, listing each act's scenes and characters to determine the logical development of the action. Each scene and the moments within it should have a relationship to the previous and future moments of the play. Acquire an understanding of how Act I, scene i, moves into scene ii, and into scene iii, and so on throughout the entire text.

To create a rundown sheet, identify *the spine of each act*, then find its component units. These may be scenes described by the playwright or designated by you. If the playwright's scenes are nonexistent, too broad, or ineffective as workable units, you may prefer your own scene divisions. (You might call these "sections.") Some directors divide an act by separating it into *French scenes*. A new French scene begins when a character enters or leaves and the grouping changes. Note, in Molière's *The Bourgeois Gentleman,* how French scene i becomes French scene ii when Jourdain enters:

The Bourgeois Gentlemen
by Molière

translation and added stage directions by Robert Cohen

> The overture ends. From rear wings on either side come two groups—a music master and his musicians, and a dancing master and his dancers. After the music master checks his student's composition, the two masters are left onstage to discuss the absent hero.

[*French Scene One begins*]

Music Master: (grinning broadly) We have found here just the man we need: our "ticket to ride," this (sniffs loudly) Monsieur Jourdain—with his visions of gallantry and noblesse oblige flitting about his head. (chortles pompously) A true "pay-trone of the ahts," this "Mon-sewer"—I only wish there were more where he came from!

Dancing Master: (mincing, with a flourish of his walking stick) Well, I suppose, but I certainly wish he knew something about the arts he patronizes!

Music Master: He knows nothing, doesn't he? (they both laugh) But he pays through the nose, and that's what counts: that's what the arts need these days, my dancing friend, money!

Dancing Master: But to PLAY for these fools! (he crosses down toward the audience, studying them while talking to the Music Master) For me, I confess I hunger more for the applause of those who can tell good work from bad, who can sense the refinements and delicacies of art, who know beauty when they see it (he poses prettily, clasping his hands upon his stick)—and who can reward an artist with the honor of their favor and praise. (he smiles)

Music Master: (following him: enthusiastically) Of course, of course; nothing is better than that—but we also must live! Praise must be mixed with something solid if we are to pay our rent: tell your people of refinement to put their money where their mouth is! (they face each other) This Jourdain, it's true, is somewhat unenlightened (the Dancing Master snorts agreement)—he speaks backwards and forwards at the same time (the Dancing Master chuckles approvingly)—and he applauds only when he's not supposed to (the Dancing Master breaks out in a burst of laughter)—but his money makes up for everything: he has great wisdom in his purse, and his praise comes in the coinage of the realm. (the Music Master ambles away, jingling his purse full of coins)

Dancing Master: (scowling) Well, you're right, as usual, but I don't like it: you're just too money-minded, my friend.

Music Master: And you? You take what he gives out, just as I do!

Dancing Master: (self-righteously) Yes, but its hurts me to do so! (the Music Master clutches his heart in mock pain) I only can wish for a more tasteful benefactor!

Music Master: (realistically) Well, of course, so would we all—but that's life, my friend. In any event, Monsieur Jourdain is giving us the chance to make names for ourselves at Court—and if you will take my advice, you'll let him pay us what the Court won't and let the Court praise us as this imbecile can't!

Dancing Master: (quickly) Shhhhh! Here he comes.[2]

[*French scene one ends*]

[*French scene two begins with Jourdain's entrance*]

> Besides French scene divisions, there are other ways of breaking down an act. Some directors divide the play like music into its component parts. They observe how a play's movements develop up to a certain point and then where a change occurs and another pattern begins. A new scene results from a shift in direction, for example, a mood change or an adjustment in tension between characters.

Problem

You cannot identify the beginning and ending of scenes in the play's act, in which there is no playwright numerical scene-division.

[2]In *Theatre* by Robert Cohen (Mayfield Publishing Corp., Palo Alto, Ca.), 1981, pp. 4–14.

Solution

1. Although there are a number of influencing factors, action dominates any division. Each scene is built on action more than any other single factor. For example, if two characters are arguing, then one wounds the other's feelings, a change of scene could ensue. The next scene might become one of apology or of repairing what hurt has been done.
2. Useful scene breakdowns may separate the work, for the actors' concentration, into sections that can be rehearsed one day at a time.
3. A workable act may contain between ten and twenty scenes or sections, each lasting from two to six pages, but usually no more than three. If sections get much larger, you are probably missing one.

<hr>

Since most rehearsals address one scene at a time, much of the actors' interpretive work results from your divisions. Many directors create rehearsal schedules around scene breakdowns. They begin rehearsals by dividing the script into its working scenes. Some distribute a rundown sheet with the rehearsal schedule printed on the back so that actors know exactly when they're called and the nature of the segment to be worked on. When the actors have confidence in the scheduling, they can relax and work on the sections assigned because they trust they'll get to the end of the play in time. Note how the rundown sheet and rehearsal schedules interface:

Rundown Sheet for *Suddenly Last Summer* (R.H. O'Neill, Director)

Script pages		
	Preset	
	Act I, *Scene i*—	
pp. 5–10	Section 1:	Set: jungle garden, New Orleans, hot, damp, 4:30 P.M., Saturday, September 1, 1936 Mrs. Venable and Dr. C to p. 10, Foxhill's entrance
pp. 10–11	Section 2:	same set, Ven., Dr., Fox., Holly, Geo. to bottom p. 11
pp. 11–16	Section 3:	same set, Dr. and Mrs. V., to top p. 16 Fox. entrance
p. 16	Section 4:	same set, Ven., Dr., Fox., Cath., Sister, Fox, bottom p. 16
pp. 17–19	*Scene ii:*	same set, 5:00 P.M., sister and Cath. to Mrs. Holly offstage call on p. 19
	Scene iii—	
p. 20	Section 1:	same set, 5:15, Mrs. Holly, p. 20–21, Geo., Cath., Sister, to Sister's exit
pp. 21–23	Section 2:	same set and time, Geo., Holly, Cath., bottom of pp. 21–23
p. 23	Section 3:	same set, 5:30, Holly, Geo., Cath., Ven., Fox., Sister, p. 23
	Act II, *Scene iv*—	
pp. 24–26	Section 1:	same set 5:45, dusk, Holly, Ven., Geo., Fox., Sister, Cath., to p. 26; Dr.'s entrance

Rundown Sheet for *Suddenly Last Summer* (*continued*)

Script pages

pp. 26–29	Section 2:	same set, 6:00, full cast, to p. 29, to exit of Fox. and Ven.
pp. 29–32	Section 3:	same set, 6:15, all but Ven. and Fox. to top of p. 32: Cath. line "ravenous mouth"
pp. 32–34	Section 4:	6:30, Dr. and Cath. to p. 34 top, George's entrance
pp. 34–35	Section 5:	6:45, Dr. and Cath., George, Mrs. Holly, Sister, Mrs. Ven., Fox. to p. 35, Fox. exit
pp. 35–44	Section 6:	7:00, full cast but Fox., to p. 44: "blazing white wall"
p. 44	Section 7:	7:30, full cast to blackout

Rehearsal Schedule for *Suddenly Last Summer*—Feb. 14–Mar. 22

February

Mon. 14	6:30–9:30	scene i, sections 1 & 3
Wed. 16	6:30–9:30	scene ii, scene iii, sections 1 & 2
Thu. 17	6:30–9:30	working of Act II, sections 3–7 (Paula and Tom)
	6:30–8:30	Sally
Fri. 18	6:30–8:00	scene iv
	8:00–9:30	scene i (Sally and Tom) sections 2 & 4
Sun. 20	10:00–1:00	*Run of Act I, lines down.* Act II with book
Mon. 21	6:30–9:30	Act I run for polish (Sally and Tom)
Wed. 23	6:30–9:30	*Act II run, lines down*
Thu. 24	6:30–9:30	Act II work for polish
Fri. 25	6:30–9:30	Work on selected scenes without Mrs. Venable
Sun. 27	1:30–4:30	Stop and go run of show. Sound.
Mon. 28	6:30–9:30	Work Act II (Tom and Paula)

March

Tue. 1		Pick up wig!
	4:30–5:30	run lines
	8:30–9:30	costume parade
Wed. 2	6:30–9:30	Act II
Thu. 3	3:30	Pictures
	6:30–9:30	Act I. Sound.
Fri. 4	6:30–9:30	Work through of scenes without Mrs. Venable
Sun. 6	11:30–4:30	Run of show for final polishing, set curtain call, including all sounds
Mon. 7	6:30–9:30	Run of show for lights
Tue. 8		Tech. work day
Wed. 9	6:30–9:30	Tech. run of Act I, twice
Thu. 10	6:30–9:30	Tech. run of Act II, twice
Fri. 11	6:00	Actor's call
	6:30	Run of show with costumes and tech

Rehearsal Schedule for *Suddenly Last Summer*—**Feb. 14–Mar. 22**
(*continued*)

Sun. 13	12:30	Actor's call
	1:30	Dress run with tech. and make-up
Mon. 14	5:30	Actor's call
	7:00	Preview and final dress
Tue. 15	6:00	Actor's call
	8:00	Performance
Wed. 16		same as above
Thu. 17		same as above
Fri. 18		same as above
Sat. 19		same as above
Mon. 21		Possible brush-up of show
Tue. 22		Performance of show for Fine Arts Festival. Times to be announced.
Thu. 17		same as above
	7:00	Call
	8:00	Performance
Fri. 18		same as above
	7:00	Call
	8:00	Performance
Sat. 19		same as above
	7:00	Call
	8:00	Performance
Mon. 21		Possible brush-up of show
Tue. 22		Performance of show for Fine Arts Festival. Times to be announced.

(Prop crew to check with me for what is reusable for rehearsal times—see TECH. SCHEDULE.)

Tech. Schedule for *Suddenly Last Summer*

February

Tue. 8		Floor marked, show roster distributed, explanation of set to Dr. O'Neill before 6:30 of 2/9/77. (May be done by stage manager.) Schedule forms distributed to crews.
Wed. 9		All actors' schedules collected and returned to Dr. O'Neill.
Sun. 13		Run of show
Mon. 14		All *rehearsal* props gathered (Dr. O'Neill's approval needed.) See p. 45 of script and additional prop list for props. The wheelchair is a must! Stage manager to supervise rehearsal props.
Sun. 20	12:30–4:30	Run of Act I with sound
Mon. 21	6:30–9:30	Act I run with sound
Wed. 23	6:30–9:30	Act I run with sound
Thu. 24	6:30–9:30	Act II work with sound

Tech. Schedule for *Suddenly Last Summer* (*continued*)

Sun. 27	1:30–4:30	Run of show with sound
Mon. 28	6:30–9:30	Run of show with sound. Final wheelchair. *Crew heads and crews present to observe show.*

March

Tue. 1	8:30–9:30	Ramps in 1st, costume parade
Thu. 3	6:30–9:30	Run of show with props (final props), sound, set, final furniture. *Prop crew to add.*
Fri. 4	6:30–9:30	Rehearsal using sound, props, and set.
Sun. 6	12:00–4:30	Run of show for final polishing, set curtain call, including lights and props.
Mon. 7	6:30–9:30	Run lights to observe
Tue. 8	?	Tech. work day. Tech. rehearsal—cue to cue. Add lights.
Wed. 9	6:30–9:30	Tech. run Act I, twice
	6:30	Call
	7:00	Run
Thu. 10	6:30–9:30	Tech. run of Act II, twice
	6:30	Call
	7:00	Run
Fri. 11	6:30	Dress run, all tech. Add make-up.
Sun. 13	1:30	Dress run, all tech
Mon. 14	7:00	Preview and dress
	7:00	Call
	8:00	Run
Tue. 15	7:00	Call
	8:00	Final dress
Wed. 16		same as above
	7:00	Call
	8:00	Performance

Spine of a Scene

Once you divide the play into working scenes for rehearsals, find the spine or major action of each one. Look for the arc, that is, the particular shape of the whole play that a scene must convey for the audience. For example, the thrust of the opening scene of Tennessee Williams's *A Streetcar Named Desire* (play's spine: to *shelter* Blanche) might be for Blanche to get a warm welcome in her sister's home; in the last scene, the thrust might be to get respectful treatment in the insane asylum.

Labeling a scene helps you identify the spine. Like character types, there are scene types, such as the farewell scene, the confessional scene, and the persuasion scene, to name a few (see Chapter 1, Classification of Scenes). The opening scene of *A Streetcar Named Desire* might be named "The reunion," another scene might be called "The confrontation," still another, "The disclosure," "The assault," or "The apology." This tag should capture a scene's essence, beneath any superficial dialogue. For example, the final scene between Lopahin and Varya in Anton Chekhov's *The Cherry Orchard* is not about "leaving and packing" but Lopahin's silent refusal to propose to Varya. He can't bring himself to ask her to marry him so they make idle conversation until he flees. The scene might be labeled, "The Rejection."

Lopahin: (Looking at his watch) Yes—(A pause. Behind the door you hear smothered laughter, whispering, finally Varya enters)
Varya: (Looking at the luggage a long time) That's strange, I just can't find it—
Lopahin: What are you looking for?
Varya: I packed it myself and don't remember where. (A pause)
Lopahin: Where do you expect to go now, Varyara Mikhailovna?
Varya: I? To Regulin's. I agreed to go there to look after the house as a sort of housekeeper.
Lopahin: That's in Yashnevo? It's nigh on to seventy miles. (A pause) And here ends life in this house—
Varya: (Examining the luggage) But where is it? Either I put it in the trunk, perhaps—yes, life in this house is ended—it won't be any more—
Lopahin: And I am going to Harkoff now—By the next train. I've a lot to do. And I am leaving Epihodoff—on the ground here—I've hired him.
Varya: Well!
Lopahin: Last year at this time it had already been snowing, if you remember, and now it's quiet, it's sunny. It's only that it's cold, about three degrees of frost.
Varya: I haven't noticed. (A Pause. A voice from the yard through the door) Yermolay Alexevich—
Lopahin: (As if he had been expecting this call for a long time) This minute! (Goes out quickly)
(Varya sitting on the floor, putting her head on a bundle of clothes, sobs quietly. The door opens, Luyboff Adrevna enters cautiously.)
(Act IV)[3]

Besides scene labeling, identifying the protagonist's action helps define the spine. For example, in a "condemnation scene" where John is accusing Mary, and Mary and her friends are listening, the main active person is John. The focus should be on the physical action of John, and the spine of the scene might read "John accuses Mary."

Scenic Movement

Some directors also do *scenic movement* analysis—the evaluation of the visual and aural progression of the scene in production. All visual and

[3]From *The Cherry Orchard* by Anton Chekhov. In *The Best Plays by Chekhov*, translated by Stark Young, 1964. Copyright 1939, 1941, 1947, 1950, 1956 by Stark Young, pp. 292–293.

aural elements of each scene must support and enhance its spine. Every moment of a production combines elements to produce certain responses in the audience. Lights, props, costumes, sound effects, music, all create such a response. Directors need to look for the explicit visual and aural choices to develop the work. Sometimes these result in an overall metaphor for the play. Note the scenic movement in the breakdown for the production of Tom Jones and Harvey Schmidt's *Celebration* in Table 4.2. Stage musicals are often more visually complex than dramas. Now observe how the scenic movement evolved from my early notes on metaphor for that production:

Possible Metaphor or Image for *Celebration*

The concept could be based on a *dream* of Orphan's. A dream is a warning from the unconscious self to the conscious self that something is wrong in the self's waking life.

Orphan is at a crisis point in his life, and a decision has to be made. His orphanage has been sold to a rich man in New York and Orphan has set out to find this man and salvage the Orphanage.

Scene I PRELUDE
Pre-set: Reality. Orphan searches to find a warm and safe place to sleep on a freezing night on the outskirts of New York City. Orphan has no place to go. He has nobody. He has no money. As a result he is thrust into a convulsive dream which exposes his conscious fears and his repressed drives.

Dream people: Larger than life—fantastic, ominous.

Potempkin is Orphan's seer into the unconscious. Potempkin represents what Orphan represses the most: aggressiveness and self-survival at any cost. Potempkin uses people to get things (material items). He is in his prime. His redeeming quality is that he admits his evil.

Rich represents Orphan's most conscious fear—success through materialism without any regard for other human beings. Rich is ruthless, and refuses to admit that evil to himself, consequently causing his own destruction.

Revelers are fawning parasites of Potempkin. Like Rich, they are not cognizant of their own evil.

Angel is two-faced. She is both an angel and a devil. To Orphan, she is an angel (he sees her virtues). To Rich, she is a devil (he sees the beauty of her vices). She is naively testing out her powers of survival without having evaluated the cost entailed: the pain which ensues from using people as things.

IMPLEMENTATION: Research Carl Jung's *Man and His Symbols* for primary dream colors—pinks, lavenders, blues; and dream images—perhaps a circular circuitous feeling—generated by a ramp, raised horseshoe effect.

Research larger-than-life masks, hats, capes for Revelers.

Use carnival lighting and fog machine?

One director, Arthur Wagner, described how the scenic movement for staging Arthur Miller's *After the Fall* was generated. He said that the

Table 4.2: Scenic Movement Breakdown

R.H. O'Neill's Production of *Celebration* by Tom Jones & Harvey Schmidt

Act I	Sets and Lighting	Characters	Costumes	Props
Scene I Prelude	Preset reality Desolate Streets Outside NYC Downstage Houselites, Gold sun hit by lite. ECLIPSE Fog, lighting effects, slow distorted speech, Drum roll	Orphan enters in reality (NYC) is lost and falls asleep Revelers enter Potempkin enters U.C.	strange old-fashioned clothes for Orphan & shoes & scarf	sack for Orphan must contain Bible, eye of God, seed, toilet paper
Dialogue as Potempkin sings. Revelers begin moving.	Transfer to Dream is complete	Potempkin & Revelers (Orphan sleeping) At end of song 6 Revelers exit to get streamer 6 stay for wind effect.		plastic bag for Potempkin
Scene II	New Year's Eve E. 90th St. Cold, Winter, Storm	Orphan & Revelers, 6 revelers enter	new costume change for Potem. (costume must have pockets)	long nylon streamers, snow, masks of Whore, Pimp, Addict, 12 New Year's Eve noisemakers, 3 hats
Scene III	Same	Orphan & Potempkin Potem. enters— applauds & sends Revelers off stage		Dirty Handkerchief, 2 cards, Potem. puts Orphan's bag down.
Scene IV	Outside Rich's House	Major-Domo— 10 Revelers in Rich People scene 2 Revs. carry on mirrors Angel carry on mirrors	Major-Domo gold "chain of office," monocle, white collar	invitations, 6 masks of rich people (real & grotesque) 2 mirrors weird
Scene V	Light change to inside Rich's	Orphan, Angel, Potem.	break away Angel outfit—to	

Table 4.2 (*continued*)

Act I	Sets and Lighting	Characters	Costumes	Props
	mysterious, eerie, cave-like		devil costume, rhinestone pasties & bikini sparkling tail	
Scene VI	Spot light on angel	8 Revelers as rich people, 3 # Angel, Orphan, Potem. Hittites	2 Hittite costumes to Angel 1 satan piece of costume	suggestive microphone
Scene VII	Drum roll	3 Revelers exit & Enter with rich Major-Domo, Angel, Orphan, Potem. Hittites, Rich	1 Reveler waiter	gold wheelchair, bib napkin, lobster, platter crushers
Scene VIII		Orphan, Angel, Potem, Rich, Domo, Revelers Hittites		eye of God out of bag
Scene IX		Orphan, Angel, Potem., Rich, Domo, Revelers, Hittites		
Scene X		Rich, Orphan-Domo 4 sycophants (exit end of song)	M.D. brings Rich	5 top hats falsies (plastic bags) artificial flower perfume spray
Scene XI		Rich, Orphan, Potem. 2 Revelers		candy, gun, 2 place cards, eye of God, winter/summer must stand up
Scene XII		Orphan, Potem., Angel, Potem. goes to up platform		
Scene XIII		Orphan, Angel		flower
Scene XIV		3 Revelers in evocative rags 8 Revelers with placards & banners Rich, Potem., Angel, Orphan, Domo	green silk rags costume addition to Revelers	4 place cards 4 banners green images of summer bracelets & rings in Rich's pockets

Table 4.2 (*continued*)

Act I	Sets and Lighting	Characters	Costumes	Props
Scene XV		Potem., Orphan rolls off wheelchair		piece of paper for Potem.
Act II				
Scene I	House lites	Revelers enter 3 from each wing 3 from each aisle Potem.	Potem. (cape)	score, baton 11 musical instr. (recorders, triangles, clickers, etc.)
Scene II	Dark & cold gentle & haunting lighting, leaf effect, country	Angel, Orphan, Potem.	Angel, rags-to-riches, Orphan—hair change	fur, jewels
Scene II	2 Revelers bring on wheelchair	Potem. Orphan, Angel, Rich, Revelers follow Rich on as exit, decorators with tree, flowers waterfall, all Revelers exit at end of Scene III	Rich needs long underwear (See props)	top hat (soft felt hat, big brim), spats, black dr.'s bag, lethal looking needle, artificial flowers (ribbon), 2 fig leaves, wheelchair, spec. vibrator, 1 tree covered with saran wrap
Scene IV		6 Revelers enter as machines UC 2 Welders, machine movement		2 welder's masks, big gloves (gray) for Machines, (Clear masks?)
Scene V	Potem., 2 welders upstage to join machines, dim ominous lights	Orphan, Potem., 6 Machines 2 Machines		
Scene VI	light change with eye of God	Machines withdraw gradually to exit Potem., Orphan		eye of God

Table 4.2 (*continued*)

Act II	Sets and Lighting	Characters	Costumes	Props
Scene VII		Rich, Potem. enters screaming	cape & mask for Orphan	mirror, white jackets with pockets, 2 surgical masks for Beauticians, Barber, caps (surgical), strap, girdle
Scene VIII		6 Revelers, beautician, Orphan enters as Reveler with costume, 2 Revs. as doctor, 1 Rev. with Orphan, Potem. will exit during Orphan–Rich mirror to get in. Father Time outfit for Rich. Potem., beauticians leave when gong is struck. Female Revel. enters with chain & noisemakers, & bat	glittering costume, white costume of Father Time	2 doctor bags, scythe, hour-glass, beard, toupee, noisemakers
Scene IX		entrance of maidens, 1 maiden must have veil and death mask— Potem. Rich after dances each will leave		
Scene X	possible projection of Rich's face (distorted) puppet-like			
Scene XI		Orphan with Angel in	cocoon silk outfit for Angel	

Table 4.2 (*continued*)

Act II	Sets and Lighting	Characters	Costumes	Props
		cocoon, 2 maidens Rich, Potem. Offstage singers	with bikini	
Scene XII	Lite change or projection for new tree brought in	Potem., Rich, Orphan with 10 Revelers, Angel enters (3 hand-held) (3 hooded) (6 Revelers with animal faces)		tinsel to put on tree, tree must be movable Orphan's unicorn mask
Scene XIII		Potem. gestures 2 Revelers to remove tree, all Revelers withdraw at end of scene, all voices needed	2 masks & armor mask simulates visor, armor simulates breastplate, gloves from welders scene (yellow, pink & silver)	
Scene XIV	clock sound gong (Phillip)	Rich, Angel, Potem. Orphan, Revelers enter one at a time with countdown	white masks	poles, mirrors on backside will be sun
Scene XV		Potem., Rich, Orphan, Angel, 12 Revelers		drums & rattle etc. (either props or toys)

idea came from a study of what the play was saying and later was developed in conferences with the designer when they both agreed that the image for the play was "the inside of Quentin's mind." The scenic movement needed to convey a feeling of the mind to enhance the words but it eventually influenced the entire design and development of the show. Basically they developed a naked stage made up of faceted platforms and six hanging screens onto which black-and-white pictures from Nazi concentration camps and images from Quentin's mind would flash at various times. The screens would "visualize Quentin's mind" during narrations about his past. Wagner had characters from Quentin's past enter the stage to play scenes from various distances and levels depending upon how far back in Quentin's mind they were. Wagner used the metaphor of "the inside of Quentin's head" to support script action from which scenic movement evolved.

To imagine scenic movement, you must see and hear how the action builds: In identifying scenic movement, begin by observing what stage directions and scenic descriptions (if any) are called for by the playwright. Differentiate between these and ones written in later for acting editions by stage managers or directors. You may not wish to reproduce exactly what playwrights want visually, but you ought to find the spirit of what they intended. Many of the great modern playwrights like Bernard Shaw, Henrik Ibsen, Eugene O'Neill, and August Strindberg, who were adept with both pen and brush, had a clear idea of what scenic pictures they required on stage (Albert Bermel).

EXERCISES

Identify the visual and aural cues the playwright calls for in the following scenes:

1. Tennessee Williams's *The Glass Menagerie*, scene iv:

> The interior is dark. Faint light in the alley. A deep-voiced bell in a church is tolling the hour of five as the scene commences.
>
> Tom appears at the top of the alley. After each solemn boom of the bell in the tower, he shakes a little noise-maker or rattle as if to express the tiny spasm of man in contrast to the sustained power and dignity of the Almighty. This and the unsteadiness of his advance make it evident that he has been drinking.
>
> As he climbs the few steps to the fire-escape landing, light steals up inside. LAURA appears in night dress, observing TOM'S empty bed in the front room. Tom fishes in his pockets for door-key, removing a motley assortment of articles in the search, including a perfect shower of movie-ticket stubs and an empty bottle. At last he finds the key, but just as he is about to insert it, it slips from his fingers. He strikes a match and crouches below the door.[4]

2. Ketti Frings, *Look Homeward Angel*, Act I, scene ii:

> The Dixieland Boarding House. The night is sensuous, warm. A light storm is threatening. Long, swaying tree shadows project themselves on the house. (Seated on the side veranda are JAKE, MRS. CLATT, FLORRY, MISS BROWN, and MRS. SNOWDEN. MRS. PERT is seated in her rocker, BEN on the steps beside her. They are drinking beer. MRS. PERT measures the socks she is knitting against Ben's shoe. JAKE CLATT softly plays the ukelele and sings, EUGENE is sitting on the side door steps, lonely, yearning.
>
> JAKE (Singing.) "K-k-katy, K-k-katy!" etc. (As JAKE finishes, FLORRY gently applauds. JAKE starts softly strumming something else.)[5]

---

[4]*The Glass Menagerie* by Tennessee Williams. (Random House, New York. © 1945 by Tennessee Williams & Edwina D. Williams; copyright renewed in 1973 by Tennessee Williams.) Reprinted by permission of Random House, Inc.

[5]From *Look Homeward Angel* by Ketti Frings, from the novel by Thomas Wolfe. Copyright 1958 by Edward C. Aswell as admin. C.T.A. of the estate of Thomas Wolfe. Reprinted by permissions of Paul Gitlin and Charles Scribner's Sons.

3. Henrik Ibsen's *Hedda Gabler*, Act IV:

> The same room at the Tesmans. It is evening. The drawing-room is in darkness. The back room is lighted by the hanging lamp over the table. The curtains over the glass door are drawn closed. (HEDDA dressed in black, walks to and fro in the dark room. Then she goes into the backroom and disappears for a moment to the left. She is heard to strike a few chords on the piano. Presently she comes in sight again, and returns to the drawing-room. BERTA enters from the right, through the inner room, with a lighted lamp, which she places on the table in front of the corner settee in the drawing-room. Her eyes are red with weeping, and she has black ribbons in her cap. She goes up to the glass door, lifts the curtain a little aside, and looks out into the darkness. Shortly afterwards, MISS TESMAN, in mourning, with a bonnet and veil on, comes in from the hall, HEDDA goes toward her and holds out her hand.)[6]

Along with noticing visual and aural cues suggested by the playwright, directors should look for suggestions in the dialogue itself.

EXERCISES

Identify the atmospheric suggestions in the following dialogue:

1. Eugene O'Neill's *Ah, Wilderness!* Act IV, scene ii:

Richard: (Thinking aloud) Gosh, that music from the hotel sounds wonderful. Must be nearly nine—I can hear the Town Hall clock strike, it's so still tonight—I'll catch hell when I get back, but it'll be worth it. If only Muriel turns up—Am I sure she wrote nine? (He puts the straw hat on the sand right of boat and pulls the folded letter out of his pocket and peers at it in the moonlight) Yes, it's nine all right.[7]

2. Racine's *Phaedra*, English version by Robert Lowell, Act I, scene iii:

Phaedra: Dearest, we'll go no further. I must rest.
    I'll sit here. My emotions shake my breast,
    the sunlight throws black bars across my eyes.
    My knees give. If I fall, why should I rise,
    Nurse?
Oenone: Heaven help us. Let me comfort you.
Phaedra: Tear off these gross, official rings, undo
    these royal veils. They drag me to the ground.
    Why have you frilled me, laced me, crowned me, and wound

---

[6]From *Hedda Gabler* by Henrik Ibsen. In *Contemporary Drama*, pp. 35–36, used with courtesy of Scribner's Sons, NY, 1933.

[7]From *Ah, Wilderness!* by Eugene O'Neill. Copyright 1933; copyright renewed 1960 by Oona and Shane O'Neill. Reprinted by permission of Charles Scribner's Sons.

my hair in turrets? All your skill torments
and chokes me. I am crushed by ornaments.
Everything hurts me, and drags me to my knees![8]

3. Shakespeare's *Macbeth*. Act II, scene i (*Inverness court of Macbeth's castle*):

(Enter Banquo, and Fleance with a torch before him)
Banquo: How goes the night, boy?
Fleance: The moon is down, I have not heard the clock.
Banquo: And she goes down at twelve.
Fleance: I take it 'tis later, sir.
Banquo: Hold, take my sword. There's husbandry in heaven;
    Their candles are all out. Take thee that too.
    A heavy summons lies like lead upon me.
    And yet I would not sleep. Merciful powers,
    Restrain in me the cursed thoughts that nature
    Gives way to in repose.
(Enter Macbeth and a Servant with a torch.)

4. Shakespeare's *Macbeth*, Act II, scene ii (*Inverness court of Macbeth's castle*):

(Enter Macbeth)
Macbeth: I have done the deed. Didst thou not hear a noise?
Lady Macbeth: I heard the owl scream and the cricket cry.
    Did you not speak?
Macbeth: When?
Lady Macbeth: Now.
Macbeth: As I descended?
Lady Macbeth: Ay.
Macbeth: Hark!
    Who lies i' th' second chamber?
Lady Macbeth: Donalbain.
Macbeth: This is a sorry sight.
(Looks at his hands)

The visual and aural elements in the above dialogue need not be created through any technical effect; they suggest the mood of the environment. Evoke this atmosphere through many means: the orchestration of the actors' voices, the intensity of the lighting, the intimacy of the staging, and most of all, through a precise interpretation of the language itself.

Implement scenic movement particularly at beginnings and endings of acts and scenes. Open each act clearly, especially the first act. While

---

[8]Excerpt from Racine's *Phaedra*, translated by Robert Lowell, © 1960–61. Reprinted by permission of Farrar, Straus, and Giroux, Inc.

the audience picks up a vast amount of information, they evaluate signals about their expected emotional responses. Opening scenes lure the audience into the make-believe world of the play.

> One of the principles of directing is that you have to get the audience's attention right away, so there must be something very interesting going on in the beginning. Simultaneously, it is another principle never to start with too great intensity, because otherwise you are taking away from the possibility of getting to the climax. So, you have to find, for the beginning, a way of making the thing rather interesting and setting the mood, without becoming too intense. To give an example, in Max Rhinehart's production of *A Merchant of Venice* he started off with the curtain going up, and Venice in hot lights, going to half lights. Then he had a dog barking at a distance, and somebody singing an Italian song. A woman came out and was hanging up her washing, a merchant came and was setting up something, and then several people were passing greeting each other. It got lighter and lighter. This long silent scene was very interesting even though very low in intensity of audience involvement. You must begin at a low intensity in order to work up to the major climax(s) of the play, saving the greatest burst of intensity for the major dramatic climax.
>
> (Martin Esslin)

Stanislavski believed that when the audience gives you their attention in these first well-planned moments, they easily watch ten to fifteen minutes of exposition. He proved that the correct *mise en scène* (scenery, lighting, costumes, sounds) holds the audience for five to eight minutes, because audiences are excited by seeing the true external shape for the given content. Delight results when the set, costumes, and props perfectly enhance the meaning of the lines.

Visual and aural effects at endings of acts should heighten meaning. The ending of Act I of Chekhov's *The Three Sisters* provides such possibilities. Masha could burst into tears as Andrei chases Natasha. Nocturnal effects and the repetition of certain sounds (churchbells, frogs, loud laughter, rough singing) from the beginning of Act I could intensify the audience's sense of the monotonous life trapping the characters. Scenic movement transports a scene to a richer interpretive level.

Beat Analysis

A *beat* is a piece of a scene, composed of action; obstacle; adjustment to obstacle; and physical action to support adjustment choices. The pattern repeats itself until the character gets or doesn't succeed in getting what (s)he wants.

Beat breakdown—dividing each scene into small sections where an actor has a single action—deepens the interpretative level.

You direct one piece or "bit" at a time, not the whole play at once. Each director's piece of it will be different. Study the play's beat patterns, examining principal emotional and informational elements of each scene, to enable you to identify acting choices that clarify the text once in rehearsals. Write beat notations in pencil, so you can easily revise.

Identifying Beats

A new beat in a scene develops from an adjustment in the action. For example, John changes his way of wooing Mary. A beat may be indicated by a discovery about a relationship between people, places, things, events. New information may necessitate some physical adjustment. For example, noise on stage could change to quiet or vice versa.

Some directors scrutinize beats prior to rehearsals. Others solidify beats during rehearsals, by investigating each character's physical life and actions.

Implementing Beats

Good directors do not set choices until work with the actor occurs. Their idea of interpretation is rooting the actor's behavior in the script's circumstances. Unique beats emphasize what an individual actor and only that actor can give to those circumstances. They match the action to the actor as the character.

To illustrate: if, when speaking, the actor leans forward or adjusts the body, you could expand on this expression by suggesting (s)he could start flirting or begin leaving at this point. To translate impulses into stage action, evaluate whether the choice is congruent with the spine of the role and the scene. Understand what physical and psychological movements for characters are in alignment with the text. You must have a clear conception of the roles to guide the actors and steer them back to center when they go off-base.

Acting choices define, either consciously or unconsciously, the beats of the play. If you do not research beats, you may not implement necessary adjustments. You could misuse rehearsal time, cement moments too soon, blur a sequence of actions, or skip meaningful transitions.

Problem

You have a preconception of what the character is doing in a beat. During its rehearsal, your direction is challenged by the actor.

Solution

1. If it's early in rehearsals and the actor has misinterpreted the character's action, do an improvisation, exercise, or discussion to enlarge the actor's understanding of the truth of the particular beat.
2. Toward the end of rehearsals, listen intently to the actor's experience. Since you are observing the role objectively, at a certain point the actor's inner sense of truth may be more valid than yours.

> When men are arrived at the goal,
> they should not turn back.
>
> (Plutarch)

Conclusion

There is no reason to pretend that a director comes to rehearsals with a complete approach to the play, into which (s)he fits actors and the space. But the director does come with an interpretation. At rehearsals, everyone is finding out; the director is simply heading the exploration. Since things rarely happen spontaneously in rehearsal without some preparation, the more you have researched the script, and evaluated its beats, the more "answers" you are likely to "discover."

You can prepare and plan for play projects in many ways. Studying the interpretive possibilities, creates a *necessary* but *not sufficient* basis for beginning work. Also try to understand the history of a theatrical work. The more knowledgeable and efficient that research, the more smoothly your production will evolve. The next chapter continues our study, examining the role of the historian.

FINAL PROJECTS

1. Select a short one-act play. (Warning: Do not do a piece of a play.) Study the play by reading it and listing its principal events from beginning to end. What do the events suggest about the spine of the play? Then describe in written, paragraph form what you consider to be the spine, core, or essence of the play. Discover a metaphor, visual design, or image for this spine. The metaphor should reflect the central feeling you want the spine to generate in the audience. Present the metaphor in a graphic image. The work could be a model, a collection of objects, or an environment, but it must be abstract and relate in size, shape, and color to the spine of the play (Sheldon Aptekar).
2. Study a play with an elusive plot, such as a Harold Pinter, Luigi Pirandello, Jean Paul Sartre, or Samuel Beckett play. Create a rundown sheet of the play based on that meaning. Bring to class some visual and sound effects for the opening and closing scenes that might support the progression of the work. Experience yourself as interpreter, as the person who makes choices about meaning.
3. Research a play of a recent historical period such as *Awake and Sing* by Clifford Odets, *Our Town* by Thornton Wilder, *Look Back in Anger* by John Osborne, *Major Barbara* by George Bernard Shaw, or *A View from the Bridge* by Arthur Miller. Decide upon your approach to this work for a contemporary audience. Then score and stage the opening scene.
4. Stage the following open-ended piece of dialogue. At rehearsal, *only* ask questions that will define the situation, the characters, the time, and the place. (For example, you might say to the actors, "Where are you, where are you going?" instead of saying, "You're here and you must walk over there.")

A: Well.

B: Well, I'm here.

A: So I see.

B: Well.

A: Is that all you have to say?

B: What do you want me to say?

A: Did you see him?

B: Yes, I saw him.

A: Well, what did you find out? What is he going to do?

B: Nothing.

A: Nothing? Do you mean to say that he . . . didn't you get anything out of him?

B: He says he can't promise anything now. He may know more tomorrow.

A: Tomorrow. That's the way it goes. After all we've done . . . I've done . . . he says tomorrow. How long is he going to go on this way? Putting things off, getting us all worked up and then . . .

B: Oh, what's the use of talking about it? That's all he'll say and that's it. What do we gain by going over it all again? Just a minute. (B EXITS)

A: Come here.

B: (ENTERS) What is it?

A: Don't you see?

B: It can't be . . .

A: You said he told you . . .

B: Yes, I know . . . but then he might . . . Do you suppose he'd have the nerve to?

A: Oh, he'd have nerve enough . . . That wouldn't stop him.

B: No, I suppose not.

A: No use our standing here gaping.

B: Strange, isn't it?

A: Now listen to me; I'm tired of all this. Between you and him I'm getting thoroughly sick of the whole business. Something has to be done and done soon. Now what I think we'd better do . . .

B: There you go. Always trying to do something. Think about it. What's the hurry? You know as well as I do we never get anywhere. We never do.

A: You mean you never do?

B: Why pick on me?

A: Why not?

B: Oh, go ahead, suit yourself.

A: That's just what I'm going to do.

B: What?

A: Go ahead.

B: Now wait a minute.

A: We've waited too long now. Come on.

Chapter **5**

The Director as Historian
Researching Period and Place

Discovery consists of seeing what everybody has seen and thinking what nobody has thought.

Albert Szent-Gydorgyi

CREATIVITY, ORIGINALITY, AND RESEARCH

In *Recollections and Reflections* James Robinson Planche writes:

> [The actors in this 1823 production of Shakespeare's *King John* at Covent Garden, starring Charles Kemble] . . . had no faith in me, and sulkily assumed their new and strange ("authentic costumes"), in the full belief that they should be roared at by the audience. They *were* roared at, but in a much more agreeable way than they had contemplated. When the curtain rose, and discovered King John dressed as his effigy appears in Worcester Cathedral, surrounded by his barons sheathed in mail . . . with correct armorial shields, and his courtiers in the long tunics and mantles of the thirteenth century, there was a roar of appreciation . . . four distinct rounds of applause . . . so general and so hearty . . . that the actors were astonished; and I felt amply rewarded for all the trouble.
>
> (London, 1901)

As historian, you should try to interpret a play's context, its time, place, and period, and employ stage conventions capturing its spirit for a twentieth-century audience. Until you can grasp the perception of playwrights within their own times and, in a sense, *see things historically*, you will have difficulty in conveying the essential reality of a script.

Try to develop a synoptic understanding of the historical period in which the text is set. A dramatic text *condenses* reality and can leap years in a matter of moments. You should know *how* to imagine and refine that theatrical reality and address its problems with authenticity. You must identify how best to translate your vision of the textual material into three-dimensional space. Research must be put to the service of making an older text speak to today's audiences. Some spectators still expect a historical reconstruction; still others want a new vision. Creative, modern directors have changed our thinking about the staging of classical texts, presenting us with new images and treatment of plays for contemporary audiences.

Researching the socio-political/religious/artistic ideas that influenced playwrights in their own environmental times should not be left to some research assistant or your design staff alone. Clearly, no one individual can apprehend everything, but you should at least know *how* to find the required information to prepare yourself for making enlightened decisions concerning historical elements. In lieu of burning the midnight oil over yet another pedantic analysis, you might read accounts by true historians, listen to some music of the time, and visit museums to see art and artifacts the playwrights might themselves have seen.

This chapter focuses on methods of—and reasons for—learning to be your own researcher. Few excuses can justify a director's poor, unfitting interpretation of a period play. Sophisticated, *avant-garde* critics and audiences will accept unusual interpretations, anachronistic settings and costumes, changes in the script, or "quirky" performance styles *if* (and this is a big *If*) they believe that directors *do* understand the historical background of a work and that lack of knowledge is not their reason for taking a unique approach. Ignorance of a play's historical context should not be the basis for producing Shakespeare in space suits, Molière in miniskirts, or Terence in tights and turtlenecks. While critics and audiences may not always *agree* with directors' choices, they should not feel that playwrights are being mistreated through acts of ignorance. A criticism for overcerebrated creativity is preferable to one for intellectual laziness.

The Period Play

Most directors and actors seek both the challenge and prestige associated with performing great works of the ages and established works of the recent past. However, many audiences and theater professionals alike have a *preconceived* idea of how these works should be interpreted. Their ideas result from the productions they have viewed before in theaters, on television, or in films—and playscripts they have studied and analyzed in theater and literature courses. You must take into account the current "tradition" of demanding historical accuracy which audiences and critics have developed in this century.

If you possess the needed historical/theatrical knowledge then your artistic/intuitive reaction can be utilized fully. Knowing a great deal about playscripts in their historical time and place should *liberate*, not inhibit,

Research—Period Plays: the performance projects the director's understanding of the formality of Victorian society.

The Importance of Being Earnest by Oscar Wilde. Guthrie Theater. Director: Garland Wright. Set design: Michael Miller and Garland Wright. Costumes: Jack Edwards. With Robert Burns and Sylvia Short. Photo: Joe Giannetti.

your creative impulses, by protecting you from anachronisms or mistakes.

Most nineteenth-century European plays (such as *A Doll's House* by Henrik Ibsen or *The Importance of Being Earnest* by Oscar Wilde) require an understanding of the highly formal and structured life of that era's privileged classes in order to interpret the behavior and language of the principal protagonists. Our late twentieth-century standards of "freedom," "equal rights for women," and economic and social mobility could distort one's perception of the leading characters, especially in the two plays mentioned above. Although your own contemporary attitudes toward character analysis and modern psychological research may connect you with the audience's likely response to a play, a *single* personal viewpoint does not necessarily inspire rich, varied, complex period productions.

Period plays encompass not only those written two hundred or two thousand years ago; but plays and musicals from the 1930s through the 1960s, and quaint relics from the bygone era of the Gay Nineties through the Roaring Twenties. Young directors today may not have experienced the social problems engendered by World War II, the Korean and Vietnam conflicts, or the "flower children" of the Woodstock generation. Soon a play about the recent 1970s will also become a period piece requiring the same amount of research as a seventeenth-century play.

"Foreign" places, including other unfamiliar areas of the United States, also require research to comprehend the behavior of the characters. For example, city dwellers may view life differently from isolated country people or from automobile-addicted suburbanites. (Consider the desperate actions of the "hero," William Holden, when his car is repossessed in the classic film *Sunset Boulevard*. Why? . . . because in Los Angeles, one cannot survive without a car.)

In ideal circumstances, we could fly to distant places whenever we directed plays with exotic settings, or step into time machines swirling us into the past for on-the-spot observation. Several famous nineteenth-century space-and-time novels (*The Time Machine* by H.G. Wells, *Around the World in Eighty Days* by Jules Verne, and *A Connecticut Yankee in King Arthur's Court* by Mark Twain) played on those popular fantasies. The same romanticized view was reflected in nineteenth-century theater. From these romantic pursuits, a concern for historical accuracy in theater blossomed in the early twentieth century. Several factors nourished this interest: educated Europeans dabbled in archeology as a faddish hobby; English gentlemen, travelling around the Empire, immersed themselves in the mystery of non-Western societies; and well-to-do Americans toured Europe seeking both *objets d'art* and "culture."

Today's students who do have travel opportunities should study other parts of the world. Holiday plans create opportunities for note-taking and for expanding horizons regarding plays you might direct. Since, in reality, you may receive rather brief notice for a directing assignment, a short rehearsal period may restrict research. (On Broadway, some rehearsals are forced into only two-week slots.) Coming into a theater production without adequate background knowledge, you are put at an immediate disadvantage.

Research Chart

When interpreting scripts with productions in mind, even the most-educated and informed directors must refresh their memories and check all historical details. If time is limited, your research must be especially focused. Directors who know *how* to identify problems and find essential information can use every hour productively. Consider making a *research*

Table 5.1: Research Chart

PLAY: *The Mandrake* (*Mandragola* in **Italian**)
PLAYWRIGHT: Nicolo Machiavelli
PLACE and DATE: Florence, Italy, about 1515

Need to Know	Act/ Scene	Role	Research Purpose	Essential Nonessential	Sources of Information
biography of playwright	all esp. Prolog.	all	To know his place in his time, people he knew, travels, education, to understand his life—know play better.	E	encyclopedias, histories of Italy and Renaissance
other works by same playwright	all	all	to understand his attitudes about life, politics, morals esp. his seeming approval of illicit lovers.	E	his famous essay *The Prince, Erotica,* letters
Renaissance history	all, esp. Pro- logue	all	understand cultural setting	E	encyclopedias, cultural and art history
religious history	all, esp. IV, vii V, iii V, vi	Fr. Timothy, esp.	explain Fr. Timothy's attitudes, and behavior	E (very different attitudes today)	Catholic Encyclopedia, books on religious history, theology
topical references, names	almost every scene	Callim, Nicea, Fr. Timothy	explain play title, refs., to Paris, Rome, Pisa, etc. position of "doctor", churches, saints.	E (may update for today's audience)	encyclopedias, history of Florence, Dictionary of etymology, English/Italian dictionary
music of time and dance	"Can- zone" (5 songs), also dan- cers?	singer, or chorus and dance	how music performed in 16th century (theater or court?)	E (update? use records?)	music history texts, recordings of 16th-century music—also read dance history and *Medici* essay
design: set, costumes, "visuals"	all (set)	all (cos- tumes)	how play, set, and costumes done in 16th century, also— fashion of time	E (update?)	museums, theater history, costume/ theater/stage design—and also art of time.

chart as an adjunct to your prompt book. By graphically laying out the
"need-to-know" facts, you can define research problems and answer
them *before rehearsals start*, as in the chart, prepared by N. Boretz, for
The Mandrake (see Table 5.1).

EXERCISE

Using Table 5.1 as a sample guide, write up *your own* Research Chart
for one of the following:

a. *Agamemnon* by Aeschylus (Greek tragedy, 5th century, B.C.)
b. *Jeu d'Adam* (*Play of Adam*) Anonymous (French, 12th century)
c. *Lovers Made Men* by Ben Jonson (English masque, 17th century)
d. *Madrid Steel* by Lope de Vega (Spanish comedy, 17th century)
e. *Faust* by Goethe (German tragedy, 19th century)
f. *Awake and Sing* by Clifford Odets (American drama, 1935)
g. *A Raisin in the Sun* by Lorraine Hansberry (American drama, 1959)

Problem

When researching Shakespeare's *Julius Caesar* for a college production, you discover that
the performers, during Shakespeare's time, wore their own clothing or whatever they
could find in their costume trunks. What kind of historical "accuracy" should *you* adhere
to: Roman dress for Caesar's "real-time," seventeenth-century dress for Shakespeare's
"real-time," or neither?

Solution

Knowledge, in this case, has opened up more choices to you. Ask yourself, "What is the
play saying that is relevant to today's audiences and which costuming style best furthers
this expression?" You could make the unexpected choice and costume the actors as they
might have appeared in Shakespeare's time. Since this performance is planned for an educational institution, you may have the unusual opportunity (not generally available in
"commercial theater") of teaching your audience. Explanatory program notes would be
helpful. If you choose any nontraditional setting or costumes, tell your audience *why*.

METHODS OF RESEARCH: PERIOD PLAYS

Detailed research need not be overwhelming. When it has a specific
goal—understanding the play and illuminating creative as well as technical decisions—then the study of the periods in question can actually
be exciting and productive. You can utilize seemingly dry facts to glean
a *sense* of the play in its own period—of people affected by their environments, of playwrights as human beings who walked and talked, not
realizing one day their plays would be "classics."

Some research has immediate application for the particular play. Other information may be stored in your subconscious to use at a later date, in another production. Often, flashes of insight emerge from ideas, facts, or observations which surface when circumstances ripen. Research time is never wasted.

A study of the physical behavior of the characters could begin your research. Especially valuable is learning about the indoor and outdoor activities of the people of the time period. For example, on a hot fourth of July in Connecticut in 1906, people might do embroidery; play dominoes or cards; swing on the porch; read the paper; read aloud to each other; or write letters, since there was no radio, television, or film. The major vacation entertainment was the conversation held over dining. All these customs provide possibilities for blocking and business for the July 4th setting of *Ah, Wilderness!* by Eugene O'Neill. For example, in one

Research—Period Costumes: seventeenth-century styles accepted by modern audiences as Shakespeare's "real-time."

A Midsummer Night's Dream by William Shakespeare. Royal Shakespeare Company. With Paul Scofield. Photo: British Tourist Authority.

Research—Mixed Costumes: a "mixture" of styles accepted in Shakespeare's own time.

Macbeth by William Shakespeare. Royal Shakespeare Company. Photo: British Tourist Authority.

Research—Updated Period Costumes: a different style due to play's relocation for the contemporary audience.

The Winter's Tale by William Shakespeare. Royal Shakespeare Company. Photo: British Tourist Authority.

Research—Customs and Behavior: in this place and time a "courting couple" might sit on the porch and read to each other.

Ah, Wilderness! by Eugene O'Neill. Loyola University Theatre. Director: R. H. O'Neill. Design: Herb Sayas. Lighting: Daniel Zimmer. Photo: Loyola University Theatre.

scene, Aunt Lily might do embroidery while Mildred practices penmanship, Nat Miller reads the paper, and Uncle Sid swings on the porch as they all worry about Richard's disappearance. Knowing about these social habits also helps you in evaluating the play's setting.

Along with tangibly assisting you in physicalizing the words on the page, understanding period behavior fires the imagination, fuels creativity, and illuminates nuances of action. You begin travelling with the playwright—seeing and sensing the moving and breathing world of the play. Numerous sources can prepare you to take this journey.

Problem

You are Guest Director for a summer theater production of Shakespeare's *The Taming of the Shrew*. The leading actor playing Petruchio stresses the rough aspects of the character and neglects the gentlemanly ones. In rehearsal, he wonders why the hero seems so "un-heroic," announcing in Act I that he has come to town to seek a rich wife.

Solution

Explain to the actor that English *gentlemen* (and ladies) in the seventeenth century regarded rich marriages as the best economic and social alternative. Until fairly recently, marriages, in many countries, were arranged by families to strengthen their financial standing. The actor's difficulty stems from our present-day attitude toward people who marry for money; we may envy them but our society does not esteem them. Knowing the seventeenth-century upper-class attitude, you can help the actor appreciate why Petruchio's philosophy is acceptable to Shakespeare's time period. Then instruct him to demonstrate this seventeenth-century attitude through his physical and verbal actions.

Books and Journals

After reading the script itself, you might study *theater histories*, describing how theater was produced in the time and place of a specific play. General theater history may contain a section on the period with photographs of artworks from the time, and pictures of recent professional productions. Scholarly periodicals, critical journals, and current theater magazines publish excellent information on contemporary productions of period plays. Articles on theater history may reveal how the specifics of plays were financed, directed, costumed, and designed. Next, you should explore *primary sources*—documents produced in the actual time period of the play—in university libraries, archives, and special collections, as well as popularly accessible magazines and newspapers. Life in Sophocles's ancient Greece might be revealed to you by reading Sophocles's other works as well as those of his contemporaries: Plato, Aeschylus, Herodotus, Euripides. *It helps the director to try to re-experience what the playwrights themselves might have known and experienced:* Plato examined innovative philosophical ideas during Sophocles's lifetime; Herodotus was writing his great *History* while Sophocles was composing *Oedipus Rex*; Sophocles himself commented on the plays of Aeschylus and Euripides.

Primary sources are also found in books devoted to selections from ancient and recent documents. Consult theater history volumes first, then materials available from other disciplines. While some collections reprint fragments or edited information, others include entire original essays, diaries, letters, and other writings by critics, artists, scientists, playwrights, performers, or politicians. Esoteric materials can be approached with a sense of adventure, with a feeling of the "director-as-detective." Regarding the information as *clues* for unraveling the mystery of a play's meaning can enliven a seemingly dull activity.

Finally, you must approach *secondary sources* in history for general information about fine art, social structure, local history, aesthetic principles, religious history, political contexts, artisan technology, and concurrent developments in theater theory and practice. These materials may be found in almost any library. Art, architecture, and travel picturebooks might illustrate what the playwrights' surroundings looked like to them. Visual information is found in scholarly books on archeology, lavish issues of *National Geographic*, or colorful books on theater costume or fashion. Encyclopedia articles are particularly good for names, dates, short biographies, and summaries of cultural backgrounds. For example, a director working on *Oedipus Rex* might first read the entry on "Sophocles" and then go on to other entries, "Oedipus," "Greece," "Mythology," ever expanding upon the initial information. Articles on history, theater, philosophy, art, architecture, and religion might reveal that the Olympian god Zeus, the ancient Greek priests, and the Delphic Oracle (a powerful "fortune teller") *are* essential components of this play because they *were* essential components of ancient Greek *life*. Thus, Oedipus's tragedy might be understood from the perspective of a society that had a different religious outlook from today's world.

Museums

Some knowledge about times and places cannot be absorbed through reading. Most visual art, music, dance, and living styles (how people moved and spoke or what they looked like) need to be witnessed. In the recent past, researching the art and music for period plays was difficult and time-consuming. Today, technology and large-scale distribution provide access to so much information that we can more quickly acquire knowledge about the play's time period. Color photographs and slides, film, television, computerized libraries, compact discs, and home videos speed the journey.

Of course, seeing or hearing the "originals" provides the optimal experience. Capitalize on your access to any *museums* in various parts of the country when you are working on plays. If a museum contains artworks, artifacts, or displays relating to your play, see and re-experience these objects. Imagine them on your stage. Fantasize how they were used by the living characters. For example, you might look at portraits. Study these paintings and try to imitate the stance of the character, the mold of the furniture, the weight of the garment, the textures of the room or landscape. You might try to imagine what the character in the painting is looking at, or what the character is thinking within the context of the place, period, and social situation.

It helps you to see what the playwright saw. Not all museums are devoted exclusively to artworks by individual artists. Some are nature museums, folk-art museums, historical museums, regional museums, and special collections supported by private associations and quasipublic institutions. Any or all of these might display grown or manufactured items produced during the periods under study such as: local flora and fauna, eighteenth-century furniture, seventeenth-century kitchen utensils, medieval musical instruments, 1940s greeting cards, ancient Greek vases, rare photographs of nineteenth-century Norway, advertising posters of the 1920s, coins of the Roman Empire, jewelry designed for kings, Chinese dinnerware imported to Colonial America—perhaps even theater costumes, drawings, photographs, and antique props.

Aside from the theater memorabilia, these items may *seem* unrelated to your immediate concerns. However, they could excite imaginative thought as well as technical or design possibilities. Seeing these objects can inspire different perceptions of period lifestyle. You may be astonished to find people more sophisticated in their living habits than your readings had suggested. For example, Greek "vases" were *never* used for flowers. These huge "vases" had many functions, from wine storage to funeral urns. Directors who wanted to use copies of them as props or stage furniture would need to understand their original purposes. And, actually *seeing* (in a museum) a decorated "vase" designed for an Olympic Games trophy might give you an *immediate* sense of the power and importance these objects had. Sophocles certainly saw them and appreciated their value.

Music

It also helps to hear what the playwrights heard. University, professional, and community music groups offer concerts with *music* of past eras that you should attend; and performances of period music are available on records and tapes. Many libraries have collections which may be listened to or even borrowed.

Books on music history can enlighten you about *when* and *where* music was written and played. For example, when working on a play by Molière (*L'Amour Medecin* or *Le Bourgeois Gentilhomme*), you might want to include music and/or dance, according to seventeenth-century practice. Encyclopedia articles or music textbooks can reveal who the composers of that era were and whether or not they wrote music in the same time and place that Molière wrote his plays. (They did at the court of the Sun King, Louis XIV.) For true aural information, locate recordings of seventeenth-century music played on authentic instruments by current performers. Listening to those pieces can "transport" you into the playwright's time, and inspire you about the musical atmosphere for your own production.

Actually listening to the music in performance generates more awareness than books *about* music. Written descriptions of music as "rhythmic," "slow," "loud," "syncopated," reveal little if you are not familiar with the works of certain composers, or sensitive to the sound of archaic musical instruments and outdated, vocal performance styles.

Twenty years from now we may have difficulty explaining to a younger generation how Laurie Anderson sang, the Talking Heads performed, or how punk rock sounded. You will have to go to a music history collection to find out.

Movies

In addition to records, early Hollywood *movies* and foreign *films* can be excellent sources for that elusive information on how people moved, spoke, sang, and behaved. Unfortunately, movies are too recent for most period research. A few "silents" were made in the 1890s, most others in the early 1900s, and "talkies" were not introduced until the late 1920s. However, research on plays written since the 1890s can provide information available in these films for: details of dress, haircut and coiffure; furniture and interior settings; social habits (smoking, drinking, card-playing); movement, acting, and dance styles; social etiquette (gentlemen opening doors for ladies, children seen and not heard, treatment of servants and store clerks); and language (idiomatic expressions, slang, and pronunciation).

Make special efforts to see these "dated" or unusual films. Some are shown on educational or non-primetime television or in university film series. Foreign films and "oldies" may be played at an area "art" movie theater and classics, silents, and art films may be featured at public libraries and museums.

See these works not only for "fun" but to learn about the time period. For example, if you are planning a production of the entirely female cast of *The Women* (Clare Booth, 1936), try to see movies made at that time, including the filmed version of the stage play, to observe the manners and customs of women in the thirties.

Current films about previous times can be insightful if you are aiming for historical accuracy or utilizing unusual settings. For example, while planning a production of an eighteenth-century play, you might see the movie version of Mozart's *Magic Flute*, directed by Ingmar Bergman. It was performed in Sweden's magnificently preserved Drottningholm Court Theater, with that theater's original 200-year-old sets. "Saturday-afternoon-at-the-movies" could create some of your more memorable, learning-intensive research hours.

To appreciate the scope of valid research, note how one professional director describes his research methodology:

Even though I have a body of knowledge that has evolved from working for over twenty years in the business, I am currently deeply involved in researching my next play, *The Lion in Winter*. I'm not doing as much research as I *should* only because it's never possible to do enough. I have read several histories of the era, several biographies of the real persons involved, and have looked rather extensively through costumes and design sources for the period. I will rescreen the film, particularly for costumes. I have done a vast amount of iconographic exploration of the period. I have traveled through all those areas and have seen them first hand. I will do a modest amount of listening to music of the period. I will go back and look at all the reviews of all the other productions, notably the New York ones. The play was selected because of the availability of two people to play Henry and Eleanor, and I've worked with them and know that they will arrive and know all the words at the first rehearsal and that it's going to be an immensely pleasant experience.

Research—Theater Sets: a modern-day production of an eighteenth-century work is being performed here in a historically "accurate" setting.
Drottningholm Court Theater. Photo: Swedish Tourist Board.

That's part of research, too. I'll spend most of my time this summer doing research.

(Tom Markus)

Problem

You are Guest Director for a production of *The Clouds*, a comedy by Aristophanes, for an in-town "experimental" theater, supported by subscriptions and grants. The troupe has previously emphasized new work and psychological drama. You sense that a "real" period piece would not suit either cast or audience. How would you handle this situation?

Solution

"Updating" an old work can be a refreshing, but also complex experience. Learn as much about the period as if you were planning a historically accurate production. Study the period/place in which it is newly being set. Some minor rewriting—especially about topical references—may be necessary, and you may need a collaborator's or dramaturg's assistance. In *The Clouds*, you might substitute local or well-known political figures and events for the ancient Greek ones. Also,

with the company's contemporary interest in the psychology of characters, include readings in the psychology of Greek life and humor.

No noble thing can be done without risks.

(Montaigne)

Updating encompasses more than just attention to costume details or topical references. *It involves a creative re-thinking of the work's basic concept.* An extraordinary illustration of updating Aristophanes would be the Yale production of *The Frogs*, with music written by Stephen Sondheim, and performed in the Yale pool! An understanding of the larger context of the play—as an idea still viable, still interesting, and still valid—was communicated through the cast to the audience.

Zelda Fichandler believes that:

Concept is the penetration of the very root thought or conflict of the play, and then its opening up. It's almost like a cubist painting where all the areas are laid open by a penetrating eye who sees through the entire object. You

Research—Updating: creative re-thinking of the play's concept and message; the setting is shifted from Europe to America's Civil War, emphasizing Mother Courage's position as a scavenger making money from both Union and Confederate armies.

Mother Courage and Her Children by Bertolt Brecht. American version by Robert Potter. Virginia Museum Theatre. Director: Tom Markus. Set design: Joseph A. Varga. Costumes: Carol Beule. Photo: Virginia Museum.

have to circle, circle, and circle the play for a long time to find the concept natural to you. We have a production of *Tartuffe* at the Arena directed by the Rumanian director, Lucian Puntilie, and he studied *Tartuffe* six months before he came to total clarity of how the play that Molière wrote at that time in his life in that culture could be opened up for today by validly stretching the material to find what was in it for our world. Everything springs from concept rightfully used; every prop, every light cue, every behavioral moment of an actor, the casting, the rehearsal method. Your concept invades every detail and triggers your imagination; it pierces the heart and circulates through the whole body of the work. Concept means fertility, birth of the work, the uniting of opposite impulses to form one that is generative: like conception.

Designing the Production

Your work as "historian" interfaces with your role in designing productions. Some aspects of design are research-oriented; however, *design* involves a deeper penetration into a play than attention to authenticity in hairdos or Louis XVI chairs. Having done thorough research, a director can bring a fresh viewpoint and fully participate in the entire design concept. (S)he can generate images, colors, patterns, and feelings for visualizations and advance the evolution of the design.

This book ends with a bibliography to help you get research started. The bibliography lists some of the most popular and essential sources for major periods. These should be useful stepping stones to further research.

FINAL PROJECTS

1. Choose a historical time period unfamiliar to you and read historical accounts, documents, and literature from the period. Then read a play from that era and evaluate your reactions: Was the play's message clear to you? Did you understand the historical context? Did (valid) ideas for production occur to you?
2. Choose a period playscript you do not know, read it carefully, and make notes about unclear concepts or details. *Then*, read a book or article, visit a museum, listen to some music, attend a lecture, or see a film related to this play. Evaluate your reactions: Did some concepts shake up your preconceived ideas? Did new facts and information encourage you to think of production in more "artistic" or "practical" terms? Compare your reactions to those of project 1 (above).
3. Choose a period play and decide whether you will have long-term research time or limited research time. Write up research time-plan lists (including all types of study) for each of these situations.
4. Ask classmates to write up a Research Chart for a period play *you* know well, but which is unfamiliar to them. Then, evaluate, and comment on their proposals. Be sure *you* know enough to make additional or alternate suggestions for *their* research.

Chapter **6**

The Director as Designer
Working with Stage Design

[The famous artist] Bernini, A Florentine Sculptor, Architect, Painter and Poet: who a little before my comming to the citty gave a Publique Opera . . . where in he painted the Seans, cut the Statures, invented the Engines, composed the Musique, writ the Comedy and built the Theater all himself.

from the diary of John Evelyn (November 1644)

Effective directing demands a strongly developed visual sense. Like the designers they may use, directors, too, are image makers, composing pictures from the varied perspectives of multi-media art. Utilizing kinetic patterns in performance, they unify text and character, enhance meaning through visual relationships, and oversee the appearance of an entire production. Every director's training should include studies in design and its conceptual and technical elements.

Educating yourself in these areas, you will gain better artistic control over your own work. Ignorance of technical terminology hampers the director's ability to illustrate ideas. A fundamental understanding of design and technical principles can help you further designers' and technicians' work, engage in meaningful dialogue, facilitate their needs, and resolve problems. To paraphrase Louis Pasteur, "Chance favors the prepared mind"; or better still, Washington Irving, "Great minds have purposes, others have wishes." Know enough to be able to evaluate the entire staging plan—and not just for its suitability to a particular show, but also for its overall excellence of design.

THE ROLE DESIGN PLAYS IN PRODUCTION

A powerful *design* supports every moment of the action and unifies all stage elements. New York director Sheldon Aptekar discusses such a design:

The design elements of *The Mousetrap* were wonderful to work with for everything fit. There wasn't one element that did not belong on stage. The characters, in costume, moving through the lighting, were totally integrated. During the murder scene the lighting effect from the stage right fireplace was coordinated to the stage left sound and the dial light from the radio. The sound of the music, announcer, static were produced by a speaker wedged inside the radio. This sound effect worked with the radio dial light which was aimed at the actors in such a way as to create additional shadows to those coming from the fireplace and the door stage right. The actors moved in space through light and dark. All of these elements were worked out within the environment in detail to enhance the dramatic moment.

The best directors encourage designers to contribute to the conceptualization process. A director who stimulates this creative participation benefits from a larger product than (s)he alone may conceive. General guidelines presented by you in early production meetings should give designers sufficient latitude to make their own discoveries. Otherwise a production will be limited to what the director alone could conceive.

The term "designer" popularly means one associated with visual arts. Like the word "artist," which commonly refers to a painter or sculptor, "designer" possesses other interpretations. Since "artist" and "designer" refer to almost any creative endeavor, these terms often combine with other descriptive words for clearer definition. Pinpointing what an artist or designer does may be difficult unless described as: *graphic* artist, *industrial* designer, *performing* artist, *set* designer, *musical* artist, *interior* designer, *literary* artist, *lighting* designer, and so forth. Today, critics, reviewers, and scholars tend to apply the term "artist" almost universally, to persons engaged in any activity of any art. The same can be said of the term "designer." A newly revived phenomenon in recent years involves the participation of "fine" artists in stage design. In past eras, the best European painters, sculptors, and architects were commissioned to design and build stage sets, interesting costumes, and technical devices for public/religious events or wealthy private patrons. Currently, fine artists and theater organizations are finding such commissions and collaborations mutually beneficial and artistically exciting.

Whether or not you eventually work with professional designers or famous artists, learn to visualize your own productions, from both conceptual and technical viewpoints. Understand the textual meaning implied by the design and utilize visual-arts methods for compositions and staging ideas. Train your imagination to "see" your scripts even before productions begin. As true artists, take full responsibility for design.

Acquiring an expertise in design and technical theater may be invaluable when you're working with inexperienced technicians in establishing light and sound cues. If a director misreads a groundplan, miscalculates the strength of a light beam, or misjudges the effect of a given fabric or prop, irreversible consequences can result. The most obvious mistakes, for an audience, are likely to occur in the design and technical

Stage Design: an exciting new setting by a twentieth-century "fine" artist for an eighteenth-century opera.

Orfeo and Euridice by C.W. Gluck. Opera Theatre of St. Louis. Set and costume design: Louise Nevelson. Photo: Ken Howard.

areas where a seemingly minor error, like a broken phone bell or misplaced chair, can eradicate the effect of an entire scene. The production's design will either strengthen or undermine the script and the acting. This chapter will examine how you, as "designer," can support the implementation of an excellent design for your production.

Visualizing the Script

Soar into the realm of fantasy and visualize your script each time you re-read it. Pictures, images, and sounds will start emerging as the script develops a life of its own within your thoughts. As Plato so wisely stated, "Thinking is the talking of the soul with itself." Your perceptions shape how you imagine the physical staging and production design. Note down when pictures or groupings flash through your head. Try to make the positions, placements, colors, contours, and design ideas you experience concrete. Even if you do not use these visions, they can serve as springboards toward identifying and developing others.

Read scripts with at least two kinds of design in mind: kinetic (choreographic/staging) and static (visual art). The composition is formed

Stage Design—Abstract: an abstract open space allows for shifts in place and time.

Black Medea by Ernest Ferlita. New Federal Theatre. Director: Glenda Dickerson. Set design: Michael Fish. Photo: Ted Lamoreaux.

Stage Design—Realistic: the closed-in feeling of this realistic set emphasizes a monastic environment.

Mass Appeal by Bill C. Davis. The Cape Playhouse. Director: Geraldine Fitzgerald. Set design: Helen Ponds and Herbert Senn. Photo: Craig Studio.

by your visual realization of the script from both movement (actor/performance) and nonmovement (scene/costume/color) viewpoints.

Movement design results from blocking and groundplans. Your sense of theatrical place/space/color/texture indicate the theme of the piece as surely as the characters' actions. For example: color may be sombre for a tragedy, bright and cheerful for a comedy. Texture is silken for a sensuous scene, rough for a poverty-street scene, opaque for a mystery scene. Vertical shapes capture the stuffiness of a structured-society scene.

An abstract environment may reveal as much about the meaning of the play as a realistic scene. An abstract scene might emphasize the characters' movements, for example, *Black Medea* by Ernest Ferlita, calls for the frenetic movements of a voodoo chorus. An abstract open space allows the women, when chanting, to psychologically transport the audience to many places. Conversely, a realistic set for Bill Davis's *Mass Appeal* supports the experiences of two religious in a contained clerical environment.

The interaction between the physical action, the dialogue, and the visual image should be clear. Directors who do not understand the importance of design may rely totally upon the emotional transaction between characters. However, transforming that exchange into color, angle, and shape could add exciting elements to it.

> The visible element of directing is the design. The better the design, the better guide the actor has for a simple line of truth, so that (s)he has less responsibility for worrying about how it looks. (S)he can just live the part, just because (s)he has confidence it's going to look right, it's going to *be* right. A proper design fulfills the play's inner truth. The director must find the harmonious relationship between the actor's inner experience and the designer's external experience.
>
> (Marshal W. Mason)

Problem

You are directing *The Cherry Orchard* by Anton Chekhov for a workshop production. Overwhelmed by the naturalism of the script, you have not considered the visual excitement of its more abstract qualities. The performers have absorbed this limitation from you and are thinking in rather mundane terms. How can you enliven your own ideas here about the "look" or the "feel" of the production and then communicate them to the actors?

Solution

1. If you can, acquire through the costumer or performers colored, paper posterboards made into a sandwich board to cover performers front and back; or long, colored fabrics to wind around them. Dressed as purely color shapes, ask performers to move about onstage while you observe patterns they create in relation to each other, to the existing stage furniture, and to the stage space. You may gain a fresh viewpoint of the actors when their function as specific characters changes. Your enlightened understanding could encourage performers to think and feel more spontaneously.

Design Problem—Solution: in rehearsal, students are seen as "color shapes" and the pattern created by their movements may give the director fresh insights.
Photo: Loyola University Theatre, New Orleans.

2. Playwrights' stage directions and descriptions provide a good source for research. (Since most scripts of past eras did not include stage directions, distinguish between additions by directors, stage managers, scholars, actors, or translators.) Some late nineteenth-century writers (Ibsen, Strindberg, Chekhov, to name a few) and many twentieth-century playwrights (such as O'Neill, Miller, Beckett, and Ionesco) include carefully thought-out ideas about sets, costumes, lighting, sounds, and action. You need not copy playwrights specifically, but use these directions to explore the *spirit* of the playwrights' intention. When playwrights possess exciting visual/theatrical senses, their textual descriptions can inspire innovative stagings.

In the rare cases where you have to be your own designer or technician, learn to identify whether your imaginative notions will be achievable. Technology in many areas has contributed creatively to both "experimental" and "traditional" theater production. These technologies can broaden design possibilities. However, they can also present problems for directors trained in standard production elements who will find themselves relying on the availability and expertise of specialized technicians. Consider some study of film, computer art, video, or projection techniques for future use in stage-production design.

Learn to experience the script as "visual" theater. Words become images, two dimensions deepen into three dimensions, and explicit visual choices can meaningfully reflect the spine of the work.

Scenographers, Designers, and Technicians

Whether choosing a bare stage or opulent setting, read and re-read your script with the actual stage and house in mind. Although you may delight in contemplating flights of fancy with forty-foot flats and fifty fan dancers, focus on the real physical space, for both aesthetic and practical reasons. The concept of the work as large or small, intimate or grandly gestural, will be affected by the space and place.

Small or intimate need not imply "unimportant." Productions can be bold and authoritative in visual concept even in a limited stage area. However, before implementing any design, consider certain practicalities. How many objects and people can fit onstage? Does the theater have enough dressing rooms, backstage areas, lighting or storage facilities for the particular production? Is there sufficient design and technical help for elaborate costumes or scene changes? Can the entire audience see all details envisioned or planned? Are there enough skilled prop people for myriad items to change hands on opening night?

Directors in commercial, professional, and well-subsidized educational or repertory theaters work with scenographers, designers, and technicians for ideas and techniques to solve problems. Directors-in-training may have minimal assistance. In either situation, you want to see some of your ideas expressing the script's visual feeling incorporated into the production. To achieve this, articulate your ideas clearly and understand the role scenographers, designers, and technicians play.

Scenographers

Scenographers are both "artists" and "design supervisors." In consultation with directors they work on both conceptual and practical ideas for production and then oversee the actual work of designers, technicians, and assistants. Although they will eventually concern themselves with set construction, costume details, and lighting control boards, their first concern will be artistic/aesthetic collaboration with directors. Scenographers are rare. Mostly available in European theater, where Josef Svoboda is a fine example, they are less a factor in professional American theater or college theater. Directors in theater organizations that can support the work of scenographers are particularly fortunate. Scenographers not only design, as artists, they also encourage and expand

Stage Houses: The size, shape, and facilities of the stage house will affect the kind of production you can realistically envision.

A. Radio City Music Hall Auditorium. Photo: Radio City Music Hall.

B. Vicenza-Palladio's Teatro Olimpico. Photo: Italian Government Travel Office.

C. Mabie Theatre, University of Iowa. Photo: Tom Jorgensen.

D. Tampere Summer Theatre (auditorium rotates). Photo: Finnish National Tourist Office.

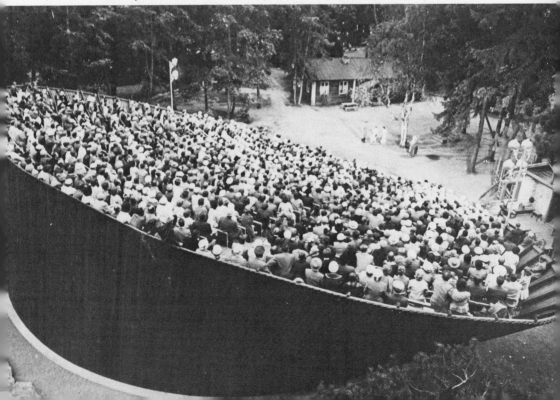

Scenographers: the concept is planned to interrelate designer's and director's ideas.
Don Carlos by Giuseppe Verdi. Oper der Stadt Köln. Design: Josef Svoboda. Photo: Stefan Odry.

upon directors' ideas. In addition, they supervise the essential day-by-day communication with other designers and technicians, thus releasing more creative and rehearsal time for directors.

Designers

Theater *designers* should be prepared to conceptualize and oversee the visual design for entire productions. However, most tend to specialize, especially in commercial theater, as *set* designers, *costume* designers, or *lighting* designers. The majority of design problems are addressed during preproduction and production meetings between the director and design staff. In commercial theater, design artists rarely oversee or take on technical tasks. The set designer may not actually paint flats, nor the costume designer sew a stitch, nor the lighting designer install gels; but, they should be expert enough in the mechanical aspects of their fields in order to design with those possibilities and limitations in mind.

When you work with a number of individual designers, interrelate design ideas and directional requirements to prevent them from clashing with each other. Collaboration among set, costume, and lighting designers enhances the visualization of your production.

Acquire enough knowledge in design areas to intelligently discuss innovative ideas and reach decisions without confusion. Communicate with designers about desired staging areas, levels, entrances and exits, and compositional-grouping requirements. If you have studied your script with visualization in mind you will be better able to work productively with designers.

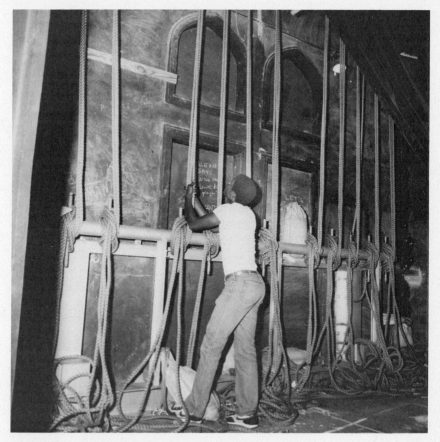

Technician—Backstage: the director should know enough about technicians' work to make realistic requests.
Photo: Loyola University Theatre, New Orleans.

Technical Directors and Technicians

In noncommercial or non-Equity theater organizations, "tech" staff are often called upon to design. Dual roles as designer/*technician* are frequently assigned in small theaters which cannot hire specialized staff for individual projects. In such situations, your understanding of design and technical areas can be invaluable.

Some knowledge of technicians' work and vocabulary is required. However, few directors who have watched lighting technicians climb around "running" cables, carpenters operate sharp table saws, or costumers hem hundreds of skirt lengths, are tempted to work in these areas themselves. The hours tech work demands would deprive even skilled directors of some rehearsal, research, artistic, administrative, and creative-thinking time.

Without some technical assistance, directors cannot mount visually complex productions. You may need to scale down your visual ideas, eliminate them altogether, or assume some technical tasks. However, arrange to avoid such work so that precious directorial time is not consumed by unusual tech tasks.

DESIGNING THE PRODUCTION

The Designer/Director Relationship

The cooperative/collaborative work among directors, designers, and technicians can be the most exciting, interesting, creative, and hazardous in theatrical experience. You might be less prepared for the possibility of friction in these areas, than in coaching actors.

A director usually accepts the possibility of eventually working with temperamental actors, prima donnas who insist on special privileges, or some "stars" who refuse to alter *their* "*style*" for individual roles. A director seldom budgets for backstage problems with costumers who "know the period and will *not* put a feather on a hat. There *are* no hats with feathers for that costume!"; lighting designers who think green is a "sickly" color and never, *never* use it if *they* can help it; or set designers whose concept this year is "Less is more" (last year it was "More is more"), and will not embellish *anything* or use colors other than stark white for walls.

Directors can hire artists or technicians whose work they know and admire only in certain situations. Guest directors, especially, usually find designers-in-residence when they arrive for preproduction meetings. You may even be told that sets have been built, costumes rented, colors chosen, lights hung, and intermission refreshments boxed in the storeroom. All *you* have to do is "direct." You may find it very difficult to make changes under these conditions for social, technical, and financial reasons. Most designers and technicians *are* willing and able to work well with directors. A director may experience difficulties if (s)he does not understand designers/technicians' perceptions of themselves in relation to their work.

First, (s)he may not realize that almost all designers/technicians think of themselves as "artists" with special conceptual talents and skills comparable in importance to those of directors and performers. They perceive themselves as *essential* members of the production staff, not as peripheral persons who labor during odd hours when directors do not see them or the work they are producing. They also regard themselves as "theater professionals" who know the script, what they are doing, and what good theater is. As individual artists, they may not consider themselves working *for* directors, but *with* them. Learn to recognize and appreciate the roles of designers and technicians in production. Although you need not accept all their suggestions, respect their knowledge.

Secondly, if the director is inexperienced, the design staff may have to take over visual production, just to get it going. A director who is not educated in these areas may resent their actions, but has no choice other than allowing skilled staff members to do their best. However, in such a situation, ask good questions: "Can it be done *this* way?; Why did you choose a brown gown for this episode? I "see" it in blue; I didn't realize my color-lighting choices would cancel out the costume colors; What would *you* substitute?" A director can learn much from the answers. You may find, also, that your idea is practical and there is no reason it cannot be done the way you visualized it.

Lastly, a director sometimes perceives technicians as mere employees who should be ready at a moment's notice to build, light, or sew. However, many technical tasks which might seem simple may take days or weeks to fulfill. For example, simply changing a painted flat from orange to purple may require specially ordered materials, extra hours and pay for scene painters, workshop space and time put aside for the project, the postponement of other tasks in order to accomplish this one, application of the paint plus one day's drying time, a second coat of paint to cover the original color plus another day's drying time, and so on *ad infinitum*. A director who puts unreasonable pressures on tech staff or constantly insists on last-minute changes in all productions will soon acquire a "difficult-to-work-with" reputation. A director who understands designer/technician functions will less likely create unpleasant work environments.

Problem

You are Guest Director for a college theater production of *Tartuffe* by Molière for a contemporary-set/modern-dress production. For the first tech rehearsal you ask if everything will be in place, and are informed that problems have arisen, they are behind schedule now, but will be ready for the final dress rehearsal. How should you react and what can you do to save the tech rehearsal?

Solution

A technical rehearsal is any practice involving the use of lights, sounds, stage sets, costumes, or make-up. A dress rehearsal refers to the last rehearsals one or two days before opening night when all technical elements are included in the complete running of the show. Do not wait until the "dress" to see what items are missing. If your technical crew is behind, a partial tech rehearsal can be called. Plan for it by observing what areas are lacking and make plans to offset problems.

Substitute other objects for missing stage furniture—boxes, tables, old chairs, anything—so that your performers have something to walk around. Ask the costumer to bring in any clothing (even if unfinished) that may cause movement problems for the actors to test. Practice lighting changes, even without color, rather than waiting for equipment on order. Never cancel or shorten a tech rehearsal for lack of tech; keep going and manage as best you can.

When a director can get together weeks ahead and intensely discuss the visual aspects of the production with the designer, it is possible to create a fertile environment for the development of innovative ideas. Such conferences may involve meetings with the set, costume, and lighting designers, or with one designer/technician covering all areas.

Directors give designers the essence or the inner structure of the show; designers give the directors the outer. Discussions bridge these domains. The inner side of the production results from the conflicting desires of the characters and is externalized through actions; the setting creates the environment to further these actions. A design should advance the possibility of action. Your responsibility is the practicality of making the script move. The designer's responsibility may be to find a visual image or metaphor for the play. Work with the designer to finalize the scenic image. Together you can begin to set spatial relationships: to solidify vertical and horizontal space and to visualize in your minds how the performers will occupy the space.

A recent trend in the designer/director relationship is design-in-progress where design is seen as part of a kinetic process, rather than as pictures frozen from the beginning. Some directors choose designers who discover the design through the actors at rehearsals, as opposed to the other way around. These designers let the space (lighting and sets) evolve from the action the actors create; they have the facility, ingenuity, and flexibility to experiment with pieces for the set, to get an effect going, drop it, and try another.

I like to work with a designer who doesn't submit the design plan in advance. The production design is worked out with the action of the actors in rehearsals. This approach gives us the maximum physical freedom to make a kind of choreography and give visual definition, that is the least confining and most evocative. I'm going to be doing *Waiting for Godot* in Stratford. The designer, whom I've worked with extensively in the past, is coming to rehearsals. He and I won't even speak before we start the action.

(Joseph Chaikin)

Narratives for Designers

Regardless of your collaborative arrangement, you need to prepare for meetings with designers. After studying the play, some directors write narratives for designers describing what they see or what experience they want the audience to have in sets, costumes, lighting, and specific properties.

Production Notes: *Tobacco Road* (directed by Paul Hostetler)

Lights: Act I—The script is not specific as to time of year, but the Novel time span runs through February–March which is early spring in the South. The climate is temperate enough that the characters do not need extra clothing as a protection against cold, which suggests fairly strong sunlight without the suggestion of oppressive heat. Time of day for Act I seems to be the middle of the day, probably sometime after noon.

Acts II and III are both at dawn, or shortly thereafter. This will give the light designer the opportunity to do some Belasco shifts of intensity and color as the sun rises and full day arrives. Temperature and quality of the day pretty much as in Act I.

Sound: The only mechanical or recorded sound effects occur in Acts II and III with the repeated blowing of the auto horn by Dude. We can probably achieve the various distances of the car from the house through sound level. Clearly the horn should be that of a 1930's vintage car that is new.

Similarly, we should have the sound effect of the arrival and departure of the car at each appropriate place, again accurate as to vintage. For the cue after the return from Augusta the motor should sound as though most of the bearings were shot, since there is a reference to their having run it without oil.

I think we can cut any cue that might suggest the arrival of Captain Tim and Payne by rationalizing that they have been visiting all the tenant farms and could have parked at some distance and walked.

Costumes: We are budgeted for grab bag design for clothes, but I am hoping that we can give a good deal of attention to the dress nevertheless.

The Walker Evans FSA books and other pictorial histories of the Depression and of the sharecropper South in particular are our models, both as to the style of the clothing and the condition of it. The palette can be very subdued and almost monochromatic—denim for the men, with the exception of Captain Tim and Payne—shapeless ginghams and cheap prints of small pattern and subdued color for the women.

Jeeter—patched, torn, ragged bib overalls, indescribably filthy and ill-fitting. Probably a faded comparable work shirt. Brogans and holey, dirty socks. There are some wonderful examples of the slouch hats affected by tenant farmers in the various picture books.

Dude—Almost a carbon copy of his father, but without hat and possibly barefoot.

Lov—In Acts I and II he is reasonably well-dressed in cleaner and newer coveralls (perhaps jeans for variety) than the Lesters since he has come from buying the turnips in Act I and from home in Act II. In Act III he will need a costume change to coal-blackened coveralls and shirt (no shirt?) having rushed away from the coal shute.

Henry Peabody—a somewhat more wholesome replica of the Lesters.

Captain Tim—Might give him riding breeches, boots, windbreaker and white Stetson. Or we could go to period suit and tie.

Mr. Payne—Affluent banker with business suit of the period.

Ada—shapeless, torn, ragged, dirty housedress. Brogans or barefoot, probably the former.

Grandma—literally rags almost not identifiable as having been intended as clothing. We might even wrap her with some of the crocus sacking as part of the costume.

Ellie May—shares the lack of cleanliness of her family with a housedress that nevertheless does not obscure her nubile attractiveness. We might go for some cheesecake for her in making the skirt somewhat shorter than the length for the period as if she had outgrown a hand-me-down from her older sisters.

Pearl—Clearly she can afford better clothes and Lov has provided them. The essential quality is to emphasize her extreme youth and her beauty, but without making her a fashion plate or out of key with the environment.

Bessie—Cleaner and a bit more affluent than the Lesters. The apron and sunbonnet suggested by the script might be o.k., although I think I would prefer an outlandish hat that in some way can suggest her essentially whorish quality. . . .

These Production Notes continue for two pages more with "Props" and "Notes for scenes." Paul Hostetler describes the detailed narratives he composes.

Through the narrative process, I try to give designers specific ideas of where I'm coming from. I describe staging elements mostly in terms of what I see but *always* supported by the text. I write out for each costume, prop, light cue in each scene *generally* what I want. In preparation for the narrative, I go through the script very carefully, underlining technical requirements with a series of colored pens. Then I go back through the script and write about what I've indicated in it. The narrative is less effective in terms of arriving at a scenic design than in dealing with those somewhat less important elements like light cues, props, or costumes. Designers like it because nothing irritates technical people more than to go to all of the trouble of assembling the actual things for the director to say, "I don't like that. Bring me something else." The narrative is a kind of contract with designers.

The purpose of bringing narratives to conferences is to suggest to designers your ideas, not only in visualization but in emotional and interpretive support of the text. You need to remain open to the input of designers and involve them in the conceptualization process. Narratives start artists communicating about specific issues.

Staging: Groundplans and Technical Plots

Along with particular ideas outlined in narratives (or verbally), be prepared to discuss the groundplan and technical plot (see Chapter 1).

Technical—Special Effects: lighting sets the ominous mood for a difficult scene.

Moon for the Misbegotten by Eugene O'Neill. Playmakers Repertory Company, University of North Carolina—Chapel Hill. Set design: Peter Gould. Photo: Playmakers Repertory Company.

You need to evaluate the location, and the types of emphasis needed, such as a moonlight effect for Eugene O'Neill's *Moon for the Misbegotten*, a staircase for Dolly's entrance in Michael Stewart and Jerry Herman's *Hello, Dolly!*, a judge's "bench" for the trial scenes in Lanford Wilson's *The Rimers of Eldritch.*

Technical plots—the maps or charts of mechanical cues—sound, lights, special effects can significantly enhance actors' performances. For example, a director may encourage light cues to direct the flow of light around the actor. This change of values influences the audience's eye. Scenes may be toned and sculpted onstage. One scene becomes amusing with a flighty feeling and the next, in the same place with no change of time, appears heavy and lugubrious. Using technical cues can make the space appear malleable, living and growing with the actors and the action. Changeable environments, even if composed of fixed elements, sway the spectators' emotions. Lighting and sound patterns create an almost cinemagraphic feeling; colors may become three-dimensional, evoking different tactile experiences.

Staging Checklist

Ask the following questions when evaluating a design's effect on staging. 1) *Visibility and focus*: Can the action be seen and is the design focused on the area where the action occurs? 2) *Plasticity*: Can and should the design be fully explored by the actors in the staging? For example, a design composed of a cloth backdrop may only function as a picture behind the actors. They may be limited to walking in front of it, rather than above, behind, under, or around it. 3) *Action*: What possibilities exist for varying movements by using doors, levels, windows, stairs, furniture, or posts. 4) *Visual interest*: Can you visualize contrast by juxtaposing color, shapes, and textures? Do the actors in costume contrast with the design, and what impression will this create in the staging? How many levels of interest will the design sustain? For example, does it reinforce the story line, establish place and time, and enhance char-

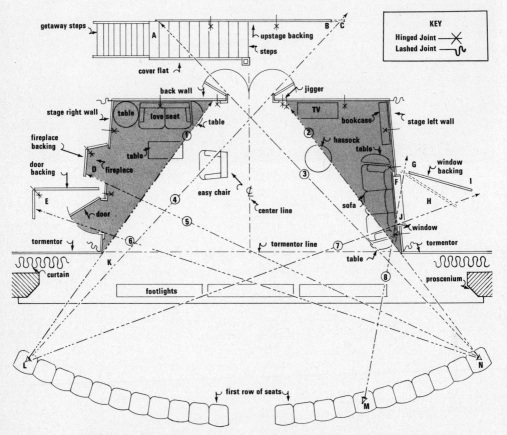

Visibility: sightlines are drawn from key seats in the house to determine which parts of the stage can be seen from those areas. Set designers find this information particularly useful; directors need the information for effective staging.

From Henning Nelms, *Scene Design*, Dover Publications, 1975.

Plasticity: the backdrop serves well in this formal setting; in "realistic" drama, it may limit movement.
Drottningholm Court Theater. Photo: Scandinavian National Tourist Offices.

Visual Interest: a variety of shapes, colors, textures creates interest on the large stage.
The Living Nativity. Radio City Music Hall. Photo: Radio City Music Hall.

acter relationships? Does the design advance the progression of the story through a series of settings or through adjustments within one setting? 5) *The entire room of the theater*: How does the set relate not only to the stage but to the entire room of the theater? Is the audience area an extension of the stage space containing the set? Does the entire visual panorama of the audience forward their theatrical experience? See, for example, the illustrations of four stage spaces on pages 170–171. 6) *Relevance*: Does the design augment the spirit of the play? For instance, if it is a farce, does the design prepare the audience for funny scenes and support their staging by the use of, say, extra doors? Should the design serve in form, shape, and color as a metaphor for the meaning of the play, a metaphor that is developed by the moment-by-moment action onstage (as, for example, the cherry orchard—central to the set in Anton Chekhov's *The Cherry Orchard*—functions as the *metaphor* for that play)?

Relevance: extra doors create possibilities for quick, numerous entrances and exits required for comedy and farce.

The Rivals by Richard Brinsley Sheridan. University of Rochester Summer Theatre. Director: Jerome Cushman. Design: P. Gibson Ralph. Photo: Rod Reilly.

Problem

You want a realistic, one-set, suggestive design.

Solution

A good, realistic set presents the hardest challenge. A nonrealistic set can have wonderful imaginings working in it but in realism, designers can't do the ordinary "shaping" that artists present. All art "distorts" surface reality. Since realism allows less adjustment, *you will have to focus on selection.* Do not make the set finished from the beginning like a painting. Allow the action of the play to fill in the design. Use props, portable set pieces, lighting and technical effects, to support the development of the action and transform the space. Juxtapose elements to shift audience impressions. If the play occurs in the same room, move the stage furniture for each act, so that spectators focus on different perspectives on the room as action progresses.

Joseph Chaikin, director of the renowned Open Theater, said this about evolving sets:

> I want to keep the eyes fluid so that one sees the set, and it changes, and erases so that you can see it again from the start. Even if I admire a set very much one of the things I'm scared about is being oppressed visually. I think "oh no. I'm going to have to look at that for 2½ hours!" And the more elaborate the set, the more likely it is *not* going to change. I like the actor moving onto or in those parts of the stage to create the scene, instead of something that's fixed. I prefer the activity of the audience to complete the set from implication (they could visualize an outdoor scene from a tree branch). I would also much rather have a color on a person than objects, the actor becoming alive with color rather than the decor.

EXERCISES

1. Rehearse a scene two ways with completely different floor patterns, costumes, props, lights, and sounds. Present both stagings to the class for evaluation.
2. Choose a play from a period in which stage descriptions are not commonly included. In class, read through the script out loud, requesting visual design suggestions from classmates as reading progresses.
3. Without a particular script in mind, search through well-illustrated books and photographs of building interiors (palaces, homes, monuments, religious structures, and so forth). Analyze them in class as possible visual sources for stage productions.

Reading and Planning Designs

After the initial conference, planning good costumes and sets requires mastering how to *read* and evaluate the visual-arts designs. Generally, artists, designers, and technicians present preliminary renderings or small three-dimensional models to convey their visual sense of the script. Di-

Rendering—Set Design: a professional designer submits sketches to give the director an idea how the finished set will look.

The Marriage of Figaro by W.A. Mozart. June Opera Festival of New Jersey. Design: Alan E. Muroaka. Photo: Fritz Conrad.

rectors may also participate in formulating place, space, shape, and color ideas. Design assistants and skilled technicians may be expected to rely on plans in these forms for producing most of their work.

In adequately staffed theater organizations, formal, detailed, technical construction plans are also submitted by good professional designers. Detailed plans are invaluable in theaters where the designer/artist does not always stay around for consultation or supervision after construction has begun.

In small theaters, directors usually hold more informal preproduction design meetings involving personal communication, discussion, and verbal description rather than presentation of drawn-to-scale plans of the set. During such conferences, designers might make a few rudimentary, quick sketches for their own reference. As conversations progress, illustrations are approved, redrawn, or discarded. Those accepted may function as visual reminders for producing more-detailed plans, or be tacked onto the shop workboard as a guide for technicians.

Rendering—Costume Design: the general look of a costume, as well as small details, may be shown to the director for approval or comments.
Costume design for Nijinsky; from *The Decorative Art of Leon Bakst,* Dover Publications, 1972.

Some directors learn to make small line sketches to get their ideas across. These can be as elaborate or as simple as their abilities allow. An ordinary doodle can explain or describe a complex spatial idea or a desired textile pattern. If you have particular colors in mind, acquire paper samples or fabric swatches to illustrate for scene painters or costumers. *Since designers are visually oriented* they will probably respond most quickly to ideas presented with nonverbal methods of communication.

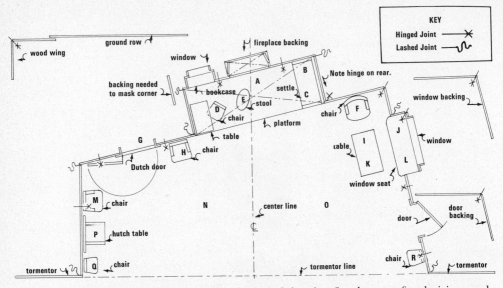

Construction Plans: detailed technical drawing for the use of technicians and workshop.

From Henning Nelms, *Scene Design*, Dover Publications, 1975.

If you conceive your own production design, try to incorporate your visual ideas while working on your prompt book. Indicate lighting, costume, and scene-design changes in this format, but use a separate section for elaborate details and technical specifications. If you know how to draft groundplans and draw light plots, include these illustrations with your basic prompt-book materials. Expand briefly written notations into lengthier information which you may add as ideas or suggestions occur.

Being exact about what you want eases your communication with costumers. The color-swatch approach can help clarify an instruction. Verbally communicating "a red dress and a blue jacket" does not describe for the costumer the shade of red or blue. Do you mean light pastels: red toward pink or red toward purple? blue approaching black or sky blue? If you need to find costumes yourself, you'll discover that knowledgeable salespeople, familiar with their own stock, can find materials or clothing more quickly if aided by your color samples.

Workshop Productions

Some workshop productions do not have designers or skilled technicians. Even part-time skilled help is not readily available.

In such situations, analyze and evaluate your theater's design, strengths, and weaknesses before making decisions. For example, if the theater has an excellent lighting system but a poor costume collection and mediocre stage-set facilities, plan the production around lighting design. Suggest mood, focus, and change of scene/place by lighting adjustments (shifts in brightness, changes in playing areas, adjustments in colors) which can be effected instantaneously. Lighting cues require fewer technicians than moving flats, shifting furniture, or changing costumes. Especially effective in stage-lighting design, color rapidly communicates emotions and ideas. Try a change from blue to red, bathing the entire stage and its performers, in a rosy (or hellish) glow to inform the audience of external change of place or internal change of motivation.

If the costume collection or rental budget is respectable but the lighting system poor, consider using costumes as the most prominent design element. Good period or experimental costumes and costume changes contribute excitement to an otherwise plain production, especially in comedies or musicals demanding spectacle. Remember intricate costumes may necessitate backstage assistants to help change, pin hair, match gloves, and effect other performance time-requirements.

Low-budget stage sets present the highest challenge. Simplify sets in the absence of technical help or funds for materials. Complexity re-

Costumes: "experimental" costumes add color and interest in a simple stage setting.
As You Like It by William Shakespeare. Boston University School of Theatre Arts.

quires *planning* and *assistance*. Streamline shapes with colors appropriate to interpretation of mood and message to build a set which creates a telling analogy for the entire work. A director who works with simple sets but imaginative concepts sometimes produces the most distinguished work.

Designing with Sound

The least expensive, understood, and utilized aspect of theater design, the careful preplanning of sound provides one of the strongest design instruments available. Learn to use sound imaginatively (live music, taped music, taped sound effects) as integral performance elements, not merely incidental afterthoughts for background.

Sound design can strengthen the texture of a scene by contrasting with or supporting the emotional chord of the performance. You should study the function of sound or music as the source of emotional impact before, during, and after a scene, especially in musicals. Some expert directors spend hours laying out the sound plot of a production so that, in addition to actors talking, sounds are traveling through the space. Musical processes and games develop a sense of rhythm. You can test musical patterns with various objects, such as bells or sticks, then use that music to enhance a scene.

Develop aural designs for production. Read and re-read your script, making prompt-book notations. Include specific sounds which explain the plot, character, or action when required by the script—a gunshot sound for Henrik Ibsen's *The Wild Duck*; cannon-fire sounds in Tom Stoppard's *Rosencrantz and Guildenstern Are Dead*—but not all texts specify sounds or sound environments.

While learning to read your script with an *eye* toward the visual, also lend an *ear* toward the aural design. Use sounds or music to emphasize text elements without scenery. For example, try carousel music to place actors—merely standing in front of a drop-curtain—at a carnival fair; city sounds—such as auto horns/fire sirens/people walking and talking—to place actors sitting at a bare table—in New York, Chicago, or Paris; ominous sounds of clanking gates/smothered screams/echoing footsteps—to suggest actors in an asylum.

Professional audio or sound designers will assist you in selecting sound effects. Well-funded theaters retain the services of experts in these areas. If you are working with sound designers, take full advantage of their knowledge.

In workshop productions, you may be able to create effective sound-effect plans without the initial assistance of a sound designer/engineer. Simplify taping and cues, and one person will be sufficient to run sound for performances.

Problem

You are directing Tennessee Williams's *Suddenly Last Summer* in a poorly equipped "studio-theater" (almost a classroom) for a college production. The low set budget requires borrowed lawn furniture and potted plants. How can you create an environment for the tropical garden setting of a wealthy New Orleans woman?

Solution

For *sounds*: employ eerie tropical sounds: harsh cries and sibilant hissing, cries of wild ravenous birds, loud caws, sounds of reptiles, a clear cry of a dying bird. Blend these sounds with the ominous fanfare of music (made by scraping scraps of tin and spoons), rattles, jungle clamor, percussive sounds, whirr of a mechanical mixer. In poetic sequences, use: various music boxes playing, a lonely bird singing, a violin melody.

For *lights*: use all the ranges of blue, orange, blood red, purple, and violet tones. Employ three side lighting units on either side of the stage for silhouettes, a "special" center stage, and angled backlighting behind wild bushes and statuary in the rear. Dress the stage with as much white as possible to reflect the lights and changes in colors. Borrow white wicker lawn furniture, patio tables, highback chair, sofa, stool, and wheelchair. Dress characters in pastels. At least six lighting areas are required onstage; the rear plants must also have at least three lighting areas besides the back lighting.

As designer, you are responsible for the integration of all elements into the total production design. Do not rely on professional designers and technicians exclusively. Your own work is the grand design, the idea for which you must learn to communicate in both aesthetic and practical terms. As master artist, you synthesize all the images around the journey of the actor. The next chapter focuses on this, your primary role.

FINAL PROJECTS

1. Choose a script you know well. Write a design project for the complete production, including all your ideas for sets, costumes, lights, and sound. For each design idea, write a short paragraph explaining or justifying your choice. Then outside classroom time, form a production group with you as director and classmates as designers and technicians in all design categories. Discuss your concept of the script at a preproduction meeting, requesting them to bring to the next meeting written or illustrated design ideas which reflect *your* concept. Evaluate completed works in the context of your original version.

2. Choose a Shakespearean play and collect materials that you might take to a design conference. These could include drawings or other pictures, paintings, photographs, records, or anything that represents the impression or tone you choose for the production. Form a production/design group outside classroom time and ask that

they bring ideas for designing to a meeting. Do not discuss your concept. Then, see how different, or similar, their ideas are from yours and from one another's. How might you use their ideas to consolidate or change yours. Submit a project book with your proposals.

3. Consider the visual sources you might need to plan an outdoor theater production. Choose one of the plays mentioned in this chapter (*The Cherry Orchard, Suddenly Last Summer, Tartuffe*). How might the play be staged without a roof or other clearly defined space? Before making any other plans, make doodle notations regarding color and design. See if these nonverbal visual approaches affect your other staging plans. Organize a design section in your prompt book to include as many illustrative sketches as you can. In class, choose your designers: a scenographer, technical director, costume designer, lighting designer. Then hold design conferences as director in a group and/or with individuals. Submit a prompt book outlining the visual aspects of the entire production.

Chapter 7

The Director
as Actor
Understanding the Acting Process

An actor is a sculptor who carves in snow.

attributed variously to Lawrence Barrett (1838–91)
and Edwin Booth (1833–98)

Knowledge of the intangible art of acting is the primary part of directing. A director utilizes the acting craft to bring the characters of a play to life and to coach the actors. Understanding acting will help you to identify with more accuracy options available for actors to fulfill the needs of the production.

Arthur Penn, professional theater and film director, says:

> When I direct I try to see the play as a member of the company, one who is up there doing exactly what the other people are doing . . . taking a chance. Doing it as openly and working out of as much personal material as I possibly can. Then, when we begin to play in front of an audience, I change hats entirely. I become the audience's emissary to the actors; I interpret what the audience is responding to.

The next three chapters will focus on your work with actors. The first two chapters introduce methods for supporting actors in developing the major components of each role. Chapter 7 overviews your function in forwarding the actor's work: creating the scene's conflict. How to deepen and expand the actor's involvement in the conflict will be explored. Chapter 8, The Director as Coach, analyzes *specific ingredients* of conflict, zeroing in on methods for enhancing the actor's mastery of each pivotal element. Finally, Chapter 9, The Director as Manager, extends the two preceding chapters, by posing thorny issues that you actually face in production, when working with actors within the context of the needs of all company members. Optimally, read all three chapters before working with actors on any individual element.

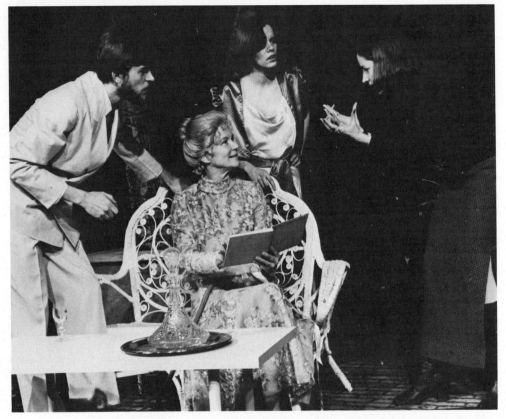

Understanding Acting: in rehearsal, the director works closely with actors; knowledge of acting is essential for effective directing.

Suddenly Last Summer by Tennessee Williams. Rider College Theatre. Director: R.H. O'Neill. Design: Thomas J.P. Sarr. Costumes: Marie Miller. With Sallie Goodman.

HELPING THE ACTOR

Other fields in the performing arts rarely demand the leader to *teach* in the process of staging. For example, conductors are not called upon to direct orchestras composed of musicians who have never played instruments, nor choreographers to plan ballets for dancers who have never danced. Directors, however, are often called upon to direct inexperienced actors, hence to *teach* acting while directing it.

You must also know acting to direct trained actors. More actors today are well informed, having studied acting at high schools, art centers, acting studios, professional schools, universities, and theaters. If you are not familiar with the techniques these actors have studied and/or employed you may impede their performances.

Regardless of the level of your actors, knowledge of the acting process saves time, a major strain in the theater. Whether three days, three

Student Actors—In Rehearsal: directors may have to teach as well as direct.
Photo: Loyola University Theatre, New Orleans.

Trained Actors—In Performance: experienced actors know their craft and may require less coaching.
Master Harold . . . and the Boys by Athol Fugard. George Street Playhouse. Director: Bob Hall. Set design: Daniel Proett. With Eric Schiff, Sullivan Walker, Lowell Williams. Photo: Suzanne Karp Krebs.

weeks, or three months, any rehearsal period must end. The more efficiently you use each minute, the further you can advance the actors'
work. In rehearsing Shakespeare's *Hamlet*, a director notices the opening
apparition scene is lagging. One pertinent experiment might be practicing the scene in the darkness or at a graveyard to stress the opposing
forces in the environment. However, this director would merely waste
time running the scene faster and having the actors work on articulation.

CONFLICT: THE CENTRAL INGREDIENT

"The harder the conflict, the more glorious the triumph." It would be
nice to think that Thomas Paine had acting in mind instead of war. Any
order of work with actors necessitates that you further the scene's *conflict*—the clash between hostile or opposing forces. A character onstage
is an opposing force in conflict. All characters have conflict, even if only
with the audience. Conflict possibilities of a character include:

conflict with one other character
conflict with a group
conflict with the self
conflict with the environment
conflict with inanimate objects

You should operate from the principle that the action of the text
generates and feeds the conflict, even when not apparent in the dialogue. Study the script prior to rehearsals and pinpoint the main and
immediate conflicts. Then assist actors in identifying, establishing, and
intensifying the opposing forces from moment-to-moment, that is, optimally—throughout each second—in every scene.

The director furthers the players' entanglement in events where they
battle to meet certain needs. Each scene marks a round in the game.
Each player has been dealt a specific "side" by the playwright. You should
encourage the actors, through their persons, to capitalize on their "sides"
by developing the role's major components: action, obstacle, objective,
and inner image. You must identify, deepen, and strengthen these elements throughout rehearsals.

The Four Basic Ingredients of Conflict

In any scene, each actor must create at least four items in *the basic unit
of conflict:*

one action (to *do*)
one objective (to *want*)
one obstacle (to *overcome*)
one inner image (to *motivate*)

Conflict—Action: actors as individual characters take action poses to physicalize the action "to demonstrate."

Travesties by Tom Stoppard. Playmakers Repertory Company, University of North Carolina—Chapel Hill. Director: Gregory Boyd. Set: Linwood Taylor. Costumes: Robbie Owen. Photo: Playmakers Repertory Company.

The actor as character does something (*action*) because of a need (*objective*) which drives the action. But something or someone gets in the way (*obstacle*). An *inner image(s)* from the actor's life personalizes the conflict and motivates the action. Motivation refers to why a character does what s(he) does. Inner images trigger motivation. To develop and sustain meaningful elements in any performance, the actor must play at least one action with one objective and maintain one obstacle and one inner image. These elements may be structured and combined variously, but all four *must* occur to generate conflict.

Actors should use all these elements when performing in *any* category of dramatic composition—whether musical comedy, Shakespearean tragedy, melodrama, or satire. No form of theater can sustain interest without these elements of conflict onstage. Without conflict, there is *no play*. Spectacle, with elaborate costumes, glamorous sets, or pulsating music, can momentarily entice the audience, but interest will dwindle in a scene without some appearance of conflict. Even in reconciliation scenes that occur in so many plays, conflict exists. Each character may desire approval from the next or some assurance of everlasting fidelity. Characters needs are not totally satisfied until the play ends. Once their needs

Conflict—Objective: the desire for happiness brings two characters together to overcome difficulties.

Home by Samm-Art Williams. Hartford Stage Company. Director: Clay Stevenson. With Delroy Lindo, Olivia Virgil Harper. Photo: Lanny Nagler.

are met, the audience's curiosity stops. If you don't support the actors in implementing the elements of conflict, you may be leaving too much "interest" to chance.

In ambiguous and absurdist plays, you may have to work with actors to establish missing moments (not articulated in the actual dialogue) in the circumstances. These create the reality or continuity for the actors to develop the intensity of performance required. As Arthur Wagner has said, "For example, although the play *The Homecoming* by Harold Pinter finally results in presenting ambiguity, directors may need to work with actors to make decisions regarding all the missing answers in the text, because actors need to play specific action."

In classic works, the words convey the circumstances and carry paramount importance. You may need to guide actors in choosing *actions*

Conflict—Obstacle: the elder Mrs. Venable tries to prevent her young niece from imparting distressing information to the doctor.
Suddenly Last Summer by Tennessee Williams. Rider College Theatre. Director: R.H. O'Neill. Design: Thomas J.P. Sarr. Costumes: Marie Miller. With Sallie Goodman.

that support the power of the language. Some American productions of period plays have ineffective acting because actors and directors overlook implementing the serious elements of acting normally applied to a contemporary psychological drama. Separating mannerisms from behavior, they mistakenly assume that certain genres require a "different" approach. Thus actors with conservatory training in performance, who have thoroughly studied and executed twentieth-century roles, may discard what they know about creating life on stage when cast in an eighteenth-century play.

Regardless of the genre, you will need a working knowledge of the action, objective, obstacle, and inner image to draw the fullest performances from each actor. Your challenge may be to set up an order of working that helps the actors implement these major components for the specific play.

Problem

Two actors, in the musical number "Anything You Can Do, I Can Do Better" from Irving Berlin's *Annie Get Your Gun*, are given no conflict. Embarrassed by the words, they perform without focus and purpose.

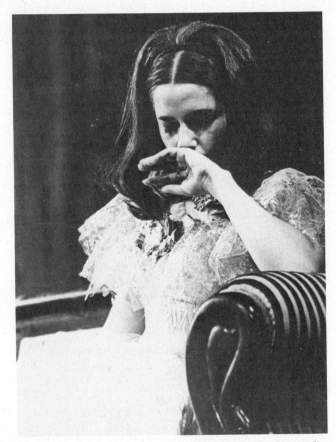

Conflict—Inner Image: the heroine faces her own death; the performer creates an inner image to motivate the action.

Camille by Alexandre Dumas. Ohio University Theatre. Director: John O'Shaughnessy. With R.H. O'Neill and Alan Langdon.

Solution

Identify the underlying conflict in the words of the song. Each character must seek to outdo the partner. Tell the actors to compete with each other, to use their gestures and movements to outdo the partner, to relish the opportunity of overcoming frustration with each other. Notice how the conflict may create more physical distance between the characters but more reality in the relationship.

The issues or circumstances surrounding conflict may differ in the various genres (see Chapter 2). In comedy, the characters are *frustrated* when unable to achieve a specific, trivial objective. Each roadblock or obstacle that prevents their completing the action leads to more frustration and sails them into an even stronger commitment to the objective. However, the frustrated character only appears to be funnier, in

Conflict and Circumstance—Comedy: characters faced with frustrations are seen to be funny.

Candide by Leonard Bernstein. University of Southern California, Division of Drama. Photo: Steve Meltzer.

Conflict and Circumstance—Tragedy: characters faced with serious loss are seen to be unhappy.

Camille by Alexandre Dumas. Ohio University Theatre. Director: John O'Shaughnessy. With R.H. O'Neill and Alan Langdon.

spite of being deadly serious about achieving the need. In serious drama, when the need is not met the character feels anguish. In both forms, the actor must concentrate intensely on the character's objective, but the seriousness of the *circumstances* differs.

Conflict in the Monologue

Breathing life into an actor's monologue may ultimately test your abilities. Whereas in a scene, two or more characters can create conflict by interacting onstage, in the long, descriptive monologue, conflict depends upon developing opposing forces within one actor. Inexperienced actors who don't have the technique to use variety to invent and sustain this "battle" may flounder here. In any monologue, the actor/character is either opposing the circumstances (talking to oneself), or opposing someone else not present onstage (the audience or an absent partner). You need to support the actors in developing a warring consciousness to create both sides of the argument. Every sentence of the monologue should promote the conflict.

The character talks to the self as a way of gaining control over the circumstances. For example, in William Gibson's *The Miracle Worker,* when Annie composes a letter to the orphanage, her vulnerable side that wants to succumb to hopeless circumstances, fights with her determined side that longs to save Helen. The physical task of the letter becomes her framework for self-confrontation.

> It is evening. The only room visible in the Keller house is Annie's, where by lamplight Annie, in a shawl, is at a desk writing a letter; at her bureau Helen, in her customary unkempt state, is tucking her doll in the bottom drawer as a cradle, the contents of which she has dumped out, creating as usual a fine disorder. Annie mutters each word as she writes her letter, slowly, her eyes close to and almost touching the page, [try] to follow with difficulty her penwork.

Annie: [*vulnerable*] . . . and, nobody, here, has, attempted, to, control, her. The, greatest, problem, I, have, is, how, to, discipline, her, without, breaking, her, spirit. (Resolute voice) [*determined*] But, I, shall, insist, on, reasonable, obedience, from, the, start—

(Act II)[1]

When a character opposes someone else (the audience or an absent partner), that adversary relationship can be intensified by stressing the basic obstacle of the listener's inattention.

You can develop introductory or expository monologues to the audience based on this principle. For example, an overall structure for

---

[1]From *The Miracle Worker* by William Gibson (Atheneum Publishers, N.Y.), © 1956, 1957 William Gibson; 1959, 1960 Tamarack Productions Ltd. and Georges Klein and Les Garel as trustees under three separate deeds of trust.

Tom's opening monologue in *The Glass Menagerie* by Tennessee Williams might be:

action: to set the stage
objective: to entice the listeners
obstacle: the listeners' lack of interest

In constant conflict, Tom must vary his actions to intrigue audiences and recapture their interest.

Tom: Yes, I have tricks in my pocket, I have things up my sleeve. But I am the opposite of a stage magician. He gives you illusion that has the appearance of truth. I give you truth in the pleasant disguise of illusion. To begin with, I turn back time. I reverse it to that quaint period, the thirties, when the huge middle class of America was matriculating in a school for the blind. Their eyes had failed them, or they had failed their eyes, and so they were having their fingers pressed forcibly down on the fiery Braille alphabet of a dissolving economy . . .   (scene i)[2]

Another page of monologue continues after this opening.

Problem

Your actor playing Tom in the above monologue is having difficulty addressing the audience.

Solution

1. Guide Tom to imagine among the real audience members, people from his own life to create and respond to their reactions. Tom can focus on his action because his opposition includes the audience but is also controlled by him.
2. Tell Tom to imagine the movement of the listeners in places where the audience won't be, so he won't spot an audience member and lose his concentration. Direct Tom to look out and imagine listeners in the aisles, windows, exit doors, backstage, or other offstage areas during various parts of his speech. (Note this advice may not work for monologues which define action in terms of audience response.)
3. Develop Tom's concentration by testing two different approaches. Have him imagine that the listeners, placed in the audience, are first attracted by and next repelled by the entire speech. Initially, the listeners might be spotted at the rear of the auditorium and then at specific locations successively closer to the stage; and secondly, a reverse procedure might be followed. Focus on making the unreal imaginary partners a real source of conflict for your actor.

---

[2]From *The Glass Menagerie*, by Tennessee Williams, © 1945 by Tennessee Williams & Edwina D. Williams. Renewed by Tennessee Williams. Reprinted by permission of Random House, Inc.

Internalizing and Externalizing

Besides trouble with monologues your actor may have difficulty expressing the conflict. Externalized and internalized performances are responses in action to a conflict different from the reality of the character created by the playwright. These problems may result from how the actor listens in character. Zelda Fichandler, head of New York University's professional actor-training program, says when listening the actor must "meet the other actor in total vulnerability, to pick up like a sensitive seismograph all the impulses coming at him."

The actor should strive to listen fully so that s(he) may interpret the situation at hand as comprehensively as the *character really would have envisioned it*. If not grounded in the character's reality, the actor's responses in action may be too exaggerated or too suppressed. The more an actor knows about the part, the more s(he) can "listen" and risk making character decisions because (s)he so identifies with that character that (s)he won't be forced to grab at ungrounded choices. (S)he becomes the character making choices in the course of the actor making choices. The actor's imagination will shape the conflict. The actor must conjure up the "hostile" world of the character. The opposition appears in the actor's listening and determines the nature and intensity of the ensuing actions.

When actors perform broadly for the audience rather than against the opponents, overacting results.

> Like a strutting player, whose conceit
> Lies in his hamstring, and doth think it rich
> To hear the wooden dialogue and sound
> Twixt his stretch'd footing and the scaffoldage.
>
> *(Troilus and Cressida,* Act I; scene iii)

Afraid of being boring, actors "play the obstacle," that is, exaggerate the struggle or try to tell the story by telescoping their feelings to the audience. You should allow for actors being most nervous at the beginning of a scene, for the quality of their listening being impaired, and for the precise actions of the characters not being generated.

Externalized performances (overacting) may occur when directors develop conflict too late in the scene; imposing it during the middle, where the obvious confrontation erupts, or randomly throughout the scene; forgetting that conflict must develop with consistency from the scene's *inception*. Loosely guided, unfocused, or missing instruction about the conflict may fuel overacting. Well-directed conflict erupts with precision and subtlety.

Problem

Actors are overacting in rehearsals.

Solution

1. Lower the actors' energy level by having a controlled number of physical and vocal warm-ups "in character" at the beginning of rehearsals.
2. Revitalize the circumstances in a scene for the actors, or increase the obstacle(s) to their action(s) to deepen focus in the conflict.
3. Start scene work on the characters' previous circumstances, what they were doing *before* the scene that influences their entrances. Creating the off-stage life of the characters forwards the scene's action from the reality of the characters' past lives.
4. Structure an improvisation on a pivotal past event, such as a last meeting, influencing the characters' mental states. Mugging is easier with memorized than with improvised dialogue. Direct the actors to focus on an inner problem of each character to curb external energy.

Internalized acting is giving too little energy, or inner life, to the action and insufficiently responding to the conflict externally. It sometimes results from the mistaken idea that "behaving naturally" and acting are synonymous or from a superficial understanding of the conflict's development in the scene.

You can diminish internalized performance (underacting) by helping actors identify a life-threatening conflict. Support them in seeing how the play's conflict endangers each character's way of being. For example, you might remind the actor playing Macbeth that his character risks slaughtering kings and heirs to the throne to capture the crown in Shakespeare's tragedy, *Macbeth*.

As an imperfect actor on the stage,
Who with his fear is put beside his part.

(Shakespeare, Sonnet XXIII)

Internalized and externalized performances frequently result from nervousness. Both can flourish in productions of classics, especially when a director believes that articulation, sincerity, and explosions of feeling will crystallize into the solid interpretation of a heroic character (internalized acting), or when too much emphasis is put on performing techniques (externalized acting). Directors must grasp the scope of the crisis and the gigantic needs of the characters that compel the action of a classic play.

Problem

The actor is not angry enough in the scene.

Solution

1. Have the actor relive a memory that generated rage (*emotional recall*).
2. Tell the actor to take the clenched fist of one hand and pummel it into the open palm of the other ferociously enough to stimulate anger (*body sensations*).

3. Ask the actor to focus on what's actually making the character angry in the play and to imagine the same thing happening in the actor's future (*projected fantasy*).

These are just a few of the techniques you can use to expand the emotions suggested by Peter Layton, director, Drama Studio, London/Berkeley.

Problem

The actors are underacting throughout the play.

Solution

1. Focus rehearsals on strengthening the actors' experience of each scene's conflict. Identify separately each actor's need in opposition to the other characters onstage. Then challenge each to focus on bypassing and overcoming the other to fully achieve that desire. If you cannot pinpoint the conflict, start by giving each actor general opposing objectives— such as to alienate and to befriend—and end with specific ones. Or, ask each character "What dreams that are being squashed could your partner fulfill for you?" Give the actors antagonistic physical actions to sharpen their sense of opposing needs.
2. Assimilate the technical process early on in rehearsal. Use lighting and sound cues, real furniture, and approximate costumes to suggest the place. Have actors bring in and use their own objects. Encourage personalization by going to a real site such as a hospital or hotel setting, exposing the actors to films, pictures, books, and music. Create an environment that suggests the size of the character's world and enhances quality listening.
3. Give each actor a structured improvisation on the character's private world to enhance possibilities for conflict.

EXERCISES

Observe and recreate a person working against a physical obstacle, for example, someone climbing the stairs with a sprained ankle, typing a paper with a broken typewriter, or cooking a meal with the wrong utensils. Then do this assignment with:

1. one objective, one action, one obstacle
2. one objective, one action, two obstacles
3. one objective, two actions, one obstacle
4. one objective, two actions, two obstacles
5. two objectives, two actions, one obstacle
6. two objectives, two actions, two obstacles

Conflict and the Structured Improvisation

You can sometimes curb actors' tendency to externalize or internalize performances by a *structured improvisation* aimed at strengthening the scope of the scene's conflict. You might suggest that listening is the key to the *reactive* structure of a character. If an actor says to you, "I am listening!" but it's not clear to you that (s)he is, you must then identify what listening produces! Demonstrate an interior monologue that could be going on in the actor's head and/or the physical adjustments occurring from listening. Emphasize quality listening and encourage actors to respond freely within the controlled structure established. Elements include:

a precise place and time
special relationships between people or between people and objects
specific circumstances from the past, present, and future
physical tasks and internal problems for each character
a specific action for each character in direct conflict with a partner's

Stage the first two minutes of the improvisation in silence, with total involvement in the wordless conflict and tasks. Remember that characters do not enter a room just to speak; they do so for a specific reason (to meet a person, to attend an event, to obtain an object) and, in the process, also begin talking. Have actors focus on their internal problems as they execute the opposing tasks. When you say "action," they should begin serious verbal conflict with no allowance for compromise, using words only when absolutely necessary. Overemphasis on words may result in a superficial conflict.

Problem

In rehearsing *The Diary of Anne Frank,* by Frances Goodrich and Albert Hackett, you notice the opening sags; the characters do not seem terrified when entering the attic hide-out.

Solution

1. Suggest what obstacles the characters overcome in getting to the place. For example, wearing various objects and layers of clothing on them (a suitcase might cause suspicion), avoiding certain streets and officials en route, hiding their anguish from loved ones, saying or not saying goodbye to relatives, hurrying to meet the scheduled arrival time, slipping away from the interrogation of a neighbor, and so forth.
2. Create a structured improvisation by asking the actors to arrive at rehearsal at a specified time as if they were actually sneaking into the real attic. Tell them not to let you see them arriving at the theater, otherwise the "secrecy" is lost. Examine how the level of fear they then generate can be developed throughout the entire play (Arthur Wagner).

THE ACTOR'S HOMEWORK ON CONFLICT

The actor's feelings and actions can be augmented by *homework* on conflict. You must clearly understand the procedures involved for this

The Lady of Larkspur Lotion

SCENE: *A wretchedly furnished room in the French Quarter of New Orleans. There are no windows, the room being a cubicle partitioned off from several others by imitation walls. A small slanting skylight admits the late and unencouraging day. There is a tall, black armoire, whose doors contain cracked mirrors, a swinging electric bulb, a black and graceless dresser, an awful picture of a Roman Saint and over the bed a coat-of-arms in a frame.*

1. Mrs. Hardwicke-Moore, a dyed-blonde woman of forty, is seated passively on the edge of the bed as though she could think of nothing better to do.

There is a rap at the door.

MRS. HARDWICKE-MOORE: (*in a sharp, affected tone*) Who is at the door, please?

MRS. WIRE: (*from outside, bluntly*) Me! (*Her face expressing a momentary panic, Mrs. Hardwicke-Moore rises stiffly.*)

MRS. HARDWICKE-MOORE: Oh. . . . Mrs. Wire. Come in. (*The landlady enters, a heavy, slovenly woman of fifty.*) I was just going to drop in your room to speak to you about something.

MRS. WIRE: Yeah? What about?

MRS. HARDWICKE-MOORE: (*humorously, but rather painfully smiling*) Mrs. Wire, I'm sorry to say that I just don't consider these cockroaches to be the most desirable kind of room-mates—do you?

MRS. WIRE: Cockroaches, huh?

MRS. HARDWICKE-MOORE: Yes. Precisely. Now I have had

65

The Lady of Larkspur Lotion	by Tennessee Williams		
ACTION	OBJECTIVE	OBSTACLE	INNER IMAGE
1. to repress nightmare	to resuscitate self as proper *virgin*	fallen past overdue rent no credit no money lack of rentals no friends faded looks	Don/N.Y.C. "nothing negative" no beauty parlor drink hidden in bath bottle
2. to inquire like a courtesan	to appraise visitor	street crime creditors	male callers? high hopes
3. to cover shock	to arrange self & room	"	rent now; hates noise, smells apt.
4. to check liquor on breath	to confirm it's hidden	heat	curly black hair Anita
5. to fawn welcome	to side track rent issue	her rage, greed, heartlessness	hard metal
6. to entreat entry	to reassure her for waiting	"	
7. to sneak in white lie	to convince of my devotion	"	
8. to ingratiate	to warm her		white/pink room, JB's office
9. to distract with bubbly conversation	to tickle her fancies	landlord's inspection	Francesca, 1st floor
10. to point out villains	get a week's free rent	landlord's ruthlessness	grown their shells
11. to encourage agreement	"	"	
12. to confirm	"	"	
13. to pinpoint enemy	"	"	manor bathtub
14. to confirm awkwardness	to seize sympathy	"	Orkin - N.O.

Actor's Score—for the *Lady of Lockspur Lotion* by Tennessee Williams: the actor scores both words and pauses, creating an individual approach to the material.

The Lady of Larkspur Lotion by Tennessee Williams. In *27 Wagons Full of Cotton* © 1945 by Tennessee Williams. Reprinted by permission of New Directions Publishing, N.Y.

From the Musical Production "COMPANY"

SHOW VERSION **THE LADIES WHO LUNCH**

Music and Lyrics by
STEPHEN SONDHEIM

THE LADIES WHO LUNCH

ACTION	OBJECTIVE	OBSTACLE	INNER IMAGE
1. to call for a toast	to arouse the audience's indignation	* SELF-EXPOSURE "drunk" humiliation of my husband two-timing me noise/music in bar Bobby's naivete others' disinterest	Sallie, G.N. "the girls" $
2. to salute my comrades	to expose hypocrisy of losers		Washington Roosevelt Hotel
3. to crack a joke	to get the audience to squeal with laughter	<u>I'm</u> the failure	Bruce/piano
4. to point out idleness	to keep audience mocking them		Sallie long red robe "writer" tennis
5. to expose their self-interest	"		Mary's birthday
6. to commend their preservation	to keep audience putting them down	avoid self-exposure	
7. to expose superficiality	to force audience to mock them	thick tongue	Spa G.N.
8. to point out their emptiness	"		cocked hat 3 spots

Actor's Score—for a song from *Company* by Stephen Sondheim. the actor's score supports the musical phrasing by identifying ingredients before the line and inserting no extraneous pauses.

homework, then identify when the conflict is or is not working. Two main types of homework include: a score and a history of the role.

In the *score*, the actor records the components (action, objective, obstacle, inner image) of each scene. In the *history*, the actor researches, imagines, and creates the character's preceding and future life-circumstances, fueling the conflict. Actors should score (analyze and record) *each* stage moment and write out character histories. Note the differences and similarities in the following two acting scores from *The Lady of Larkspur Lotion* by Tennessee Williams and *Company* by Stephen Sondheim. The major distinction is that the strength and length of the action in a musical must correspond to the structure of the musical phrase.

The Function of a Score and a History

When actors do not create a score or history, they construct the conflict without a blueprint or map for a reference. Experienced actors can recreate from memory, but if they should lose focus they must have some structure to consult or the scene's conflict could collapse.

> . . . Like a dull actor now;
> I have forgot my part, and I am out,
> Even to a full disgrace.
>
> (*Coriolanus*, Act I; scene i)

A score and history provide actors with a record of acting choices discovered privately and in rehearsal. Many actors, whether because of inexperience, arrogance, or laziness fail to do this work, and urge directors to spend extra rehearsal time assisting them in discovering the lives of the characters and their actions for each individual moment of a scene. Directors are then forced to encourage the actors to annotate the choices they have made during rehearsal. A score and history clarify the path of development of the characters for actors, so that distractions cannot sidetrack them from the path of truth.

Scoring solidifies what the actor plays from moment to moment; unconscious performance choices become conscious. At any given time, the actor can review the score to discover elements missing in a performance. If an actor cannot put into language an acting choice, you may never see it again. The longer the run of the play, the more valuable becomes an accurate score. The actor should record on the score discoveries in rehearsal and alone about what the character is doing, wanting, avoiding, and identifying with at each moment of the play.

Finding the Score in Rehearsal

To find the score in rehearsal, encourage actors to test a variety of actions, objectives, obstacles, and inner images. When an action captures a moment, praise and tell the actors to record its components. Urge them to write down specific acting choices for their roles with a beginning, middle, and end, or even better, with line-by-line actions, objectives, obstacles, and inner images. Ideally, a score breaks a role down into line-by-line and moment-by-moment components. Again, the four basic ones are: the *action*—What is the character doing?; the *objective*—What does the character want?; the *obstacle*—What's in the way?; and the *inner image*—What is the substitution or personal source? *Private sources may be abbreviated in the written score.*

Some acting coaches use a fifth component of *motivation,* why a character does something or wants something. We address motivation in connection with the inner images sourcing it. Inner images fill the actors thoughts and feelings fueling the reasons behind the actions.

The line-by-line components of an actor's score may be grouped into beats. A *beat* is a small section of a scene in which an actor has a single action–obstacle–adjustment–physicalization of action until achieving, or not achieving, a specific goal. The beat changes when the action changes. One actor may change an action without the other actor(s) changing, but that shift in action moves the scene in a new direction (see Chapter 4). There are many differences in one action possible in a beat. (Think of all the variations in behavior in a farewell action.) A typical beat pattern of an actor might be:

BEAT: objective→action→obstacle→adjustment→physicalizations

Physicalizations, external expression of the action, are not always there, but usually grow out of the intensity of the need.

Problem

Actors have done detailed scene scores, but the acting remains uneven.

Solution

1. Have actors look over and eliminate from their scores whatever they aren't playing onstage. Inexperienced actors frequently include material which is never used. A score should only record what the actor is actually doing. Ask actors what sections of their scores have the largest gaps for *them.* Work in detail on various choices for these areas; discover missing elements by testing choices opposite from those being played.
2. Explain that a score is only as good as its first missing link, connecting moments in a chain of development. One or more transitions can stop one moment evolving into the next. Too long a pause, an afterthought, or an inappropriate adjustment between lines can throw off the truth and momentum of an entire scene. Work the scene for transitions between beats and then for its pauses.
3. Run the entire scene without words. Observe where the character's physical life looks weak or unclear and work on these gaps. Once the physical life becomes solid in each beat, reintroduce the words.
4. Encourage actors to freely test different thoughts behind certain beats and not worry about making mistakes.

A life spent in making mistakes is not only more honorable but more useful than a life spent in doing nothing.

(George Bernard Shaw)

The Score/Prompt Book

Encourage actors to annotate the beats of their scores. Many actors make use of a *prompt book,* which may contain on the left a blank sheet of paper for notes, and on the right a page from the script affixed to an 8½ × 11 sheet. The script can be pasted face down if an actor has two copies. In the script next to the first line the actor writes the number "1," referring to number 1 on the left scoring page. On the scoring page, (s)he writes in pencil number "1" in the left-hand margin. (S)he makes columns for "action," "objective," "obstacle," and "personal source" for each particular line or moment; and uses direct infinitive phrases for the action and objectives (see former examples of working scores for a scene and for a musical number earlier in this chapter). The value of a score may be observed in its clarity, specificity, and aliveness—how it actively empowers the conflict.

Histories for each scene can also impact the conflict by making real: 1) the *who,* the character; 2) the *time,* including century, year, season, date, minute; 3) the *place,* including country, city, neighborhood, house, room, area of the room; 4) the *immediate surroundings,* including animate and inanimate objects that influence the character's life onstage; 5) the *given circumstances,* the past, present, and future, and the events influencing the scene; and 6) the *relationship,* the character's relationship to other characters and objects in the scene. When actors don't make decisions regarding these six areas, their choices onstage may be too general. You may need to suggest areas in developing the character's history that should be explored or expanded.

The British actor, Roger Fox uses the following approach in creating a history:

> What I do first of all, is to read the show five or six times before I even start to work on it. Then I have a simple formula of questions that create a foundation from which I can start to examine the individual. 1) *What does he say about himself?* It doesn't necessarily mean that he's telling the *truth,* but what my character says will inform me about who he is. 2) *What is said to him,* which gives me the perspective from the other characters. 3) *What he does,* is often the most important question. What does he achieve or do to other people? 4) *What is done to him?* These questions give me an idea of where my character is at that particular time in his life. Because a play is really a little window through which we see the character's life as a big sort of cartoon strip. Every square is something that happened, that is the character's life within this world. Now it may be a play that puts a frame around one day, one hour, or thirty years, but that's the storyboard for the character.
>
> After I've got that storyboard, I've got to fill in the blank spaces. Is there

a clue in the script which will tell me what happened immediately before the play? That's probably the most important first step. I start to work way back, as far as I can go drawing from the play—then I start to work forward as far as I can go, giving a logical conjecture of what is going to happen next. After that, once I've taken everything I can out of the play, I then start to invent it, but a lot of that invention will be as a result of the way people are reacting to me, my character, in rehearsal.

FINAL PROJECTS

1. Direct two actors to perform the same physical task for two different objectives. Then create a structured improvisation where these objectives totally conflict. Support the actors in scoring the action, objective, obstacle, and inner image of each moment.
2. Perform a ritual (getting dressed, preparing a meal, cleaning a room) with a physical obstacle or handicap. Then direct a scene from a play where a character has a similar handicap; have the actors explore and record the focused actions and negative inner images generated. Possible scene choices include: Brick (a broken ankle) in Tennessee Williams's *Cat on a Hot Tin Roof;* Eva (crippled) in Lanford Wilson's *The Rimers of Eldritch;* Danny (blind) in Leonard Gershe's *Butterflies Are Free;* Ruth (pregnant) in Lorraine Hansberry's *A Raisin in the Sun;* Merrick (deformed) in Bernard Pomerance's *The Elephant Man;* Helen (deaf mute) in William Gibson's *The Miracle Worker;* Edmund (consumptive) in Eugene O'Neill's *Long Day's Journey into Night;* Deaf Mute (deaf) in Jean Giradoux's *The Madwoman of Chaillot.*
3. Direct a monologue from the perspective of the character at adolescence. Have the actor create a history, basing the speech on one unsettling early experience or unresolved childhood obsession. Research the actor's childhood to intensify connections. Possible choices include Ketti Frings's *Look Homeward Angel* (Eugene), Elmer Rice's *Dream Girl* (Georgiana), Nitozake Shange's *For Colored Girls* (lady in red).

Chapter 8

The Director as Coach
Sharpening the Actor's Technique

One of the things that you have to have in your lexicon, in your knowledge, and in every way in which you contact an actor is a knowledge of the actor's process. It's a pure act of empathy. If you don't recognize what a courageous thing the actor is doing by stepping out in front of the audience and touching on some emotionally tender spot, then the actor will be wary of doing that, and indeed will retreat from that. If the actors sense that you recognize the risks they're taking, they'll sense that you will also be careful to not use a moment in which they are not at their best.

Arthur Penn

You cannot emphasize enough: Every role is sustained by the four basic ingredients of *conflict*—action, objective, obstacle, and inner image. This chapter focuses on methods used by directors, as coaches, to help actors develop these working ingredients. *Coaching* refers to the strengthening and developing of an actor's technique within the bounds of, and isolated from, a specific role. To coach actors, each component of conflict, and its impact on the performance, must be examined. In this chapter we will define the nature and function of these root elements from *action* to *objective* to *obstacle* to *inner image* and how they feed and nourish acting. You must understand what the actors are doing (and not doing) with these ingredients to coach their work. The chapter will conclude with some suggestions for critiquing actors.

ACTION: WHAT IS THE CHARACTER DOING?

The core ingredient of conflict is *action*. What is the character *doing*? Basic coaching involves identifying playable actions. Line by line each character *plays* an action (as in *to please* my father, *to enrage* my sister, *to captivate* the visitor) in order to meet a specific goal. Action is not just logistics. Connected to the inner life of the character, it can be a thought (*to consider* dating a friend), a memory (*to remember* an ornament), or talk (*to flatter* a student). All words involve and make specific action. Most actions are psychophysical having an interior (mental) and exterior (physical) connection. Again, the main principle to recall is: *Action is what the character* does *every second on stage.* The action thrusts itself through a beat, a scene, an act, and then the play itself.

Action and *physical action* are not interchangeable concepts. An action sometimes has little manifestation in physical actions. Eighty years ago Constantin Stanislavski revolutionized the study of acting by discovering that physical action, more than anything else, creates truth onstage for actors. Physical action refers to the characters' body movement; it deals with material or natural objects as opposed to mental, moral, spiritual, or imaginary elements.

Although the terms "movement" and "physical action" are sometimes used interchangeably, physical action is a more-focused concept. *Movement* implies a change of location or gesture. Physical action or physicalization includes *only movement that evolves from the character's objective in the scene.* Physical actions either advance or retard the conflict. For example, the way one character touches another—or responds to a noise in the parlor, a knock at the door, or the closing of a window—may or may not forward conflict. Conscious physical actions, truthfully performed, open the doorway to an actor's unconscious mental actions— the less tangible, but powerful springs of creativity. At least eight or nine different possibilities exist for directing every physical action. Work specifically with each character's physicalizations and remember that movements of light, sound, objects, and stage furniture will affect how these are received by the audience.

Relaxation and Physical Action

Relaxation releases the actor's imagination so (s)he can fully engage in physical action. Relaxation and physical action enhance one another. Unnecessary tension blocks expressive physical action and may be misconstrued by audiences as a character trait. Actors are more prone to tension during passive activities (like reading) than during strenuous physical tasks (such as pouring a bucket of water or jumping through a hoop) because physical actions lessen the residue of energy which manifests as tension.

Problem

Actors cannot relax in a scene.

Solution

1. Lessen tension by solidifying the characters' objectives. Run the scene while actors focus everything they do on what the characters want to achieve from *each other*. By concentrating on their partners, actors take concern away from themselves to lessen stage fright.

2. The blocking may thwart relaxation. Give the actors *physical tasks* which immediately root them in the reality of the scene as soon as they enter. The task can be simple (like eating an apple or wafting a scepter) but should propel the action. Test and adjust blocking to make sure it works logically. False movements make actors look unnecessarily stiff.
3. At the outset of rehearsals, give actors warm-ups to do (running for two minutes, stretches, vocalizing, and so on), *in character*, to facilitate transition into their characters' worlds. Such exercises also help the actor identify and relax areas of tension in the body.
4. Guide the actors through relaxation exercises.

Useful exercises to augment relaxation include: 1) *relaxation count-downs,* where actors lie on the floor and relax all areas in the body from their toes to the tip of the scalp; 2) *relaxation/tension exercises,* where you guide actors to work through the entire body, tensing, then relaxing its various parts; 3) *"heavenly" experiences,* where you encourage actors to relax to pleasant experiences such as listening to music. Shorter relaxation exercises include head rolls (for neck), shoulder lifts (for upper back), shaking out fingers (for hands), circling arms (for shoulders), pliés or squatting (for legs), flexing toes (for feet).

Physical Action and the Text

Guide actors in physical choices that reflect the play's message. Often actors think *their* feeling something heightens *the audience's* perception automatically. On the contrary, inappropriate feeling may blur the action. Actors communicate emotions to the audience through their deeds which clarify the text, and not necessarily by reflecting their own inner natures.

Beware of giving actors inappropriate movements that falsely distort or retard the action of the scene, as in "Move to the edge of the stage and say your lines to a character who has entered behind you." Few people stand in front of their livingroom furnishings to speak to someone who has entered behind them. Good directors understand the essence of the play so that they select actions which illuminate the text.

The physical action of the protagonist supplies the primary ingredient of conflict. You must identify this lead player and the action. For example, in the balcony scene from *Romeo and Juliet,* the focus is on Romeo and his action is *to woo* Juliet. Ask yourself, "What might Romeo do while wooing with words?" Could he leap the wall, throw her a rose, swing from the balcony, whistle, caress her cheek? If Romeo's physical actions seem static, tell him to physicalize action in the dialogue. For instance, have Romeo rush toward Juliet when saying "For stony limits cannot hold love out." Visualized words are powerful. The moving body, reinforcing the voice, is more dynamic than the voice alone.

Selecting Objects

From the moment actors go off book, give them specific tasks and appropriate objects to deal with. Objects fitted to the correct action serve to root the actor in the make-believe reality by providing a physical expression for the action.

The *selective* use of *objects* visualizes action. Try staging the following scene from Tennessee Williams's *The Glass Menagerie* in an empty room. The characters can do little (except scream) since there are no objects to extend and sharpen their actions.

Amanda: (as he passes her) Son, will you do me a favor?

Tom: What?

Amanda: Comb your hair! You look so pretty when your hair is combed! (Tom slouches on sofa with evening paper. Enormous caption "Franco Triumphs.") [Ignore stage direction.] There is only one respect in which I would like you to emulate your father.

Tom: What respect is that?

Amanda: The care he always took of his appearance. He never allowed himself to look untidy. (He throws down the paper and crosses to fire-escape.) [Ignore stage direction.] Where are you going?

Tom: I'm going out to smoke.

Amanda: You smoke too much. A pack a day at fifteen cents a pack. How much would that amount to a month? Thirty times fifteen is how much, Tom? Figure it out and you will be astounded at what you could save. Enough to give you a night school course in accounting at Washington U! Just think what a wonderful thing that would be for you, Son! (Tom is unmoved by the thought.)

Tom: I'd rather smoke. (He steps out on landing, letting the screen door slam.)[1] [Ignore stage direction.]

By adding certain objects to the room—newspaper, sofa, and a cup of coffee—you introduce options for the actors. Amanda could strenghen her criticisms by straightening the newspapers and sofa. Tom could rebuke his mother by slurping coffee, sprawling on the sofa, crushing the paper. Objects picture past reality, present circumstances, and future possibilities. They are weapons actors use to implement the verbal battle waged in the scene.

Personalizing Objects

Using their own personal objects will assist actors to find choices for their characters. Actors would not handle prized possessions (a favored watch, special cologne, house key) in the same artificial way they might

[1]From *The Glass Menagerie* by Tennessee Williams, © 1945 by Tennessee Williams and Edwina D. Williams; renewed 1973 by Tennessee Williams. Reprinted by permission of Random House, Inc.

use fake props. Personal items conjure up specific meanings, histories, and rituals. Although the character may deal differently with an item, physical action can be discovered when the actor uses a personal object. For example, in *The Glass Menagerie,* Laura must handle her glass unicorn in a way which will show the audience that it is her favorite. Have your actress rehearse the scene with a favorite object of her own, a child's first curl, a mother's cameo, perhaps even a small bird. Let her experience the special way she handles her own object, and then transfer those feelings and actions to the foreign prop—the unicorn—which will now be transformed into a thing of wonder.

Character Action: How the Action Is Performed

Identifying Spine, Action, and Attributes

You will need to analyze a play prior to rehearsals to find each character's driving action (spine) and the barriers to it in each scene. Some directors read all the parts separately as if they were playing them to identify the spine behind each one. A response in action to a character's need, the spine should be stated as an *active verb.* For example, Oliver's spine in Charles Dickens's *Oliver Twist* might be "*to find* a home" (active) rather than "what Oliver Twist *is looking for* (passive) is a place to live."

The spine of Blanche DuBois in Williams's *A Streetcar Named Desire* could be *to find* a nest (play's spine: *to shelter* Blanche). Each character's spine should be generated by the play's main action. Some characters' (like Stella's) actions forward the play's spine, while others (like Stanley's) may block it—for example, thwarting Blanche by his hostility. Each role's spine contributes to the through-line expressing the spine of the play. You will need to know both the character's spine and the play's spine (see Chapter 2) to help actors implement their individual character actions in each scene.

The principal work on characterization involves developing the character action, *how* the character performs the action. The actor cannot play an adjective or quality, only a verb. For instance, an actor does not play "obnoxious" but (s)he can sass, insult, irritate, or behave in an obnoxious manner. In rehearsal, you help the actor discover how the action is done. For example, the action *to share* might be performed differently by various characters. A pompous person might share sanctimoniously or preach, while a gentle person would share quietly or disclose. Similarly, with the action *to eat,* an uncouth person might *grab,* a dainty person might *pick,* a sly person might *sneak* the food.

Physical Attributes. A character is marked by notable *physical* and *personal* traits influencing action. For example, if the character's action is *to teach,* the physical attributes of weight, health, and age might affect the *how* of the action—whether (s)he moves around demonstrating or sits immobile. Personal traits could also condition the teaching: a *tedious* person might inundate, a *spiritual* person might enlighten, a *lively* person might entertain.

Dramatically influencing costumes, physical traits shape all action. Many directors visualize development in character through adjustments in their physical movements, patterns, and external appearances (costumes, hairdos, make-up, accessories) of the characters. Physically, Willy Loman in Arthur Miller's *Death of a Salesman* is a destitute salesman, past sixty. His eyesight is failing so his clothing may be ill matched, worn, and dated; and his feet hurt so he wears arched supports in his shoes. He carries two heavy sample cases which keep his palms feeling sore and his shoulders drooped.

The following questions can help you evaluate physical traits:

1. *Well being.* How do the age, health, and fitness of characters impede or further their actions? How physically adept are the characters? Do any suffer from aches, colds, tiredness? Have they gained or lost weight? Are clothing or accessories confining, expanding, or qualifying their movements?
2. *Circumstances.* How do the profession, family habits, and social conditioning of the characters influence their movements? How civilized and how work-oriented are the characters? For whom and for what are the characters attired? Have they changed their style of dress, outfitted themselves inappropriately for the time, place, or weather? How does money (or the lack of it) influence their appearance?

Personal Attributes. Along with physical traits, distinguish personal traits of each character. For Willy Loman, they might be a *forced enthusiasm* to cover his tired gestures and *daydreaming* to distract himself from his failures by mumbling. Willy increasingly loses hold on external reality throughout the play.

Identify key traits before auditions so you cast actors who can translate those traits into the characters' actions. Search for the central characteristics of each part necessary to the unfolding of the story. One approach, the *two-pole technique,* involves studying the script and interpreting the two major extremes of personality—one positive and one negative—crucial to each role. (For example, Romeo may be seen as daring and also pensive; Juliet as impulsive, but frightened.)

Although a character has many qualities, poles define extremes of identity that create the action. Annie Sullivan in William Gibson's *The Miracle Worker* is vulnerable and determined (play's spine: *to reach* Helen), and Othello in Shakespeare's *Othello* is passionate and suspicious (play's spine: *to secure* marital fidelity). While subtler versions shape much action, these poles identify the edges the characters must reach. One pole frequently triumphs over the other by the end of the play. Smaller roles with undefined physical and personal qualities provide opportunities for imaginative casting, that is, for fitting the role to the interesting traits of actors.

Knowing character poles can help you keep focus in rehearsals and create from action. When naming poles, choose positive adjectives because actors may feel uncomfortable playing, and therefore resist, repulsive characteristics. Table 8.1 shows a breakdown of character poles for audition and rehearsal purposes.

Describe the poles using enticing, emotional words to propel and shape action. For example, the two poles of Annie Sullivan, teacher of the blind, deaf, and dumb Helen Keller, stretch from *driven* to *vulnerable*. Pick *driven* rather than *aggressive, arrogant,* or *bossy,* although all these words describe a similar characteristic. *Aggressive, arrogant,* and *bossy* sound pejorative, whereas *driven* compels. *Driven* is a positive cover-up for the negative characteristic *bossy.* Since this trait sustains the role of Annie, the actress must be encouraged to value it.

Remember that the more imbedded the negative trait, the more likely it is to be camouflaged. Human beings excuse and hide their distasteful qualities not only from each other, but from themselves. Describing a character sympathetically predisposes the actor to incorporate your interpretation.

Rehearsing with Visual and Aural Aids

The more you do visually and aurally to entice an actor to implement a specific trait, the less you may need to discuss characterization. For example, you are working on the opening scene of Henrik Ibsen's *A Doll's House* during which the fun-loving Nora prepares for Christmas. Encourage the development of that quality by practicing with festive lighting, colorful decorations, Christmas music, and holiday attire, even if these elements are not incorporated into the final staging. Then insist that Nora rehearses in shoes appropriate to the role. Shoes affect the *how*—the carriage and overall movement of a character.

Problem

The lead actress has difficulty developing the essential "delicate" trait of Catherine, in Ruth and Augustus Goetz's *The Heiress.*

Solution

Dress her in a nineteenth-century spinster costume during rehearsal. Clothing unique to certain periods and personalities needs to be "lived in" by an actor. It can drastically affect and even generate a character pole. Since Catherine wears items like a hoop skirt, waist cincher, veiled hat, kid gloves, and tightly laced shoes, her "delicate" behavior can be produced by the constricting attire. Encourage her to move, to perform tasks, to discover how her costume necessitates delicate behavior. Help the actress to create the same feeling from

Table 8.1: Two-Pole Character Breakdown (R.H. O'Neill)

The Miracle Worker (by William Gibson)

Character	Attribute	Pole
the doctor	sophisticated	positive
	anguished	negative
Kate	loving to exhaustion	positive
	tormented gentlewoman	negative
Keller	doting	positive
	domineering	negative
Helen	affectionate	positive
	savage	negative
Martha	congenial	positive
	snippy	negative
Percy	respectful	positive
	frightened	negative
Aunt Ev	indulgent	positive
	disciplined	negative
James	sensitive	positive
	defiant	negative
Anagnos	paternal	positive
	worried	negative
Annie	vulnerable	positive
	driven	negative
Viney	devoted	positive
	arrogant	negative
servant	enthusiastic	positive
	docile	negative

within as well as with costume and environment. Explore what makes Catherine so delicate psychologically. Does she hide in her own world? Is she afraid of stating her own opinions and feelings for fear of reprimand, ridicule, or rejection?

Personalizing the Character Action in Rehearsal

Character traits indicated in the text must grow through the actors themselves. A preconceived idea about a role can stifle development of character poles in rehearsal. Actors will repeatedly play the same image. If a script only contains some general reference to a character, beware of imagining a stereotype for the part such as a "dumb blonde" or "cranky, old miser" and encouraging or imposing your own image on an actor.

To avoid cliché character action, guide actors to try to experience the play as though seeing it for the first time. Actors need to create for themselves first before doing roles for others. At rehearsals, allow actors to explore *who the characters are* and how they mesh with the other characters.

Help actors create comprehensive *histories* of the characters' circumstances and life prior to the play and before each scene. The history is grounded in the actor's life and provides the framework for connecting past experiences with the character's. Avoid prying into private areas or secrets, while encouraging actors to fantasize a history from the point of view of the character, unaware of future mistakes. Sometimes you may suggest an actor create the history from the character's perspective at a given age (growing up, before marriage, working, in ill health) so the actor considers the effect of time, another person, or a particular event on the character.

EXERCISES

1. Choose a play and break down the two poles of each character. Justify precasting specific stars for each role.
2. *Observation.* Scan the classroom and list all the objects surrounding the students: books, pens, hats, scarves, and so on. Distinguish which items influence the behavior of students prior to class, during class, and after class. Pick three essential props for each student.
3. Direct a monologue with the actor using an object to forward the physical action. Possible choices: Blanche in *A Streetcar Named Desire,* Anne in *The Diary of Anne Frank,* Lorraine Hansberry in *To Be Young, Gifted, and Black,* John Proctor in *The Crucible,* Jamie in *Long Day's Journey into Night,* Brick in *Cat on a Hot Tin Roof,* Biff in *Death of a Salesman,* and Walter Lee in *A Raisin in the Sun.*

Problem

Actors are playing stereotypes about their characters.

Solution

Eliminating a stereotype is tricky because the actor may have seen the part done a certain way so often it seems integral.
1. Suggest the actor think about an actual person (like one's own father, mother, or brother), whose emotional presence is concrete and at the same time similar to the character's. Ask the actor to compare this person with the stereotype. The descriptions will rarely contain a connection between them. Break down the scene into specific actions that could be performed by the "real individual" and work on one beat at a time.
2. Videotape, then play back the scene so that the actor has the opportunity to observe the falseness of the stereotype choice. Ask the actor to photograph or videotape, if possible, the behavior of similar characters from life.

3. Work with actors to explore the opposites in their character's behavior. Stereotypes falsely limit a character to one trait: the blonde bombshell is *only* sexy, the miser is *only* greedy, and the soldier is *only* tough.

4. Direct the entire scene as a comedy, then as a tragedy. Tell actors to first play every moment to make the partner laugh and second to make the partner cry. Though it distorts certain moments, this technique reveals options in the text to stretch the range of character action.

Joseph Chaikin discusses balance as a missing ingredient in stereotype performances:

> There are several balances with actors . . . that have to do with release, abandon, and restraint. You give yourself, surrender to something, you let it open, and you control it. As you open it, you monitor it, you sort of abandon and control. If you just control, or if you just spurt it out, then there's not that balance one must develop. So, the more you release the more you also shape. In other words, when an actor maintains a certain amount that's not played out there's a constant replenishment of inner resource. When it's all played out it's like steam that evaporates and there isn't any more replenishment. So just purely technically it's of value to an actor, no matter how fully one is playing, to have something that's not played out. A director should get the actor to contact the material of the moment, like it's an iceberg with all that underneath the water and just a little bit coming out of the water.

Personalizing character action may require supporting actors in controlling the shape of the visible action.

Relationships: Who Is Influencing the Character Action?

The principal work on characterization involves how the character performs the action. For example, two people might chat and drink tea differently. Ancillary to that task is developing character relationships because relationship influences character action. The *receiver* of the action shapes the character's manner of behavior. A teacher might lecture (action) in a different manner to a favorite niece than to a school official (relationship). Whom you are talking to or doing something to influences *how* you act. *Prior to rehearsals you must study* the central relationships in the play. Audiences experience characters through their relationships. Often intangible and abstract, relationships are revealed through character actions. Because of the nature of relationships, characters will perform actions differently. For example, how one character greets another could reflect a relationship of affection or disdain.

Characters develop onstage through their interrelationships or connections to other people, places, things, and events. Directors should consider the following question: How do the main relationships adjust throughout the play?

Relationships between two people greatly influence character development. Meaningful, volatile, and diverse relationships intrigue audiences. Look for contradictions in any relationship. For example, in a loving relationship, identify the hatred.

Character development may next be influenced by whether relationship to place changes throughout the play. Some useful questions to explore include: What does the environment tell you about the characters? What are the boundaries in the room between characters? Are certain places off limits to any characters? From what spot does each feel most comfortable in this space?

Finally, examine characters' connections to certain animate and inanimate objects and events. Witness the significance of relationships to animals such as the birds in August Strindberg's *Miss Julie* and John Steinbeck's *Of Mice and Men,* and the rabbit in Paul Zindel's *The Effects of Gamma Rays on Man-in-the-Moon Marigolds.* (All three animals are murdered by the protagonists.) Evaluate how each character's relationships to the principal events throughout the play (the selling of a house, marriage, and so on) shape the character actions. Although relationships include connections to people, objects, and events, in this section we focus on relationships between *people*.

Rehearsals: Working for Truth in Relationships

In rehearsals, you must transform fictitious relationships in a written script into believable people interacting onstage. To nurture sensitive performances from the actors, you need a heightened sense of truth in human relationships. You can encourage such integrity by directing actors to continually tie the stage relationship to their own worlds.

At rehearsals, test various actions with actors to see which ones affect their partners. Implement acting choices that develop a *relationship* between the specific actors as the characters. For example, if you notice that your "Willy" in Arthur Miller's *Death of a Salesman* responds to joshing from your "Biff," incorporate that action whenever appropriate.

One technique for illuminating stage relationships is asking actors the right questions, such as: "How much does your character care about this relationship? What does (s)he resent in this relationship?" Characters always come from and move toward particular choices about affection in a relationship. The degree of attraction molds their action.

In every relationship, there is usually an order of power. Identify and work with actors on *who* has the most control in the relationship; *why;* and *how* the domination/submissiveness in the relationship influences character action. For instance, the former order of power between spouses may be reversed because of some crisis (divorce). The new order may impede communication, restraining the characters' energy and contact.

The more vested stake the character has in the partner, the stronger the responsiveness, whether positive or negative, may be. Hamlet's responsiveness to Claudius (his father's assassin) is more intense than his responsiveness to Rosencrantz.

Identify *changing* relationships which develop throughout scenes. Does the protagonist's development influence that of a secondary character and does their interrelating affect a third character? For instance, Romeo's falling in love with Juliet affects Juliet's relationship with her fiance, Paris. Juliet's breaking off her relationship with Paris affects her relationship with her mother. An adjustment within a primary relationship can shift all other relationships in the play. Blanche DuBois's arrival to live at her sister's house affects the entire household in *A Streetcar Named Desire*.

Frequent Mistakes in Directing Relationships

One trap is to direct a "general idea" about a stage relationship rather than the specific range of realities within the action. For example, a director who has a limited image of what a love relationship entails might tell an onstage couple to smile, flirt, or cuddle and never respond to each other negatively. (S)he feels "being in love" precludes negativity, when in real life, this state usually involves varied emotions and some negative behavior!

Another mistake is to direct choices about relationships that run contrary to the text. Sometimes directors do this because they have no background to help them comprehend the events and circumstances of the play. An unmarried director chose, when directing *A Doll's House* by Henrik Ibsen, to delete all references to the Helmers' children and focused the play on *Torvald's* tragedy in losing his wife Nora. This tactic is at odds with Ibsen's play which quite clearly focuses on *Nora's* tragedy at having to abandon not only her husband but her *children* (whom she has identified with and raised) as well. At other times, directors support incorrect choices because they don't like what the script is saying about relationships. For example, one actor, fresh from a heartbreak, chose to play he secretly hated his wife, although his character continually expressed the opposite.

Problem

Actors are creating inappropriate relationships that work against the text.

Solution

1. In private meetings, ask actors to describe the play's principal sequence of events and their characters' attitudes toward *each* event. When actors realize where events are taking their relationships, correct adjustments usually evolve.

2. Do a structured improvisation on a past, future, or dream encounter in the script. When actors reexperience a pivotal offstage event, their stage relationship often becomes anchored in the reality of the character's life. For example, for the opening of *A Streetcar Named Desire,* an improvisation with old, heavy luggage in a dirty bus station, then on a hot streetcar, then on some faded streets could give Blanche DuBois a sense of how she feels when arriving at her sister's apartment. Reliving a crucial circumstance of the character

creates a true perspective on the stage situation. *Or*—have the actress playing Blanche bring in sentimental or valuable clothing, memorabilia, and jewelry for Blanche's trunk. Then improvise a scene with Stanley when he "attacks" Blanche by ravaging through "her" possessions so that the actress must protect what is "hers" both in fact and fancy.

Problem

Totally self-absorbed, an actor is not communicating with a scene partner, causing their interaction to become dull.

Solution

By heightening the possibilities within the relationship, directors can keep actors alert and on guard.

1. Require the actors to make physical contact with one another, to bring the relationship from the mind to the body.

2. Tell the actor to observe what the partner does during the scene—every facial gesture, sound, pause, breathing pattern before responding—then describe in detail everything noticed. Ask how (s)he could use this growing knowledge of the partner to obtain the character's needs in the scene. The actor should wait to say a line in response to the partner until (s)he knows the reason to speak.

Relationships and Audience Impression

Remind actors of the power of relationships over audience response. Except in one- or two-character plays, each character is perceived through a series of relationships with partners. If an actor plays a scene with another actor whom (s)he actively dislikes, the audience can pick up the dislike whether or not it fits the stage relationship. More than any other factor, the progression of *relationships* creates the story for the audience. These relationships are formed by everything actors *do* onstage. How Nora relates to her husband, Torvald, and the other characters in each scene of Ibsen's *A Doll's House* reflects the growing alienation that results in her final exit.

Place: What Is Influencing the Character Action?

Place also shapes character action. Notice Nora's changing relationship to her home from the opening holiday scene to her exodus. Place is the specific location (area of room, building, neighborhood, state, country) at the precise time (second, minute, hour, day, season, year, century) of the action. Second only to relationships, is place's influence over how a character does an action. The place can heighten or restrict character action. One place presents more obstacles than another (for example, a crowded bus depot at 5 P.M. could limit a "flirting" action). Your attention to how places affect behavior in real life will heighten your sensitivity to truth and detail onstage.

Table 8.2: Relationships

Characters	Relation	Action	How	Place
J. Palmer *vs.* P. Snow (pros)	leading U.S. rivals	to play golf	(to slaughter) mercilessly	sunny, championship course
K. Smith *vs.* M. Doe (amateurs)	twins recovering from heart surgery	to play tennis	(to protect) cautiously	grassy hospital field

Since place conditions physical action, explore the specific character-istics of the play's setting. Show actors how to endow the place negatively when the conflict in a scene is spurred on by adverse relationship to a place. Brick wants to stay away from the bed in Tennessee Williams's *Cat on a Hot Tin Roof* because he refuses to have relations with his wife. Helen wants to break away from her seat at the diningroom table in William Gibson's *The Miracle Worker*. Romeo must sneak from the gar-den wall to Juliet's balcony and back in *Romeo and Juliet*.

Table 8.2 shows how relationships can shape action. Notice that the characters' objectives for the contest remain unidentified. However, re-lationships to the very different places and partners should drastically affect *how* the action is done. The pros might play tennis mercilessly, while the amateurs play cautiously due to these influential relationships.

Problem

Actors look awkward in the stage relationship.

Solution

Their discomfort may result from inability to relate emotionally with the partner or with the place.

1. Have actors personalize the partner with someone meaningful in their own pasts. Ask them: "If these were your circumstances and your partner were actually your sister, mother, or best friend, how would you behave?" If the analogy isn't useful, they can choose *any real* significant person who even partially parallels the other character and imagine that person within the body of the partner by making some inner connection be-tween the two—such as, both are dark-eyed, German, possessive, or stubborn—playing the scene to that *real* person.

2. If unfamiliarity with the environment brings on awkwardness, have actors pretend that the set is like an environment they inhabit. Ask questions that stimulate appropriate emo-tional ties between the actors and the place. As actors move in the space, suggest connec-tions by saying, "Is this desk like the one in your room?" or "Which hotel does this carpet remind you of?" or "What park have you been to (or seen in a movie) that reminds you of this place?"

3. The actors may be missing objectives for their characters.

EXERCISES

1. With one garment, capture the physical and personal attributes of a character in a classical play. Demonstrate its use by the character.
2. Study the character, Louise, who appears at the beginning and ending of Edna Ferber's *Stage Door*. Visualize Louise's development through a change in physical traits (differing hairdos, clothing, movement) personal traits (intensifying or diminishing poles), and relationships (adjusting differently) in the last act.

OBJECTIVE: WHAT DOES THE CHARACTER WANT?

The action is what the characters do to achieve their goal. The *objective* is the goal they *want*. Although influenced by relationships to people and places, character action is driven by the objective. The following eulogy written on the death of Richard Burbage, Shakespeare's leading actor, captures the passionate intensity with which he performed. Today we might say he played strong objectives:

> He's gone, and with him what a world are dead
> Which he revived, to be received to;
> No more young Hamlet, old Hieronymo;
> King Lear, the grieved Moor, and more beside.
> That lived in him, have now forever died.
> Oft have I seen him leap into the grave.
> Suiting the person which he seemed to have
> Of a sad lover, with so true an eye
> That there I would have sworn he meant to die.
> Oft have I seen him play the part in jest,
> So lively that spectators and the rest
> Of his sad crew, whilst he but seem to bleed,
> Amazed, thought even then he died indeed.[2]

Actors must be compelled by specific needs to play actions with purpose. Like a game, the action is directed toward a goal where each character wins something from someone or something else. Without the objective, the action remains purposeless and unfocused. Like bait, the objective lures the character and motivates each action. *Motivation* is why (the reason) characters want the objective. Refer to objectives by using the infinitive phrase, to want—from. In a scene, the objective is what the character wants from the partner or an offstage character. In a monologue, the objective is what the character wants from another side of the self, the audience, or an absent partner.

In the following scene from *The Heiress* (script by Ruth and Augustus Goetz from a Henry James novel), the characters' opposing objectives

[2]From *Theatre in Its Time* by Peter Arnott (Little, Brown & Co., Boston, 1981), p. 188.

are relatively clear: Morris wants to make up with Catherine while she wants to break off with him.

Catherine: (calling out) Come in, Morris.

Morris: (entering) Good evening, Catherine.

Catherine: Good evening.

Morris: I have been sitting in the Square for the past half hour watching your windows. I knew you were at home. Do I offend you by coming?

Catherine: You should not have come.

Morris: Didn't Mrs. Penniman tell you my message?

Catherine: I did not understand it.

Morris: It's easily understood, Catherine! I have never ceased to think of you.

Catherine: Morris, if you cannot be honest with me, we shall have nothing more to say to each other.

Morris: Very well, Catherine. I have ventured—I have ventured—I wanted so much to . . . May we not sit down?

Catherine: I think we had better not.

Morris: Can we not be friends again?

Catherine: We aren't enemies.

Morris: Ah, I wonder whether you know the happiness it gives me to hear you say that!

Catherine: Why have you come here to say such things?

Morris: Because since the night I left it has been the desire of my life that we should be reconciled. I could not break up your life with your father. I could not come between the two of you and rob you of your due.

(Act II; scene iv)[3]

In rehearsal, work with actors to find conflicting objectives that are compelling, that fire the action with purpose and commitment. For example, Romeo, in Shakespeare's *Romeo and Juliet,* yearns to *secure* Juliet's eternal love. Amanda, in Tennessee Williams's *The Glass Menagerie,* longs to *capture* a husband for her daughter. The fact that objectives cannot be *seen* makes them difficult to work on. Only the action is visible. Objectives empower action by generating, conditioning, recharging, and intensifying it. An unsuitable objective may be signalled by resulting action that appears unfocused or uninspired.

Note how the action in the following monologue differs depending upon which possible objective is chosen: *to inspire* laughter; *to obtain* sympathy; *to motivate* artistry; *to win* an audition; *to get* a date.

> I should have been an actor. I had the talent for it. I was always the class clown, the first to speak out. But it was impractical. I went into real estate—then the market fell, interest rates went up. You should see the acts I put on now.

[3]From *The Heiress* by Ruth and Augustus Goetz (Dramatists Play Service, N.Y., 1949).

While some flexibility exists within any character's objective, actors cannot implement objectives that contradict the play. For instance, the objectives *to close down* theaters or *to entice* someone into real estate would be hard to play in the above monologue. All the objectives should develop the character's overall or *super objective* in the play.

Problem

The actors cannot find their characters' objectives.

Solution

1. Ask them, "Why would you behave this way?" Work from the general—such as *to win, to please, to find comfort,* and so on—to the particular desires of the characters in the situation.
2. Test several possible needs when running the scene.
3. Analyze the closing of the scene for what each character obtains or does not obtain, then have actors work to achieve those needs from the scene's inception.
4. Deduce the characters' objectives in a scene by first identifying their super objectives in the play.

The super objective is the core, or major need of a character that thrusts through the play and ties together all subordinate needs. Blanche DuBois's super objective in Tennessee Williams's *A Streetcar Named Desire* could be *to find a refuge* while Walter Lee's in *A Raisin in the Sun* might be *to prove his manhood*. You should support each actor in identifying the super objective because all the character's other objectives are its subsets.

Actors need to work scene-by-scene to discover the character's major objective, minor needs for the various beats, and sometimes line-by-line needs.

Arthur Penn warns about setting ideas too soon:

> One of the mistakes that happens early in directing is that we set up a climate which presupposes that there is an exact way to do something, and that there's a director's image, which already exists as a mold, which the actors have to strive to fill out. When an actor says to me, "What do you want me to do here?", I most frequently respond, "I don't know." It's true because at the heart of the matter, I really honest to God don't have an answer. And that's what you have to hang on to, to keep the circumstances open, open, open so that the actors feel they have a right to make a choice. Watching a process emerge, watching actors convert chaos into a kind of order is absolutely fascinating. And it's at that level, directors should be making a selection of values.

A scene's values are largely determined by the objectives actors play. In every moment an actor is onstage, there should be an objective operating. Characters either achieve the desired results, then intensify the objective or shift to a different one; or fail to get what they want, after which they may leave, give up, or try another strategy. A character is continually playing actions to achieve a particular objective.

OBSTACLE: WHAT IS IN THE WAY OF THE ACTION?

Besides the action and objective, a third component of conflict must thrive onstage: the *obstacle*, or what impedes the character's action. An obstacle can be an idea, person, object, event, or space. A barrier to action, the obstacle generates the conflict. While the objective inspires the action, the obstacle blocks it, placing the character in constant jeopardy, much like a player in a game. The stronger the goal or objective, the more intensely the character strives to surpass the obstacle.

You should support each character's actions to overcome impending obstacles. Like a contestant, each character performs actions (like hitting a ball) but various obstacles (like the opponent, time, disappointments, weather, distractions) stop the ball from reaching the goal. The character should be directed to concentrate totally on performing the action so (s)he doesn't fall prey to "playing the obstacle" or indicating the struggle. The obstacle functions to intensify action. Guide actors to commit themselves 100 percent to what the characters *do to overcome the obstacle* and reach a goal.

Identifying Obstacles

Pinpoint which obstacles impede the characters' action during every moment. The obstacle could be nature, when it's raining; it could be the partner, when the partner isn't listening; it could be a failure, when the character is fighting depression. Identify with the actors the major obstacles running through scenes, the minor obstacles for various beats, and individual obstacles at certain moments.

To sustain interest, a scene must have at least one primary obstacle, surging below the surface, like an undertow, opposing the characters. When they are not working against an obstacle, its force will disappear, and their focus may dissipate. If a major obstacle in a scene is the character's blindness, the scene must be directed from beginning to end with the character working against the vision problem. If the character stops trying to overcome blindness, it will disappear as an obstacle.

Problem

You cannot identify the obstacles in a scene.

Solution

1. Identify the action of the protagonist; decide what obstacles block the action from total completion. Use the stage environment (smells, textures, sounds, shapes) or other people (actions) to stop the action.
2. Perhaps the protagonist has a mental obstacle not readily apparent to the audience. The audience need not identify the obstacle for it to influence the scene. Give the protagonist a physical task to further the action; for example, one contemplating murder could sharpen a knife. A mental obstacle may require a physical task to give the actor some tangible activ-

ity on which to release inner anxiety. Otherwise the mental obstacle might neither be seen by the audience nor experienced by the actor as a moving force.

Easy to implement, physical and external obstacles automatically block character action and do not have to be imagined by the actors. For example, a stuck drawer physically impedes a thief from finding money. Psychological or mental obstacles (such as guilt or worry) may require more technique of actors because they must simultaneously create an interior, unseen block and work to overcome it. Find a physical expression of a psychological obstacle, such as a worried person might grind teeth, twist a handkerchief, and so on.

When working with inexperienced actors, you may have to emphasize physical obstacles—time running out, physical handicaps, broken objects. Visualize obstacles as opponents in the scene rather than ideas in the minds of actors. Look for clearly defined, functional obstacles actors can hurl themselves against.

Rehearsal Techniques for Opposing Objectives

Two onstage characters should always have a major obstacle between them because *characters must have conflicting needs.* Conflict of opposing needs generates and reinforces distinctions between characters. Opposition need not be vicious. Two characters, wildly in love, might differ about when to express their affection.

You can set up this conflict by identifying opposing needs of characters, then pitting the action of each against that of the other. Each character must then overcome the *action* of the partner to win the objective. Three outcomes can result: 1) the actions of both characters are evenly blocked; 2) one character overcomes the other; and 3) one character is nearer to overcoming the other.

You can intensify actors' commitment to performing actions to overcome each other. Tell each actor privately that (s)he is playing a game that only one will win. To win (s)he must play actions fully and respond completely to the partner. Each actor must interpret everything the partner says and does as adversary. Compromise is not possible, the conflict is irreversible, and even though the words are fixed, the character with the most conviction will win.

By working independently with each actor, you maximize the secrets used to fire the confrontation between partners. Some directors might confer privately with an actor about a choice to use against the partner. Others might ask actors to draw on what was meaningful and/or difficult in their lives with specific reference to a period of pain, joy, or the type of emotion being experienced by the character. For another actor this approach might appear too direct. Something paradoxical might work—like suggesting to an actor playing the "bigot" journalist in Lorraine

Hansberry's *To Be Young, Gifted, and Black*, that the character is really a "genius"—and see where it leads!

You might tell an actor to see disaster in the partner's motive, to let it offend and upset the character action. People can read anything into behavior: others might view your sweet smile as an insulting smirk or sign of contempt. By telling actors to interpret their partner's action as adversary, you enhance responsiveness and the need for, or stimulus to, a counteraction. Most acting is a response-in-action to increasingly stressful circumstances. One final ingredient, however, is needed for conflict to erupt: inner images.

EXERCISES

1. Direct two actors in an intense game (ping pong, wrestling, tennis, cards, karate, fencing, checkers) and have each thwart the actions of the other.
2. Stage the open-ended scene on page 146 as a crisis during which the characters' needs and their resultant actions conflict. Possible opposing objectives: to separate/to get married; to evict/to move in; to get peace/to have a party.

INNER IMAGES: WHAT IS GROUNDING THE CHARACTER ACTION?

Inner images are the unconscious, automatic mental pictures we attach to words, thoughts, or feelings. All action is connected to inner images. When interacting with people, places, or things (even unknown entities) we act from our mental pictures, true or fantasized. (We respond to the constant stream of inner images running through our heads—like a film.) Especially important, our self-image colors our subjective pictures which often differ from objective reality. Our view of reality shapes our reactions. Even when no connection exists with the truth, inner images influence all of our actions.

While inner images influence action, they aren't action. You can only gauge their effect on the action. When the actor contacts an *inner thought*, creating a *response* which propels the *action*, you see that in action. If the response is not appropriate, you can suggest the actor use another inner image to elicit another response. Some actors with limited techniques employ an array of images that provoke similar actions and responses. Stanislavski's studies on concentrated imagination and emotion memory provide in-depth knowledge of this domain.

Inner images can be referred to as *personal sources, substitutions*, or *inner objects*. Personal sources or substitutions imply vivid memories rooted in the actor's experience. Inner objects, remembered physical objects, serve as triggers for a series of highly emotional images. A ring may remind one of a broken engagement, a friend's death, or a graduation triumph. When the actor visualizes the ring, the film of emotion-charged images may be recalled. Actors piece together their live stream of images for the characters.

Encourage actors' fertile use of inner images as *levers to the action*. Zelda Fichandler advises:

> The materials are inside of the actors. And the craft in acting is knowing how to use what's inside of you so that it can be objectified. Start out by making actors aware that the light is in them and that . . . the process of finding the channel into themselves is not narcissistic. It's absolutely essential to discover the connection first to what they're thinking, feeling, smelling, tasting and touching—what they're knowing, perceiving—and to take that as the *only* starting place for action.

Actors need inner images to spur physical action. When playing a card game, the contestant's mind is filled with images about the opponent's hand, payoffs from winning, people to please, and so forth. Inner images give the tools to root action in personal experience and keep the performance charged by a stream of active, ongoing thoughts.

In scenes with strong physical action, inner images may claim less focus. Actors often have greater control over their hands and feet than over the intricacies of feeling and thought. Conversely, in scenes with little physical action, actors need to develop more inner images for sufficient variety of action to sustain audience interest.

Verbal Life and Inner Images

Although inner images stimulate all character action, the richness of verbal life depends on them. Before we speak, we contact mental pictures to send to others through our words. Even as we listen, we understand what others say via our own inner images. Encourage actors first to conjure up specific images for every person, place, or thing related to, talked about, or listened to onstage; and then use words to provoke the partner to experience their personal "moving pictures." For example, a Eugene Ionesco play like *The Lesson* or Samuel Beckett's *Waiting for Godot* employs, or requires, this technique.

Problem

Actors are misinterpreting the direction "Use a high energy level" as hysterics and not sending images—only stomping and screaming.

Solution

Tell the actors to use the words actively, as weapons to get what they want, rather than interject them between screams. Critical language for extreme circumstances must inspire the partner to "see" these personal "moving pictures."

You may have to slow actors down periodically, work on pauses, and observe how their mental pictures actually affect their partners. Check on how the communication is being received and perceived. Pauses allow the partner to take in what is being said. If the actor does not stop, the partner (and audience) can't absorb the mental pictures, so (s)he is speaking to no one.

Sometimes actors just go on talking, without noticing if the partner is listening or misinterpreting them. It may be necessary to stop actors in rehearsal, to experiment with pauses, and to have them annotate pauses with "X" marks, placed in their scripts, where they stop to evaluate the partner's response.

Rehearsal Techniques for Maximizing Inner Images

You may need to encourage actors, who use few personal sources, to continually generate *more* emotion-packed images than may be absolutely necessary for the communication.

Using the Text. Actors may strengthen inner images by identifying which sense is strongest in the scene. For a hot day, the sense could be touch (the cool wetness of perspiration or sticky sensation of damp air) or sight (the fizz on a cold drink, a winter landscape at dawn).

Adjusting Focus. In some cases you may have to *adjust actors' focus* to allow their inner images to flow freely. Inappropriate external focus impedes the flow of inner images. Actors' eye contact with each other restricts inner images because the focus is external. To contact inner images, they may need to look away from the partner and inward for an instant to recall the source of memory.

Ask actors to recite to a partner the details of their day's behavior. Note that they cannot simultaneously recall events and retain active eye contact with the partner. They need to look inward at specific images of events periodically, if just for a second, before speaking directly to the partner. Adjusting the focus inward, where necessary, creates the structure for actors to conjure up images. Allow eye contact to remain an organic process before imposing this technique!

Using External Means. You can employ *external means* to heighten the actor's inner life. Sound effects (such as music) or physical adjustments (such as lighting effects, costumes, meaningful objects, stage furniture) intensify inner life. For example, a sound cue used to underscore the initial meeting between Jean Brodie and her favorite pupil (in *The Prime of Miss Jean Brodie* by Jay Presson Allan), when replayed at their final parting (after the student has betrayed her) could evoke inner images bringing tears to Jean Brodie's eyes.

Recreating the Subtext. To forward actors' use of inner images, assist them in *recreating the subtext*. Such work requires time because actors are exploring both the characters' inner life and their own. Between rehearsals, an actor may spend several hours experimenting with images for just one scene, only to have the director discard much of the work. Encourage actors to write down the images used. The more inexperienced the actor, the more images likely to be forgotten between rehearsals.

Using Emotional Memory. An emotional memory exercise deals with recalling inner images from events. If appropriate, you can use an *emotional memory exercise* to help actors reexperience inner images. However, caution is advised. Emotional memory could cause serious problems if used improperly. Allowing the actor to practice alone the full technique of emotional memory can be dangerous. It should be attempted only in rehearsal after careful explanation with the strong guidance of a qualified director.

The actor may be asked to recall an experience, similar to one used in the script, in full detail (the exact facial expression, colors in the room, textures, smells). If and when a remembered event triggers a feeling, the actors should note the exact moment that "button" sets them off. A director can use part of this technique to evoke an emotional response onstage by advising actors to bring into rehearsal several "buttons" to contact at given moments in the scene or as preparation for entrance onstage.

Problem

Actors are not sending sufficient inner images to their partners.

Solution

1. Tell them to run the scene and let the inner film of personal images flow freely in the mind's eye. After saying each line, let them describe under their breaths what they are experiencing. Notice which areas have the greatest gaps, then rerun the exercise focusing on those sections.
2. Advise actors to test different associations that might stimulate lines, to uncover meaningful options for inner images.

State of Mind Generates Inner Images

Before an athletic event, journalists often interview players to uncover their *state of mind* regarding the contest. State of mind *generates* inner images, which give the impulse to action. Good directors explore with actors the character's emotional state that, like a mental net, supports and contains all the inner images. *The state of mind is fed by an inner problem,* or unsettled question, a source of perplexity or delight that the character is dealing with. The inner problem sends out inner images and fills the character's mind with thoughts in a stream of consciousness. In life, we may hear only a fraction of a communication because we are concentrating on our own problems. Inner problems fuel the mental state of players.

To develop an inner problem, an actor can initiate a process of considering, then rejecting, solutions to it. The thinking process agitates the state of mind with inner images. The inner problem functions as an obstacle, pressuring the state of mind. While they may not surface in the scene, inner problems may fuel the "troubled" relationship between characters onstage.

The more complex the character's inner problem, the more you may need to encourage the actor to use a variety of physical choices. Physical action externalizes the character's inner problem. Connected with a physical task being performed, the activity may strengthen the problem. For example, the task of covering her wrinkles with make-up may heighten Blanche DuBois's problem of attracting a husband in Tennessee Williams's *A Streetcar Named Desire.* The intensity is observed through her manner of handling the make-up. An inner image intensifies the obstacle which intensifies the objective which intensifies the action. These ingredients of conflict continually recharge each other in any solid performance.

EXERCISES

1. Direct an actor to answer the telephone three times with the word, "Hello." (S)he should contact a different series of five inner images while crossing to pick up the telephone. Use a real telephone and set the number of times it is imagined ringing.
2. Have an actor focus on resolving one major inner problem while doing some routine physical task such as making a salad, setting the table, or shining shoes.
3. Create a stage conflict with both characters concentrating on their own inner problems.

Importance of Moment-to-Moment Work

Within the time constraints of each rehearsal schedule, initiate as much moment-to-moment work on the four ingredients of conflict as possible. (Working moment-to-moment means rehearsing actors from one moment or second of the script to the next.) Few actors can remember all the nuances of a two-hour performance without directors taking the time to work with them in detail on their characters' actions, objectives, obstacles, and inner images.

Moment-to-Moment Work and Truth

This moment-to-moment work, more than any other approach, leads to actors' belief in the "stage reality." Stage truth is *not* real truth. It happens within a compact form, an *arranged* reality. The feeling of truth results from the *"magic if"*; when actors say: *If* the stage conflict were true, I would do such and such, then I would behave in this manner."

Use the "magic if" by relating to the actors as though the stage confrontation *were* true. Deal with the stage elements—properties, make-up, costumes, sets—as if each alone established the conflict. Support ongoing use of the "magic if" by actors to transform themselves into the characters. Stage truth emerges within the actors as *characters* as they confront the opposing events, elements, and people in the world of the play.

Work to insure that each objective, obstacle, and inner image secures belief in the action. While actors *must* trust anything and everything that takes place onstage, above all they must have faith in their actions.

Moment-to-moment work discovers and deepens actions that clarify the playwright's intent. Rehearsal on each section is not magically created. It must be systematically prepared for. The more you study the script and work on beats, even without finalizing choices, the better possibilities you will uncover when you start practice with the actors. Few good things happen spontaneously for actors without *preparation!*

Reinforcement through Scheduling

Each piece of work needs reinforcement not only from praise, but also from rehearsal schedules constructed to identify and repeat actions in small sections. Good directors locate the action of each beat out of which every stage choice grows. They rehearse the scene in beats, working first on previous circumstances—what happened before characters entered—then spending time on the opening beat since it sets up the scene's conflict.

Smart coaches remember each piece of an actor's work may be responsible for a second of audience attention. How that attention is focused and maintained depends primarily upon the structure of conflict in the acting. It is impossible to know too much about the essential ingredients of conflict nor be too effective in coaching their implementation. Joseph Chaikin describes the lengths he would go in coaching a role:

> If I were working on *Medea*, I would execute it through the actor playing Medea. I would talk to her as she is experiencing things. I would support and challenge her to open up to Medea's rage, planning, and strategic lunacy, and that's very difficult for an actor to do, because it's an incredible thing for an audience to witness these extremes. So for the actor to put herself on the line and go through them requires a relationship of trust with the director that I would undertake. I would move with her in the journey of her extremity!

CRITIQUING ACTORS

Besides moment-to-moment work, you need the perception to accurately critique actors. Establish a positive climate of emotional support so that they can explore choices and develop a deep affinity for their roles. Sometimes you may need to gratify an actor's immediate need, without necessarily resolving the problem. By giving the actor something to do, you put energy into the work and avoid wasting time in abstract discussions.

Focus critiques on the main aspect of each character's motive or action. Encourage the actors to immerse themselves in their characters and intensify different choices. While they must do their own soul-searching, you should provide the feedback necessary to assist them in mastering difficult moments.

As coach this feedback may sometimes entail suggesting another approach for them to explore. Sometimes you should help actors break down the text into choices that better suit them as the characters. At other times you must explore ways for them to avoid mere illustration of a character and to root the scene in an intense personal connection.

The actors' bodies may reveal whether the situation is actually being experienced by them. (For example, Blanche in hunting for alcohol in Tennessee Williams's *A Streetcar Named Desire* would have certain physical reactions in her body. Her speaking might be different because her inhaling and exhaling influences the way she speaks.) You might identify certain body sensations of the character (hot or cold; alert or tired; regular, slow, or rapid breathing) and work from there to develop the actions called for in the scene.

You can also locate playable actions by asking questions that assist the actor in *discovering* what the action is, such as "What is the character trying *to do to the other characters?*" In real life we aren't always saying, "What am I feeling?" But we do say, "I want you to see this my way; so I try to show it to you, by saying this or doing that."

Sometimes suggesting an improvisation on the character's experience can help the actor generate some present action in the play. Try having actors experiment by not saying the line because they remember it, but wait until they know *why* they are speaking it. Ideally you should test many different choices. However, realistically speaking, time constraints limit experimentation.

The good director suggests an approach based on the *specific talent* of each actor and will change a prejudgment or even a clever approach to a less intriguing one to try to suit the performer's ability. Tom Markus, a director at Yale University, described such an adjustment:

I was hired to direct a production of *As You Like It* in a professional company. The people had been cast before I arrived, which is not at all uncommon, and I gave a description of what I thought the show was like at the first session. We went to have coffee, and the guy doing Jacques came to see me and he said, "You know, that is the most intelligent and interesting approach to a play I've ever heard. But I think I'd better tell you, I don't do that. What you have suggested for Jacques is not something I do." And I realized I was talking to a 58-year-old man who had made a living doing a certain kind of acting, and he knew exactly what he did and didn't do. And I said, "Please tell me what you *do* and I will find a way to make that happen within the production which I am to create here."

While supporting individuals, you must focus on how their stage actions clash to develop the scene's conflict. Encourage a climate that invites intimacy and challenges actors to confront and go through extreme passions with each other.

"Loading a scene" or heightening its emotional level intensifies conflict. For example, you would unload Brick's scenes in Tennessee Williams's *Cat on a Hot Tin Roof* by suggesting to the actor that Brick doesn't care that Maggie is in the room, doesn't expect to get the "click," and is indifferent to the marriage. By weakening the repetitive collision that occurs between Brick and Maggie, you would deactivate the scene. Conversely, to activate it, you might encourage actors to heighten their characters' investment in each moment. For example, you could suggest that Brick is so upset about Maggie being in the room that he refuses to look at her, that he is anticipating the "click" momentarily, and is repelled by their marriage.

Problem

High-strung actors, trained to depend on your "workshop processes," request you to explore all emotional values in every sequence, including sense memory or recall. Your time schedule is tight.

Solution

Acknowledge actors' needs but do not sidetrack rehearsals into acting classes or therapy processes. Keep the demands of the entire production in perspective. Tell actors to think through sources for emotional values at home, write a few notes, and bring in choices. Handle any problems at especially scheduled rehearsals where you can suggest any necessary adjustments.

Your critique should vary according to the actor's perspective. Speed up the communication process by using the terminology of actors rather than results-based language which relates to the end product seen by the audience. Use process-based language, addressing what actors need to do to produce certain results. When you tell an actor the *result* you want—that is, tears, fear, excitement, empathy with the partner—(s)he must stop and consider the method to use to produce the result. If you use the shorthand by giving the actor the action to perform (s)he can simply do that.

Obscure critiques intensify acting problems. When does the critique create an impasse for actors? When it is a symbol, a literary analysis, an abstraction, incapable of being translated into action. For example, the direction: "On these lines, I want you to remind me of the Chapel of Saint Mary's at dawn on Easter Sunday" practically defies enactment. Clear directions stir the impulse to action. The former direction is more concretely stated as follows: "Use these words to mystify your partner."

Besides undermining actors, a director can mistakenly overencourage them. Pretending something works effectively when it does not only falsifies a situation. Even after a play has opened, you can transform performances from one night to the next with accurate critiques. Most actors would rather be presented with a positive approach to try than glib answers reflecting the director's despair. In *extraordinary* circumstances, you may need to work as coach throughout the performance, go backstage during intermission or even the performance itself to put players back on the track when they are losing direction. Exercise this technique with great caution, since going backstage may disrupt rather than support actors.

> The play is done; the curtain drops,
>   Slow falling to the prompter's bell:
> A moment yet the actor stops,
>   And looks around to say farewell.
> It is an irksome work and task;
>   And when he's laughed and said his say,
> He shows, as he removes the mask,
>   A face that's anything but gay.

> (William Makepeace Thackeray, *Doctor Birch and His Young Friends*)

FINAL PROJECTS

1. Observe a major relationship in a beginning scene of a play, such as the reunion of Blanche and Stella in Tennessee Williams's *A Streetcar Named Desire* or of Biff and Happy in Arthur Miller's *Death of a Salesman*. Identify the poles within each character that can be widened to support varied actions. Explore how the events in the play have changed the characters' relationship in a subsequent scene. Stage the two scenes to visualize the development of the relationship through changes in the characters' actions. Adjust their personal habits, clothing, hairdos, and environment to intensify the action.

2. Direct two actors to recall and describe in detail all the physical characteristics of a place from their own lives, similar to a setting in a play, like a living room at Christmas in Henrik Ibsen's *A Doll's House*, an attic in February in Frances Goodrich and Albert Hackett's *The Diary of Anne Frank*, a kitchen in the summer in Arthur

Miller's *Death of a Salesman*. Have each actor walk around the stage and demonstrate precise physical characteristics of the place. Then agree on certain spatial elements for both actors, and collaboratively recreate the place onstage. Stage the scene focusing on the actors' personal connections to the place. Encourage them to score their work.

3. Stage people in conflict in an intense relationship in an adverse place, such as an abandoned building at dusk on July 4th, a cramped disco at midnight on New Year's Eve, a hospital waiting room at 2:00 A.M. on Labor Day, a stalled train in bad weather on Christmas.

4. Could you do Project #1 in a purely improvisational situation with actors creating two poles in a character, given circumstances, scenic objectives, and time and place? This could be implemented on the spot, rather than having to go home and read a play.

Chapter 9

The Director as Manager
Coordinating the Ensemble

Where is our usual manager of Mirth?
What revels are in hand? Is there no play,
To ease the anguish of a torturing hour?

A Midsummer Night's Dream (Act V; scene i)

This chapter deals with the integration of all theater artists and production elements. Expanding upon the preceding chapters on acting, it poses actual dilemmas and troubling problems that occur. Your role of coach expands to that of manager as you begin incorporating the needs of other production personnel. The actors' work is central to effective public presentation, but all the players support or stifle it. Marshall W. Mason, artistic director of Circle Repertory, New York, says: "Although the director works primarily through the actors, (s)he must possess a larger vision than just one human being in the play. The director must collaborate with other artists, especially designers and technicians. (S)he must work through space, color, light, shadow, and dimension and through the proximity or distance between the audience and the stage. Otherwise, the actors' work may be invisible to the audience."

In the process of coordinating personalities, your "role" of manager may vary from one of dominating all the players to one of bending and adjusting to individual circumstances. Any style you choose should reflect who you are as well as the specific situation at hand—ultimately resulting in the assumption of your role as final authority on the production.

This chapter will present procedures of directing that affect managing others, such as designers, actors, producers, technicians, from initial meetings to tearing down or "striking" the show. Initially we will examine some of the qualities of a good manager: enthusiasm, high standards, communication, discipline. Then we will observe the role of the manager throughout the directing process. Finally, we will examine special problems in management: directing the musical.

THE QUALITIES OF A GOOD MANAGER

Enthusiasm

> There has to be one leading perception in the creating of a production. And in the modern age that perception has commonly fallen to the person called a "director." It's a case of a subtle recognition by all that the director has the roadmap. And that only works if the director convinces her team. The director does this by a kind of proselytizing, by artistic leadership, by exciting people by her belief or insight that this is a thrilling route to go. Then everybody's creativity, instead of being squashed, will be released to enliven and enrich the journey. There is creative interchange, but someone has to be the guide so that a seamless experience occurs for the audience where everything fits together as if by some law of inevitability.
>
> (Zelda Fichandler, producing director, Arena Stage)

A theatrical production is ephemeral. Yet it requires intense dedication, long hours, concentrated effort and, above all, it demands your *enthusiasm* to motivate people to do work that under different circumstances might appear as drudgery. "Enthusiasm" comes from the Greek word, "enthousiazein," which means "having the god within you." The hallmark of an inspired director, enthusiasm is the quickest way to rally people to an idea and to a project. The enthusiasm of artists comes from optimism, a spiritual feeling that what they are doing will make a difference, and mean something in the cosmos. "Only the artist, or the free scholar, carries his happiness within him" (Ludwig van Beethoven to Karl von Bursy, 1816). To evoke optimal performances from others, you have to believe that too. Delight in the meaningfulness of your work. Ted Swindley, artistic director of Stages says, "It all comes down to a question of significance. I have to believe that my work is significant. I have to make sure that, for every play we do, everyone involved in the production side *knows why* and *likes why* we are doing the play."

Since factions can devastate a company, recharging enthusiasm may be necessary to uplift the company at times of disillusionment. You can inspire a commonality of purpose—whether the production is a grand spectacle with hundreds of performers or a drama played on a small stage. Theater profits most from a collaboration of talents, from one great mind influencing the next. Drama during the Golden Age of Greece, Shakespeare's England, the Spanish Golden Era, and the French Baroque Period triumphed with many talents inspiring each other.

Problem

When working with an ensemble, you notice that company members are bickering among themselves.

Solution

1. Try to channel the bickering into the performance or into something positive.

Management—Grand Spectacle: the director must relate to many performers as well as the demands of a large-scale production.

Die Meistersinger Von Nürnberg by Richard Wagner. Landestheater. Photo: D. Kirchner (courtesy of the Austrian National Tourist Office).

Management—Small Theatre: the director must relate to actors and technical requirements even in a small-scale production.

The Good Hope by Herman Heijermans. With Rien van Nunen. Photo: Consulate General of the Netherlands.

2. Find an external adversary for the company to fight against—for example, Joseph Chaikin had one company unify against the absentee landlords, who were endangering the use of the space.
3. Give special encouragement to company members whose morale is low.
4. Inspire the company to unify by dedicating a performance to some person they care deeply about.
5. Be ruthless in your commitment to the work and keep the company busy.

High Standards

Besides enthusiasm you need to implement *high standards*. Wanting to create truthful, meaningful stage reality does not necessarily evoke these goals in others. If you possess high standards, look for superior players interested in giving fully of themselves to produce quality results. Most participants will do their best, but sometimes their best falls short of your standards. Something awesome occurs when a company plays with important stakes and gives their all to a production. High-spirited performance overcomes many problems, both predictable and unpredictable, and miraculously affects audiences. High standards, while enforced by the players, must be evoked by the director. Apropos of this director/cast relationship, Proverbs 29:18 tells us: "Where *there is* no vision, the people perish."

Effective Communication

Along with high standards, you must *communicate effectively*. This frequently involves communicating what is *not* working. While they may resist hearing, actors, designers, and technicians sustain their confidence in a director who seeks the best from each player by specifying when and where adjustments are needed. Using language carefully minimizes the possibility of wasted efforts and misinterpretations. If uncertain as to whether you are being understood, have the player repeat the message. Besides being explicit, you should be able to correct, without insulting.

Acquire a nonpejorative, working vocabulary. Replace words such as "awful, ugly, ridiculous, foolish, and terrible" with phrases like "not functioning, not useful, not working, not clarifying, not enhancing." Always correct the *activity* rather than the individual. Good directors have a bias toward action-oriented communication. They test rather than debate choices.

Discipline

Communications skills must be coupled with *discipline*. You need discipline to target goals, results that must occur by specific dates, to motivate people and keep them on schedule. Do not fall into the trap of drowning in individual problems and losing sight of the production's purpose: *the audience's experience of a quality theater production.* In managing, you work with specific players and imaginary audiences. Your ability to balance the two perspectives may keep you focused on the player's *real* needs and keep production progress on target. Remember Edison's maxim: "Genius is one percent inspiration, and ninety-nine percent perspiration."

In some circumstances, to maintain goals for the production you may have to operate as a "hatchet" person and implement strongly unpopular decisions. Your value may increase with your courage to revoke a decision or say, "No." Sometimes you may have to alter an entire scene. *No matter how you say it,* such surgery often offends someone involved. Good directors may appear dictatorial: insisting on high standards in a scene, requiring deep involvement of the actors, effecting rigorous deadlines in technical details, or revoking a decision. Arthur Penn reflects that "one of the toughest things in the world is to change your mind. It's very easy to be a nice guy and go along, because it has the air of being efficient and everybody thinks you're the boss and you know what you're doing. Every once in a while, it hurts, but it's inevitable for you to stand up in front of people and say 'I don't know' or 'I was wrong. I want to do it the other way.' "

To revoke, sustain, or initiate any decision, you must understand the progressive steps in working with others from the beginning to the last meeting.

> Directing is a series of decisions, the most important being do I want to do this play and is it worth doing? Then comes the casting, which includes the choice of designer and costumes. Next follow the actual decisions about the structure and style of the play. Only after that does the actual work of rehearsal start. Most plays have already been failures or successes before the rehearsals begin, because the basic decisions, on which everything else depends, have already been taken.
>
> (Martin Esslin)

INITIAL CONFERENCES AND ONGOING MEETINGS

Directors shape a production at initial and ongoing meetings where the plan is mapped out, charted, and refined. To maximize time during meetings, trouble-shoot production traps. *Study the project in advance*, then create a plan to strengthen its weak spots. By coming in prepared, you open up time and space for solving other unpredictable snags. Ideally, your designers should have been previously involved in the conceptualization of the production, so they come in open and enthusiastic to the conferences on the visual aspects (see Chapter 6). At these meetings you can further the quality of your designers', administrators', and assistants' contributions by coming in both knowledgeable, and interested in their creativity. You lead most through example sending out subconscious signals by allowing time for thorough discussion and investigation in each area.

> The problem is the same when working with actors or with scene designers, especially in America, where everyone is an independent contractor who has ideas and resents the fact that there are other ideas. I have this medieval concept that fundamentally the director is not the boss. When I started directing, I thought he was the boss, and I got into terrible trouble. But the director seems to be first among equals. In the end, as director, not as Alan Schneider, it is ultimately my decision to choose among the things that have been given me.
>
> (Alan Schneider)

Remember that the essence of an artist is that (s)he should be, as Swinburne says, "articulate." Use weekly production meetings to keep in touch with company members, identify problems, and avoid calamities. At the minimum, the head of every area, the stage manager, designer, technical director, assistant director, house manager, and director of publicity should participate. Explore how the technical and managerial aspects are aligning with the performance ones, so people do not work in a vacuum, totally unaware of how their choices influence one another. Leaving assignments vague can generate numerous disasters during performance including: backstage phones ringing, actors pressing wrinkled costumes and missing entrances, minor actors partying in the light booth, stagehands removing the wrong furniture and crashing into unsuspecting actors.

AUDITIONS/CASTING/REHEARSAL SCHEDULES

Tryout Procedures

> Nay, you may call me coward if you will; but if that little man there upon the stage is not frightened, I never saw any man frightened in my life.
>
> (Henry Fielding, *Tom Jones*)

After pre-production planning and work with designers, you must tackle the sensitive tasks of *auditioning*—often in less than ideal circumstances. If you come to the first audition with an insufficient supply of scripts or without having set standards for auditioners, you may create an impression of disorganization which may never be erased. And, if you are solely responsible for details, you should be especially alert to their importance. The notes prepared by Florida State University are an excellent example of how to prepare prospective performers for auditions.

AUDITIONS

Casting for Mainstage and Studio productions occur four times each year. General auditions for the first third of the regular season are usually held on the Sunday before the first day of Fall classes and on the first day of classes as well. For the middle third of the regular season, auditions are usually held before Christmas break (often in late November), and for the final third of the regular season, general·auditions are again held during the first days of the Spring semester. Summer production auditions are usually held at the beginning of the first summer term. In short, there are four opportunities to audition for casting, and at each audition up to four productions are cast. Auditions are open to all FSU students.

Following each general casting audition, callback lists are posted on the callboards which are located in the hallway adjacent to the Fine Arts Building lobby (majors should check the callboards twice each day, every day!!!). After callback auditions, cast lists are posted.

How to audition? At least two weeks in advance of each general audition, application instructions are posted on the callboard along with audition time slot reservation forms. Students enter their names on the reservation forms indicating the·day and time slot of their preference. Once you have signed up to audition, complete an audition application. The applications are posted in a large envelope on the door to room 207 in the Fine Arts Building (FAB). You must bring your completed audition form with you when you check in for your audition. Make a special note: unless otherwise instructed, you must check in at the FAB lobby *twenty* minutes prior to the hour of your scheduled audition. Example: You have reserved an audition slot at 5:22 P.M. You must check in at 4:40 P.M. After you check in there is ample time for warming up (unless auditions are ahead of schedule, which often is the case). When your audition time is near, an audition staff person will escort you to the audition site (usually in room 117 of the Fine Arts Annex (FAA), or the Mainstage). Those who fail to appear after reserving an audition time are barred from the next general audition.

The following lists of what to "DO" and "DON'T DO" should be helpful in preparing for the School of Theatre general casting auditions:

DO!

1. Be prepared. Know your audition selection.
2. Avoid overused material—you may be remembered for the originality of your selections.
3. Be relaxed. Space will be provided for warm-ups, use it.
4. Be on time with completed application form in hand.
5. Cooperate with the audition staff.
6. Choose clothing that is simple and allows for freedom of planned movement.
7. Generally, your audition selection should reflect your casting type or potential.
8. Time yourself. You will not be allowed to exceed the two minute limit.
9. Begin your selection by clearly stating your name and the selection you will perform. EX: Hello, I am Jennie Lancaster. This is Heavenly from *Sweet Bird of Youth.* Your introduction is often more important than the audition itself. Take your time.
10. If a musical is being cast, you may have to reserve an additional singing and/or dancing slot. If not, you may include sixteen bars from a song (sung *a capella*) as part of your two minute audition time.

DON'T!

1. Don't make noise while waiting to audition.
2. Never use a script.
3. Avoid audition material which requires heavy use of props.
4. Don't look at those auditioning you during the performance of the audition selection—find a focus point slightly above their heads to represent your imaginary participant.
5. Don't audition to a chair.
6. Don't name the playwright in your introduction, and never describe the scene or provide exposition.
7. If you go blank, try to be charming—don't make excuses. If you must begin again, say so with a smile and do so.
8. Do not use a dialect piece unless it is specifically requested.
9. Don't fail to extend your last moment slightly before breaking out of the "moment."
10. Thank those who auditioned you before exiting.

General auditions for mainstage and studio productions are not to be confused with auditions for Acting I (TPP 3110) and auditions for the B.F.A. Programs in Acting and Musical Theatre. Auditions for Acting I are held during the FSU orientations and three weeks prior to each School of Theatre preregistration day. Consult the callboard for place and time information. The audition requires one selection no more than two minutes in length. Auditioners for Acting I should report to the audition site fifteen minutes before their scheduled audition time. A list of those approved for Acting I will be posted on the callboard.[1]

Effective planning of the audition, as outlined in the above schedule, allows the director to focus on the creative aspect of evaluating the actors. Available resources will influence these procedures. With multiple spaces and staffing available, various procedures can be implemented simultaneously. For example, you could be casting actors in one room, while the choreographer evaluates dancers in another, and the musical director auditions singers in a third space. Instructions about the nature of auditions, audition selections, and actor information forms should be provided. At one New York theater, actors who resist filling out the form or insist on submitting their own resumes are not asked to audition because they are viewed as uncooperative. During auditions, some directors rate actors on the forms for acting ability (on a scale of 1 to 10), vocal or physical attributes, and suitability for certain roles.

[1]From "Auditions," Florida State University/School of Theater *Handbook*, Tallahassee, pp. 19–20. Used by permission.

Sample Audition Form

```
                                              ————————, 198——
Play: ——————————————————     at —————————————————— Theater
Name: ——————————————————     Age:—— Sex:—— Ht.:—— Hair:——
Address: ————————————————                  Wt.:——

——————————————————————     Phone: ——————————————————
                                              ——————————————————
Role auditioning for:  1. ——————————   2. ——————————   3. ——————————
Production Position:   1. ——————————   2. ——————————   3. ——————————

Previous Experience and Special Skills:
——————————————————————————————————————————————————
——————————————————————————————————————————————————
——————————————————————————————————————————————————
Times NOT available: ——————————————————————————————
----------------------------------------------------------------------------------
Director's Comments:
```

Open versus Closed Auditions

Along with tryout procedures, you must decide upon an open versus closed audition. At open auditions, everyone auditioning is invited into the room so you can call freely upon a range of actors. Most helpful for casting ensemble productions and for testing combinations in final callbacks, open auditions sometimes unnerve actors forcing them to confront their competition and to audition in arbitrary order.

Closed auditions only permit performing actors to enter tryout areas so you can focus on them, and get more relaxed performances. Although closed auditions are more controllable, directors can lose sight of the larger talent pool, extend gifted actors only one chance at a reading, and forget to evaluate combinations of actors.

Types of Auditions

Whether open or closed, all auditions incorporate three basic methods of evaluation: scene selections, interviews, and improvisations. Since none are mutually exclusive or set in stone, a good director creates auditions combining elements from all three, to capture the real demands of the roles. You should set up the kind of audition that will best identify the actors most qualified for specific roles. For example, when casting a free-style production, evaluate actors in improvisations; in classical roles, see how actors handle poetic sequences, both in monologues and scenes. For a script like Jane Martin's *Talking With*, which is a series of monologues, a straight monologue audition may be fine, but not for a Shakespearean play in which most of the characters appear only in scenes. A broad range of auditions will allow you greater possibilities for testing different strengths of actors.

Scene Selections

Scene selections dominate the market of audition materials. Since you may know within the first few minutes whether an actor engages your interest, encourage short selections that focus on the major traits of a role (determined, vulnerable, protective, cautious, daring, refined, and so on) rather than stopping actors in the middle of an audition.

Choose scene selections that are self-explanatory, engaging, and capable of being typed on one sheet. Beware of distributing scripts at initial auditions, because finding the beginnings and endings of selections in scripts can unnerve actors, and scripts do get lost. However, using scripts at callbacks, with a limited group can let you test them in a range of scenes.

Problem

You are about to fall into the trap of being misled by first readings, not identifying which of your less-trained actors can most fully develop the role.

Solution

1. Audition all actors with the same reader to pinpoint the distinctions between performers.
2. Identify the expressiveness of the actor's body from the neck down during the reading; does the actor move the legs, the hands, the torso, revealing a physical connection with the role?
3. Use the audition to redirect the actors, such as giving them a strong, but different, objective from the one they are playing. Their responses should reveal if they can *quickly* respond to and incorporate changes.
4. Read with the actors yourself to see what responses they give *you* as a performer.
5. Videotape and replay auditions to reflect on their qualities away from the pressure of tryouts.
6. Talk with actors about the seriousness of their commitments to play the roles.

Personal Interviews

Personal interviews can be valuable at the beginning and ending of auditions. At a personal interview, actors bring their pictures, resumes, and play notices, and chat with you, casting personnel, and producers of a play. Outline what is needed in the roles and assess the actors' qualities. At callbacks, interviews can reveal the kind of individuals you are dealing with, the seriousness of their commitment, and their willingness to do independent work. The disadvantage of interviews is that charismatic actors can beguile you into believing they have more ability than they do.

Improvisations

Improvisations consist of ad-libbed, spontaneous scenes, freely interpreted by actors. A typical instruction might be, "Pretend you are looking for a bomb that is about to explode," or "Imagine you are preparing for a party and dreading your date." Improvisations test concentration, ingenuity, openness, and imagination. Notice how completely actors respond to different directions, to group interactions, and to fictional circumstances. An actor willing to risk on-the-spot choices may require less explanation before attempting any direction. However, excelling in freestyle work does not mean that actors can master a structured scene with set dialogue onstage.

Casting Traps

If you pick actors who cannot do what is required, the play could be a disaster. Casting is a chancy proposition because you cannot always find the perfect performers and might have to compromise when casting.

Problem

You are Guest Director for a regional theater production of Anton Chekhov's *The Three Sisters*, with paid professionals in the leading roles. Open auditions are held for community-based performers in smaller roles. Scripts have been available for ten days in the theater office and prospective performers have been asked to read them before auditions. At the first audition only 3 of 10 people have studied the script; the others are unprepared.

Solution

Explain to this group *why* knowledge of the play is important and why seriousness of purpose is a quality you, as director, should and will consider in auditioning and casting. Audition first those who *are* prepared. Ask those who have not read the play to do so now, in the lobby or lounge, and give them sufficient time to read it.

Problem

You are directing Henrik Ibsen's *A Doll's House* in a regional theater. The leading performers are members of Actors Equity Association and expect to devote most of their time to rehearsals. Three of the cast members are community residents who have worked with the group in previous seasons but have daytime jobs. These three are disappointed not to get larger roles, but claim they cannot come to all the rehearsals.

Solution

Casting and rehearsal schedules are often closely related. Accommodating some (volunteer) performers in certain roles may not be possible if their schedules do not allow sufficient rehearsal time. *At the first audition,* distribute a list of rehearsal times and the minimum amount of time performers should expect to spend in rehearsal, practice, or coaching. Explain that minor adjustments can be made for unusual situations, but that casting may depend on *availability* as well as *willingness* to work. Potential performers should advise you at auditions or callbacks if the scheduling makes them unavailable for particular roles. (Use Tables 9.1 and 9.2 as models for your own rehearsal sheet and scene breakdown *to be distributed at auditions.*)

Table 9.1: Rehearsal Schedule (prepared by Paul Hostetler)

The Corn Is Green by Emlyn Williams

Mon 4/6	3:00	Block 11	Wed 4/22	3:00	Special scenes (set in lights)
	7:30	Work 11			
Tue 4/7	3:00	Block 12		7:30	Act III
	7:30	Work 12	Thu 4/23	3:00	Special scenes
Wed 4/8	3:00	Work 11		7:30	Acts I & III
	7:30	Block 21	Fri 4/24	3:00	Special scenes
Thu 4/9	3:00	Work 12		7:30	Acts II & III
	7:30	Work 21	Sat 4/25	2:00	Run-through
Fri 4/10	3:00	Block 22	Mon 4/27	3:00	TECH REHEARSAL
	7:30	Work 21		7:30	Run-through
Sat 4/11	2:00	Block III	Tue 4/28	3:00	Open call
Mon 4/13	3:00	Work 22		6:00	REHEARSAL (actors arrive for costumes 6 P.M.)
	7:30	Work III			
Tue 4/14	3:00	Work II			
	7:30	Work 21	Wed 4/29	3:00	Open call
Wed 4/15	3:00	Work 12		7:30	TECH REHEARSAL
	7:30	Work III	Thu 4/30	3:00	Open call
Thu 4/16	3:00	Work 22		7:30	TECH REHEARSAL
or	7:30	Work III	Fri 5/1	3:00	Open call
Fri 4/17	3:00	Act I		7:30	DRESS REHEARSAL
	7:00	Act II (See costumer) *PHOTOCALL* (costumes)	Sat 5/2	7:30	DRESS
			Sun 5/3	7:30	Possible Preview Dress
			Mon 5/4	7:30	Preview Performance
Sat 4/18	2:00	Run-through	Tue 5/5	8:00	Opening Night (actors arrive 6 P.M.)
Mon 4/20	3:00	Special scenes	through		
	7:00	Act I and *PHOTO-CALL*	Sat 5/19		Please check the callboard *daily* for changes.
Tue 4/21	3:00	Special scenes			
	7:30	Act II			

Note that rehearsals have been scheduled *during* the week of University Recess (April 6–12).

Days and times of rehearsals are scheduled to accommodate day and evening classes.

Photocall Monday 4/20 at 7 P.M. *SHARP!* See costumer Friday 4/17 for your costume.

Table 9.2: Cast/Scene Breakdown (prepared by Paul Hostetler)

The Corn Is Green

Act I—Scene 1

Ronberry	Sarah	Moffat	
Jones	Bessie	Squire	
Idwal	Watty	Groom/Morris	

Act I—Scene 2

Watty	Glyn Thomas	Bessie	Squire
Morgan	Will Hughes	Watty	Sarah
Robbart	Jones	Idwal	
John Owen	Moffat	Ronberry	

Act II—Scene 1

Ronberry	Watty	Glyn	Mary
Jones	Squire	Will	Mother
Moffat	Groom/Morris	Old Tom	
Bessie	Robbart	Sarah	
Morgan	John	Idwal	

Act II—Scene 2

Watty	Bessie	Morgan
Ronberry	Jones	
Moffat	Squire	

Act III

Ronberry	Moffat	Sarah
Jones	Morgan	Old Tom
Idwal	Bessie	Robbart
Squire	Watty	John

Consult *Rehearsal Schedule* for days and times for your scenes.
Full cast *must* be available for TECH and DRESS.

A casting mistake can have long-term ramifications throughout rehearsals; it can downgrade the quality of the other acting performances and distort the interpretation of the script. Temperamental actors resist direction, miss meetings, and/or throw tantrums which threaten the progress of the play. They create havoc in the technical department by missing lines, entrances, or exits that influence lighting, sound, or other effects. Many a director has a favorite "war story" about an actor refusing to wear a costume and storming off the set. No veteran director is immune to the emotionally draining, terminal casting mistake.

Beware of certain basic traps in casting: not knowing the play; overemphasizing physical looks; overlooking the "throwaway part"; disregarding vocal sounds; and mistaking the lead actor.

Not Knowing the Play

Directors who study the play generally may not know the precise needs and actions of each character. You must understand the parts well enough to recognize actors who, besides looking or feeling the parts, can develop that physical and emotional life *through specific actions called for in the text*. Actors must be able to relate to the director's interpretation of the characters and play actions in a particular way (the *how*) under contrived, stage circumstances. They must be able to connect with the character's basic action unit: what a character wants; what's stopping getting it; what the character does to get it. How the action is performed comes after that, further delineating the action.

Overemphasizing Physical Looks

A wide selection of actors may lure you into the trap of stereotype casting—casting for physical characteristics rather than for character action. Discovering if a person can act is harder than identifying a type. Rather, you should put actors into the parts that are going to make the play work. For example, you may have to cast the best actors (but the wrong types) into the lead roles—even if it means their wearing wigs and adjusting behavior. *The strongest talent needs to be cast in the strongest roles.*

When auditioning, remember how the action is done *makes* the character. The *how* of an action differs depending on whether the character is a shy student, a macho truck driver, or an office worker. The *how* expresses both the individuality of the artist and that of the character. At auditions, inform actors of two major qualities or poles (the how) of each character, and notice how extensively they are incorporated into actions. *How* the action is done reflects *who* the character is.

Besides individuals, you also cast groups:

> When casting, look for the external shape of all the family of characters playing the parts; all of the characters fit together to create a certain external shape, or the family of characters. The likelihood that you will be able to cast all roles exactly as envisioned is rare, because ideal actors will probably not be available. However, you can usually get the external shape from adjusting the individuals within the group. Although you might not be able to cast the individuals exactly, you can usually get the external shape needed.
>
> (Tony Distler)

In casting the family of characters, evaluate the unity of the whole group and the distinctiveness of individuals. Besides functioning as a unit, an ensemble must contain smaller combinations of actors who can in an interesting way interact with the scenery, lighting, costumes, and mise en scene. Many ensembles also contain the "throwaway part."

Overlooking the "Throwaway Part"

Do not think the "throwaway part," i.e. small and shapeless, can be performed by anyone or you may complete the stage with dull actors. Less appealing dialogue needs to be played by intriguing actors. For example, an opera singer, wrong for a lead, might be perfect for a "throwaway part" such as the nurse in Tennessee Williams's *Suddenly Last Summer*. She could exercise her vocal chords while wheeling Mrs. Venable on and offstage. Clever variety, unusual characterization, and unexpected approach create suspense and heighten interest. The "throwaway part" should not be so exaggerated that it distorts the action and focus of the scene.

Disregarding Vocal Sounds and Appearance

Audiences respond to the voices and bodies of actors as well as their spoken words. Listen to how actors sound alone and together onstage. The tuneful sound or melody, pleasing or congruent arrangement of voices when two or more people are talking onstage should harmonize.

Similarly, assess the physical appearance and prowess of the actors because a human being standing onstage represents humanity for us. Since audiences observe an actor (especially a lead) for two or more hours, (s)he should be palatable to watch and capable of varied stage movement.

Not Distinguishing the Lead Actor

Some directors mistakenly believe that any actor with talent can play a lead role; however, smart directors look for the compelling person.

> What distinguishes a leading actor, along with ability, is the magnetism of the individual; this actor seizes your attention. One reason audiences may like certain performers is because they are interesting personalities. Good actors, who are rather ordinary personalities, should play your supporting parts because they can fill a scene or two but they are not Prince Hamlet, nor were they meant to be.
>
> (John Bettenbender)

Identify the appealing aspects of each lead's personality because leads should look better than the others onstage; even an actor playing Quasimodo, like Charles Laughton, was an attractive ugly hero.

According to Martin Esslin:

> A lead actor has to have complete control over his physical apparatus, considerable either instinctive or conscious intelligence, and a fascinating personality. For example, Shakespeare's Juliet is supposed to be a fascinating girl. The lines can be as fascinating as they like, if the girl is not attractive, if she doesn't overwhelm me when I look at her, she is a second-rate Juliet. That's what performance is all about.

Miscasting creates a missing link in the performance. Mistaking the qualities necessary for a principal role may be a fatal error because a lead unifies the entire production.

Problem

You'd like to cast an actor who is perfect for a part, but has a reputation for being uncooperative.

Solution

1. Arrange for a meeting with the actor alone, confront the situation head on. Say, "I've heard that people don't get along with you. Could you make a commitment to cooperate with this particular group and handle the part?" Make your casting decision based on the actor's forthcoming response along with the actor's ability.
2. Evaluate the group nature of the performance; will (s)he be working with other actors who have a built-up resistance, or primarily alone with you? Other casting may have to change should you choose this actor.

Avoiding Miscasting

If you have *miscast* in the past, you may live with a terror of miscasting again. Avoid this calamity by taking your time and profoundly observing as much auditioning as you can.

> Look for specificity and honesty in actors. Identify those who can create the logical moment-to-moment reality of the characters and believe it with their imagination. Then, honest emotion and everything else will follow. Also search for actors who don't know how to lie on stage. An actor who has an immediate sense of giving oneself over to the present-tense moment, is so much "of the moment" that (s)he performs fully every single time. . . . Encourage actors to give their best auditions by helping them relax.
>   . . . I've never had an audition where I haven't said to the actor before it started, "Take your time," because the big problem with auditions for actors is their coming in and starting to act before they're ready. Relaxation, concentration, and the ability for the imagination to take off are essential before any good work can be done. If you feel the actors are nervous, you can do things like rearrange the room, have them start again.
>
> (Marshall W. Mason, artistic director, Circle Rep.)

EXERCISES

1. Rehearse an audition scene with actors of different physical types, then present both versions to the class.
2. Direct an audition monologue with three different actors, and identify how their bodies and voices influence the presentation.

Scheduling Quality Rehearsals

Many mediocre productions result from *insufficient rehearsals,* which force directors to edit performances and slavishly work to achieve minimal quality. A good schedule sets up adequate rehearsal time for each area and the entire play to be developed. Like a map, a schedule charts where a director needs to be at given points in rehearsals, so (s)he can check it to see how often a scene has been worked or when an act will be reviewed. However, any schedule should allow for change.

Most plays require an overall rehearsal period of four to six weeks, six days per week, three hours per day. Professional productions may halve the rehearsal period and double the practice time each day (3 weeks of rehearsals, 6 days a week, 6 hours a day). Too few rehearsals can make you *push* for results, while too many can flatten enthusiasm as actors begin slipping away for other commitments. Although private coaching sessions of thirty minutes to an hour can be effective, little can be accomplished with groups in less than two hours. Ideally the scheduling would allow work to be finished before the last one third of rehearsals, so time is available for trouble spots—confusing sound cues, sloppy dance numbers, dead monologues. Booking all-day rehearsals on the two weekends prior to opening night reserves you long periods at the end for in-depth work on problem areas. You can cancel these rehearsals if you are on schedule.

Types of Rehearsal Schedules

Rehearsal schedules should fit the production—for example, a spectacular musical requires more technical rehearsals than an intimate staged reading—and address the different parts of a play. Do not take too long with opening scenes and then rush through middle or final scenes, especially if the real changing points and emotional peaks occur near the end.

Allow time for coaching diverse individuals and groups. Beware of potential trouble with actors executing minor parts that few people want to do. Although untrained and inexperienced, they may not donate much time to their assignments and may become resistant or unreliable when pressured to do so. Formulate a considerate rehearsal schedule that maximizes the input of these actors. Clarify which kind of session is being called. Individual sessions addressing the amount of vulnerability, depth, and range each actor brings to a part work best in private. Group work may benefit from imaginative situations. For example, you might take some actors to an actual location, or begin rehearsals with them moving to music evoking the emotional state of the characters.

Schedules should include blocks of time for shaping the totality of the production through work on units and run-throughs. Two scenes together might compose a unit relating to a singular event (say, before and after a party). Try practicing these two scenes before running the entire act; then explore another unit in the act.

Build rehearsal schedules around *reinforcement*—in small, then in slightly larger sections—so actors can experience, repeat, perfect, and expand upon a direction. Marshall W. Mason reinforces as follows: "Basically my process is to review scenes in the morning, to go to new work in the afternoon, and then to review that material the next morning. For example, from 11:00 A.M. until 2:00 P.M. I may go back and repeat scenes 1, 2, 3, & 4; and then I'll go on to scene 5 in the afternoon."

The effectiveness of any schedule depends on the quality of your rehearsals. Try to: 1) Call only actors whom you rehearse, because actors waiting in the sidelines distract those working. 2) Allow time for the actors to get into character, for musicians and dancers to warm up, and for technicians to set up, to focus everyone at the beginning of rehearsal. 3) Eliminate extraneous talking and socializing inside the work area. 4) Have each person take responsibility for the concentration of the entire group. 5) Target what you expect to accomplish and hold to the time limits. 6) Insist that people arrive on time for rehearsals and return promptly after breaks. 7) Make sure that actors *understand* the time and place of each session and rehearsals policy.

Problem

Absenteeism and tardiness is prevalent at your rehearsals.

Solution

1. Review or formulate (for the first time) rehearsal ground rules. Adjust any that the actors cannot adhere to, for instance, do not rehearse on Friday or Saturday if complex social schedules are involved. Put rules in writing, and present them to the company. If possible, draw up individual contracts for each actor to sign.
2. Establish a system for whom to call in case of emergencies. Having to report in minimizes absenteeism. Commit actors to agree to support promptness and reliability in each other.
3. Replace those who break rules; so don't establish any you can't live by. Set an example by imposing tighter standards on yourself; always be early, alert, and well-rested yourself.
4. Postponing or canceling a rehearsal because of missing performers may shock those who do show up into coercing delinquent actors into promptness.
5. Next time, if you sense similar problems, get actors' written agreement to the schedule before casting.

FIRST REHEARSALS

Everyone involved in the production needs to be present at the opening rehearsals when the play is presented and procedures defined. The first sit-down rehearsal is crucial because that is when you tell the entire company *where* the production is going and motivate them to head in that exact direction. "The purpose of the first rehearsal is to establish those open relationships with everybody, assuring them that you're going to hear what they have to say and you welcome their contribution. At the same time, put forth your plan. Establishing their trust at the beginning is very, very hard" (Marshall W. Mason). It's best to let go of an antagonistic individual early on, because a limited rehearsal situation does not allow time to persuade someone over to an approach. If, from the outset, company members support the approach, you will not waste time and energy "justifying" decisions. Joseph Chaikin says:

> I find the very first stage in rehearsal to be the most difficult because I don't know what to do, I can't keep my hands off it. Anything I do follow is probably going to impede the actor. I need to hold back, because in some way my imagination is rushing faster than the process is ready for. Since I've been thinking about it, dreaming about it, I'm ready to go to stage #4 instead of stage #1. So I find always the first part the hardest.

Consider having the actors read through the play during early rehearsals. Some directors have the actors read the play slowly so that they don't interpret dialogue too soon at a performance pace. Other directors urge actors, while reading, to abandon the inhibiting seated position and move around freely. Don't let the actors rush into interpretations of the roles. "You encourage the actors to touch the material like skin— not claim it, not to possess it, not to make performance choices too early" (Joseph Chaikin).

Arthur Penn warns:

> Actors familiarize themselves with a script immediately, because they don't want to be in that vulnerable situation of being unprepared. And the most important thing is to try to keep them in that state of grace, of being unprepared; to not acquire the language of the play too soon, the intellectual postures, or even the emotional ones too soon. There's a long period where if you can keep an actor open to their own resourcefulness and yours, you might be able to find materials that neither of you ever dreamed you were capable of.

As actors start relating to lines, support them in experiencing what feeling comes up, whether it be a word, a silence, a gesture, an image, or a repetition. Encourage actors to let such moments occur, to register, and to savor them. Help actors find instances in the play—a moment here, a line or word there, a pause somewhere else—that come alive for them so that they can expand upon and build from these sources. Tell the actors to let their bodies experience the lines and to allow physical or internal images to move in and stir their emotions. Letting actors discover elements of the characters' behavior in rehearsals produces more interesting portrayals than set ideas that directors present for actors to enact.

Trust leaving beginning rehearsals with some work incomplete to avoid having rehearsals run into the wee hours. Company members can live with loose ends when appropriate schedules are followed. Stopping a rehearsal with partial work done creates space for participants to do homework and return with fresh ideas and revitalized energies.

Problem

At your first read-through, actors nervously glide over the meaning of lines.

Solution

Peter Layton suggests asking actors to preface every line of dialogue with the phrase, "and then so-and-so said." In other words, if the character's name is Mary or George, (s)he says before every line of dialogue—even if just a grunt or a yes or a one-word response—"And then Mary (George) said, 'would you mind going out of the room?'" It's an excellent device for stamping out "acting" and finding out the content of the play. By momentarily standing outside the character, the actor can discover what the character *is saying*.

Problem

The actors cannot relate to the first part of the play.

Solution

Begin working on another part which the entire company can understand. Perhaps, scene iv is extremely clear and everyone relates to it. Begin there, then work back to figure out how the characters got to that point.

Problem

Actors are squeamish about playing an intimate love scene.

Solution

Marshall W. Mason suggests having actors do the "baby" exercise. Tell the actors that they're babies, not talking yet, and they're to explore each other's hair and eyes, feeling and touching each other. This exercise makes strangers behave like lovers. It can also create exciting possibilities for blocking.

Reblocking

After read-throughs, many directors do blocking, working out the actor's principal positions, movements, and gestures, including entrances and exits (see Chapter 1, Movement). You may also do *reblocking* or changing the original blocking, when the impressions created by it are deficient. Since you cannot freeze movement in time, you must instantaneously evaluate moving images to identify those that accurately reflect the action of the scene. You put together little pieces into bigger and bigger sections, then run these sections in larger and larger groupings.

British actor and director Roger Fox claims:

Any show that does not change during a performance is a bad show, it has to change. A lot of directors are extremely dictatorial, they say, "Ah, yes, fine, you will do this and you will do that." If a director says to me, "You will get up on that line and walk across the stage," I'll fire him, simple as that, because he's not a good director. If a director says to me, "Do you feel that you would like to move on that line?"—then it gives me cause to examine that. I say, "Okay, maybe." I see if I need to move, if I'm driven to move, and if not I say, "No." That's the difference between good directing and directing traffic.

At the heart of directing, accurate blocking develops the characters. It visually enhances the action of the script and/or helps to develop the movement of the plots and characters.

Line Memorization

Once the blocking has been roughly delineated, you may require actors to begin *memorizing* their lines. Lines should be learned by mid-rehearsals. The sooner actors can comfortably put down their scripts, the better. Let your actors know from the outset when you want "lines down." Some directors require memorization by professional actors after one rehearsal exploring a scene. They develop the blocking by then working with the actors "script free" in rehearsal. However, some amateur actors freeze mechanical line readings, if they memorize the dialogue too soon. Situations vary, but normally, with "lines down," actors are more receptive to notes. When the actors trust the lines, the road map of the characters' experience, you can strengthen their interpretations.

Taking Notes

Notes are specific, informal suggestions you give to company members, especially actors, at the ending, beginning, and sometimes throughout rehearsals.

A good acting note is one which stimulates the performer to embody the thing—the wish, the action. Even an articulate director may not be able to state something to actors. Such directors might state things well but the statements might absorb the activity; whereas something which is not stated as certainly and as finally might require the actors to extend the activity from the beginning thought.

(Joseph Chaikin)

There is a measure between understanding the processes of acting and your ability to generate helpful notes. Similarly, capable actors usually feel less defensive about receiving notes. A recent *New York Times* article cites how Alan Schneider always gave detailed notes—six pages to Hume Cronyn after *one* rehearsal. Conversely, inexperienced actors not realizing they aren't expected to be perfect may be less secure with any note.

Some directors prefer "stop-and-go" run-throughs during which a performance is stopped, notes are given, then the section is rerun incorporating them. However, as opening nears, schedule nonstop run-throughs, because company members need to experience the total running of the show.

At nonstop run-throughs, you can take (or have an assistant take) detailed notes which are written on blank pages in your prompt book. (Bringing a flashlight to rehearsals facilitates note-taking in a darkened theater.) After rehearsals, call the company together onstage and give notes. Encourage actors to write notes down so they don't forget or misinterpret them. The process of writing often clarifies the note. Mention moments you liked as well as disliked. Good moments are often lost because directors failed to mention them and actors forgot what they did. Notes should be expressed in a positive fashion so they forward creativity and self-esteem. If rehearsals run late, consider giving notes before the next rehearsal rather than racing through them. Use the time in-between to consolidate ideas, so that note-giving does not devour time that could be spent in implementation.

Near opening, simplify your notes into fewer more encompassing ones. Too many notes confuse inexperienced actors and jeopardize entrances, dialogue, and action. Instead of adjusting a moment or line, you might have to eliminate a section or stress only one direction to strengthen the entire scene.

Due to the sensitivity of company members, you may choose to give some notes in private, or write out comments for each participant. Seek out individuals before or after rehearsals: The actors' receptivity to a delicate note may depend upon the relationship you develop with them during coaching sessions.

MAIN REHEARSALS

Middle Slump

During middle rehearsals, time grows increasingly precious. Guard vigilantly against the seeds of discouragement, in yourself and others. Devise schedules that allow space for people to recharge. Creative energy does depend upon good health patterns of eating and sleeping.

Midway, you may also begin doubting the success of your efforts and sometimes you have to admit error. Occasionally, when an actor seriously jeopardizes the quality of a production, (s)he may have to be replaced. Determine if enough time exists to orientate a new player, and if so, expeditiously replace the individual. Sometimes you can phase out an actor so the termination does not agitate the individual and the remaining players. Other times, communicate directly to the person concerned. Beware of debates, which can lead to prolonged upsets if other players enter the argument.

Problem

Not knowing lines, a difficult actor is throwing off other actors in several major scenes. When criticized, the actor storms off the set.

Solution

1. Meet with the actor privately to identify the problem. You may need to rework the scene, minimize the actor's contribution through adjustment of another character's action or dialogue, change the physical setting, or make additions in a program note.
2. If (s)he lacks self-discipline, set reasonable standards and deadlines. Restructure the rehearsal schedule to allow space for the actor to learn the lines.
3. Do not have a prompter at rehearsals, forcing the actor to handle line lapses while remaining in character.
4. Do an improvisation on the scene to reveal motivation behind words if you think (s)he is forgetting lines because they are not rooted in the situation.
5. Caution the actor, set rules, and hold to them if you suspect drinking or drugs are causing memory lapses. Your only solution for such irresponsibility may be replacement of the actor. Remember to include comprehensive standards for yourself when requiring alertness from others as a prerequisite for artistic work.
6. Give the actor a cue word to signal the partner when lines are forgotten, and give the partner instructions on how to respond when the cue is given. Near opening when you cannot arbitrarily replace the actor or significantly adjust the scene, your only viable choice may involve camouflaging the problem.

Routinely thank participants after each work session, especially following a difficult rehearsal. Acknowledgment revitalizes player participation. Thank *all* involved, including those members doing the least obvious tasks, such as holding the prompt book or xeroxing line changes. The morale of the company may hinge on the attitude of these "hidden" people who have more time to support or undermine others.

Difficult Sequences

Besides unexpected problems, you will need to work on some difficult sequences—run-throughs, beginnings, scene changes, crowd scenes, and curtain calls. Don't underestimate the time required for mastery of these troublesome sequences.

Some directors spend too many hours on *run-throughs* and do not allow enough time for detailed scene work. Others do the opposite. Don't postpone the first run-through too late because you must sense the development of the entire production along with individual scenes. Get informed during mid-rehearsals about the general state of the work, evaluate and compare problem areas. Since the run-through may be ragged, company members will want to put it off; don't cancel or accept piecemeal run-throughs. Early run-throughs allow company members to experience the flow of the work and give you time to handle incipient problems.

Enhance the run-through's effectiveness by requiring all company members' involvement (sometimes costumes and lighting instruments have been changed because designers dropped their fictional notions about performances after seeing a run-through). Insist on nonstop run-throughs, avoid the temptation to patch problems, and restrict breaks to any intermissions or act changes. Nonstop run-throughs force those involved to bail themselves out of difficulties; artists and technicians have to be right the first time.

Besides run-throughs the *beginnings* of acts and scenes need special attention. They must capture interest, suspend disbelief, and provide information. The scenes closer to the play's outset must be directed at a slower pace for the audience to experience the action. Ironically, these are the moments actors will tend to race through. Work in detail on the actors' first interactions because the audience will invent their expectations of the production based on first impressions.

Each scene's beginning establishes the time, place, relationships, and circumstances. If the audience responds positively, they will listen attentively throughout the scene. Inexperienced directors often glide over the first minutes of a scene, then keep flattening its various values by rerunning it. Competent directors work on each scene's opening and limit actors from progressing to a subsequent sequence until these values are clear, fully drawn, and under control. Investigating the moments before a scene opens can deepen the actors' involvement onstage. If the opening is rooted in the actors' experience, the following moments can develop that truth. Conversely, a phony beginning perpetuates falseness throughout the scene.

Scene changes, another difficult sequence, can drastically affect scene beginnings and endings. Transitions should forward the intention of the playwright rather than destroy the scenes they follow and precede. Your tendency may be to move on to a more "meaningful" part of the production and to forget that if scene changes are not smooth, they may be emphasized instead of the play itself. To develop transitions, start rehearsal with the ending of the preceding scene and finish with the beginning of the following one.

If it is a *crowd scene,* the logistics of the work required on this troublesome sequence may be substantial (see Chapter 1). Before rehearsing with a potentially impatient mob (15 or more), consider experimenting with a copy of the groundplan or model of the set (even a makeshift facsimile will do), pacing out various combinations on the stage floor, or breaking crowds into smaller groups.

The *curtain call* is the final difficult sequence because it involves a "crowd" of actors playing themselves. The curtain call, your final statement to the audience, acknowledges your company. Do not skim over it. Include curtain calls even after a tragedy, as the audience's acknowledgment serves as their transition to the realm of reality. In the 1960s and 1970s, curtain calls were often omitted so that the statement of the play, not the performers, made the final impact. However, most audiences today expect and should receive curtain calls.

Actually the curtain call can underscore the statement of the production. The curtain call can be treated in either of two ways: as a part of the play; or as a return to real life outside the theater. Each approach affects audiences differently. The first method implies that life *continues* the "story" of the play. The second, that life *ends* the realm of make-believe. A curtain call that contains a restaging of action from the play must be carefully monitored to prevent audiences from confusing it as a continuation of the story and stopping applause.

Curtain calls should build the audience's interest until the final bow is made. You should assess, prior to rehearsal, the order of separate bows to be given by taking into account the actors', the audience's, and your own points of view. Actors' egos can be bruised by thoughtless mistakes in order of importance.

Practice your curtain call meticulously. Rehearsed at run-throughs, it should evolve from and heighten your play's closing. Synchronize the curtain call with the music and lights. The swiftness of entrances and depth of bows should evoke applause. Actors can use objects "in character," such as a fan or a cap, to enhance the bow. Amateur actors may need a week of curtain call rehearsals, a professional group only one or two. Have amateurs stage an exaggerated "mock curtain call" by devising secret stories justifying their personal importance to the play, then instruct each to out-bow preceding actors.

Traps Midway through Rehearsals

Along with difficult sequences, watch out for certain potholes midway through rehearsals. One, *loss of objectivity*, results from being so enamored or repelled by a particular scene that you are blind to the message it is *really communicating*. To regain a visual awareness, run the scene as a "dumb show." Have your actors go through the actions without dialogue while you, acting as audience, describe out loud *only what you actually see*. For example, if an actor is staged walking proudly with his head held high, you might observe, "I see an important-looking man coming in," but you couldn't say, "I see a king coming in" because the performer's action does not reveal a regal status. Conversely, the activity of removing a crown might indicate royalty. (Perform a similar exercise for aural objectivity by listening to a scene with eyes closed and saying, "I hear. . . .")

Sometimes you may find yourself bogged down by a drab performance when the actor becomes so complacent running it that all inspiration vanishes. To give actors a shake up, recharge, or fresh point of view, use a *mirror-images* exercise. You reverse the furniture on the stage-set and actors perform in the same room with the same furniture, except their mirror image is changed. Finding everything backwards, they must rediscover the thought processes that led them to choose specific actions. Facing new directions forces them to intensify concentration in the make-believe stage reality and heightens your interest.

When your interest is engaged, you will less likely fall into the second trap of *making final directing decisions too early*. This trap often surfaces when a choice involving a degree of compromise must be made. As the late director Alan Schneider put it: "My biggest people-oriented problem is to compromise without compromising." When debating between choices, take time to weigh their limitations and do not make instant decisions while involved with other activities such as another rehearsal, meeting, or deadline. Don't let company members (actors, designers, technicians) corner you into an irreversible choice. For example, a costume once dyed cannot be undyed, and lines practiced one way may be hard to reinterpret.

When you know more about the script than any player, do not fear owning that you do *not know what to do at a given point*. However, do not say too many "I don't knows," or the company may judge you incompetent and seek to control the production. If unsure how to handle a problem, admit that confusion exists and table presenting solutions until the next rehearsal.

Arthur Penn urges this open-ended approach:

> The thing that I would suggest for myself, and it's not easily obtainable, is not to panic in the face of not knowing how it should look. If you keep going with it, you're going to come to a point where something is going to click and you can say, ah, now I see it, and indeed you do. But directors need to try and hold off that point as long as possible. Now that's not easy to do, because you have a bunch of people who are constantly saying, all right, look, I want to set this or fix that. . . . So you're being forced into decisions that in themselves seem just logistical, but in point of fact have their roots in what your vision is going to be. So before you're aware of it, directors have already committed themselves to a vision. And one of the toughest things is to ever change that.

Along with cementing a vision, beware of a third trap: *mistakes of omission*. Some directors sequester actors in an ivory tower and ignore such "mundane details" as publicity. They may refuse to relinquish rehearsal time for a scheduled photography session for production shots—black and white 8″ × 10″ glossy photographs of several characters in costume. Newspapers and magazines are more likely to publicize an upcoming play if they receive a striking production shot along with a press release several weeks before opening. However, to obtain such photos, you may have to spend time devising makeshift costumes and sets, to represent the production for the reading audience. The impact of this inconvenience should be weighed against the alternative of poor audiences.

Don't overlook the opportunity for artistic growth that a photo session can provide by pressurizing the director, actors, and designers into a visual expression of the production for a detached observer. The impartial photographer expects the actors' movements, the costuming, and the sets to picture the idea of the show. Managing the creative and technical aspects of a photo session can serve as timely practice for your technical rehearsals.

Technical Rehearsals

While alert to the traps of losing objectivity, finalizing decisions, and omitting publicity, keep vigilant about the technical development of the production. Some technical coordination should begin during mid-rehearsals, when designers and technicians test and practice their operations, usually in conjunction with actors' movement and dialogue. At some "techs," scenes are run and cues experimented with to discover which provide the best visual and aural support for the acting. In "cue-to-cue" rehearsals, only run sections that cue predetermined technical effects.

The success of technical rehearsals depends largely on the quality of your communication with designers. You discover whether the design reinforces your rehearsal work, or whether you have to start over and adjust, adjust, and adjust. Technical rehearsals can be twelve hours of endless light and sounds cues that are wrong, that don't match the stage action.

Postponing the first technical rehearsal may cause catastrophes in productions where beginners are working with equipment and materials for the first time. Colors, textures, and lighting may diffuse focus onstage; costumes glamorously sketched on renderings can distort actors whose real-life bodies are not cut to size. If you have misread a set's dimensions, scenes may have to be overhauled. If you have misinterpreted where lighting units are focused, instruments may have to be rehung and/or actors reblocked; all at added expense.

As a general rule, inexperienced company members and complicated productions need more technical rehearsals. Wisely schedule in extra ones then cancel some if the "tech" is mastered. Nothing can make a production look shabbier than technical calamities—misread cues (lights going out), missing cues (phones not ringing), or misplaced cues (curtains inappropriately descending).

Problem

At dress rehearsals, the choreographer complains the music cues are too *low* while the playwright insists they're too loud. Should you use louder music that creates a needed kinetic impact but obscures the words?

Solution

1. A tripartite compromise can be effective. Use loud music when dancing predominates; average during noninformational dialogue; low to none during important language.
2. Consider using body microphones on some actors so their dialogue can be heard over the music.
3. Adjust the placement of musicians or (if music is taped) speakers to measure the resulting impact on the words.
4. Next time, integrate technical elements into the production as soon as possible so they don't become ingredients for crisis.

If the technical elements are filtered into and evolve from rehearsals, you will not be assaulted with adjustments near opening. You will arrive at a finished production earlier. The actors' experience is heightened by incorporating technical elements which realize the changing relationships of the play. Costumes, make-up, hairdos, lighting, and furniture influence the development of the characters. For example, as characters mature, they might read a book, change clothing, use different furniture, and adjust the lighting; these choices depend upon technical items.

Try incorporating the various technical elements at different rehearsals. From the beginning, mark out the groundplan on the stage floor and use rehearsal furniture and props similar to production pieces. Require actors to simulate costumes in rehearsal from which stage choices, intrinsic to the characterizations, develop. Be sure the actors experience the rituals of unfamiliar costumes and accessories.

Besides practice with rehearsal costumes, keep informed about the actual costume development. Possibly schedule dress parades, a filing of actors in costumes across the stage. A costume parade, where actors try on their costumes then test them out onstage under lights, is extremely valuable. It allows the director, actor, and costume designer to judge the effect of the costume on the actor, individually and in groups, within the developing set. Any needed adjustments can then be made. Dress parades midway through rehearsals reveal if the costumes are visually evolving as the actors are developing. Designers who are abreast of rehearsals should show actors how their costumes can enhance their characters' physical lives.

Problem

The costumes inhibit the actors and make them look artificial.

Solution

Without some experience of *why* the costumes were worn, actors may be stifled by the costumes. Designers might explain the characters' environment. Then have the actors do an improvisation on what the characters are *doing* in the clothes. For example, the costumes of characters in a warehouse may result from their tasks there. Finally, have the actors wear the costumes (or a makeshift version of them) as much as possible before opening.

Consumed with scene work, many directors neglect the opportunity of having dress parades. Don't overlook the significance of costumes. More than any other factor, they signal to the audience who the characters are. Wise directors reserve at least one part of and often two rehearsals for dress parades. With a second session, designers or actors themselves (if they are providing their own costumes) can incorporate previous suggestions and present new options.

Your last technical responsibility may be planning for *striking the set*. Usually run by the technical director, a "strike" involves dismantling and storing scenery, putting away costumes, accessories, and props. In small-scale situations, you should include the strike in your rehearsal schedule and list its participants, length, and date. You can motivate company members to help by following the strike with some forthcoming occurrence: auditions for the next play, a social event, release from an assignment. Procedures regarding the strike should be clarified before the opening and run.

FINAL REHEARSALS AND THE RUN

The last week of rehearsals will excite and frighten you. More combinations of costumes, make-up, sets, lighting, hairdos multiply the potential for problems. Company members will require rest and relaxation as their charged participation at each rehearsal becomes crucial. Keep rehearsals contained and efficient because illness can result from the overwork and exhaustion of participants.

Encourage everyone to minimize their mounting nervousness. Give fewer directions. Limit your words to one or two unifying directions stretching through the fabric of the play. For example, to sharpen conflict or contrast: advise actors to strengthen their characters' basic drives, tell designers and technicians to focus on a principle like sharpness of color, costume, or change.

Scan the theater for any physical details that might need adjustment. Starting with one corner of the stage, scrutinize every shoe, sock, hem, hand prop, and last detail. Often people responsible for technical choices are flattered by such careful observation, demonstrating your attention to visual excellence and your recognition of backstage contributions.

Listen meticulously to run-throughs and make sure lines setting up the "story" are clear and not obscured by technical effects so the audience knows what's happening. For example, the words "You are going to pretend you're deaf" could set up the entire action in a subsequent scene.

Dress Rehearsals

A key time for aural evaluation, *dress rehearsal* is a complete technical run-through with costumes and make-up, usually the last nights before opening. Concentration should be sharpened to keep the momentum of the run-through going and offset errors. Participants must sustain a heightened consciousness: playing each moment fully and keeping alert to impending demands. Dress-performance level is like driving a car on a freeway at rush hour after cruising on a country road. At a "dress," actors may panic when presented with all the ingredients in a full stage production. You may need to calm them down and remind them of technical demands—to stay clear of the audience sightlines, whisper backstage, avoid technical instruments, close doors, and exit properly.

Dress rehearsals are an excellent time for production photos. The best moments for pictures happen in performance as actors, deeply involved in their parts, interrelate onstage and mood lighting enhances their action. So, plan to take pictures en route, during a dress rehearsal, and if not, during a preview. If circumstances dictate that you take pictures before or after the performance, do so beforehand when actors' energy is high; any actor unavailable then could be photographed after the performance. The photographic session may be one of your last creative jobs.

Opening Night

The House, Backstage, and Actor's Quarters

Expect the players' tension to skyrocket near opening night. Actors are operating from a state of heightened emotion. The technicians are risking greater jeopardy by using real items; costume and make-up people are fussing over adjustments in the dressing rooms. Everyone seems fully involved, while you slip around acknowledging people and subtly suggesting what is not working. Your ultimate goal, rendering the director's presence unnecessary, approaches completion. Drama critic Martin Esslin claims "The best directors are people whose work you don't notice. They are invisible."

Opening night presents one of the loneliest times for directors because your creative job is over. If you also function as artistic director and/or manager, you may arrive at the theater early to supervise operations, to see that stage and house are cleaned, actors have arrived, refreshments are stocked, technical equipment is checked. You go dressed for work and bring a change of clothes for meeting the public.

A significant gesture directors extend in many communities is greeting audience members. Some also bring token gifts or thank-you notes for company members on opening night. This favorable custom encourages morale. It is wise to bring some extra mementos for people inadvertently overlooked.

Extend yourself backstage and boost morale by giving a brief pep talk before the production, in a dressing room, backstage area, or on the stage itself about thirty minutes before curtain. Besides applauding the group, you can warn them of their possible tendency to override the audience's response and race through the show.

Running the Show

Once opening night and its jitters have passed, the actors sometimes incline, during the run, to "milk" every moment and go too slow. They add, change, or embroider on original performances to the point they are unrecognizable. While character development throughout a run strengthens acting, changes made to please audiences, weaken it.

Problem

During the run, the actors begin anticipating and pushing for certain responses from the audience.

Solution

The second and third performance after a successful opening, actors often feel comfortable and stop listening onstage. They begin to expect and play for audience response rather than focus on stage actions. When the audience fails to react, the actors overact. Tell them to return to the simplest logic underlying what happened in the scene, to go back and make the scene simpler, then come forward again.

Problem

After bad reviews, a glum cast worries about the audience's reception.

Solution

1. Give your discouraged cast a pep talk before the show. By demonstrating your unconditional support of the company, you can stimulate the enthusiasm needed for *their commitment to the performance.*
2. Encourage the actors to withdraw, relax, and focus on their character's action for a few minutes before going onstage. Then, tell the actors to concentrate on and play fully to get what their characters want most—be it love, money, fame, or whatever.
3. Put the review in perspective. Are your company members playing for that reviewer or for *this night's* audience? Do they believe *all* reviews? Why, why not?

Good directors keep tabs on their productions. They continue to give notes during the early days after opening. Previews and "taking shows on the road" are special performances aimed at fine tuning a production. While the stage manager is in charge of maintaining quality during the run of a show, sharp directors drop in periodically on their productions to assure performances meet their standards and to delete any harmful "additions."

The director as manager requires tenacity:

Directors have to be indomitable. You cannot be conquered. You have to keep persisting, and persisting, and persisting. I've battled the play right down to the very last hours before we played it to the critics, changing, changing, working, working. The only sin is to give up in the face of it. You have to believe that some kind of poetry is going to suddenly emerge, that the components will come together in a sublime order that will speak to the hearts of people. You have to build your own little arcade and over its door you have to say, to the company, "Abandon all wish to abandon!"

(Arthur Penn)

SPECIAL PROBLEMS: DIRECTING THE MUSICAL

Because of its scope, a musical will test your managerial skills more than most plays. The musical comedy consists of song, dance, and dialogue with a plot, called a "book." Besides supervising the complete work, the director stages dialogue sequences, principal songs, and routine numbers not requiring dance choreography. The director of a musical synthesizes the entire visual, acting, and musical effect of a production.

If you approach the medium as if *others* are responsible for musical areas and your own work is limited to dialogue, you are not directing the musical but coaching dialogue.

A director of a musical provides the vision for the *entire* production, defines the overall image to be conveyed, and evokes this meaning in the acting, visual statement, and musical design. Musicals add another layer onto the play: *music*. So arresting is this component, that it becomes the major channel of the production.

> Music has charms to soothe a savage breast,
> To soften rocks, or bend a knotted oak.
> I've read that things inanimate have moved,
> And, as with living souls, have been inform'd,
> By magic numbers and persuasive sound.
>
> (Congreve, *The Mourning Bride*, Act I; scene i)

Since directing a musical requires mastery over its most important and persuasive element, disastrous mistakes result when directors give the music secondary consideration. If you know nothing about music, cannot play an instrument, sing, or dance, beware of choosing a musical to direct. You will be helpless, ineffectual, or at the mercy of others when problems appear in musical areas. For example, you might direct an actor to sing a number (s)he cannot sing not knowing the song could be transposed to another key; or the sequence "talked" through.

Staffing for a Musical

Musicals require a more complex staff than nonmusicals, including the pivotal position of *musical director* to rehearse singers and/or lead the orchestra. Put all your energies and monies into assuring you get an expert in this position. The quality of the musical director is key to success. (S)he needs intensive knowledge and ability to motivate, lead, teach, and coach within a brief time period.

A *choreographer* or dance director stages the principals, dancers, and chorus in all movement numbers. If a director has background in movement, and musical numbers are simple, (s)he sometimes doubles as choreographer. Large-scale musicals usually require a *chorus director* to rehearse the singing chorus and a *rehearsal pianist* (possibly the chorus director or music director) to play at all music rehearsals.

Along with a good rehearsal pianist, you might need a *vocal coach* to coach individual singers. The vocal coach works principally with leading singers for projection, quality of sound, and interpretation. Singers need to relax and concentrate to eliminate tension in their voices. Vocal coaches help actors relax and warm up vocally before the performance. In the absence of a vocal coach, the music director or rehearsal pianist may do this. Many directors assume incorrectly a conductor or rehearsal pianist also has the skill of a vocal coach.

Budget for a Musical

The budget places special restrictions on the musical organization: on the size and quality of the musical leadership—musical director, vocal coach, choreographer, rehearsal pianist, conductor—lead singers, chorus, and orchestra. The budget influences how many musicians, singers, and dancers can be used for a production. Musicians cost money; singers and dancers need supervision and guidance. If budgets are limited, you may have to make do with smaller choruses and fewer (nonunion only) musicians.

Although some theater artists volunteer their services, trained musicians rarely fall into this category. If you do not reimburse them and they receive paying assignments, musicians may not appear for performances. Nontheater employment opportunities arise for musicians at various entertainment centers and clubs. Unlike actors, who need time for rehearsal and memorizing lines, skilled musicians can perform from music sheets on the spot. Unless you can reward them in another fashion (for example, course credit for the college production), plan for paying musicians for rehearsals and all performances into your budget.

At early rehearsals, you might be able to manage with only a rehearsal pianist; but as opening nears, you will need full orchestra or ensemble. If musicians play in the orchestra pit and actors can see the conductor from any stage position, (s)he can easily cue in their songs; but if the orchestra is performing under the stage or backstage, you will need more rehearsals for coordination.

Rehearsal Considerations

Musicals require more complex rehearsal scheduling. At least half of the rehearsals should involve working with singers and staging song-and-dance numbers. Establish a schedule to allow time for: acting, singing, and dancing rehearsals.

An effective schedule might designate Mondays and Wednesdays for music and dance rehearsals, Tuesdays and Thursdays for acting rehearsals, and Friday for coordinating various areas, group movements, and run-throughs. When space and staff permit, schedule simultaneous musical and acting-rehearsals with different actors. Some directors allow too little time for song and dance rehearsals, which require ongoing practice and development. If rehearsal time is short, consider advance work or private coaching of dialogue sequences.

Once into major rehearsals, songs and dances must be practiced on a regular basis. Problems in those areas can force you to cut acting rehearsals and underrehearse the dialogue segments in performance. Set up schedules so that if you need more rehearsals of song-and-dance numbers toward the end, you can streamline dialogue rehearsals, acting problems having been handled in advance. Such a plan might require additional meetings apart from the regular schedule.

Weaknesses will first appear in dance or vocal numbers because an actor is under more stress when doing several things simultaneously. (S)he is interpreting the words (playing the character action), regulating the breath, synchronizing timing with the orchestra, and preparing for difficult notes. Because of musical numbers' complexity, more can go wrong.

Smart managers schedule run-throughs so that performers can experience connecting song and dialogue sequences. Design your rehearsal schedule to further actors' work in all sections so that one scene evolves seamlessly into the next and the whole process develops organically from moment to moment. Dialogue sequences should build *to* the songs or dances rather than float along as separate sections of a straight drama, or only "rests" between songs. The additional ingredients of musicals form a complex pattern challenging the director/manager.

> If music be the food of love, play on;
> Give me excess of it, that, surfeiting
> The appetite may sicken, and so die.
> That strain again!
>
> (*Twelfth Night*, Act I; scene i)

FINAL PROJECTS

1. Plan the presentation you would make for your first audition. Pick a major play, like Bernard Shaw's *Pygmalion,* and a theater that you can study. Describe your concept of the play for today's audience and your specific approach to staging, text, and acting. Clarify the time commitment, rehearsal procedures, and six-week production schedule required to motivate the class to participate in the production. Submit a two-day audition format, including audition instructions, scene breakdowns, and three audition selections.

2. Plan a rehearsal and technical schedule that allows for the development of the play's text and characterization. Project description: You have a month, five nights a week from 7:00 to 10:00 P.M. to rehearse a group of actors in a community-theater production of Tennessee Williams's *The Glass Menagerie*. Laura Wingfield is available Monday, Tuesday, and Wednesday nights; Amanda Wingfield is available Tuesday, Wednesday, and Thursday nights; Tom Wingfield, Wednesday to Friday nights; and Jim O'Connor, the Gentleman Caller, Monday through Friday nights. All actors except Mrs. Wingfield are unavailable days and weekends. All have played lead roles at the theater except Jim, who is new in town and has never acted before with this group. You have a $500 budget and one underpaid, inexperienced assistant doing lights, sets, and costumes, most of which must be pulled from the theater's and actors' available resources.

3. Plan procedures to resolve the following house-management problem. As director, you have also been assigned box office, ushering, and intermission refreshments for *The Glass Menagerie*. The play will be performed for two consecutive Thursdays through Sundays in a 200-seat theater with two side aisles and one major, double-door entrance. You have one seasoned assistant being paid for six hours of work and four inexperienced volunteers who have agreed to work three hours each. Two have offered to bring their dates along to work, if it's a Friday or Saturday night. One actor, Jim, is not in Act I. You cannot be present to supervise the last performance.

4. *Musicals:* (a) Try to see some live musicals. Evaluate what you consider to be the production concept or metaphor of each production. Note productions lacking a concept. (b) Select a musical. Describe a production concept for staging it at a specific theater to the class who might represent the Board of Trustees and a group of designers and technicians.

Chapter **10**

The Director as Audience
Evaluating the Production Objectively

The applause of a single human being is of great consequence.

Samuel Johnson

Throughout time, the structure and shape plays take have been greatly influenced by the changing composition of the audience. Transporting these time-honored plays to the differing audience of the modern age may necessitate adaptation to allow for these changes. Audiences of today differ in both expectation and behavior from those of the past, and they attend theater for different reasons. New York director Ned Bobkoff claims: "The biggest mistake in script selection that directors make is not being able to discriminate between their own concerns and what the audience can deal with. Directors need to know how to step back from themselves and become a proxy for the audience." Most people, today, think of theater as live entertainment, a social evening out, or an escape from their usual work schedule. Some, especially those living in large cities or affluent suburbs, consider it a culturally broadening experience.

Some communities maintain a resident-professional or skilled-amateur theater, where the audience enjoys expressing loyalty to the company by subscribing for season tickets and attending every event. College campus productions of classics, or off-off Broadway productions of "serious" theater attract a special audience, which is both highly supportive and intensely critical. Each theatrical organization must evaluate the nature of its own audience, a challenging task in our complex society.

I'm one of those directors who sits out there in the house taking notes, and I think in terms of what you're saying to *us*, me being a part of the audience. And I've gone to so many meetings of artistic directors where they start talking about *my* art. Nothing turns me off sooner because it is not my art, it is *our* art and that is frequently denied. Many of those theatres that have that

278

type of artistic leadership, actually have failed. They've started closing down, because they're not addressing what the heart of the theatre is about which is a shared process. So the audience is very present when I read a play.

(Cliff Baker, artistic director, Arkansas Rep.)

A BRIEF HISTORY OF THE AUDIENCE

Past audiences could not select from such a varied theatrical menu as we have today. For "theater" functioned less as a theatrical event than as a religious or social requirement. Theater first manifested itself in the ritual expressions of prehistoric societies. The entire population of ancient Athens attended Greek productions in huge, open-air theaters, as part of a religious festival. Peter Arnott says, "We need to remind ourselves that the Greeks were, then as now, vivid, excitable, prone to rapid anger and equally rapid appeasement, and given to loud, colorful talk and emotional display" (*The Theatre in Its Time,* p. 36). Here the dominant factor was the theater's size. The acting area was dwarfed by the auditorium, a crowd of 14,000 people filling up the tiers of seats. "It has been calculated that to the spectator in the back row of the Theatre of Dionysus, the actor looked about three-quarters of an inch high" (Arnott, p. 37).

In Rome, theater was also given in huge arenas seating 8,000 to 14,000 people as part of a religious festival. However, the Roman public was fickle and interested in grandiose, sentimental, and diversionary entertainment. The audience was free to come and go during a performance and even to buy food and drink which were sold just outside the theater. Roman festivals, often given in conjunction with fairs, included besides dramas: acrobatics, trained animals, jugglers, athletic events, music, dance, prizefighting, horseracing, and competitive sports (Brockett, *History of Theatre,* pp. 51–52). "Furthermore, other attractions competed for the audiences' favor. The first two productions of Terence's *Mother in Law* were failures because at the first the audience left to see a rope dancer and at the second to watch gladiators" (Brockett, p. 61).

Throughout the middle ages, audiences from all classes and from both local and neighboring areas flocked to see free theatrical performances reflecting the teachings of the Catholic Church. Cycle plays, commemorating religious holidays, were staged outdoors during the spring and summer months. However, the interval between productions ranged from two to ten years—and some of the more elaborate performances were *never* repeated. Distinguished citizens most likely watched from the windows of surrounding houses; scaffolding was erected for lesser personages; the lower orders stood. Often spectators began to take their places as early as 4 A.M. (Brocket, p. 114). In Elizabethan theater, though performances only cost a few cents, artisans and craftsmen who attended the public theater (which held around 2,500 people) did so at the cost of working. A sprinkling of the nobility and leisured classes would attend and sit in the gentlemen's rooms, higher priced, segregated seating in the gallery. However, the deep thrust stage carried the actor into the midst of lower class groundlings (Arnott, pp. 183; 191).

Although French royal theaters in the seventeenth century were roofed, performances were still restricted to afternoons, as the negligible street lighting of Paris made later hours impossible. The audiences were mainly composed of those not bound by working conditions, freeloaders, and members of the royal household staff (vast numbers had to be admitted without charge) (Arnott, p. 247).

"The peculiar flavor of the Chinese theatre also owes much to the audience. Most of the early public theatres were temporary, but in the seventeenth century, actors began to perform in teahouses where customers were seated at tables. When permanent theatres were built, this arrangement was retained and the ground floor was fitted out with tables and stools at which spectators were served tea while watching the play" (Brockett, p. 246).

Conversely, riots were not uncommon in the Restoration audience. "The relationship between audience and the performers was close. Actors often took their grievances to the spectators who sometimes refused to let performances proceed until explanations from alleged offenders were forthcoming" (Brockett, p. 297). "The theatre served as a veritable clubhouse for its audience. Seated in their boxes, gathering in the loges, milling about in the aisles and even perching upon the skirts of the stage, the courtly audience came to the theatre to see one another and to be seen, to make contacts and conduct business, to dally and contrive assignations" (Cohen, *Theatre*, p. 169).

> Afternoon performances began at three o'clock, but, again as in Paris, the door opened well before then to allow the patrons a few hours of pre-performance frivolity and social intercourse. The performers' splendid satin and silk costumes, high heels (for both men and women), towering "perukes" (wigs), handkerchiefs that draped almost to the floor, and elocutionary acting styles created a spectacle well suited to the tastes of a court conspicuously preoccupied with sexual assignation and dalliance. Indeed the whole mood of the Restoration theatre was one of blatant sexual provocation.
>
> (Cohen, p. 202)

If the Restoration audience was small and limited to the aristocracy, nineteenth-century American audiences were diverse and rough. In nineteenth-century American theater, democratization revealed itself in the disappearance of differentiated seating, specifically boxes. Both auditorium and stage were lit with gas lighting, but manners had not improved with the surroundings. There were complaints of noisy and unshaven patrons, of the spitting of tobacco juice, and of assaults on the audience in the pit from the balconies above (Arnott, p. 447).

The Expectant Audience: waiting for a play to begin; the director's work
must engage and sustain their interest.
McCarter Theatre. Photo: McCarter Theatre.

Some historians trace our current concept of the silent, rapt audience
to the late nineteenth-century approach of the opera composer, Richard
Wagner. Today, audiences expect the director to create an environment
to sustain their interest. You must weigh this expectation seriously, if
you expect audiences to appreciate and benefit from your creative work.

OBJECTIFYING YOUR RESPONSE

When the curtain goes up on opening night, the set, props, costumes,
sound and lights are all on stage with the actors; but the director is alone
with the *audience*. At this point an inexperienced director—and often
an experienced one—suffers unexpected shocks. Much of what seemed
"cozy" alone in rehearsal suddenly appears unfamiliar and strange. For
the first time, (s)he realizes the impact of this partnership with the audience, as well as with the cast and crew.

A good director maintains a dual consciousness rotating between the perceptions of "creator" and "observer" while working on a production. (S)he acknowledges the outside audience factor, while simultaneously creating from inside the world of the play. Directors who do not incorporate both vantage points may be startled by audience reaction to their work.

No single formula codifies how to apply such a double awareness, but maintaining a dual consciousness throughout pre-production planning and early rehearsals assists you.

A tricky concept, artistic objectivity can evade beginning directors. Most amateur artists in any creative endeavor—visual arts, music, playwrighting, theatrical performance—anguish over changing or discarding unworkable ideas. But learning to see your own directorial faults, which the audience might perceive, is the first step in expert directing. For example, you may study the play so carefully, rehearse the beats so well, and become so enchanted with certain imaginative moments, you forget that the audience may not cherish the play as you do. You have not developed artistic objectivity.

This chapter will deal with reasons for developing objectivity and ways to examine a performance from the viewpoints of audience as well as director. Beginning directors evaluate results too late. As *audience*, the director functions as judge, responding to and analyzing results. Judge *what* changes need to be made, then decide *how* to effect them.

Research your audience. If you do not live near the theater, get information about it. Some professional theaters have had a marketing analysis done; others have devised their own form requesting information from a typical audience. If such a survey is available, you should evaluate it. Use Table 10.1 to help you learn and assess who your audience is.

Jerome Lawrence described one of the director's duties:

> A major function is for the audience to be able to *hear* the play. If an audience just isn't receiving a play, it's like turning on a radio with a dead battery. An audience is a great collective genius and can tell you a great deal. The first time your play hits an audience you will know things about it that you weren't aware of in the rehearsal process. The audience wants to be challenged; they want the dancing ideas; they want to be astonished, surprised, delighted, stirred. And it's sharing that same area: living, breathing actors and a living, breathing audience. The major function of the director is making the play live for the "first" time at every performance: reaching the audience, affecting them, and making sure that the ideal spine of the play, the essence of the play, is conveyed.

Another director, Ron Gural, suggests: "You the director, read the play first *as audience*. If something speaks to you as audience, if it comes to you fresh, and if it's something that *you* experience . . . then you will have a stake in it and want to do it. At the end of rehearsals, you reconnect with that original experience you had for wanting to do the

Table 10.1: Audience Analysis Form

1. Age.
2. Sex.
3. Address (incude zip code).
4. If suburb, how often do you get into the city?
5. Mode of transportation used to get to the theater.
6. Education.
7. Job.
8. If student, what year and major?
9. How often do you go to the theater?
10. How often do you go to *our* theater?
11. Other entertainments you attend.
12. Why did you select this theater and this play?
13. How did you hear about it?
14. Price of ticket.
15. Would you come again?
16. Performing day, times—are they convenient?
17. What other kinds of plays would you like to see?
18. Do you subscribe to any theater group's season?
19. Other interests you may have.
20. Was the production well-communicated and well-received? Comments.
   (Some theaters ask a series of questions about the play. This often determines how theatrically knowledgeable the audience is.)

Goal: To identify the type of persons in the house, how they heard of the particular production, and if they liked it.
Procedures: Survey all audiences for a particular run of a play: preferably all productions during one year.

play and you reassess whether or not the audience is going through the same experience that you had in reading it. The director is the representative of the audience during the rehearsal process." Work to assure that the impression that you initially received from the script is conveyed to the audience, that your need to tell the story in a particular way so compels your directing that you will do whatever necessary to create that experience for someone else.

Emotional Goals: Responding to the Text

Reading, researching, planning, blocking, and scoring the text, will help you imagine what you want the *actors* to express at every moment in each scene and, simultaneously, what you want the *audience* to feel. While complicating the pre-production process, scoring the text this way will introduce a double-awareness into your thinking and better prepare you for audience reaction on opening night.

THE MANDRAKE, I, i, PROLOGUE: TEXT

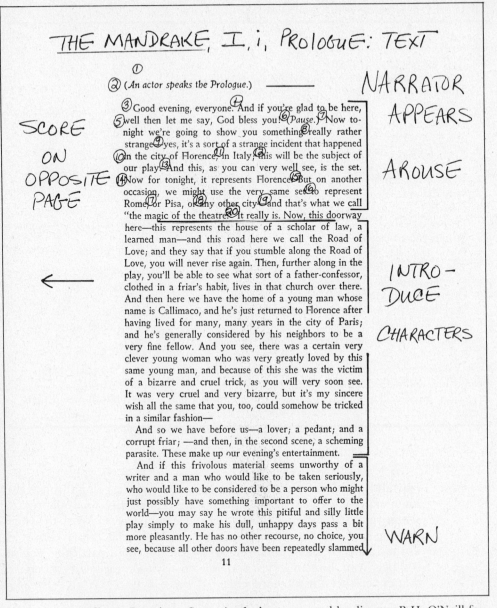

(An actor speaks the Prologue.) ———   NARRATOR APPEARS

SCORE ON OPPOSITE PAGE

Good evening, everyone. And if you're glad to be here, well then let me say, God bless you! (*Pause.*) Now tonight we're going to show you something really rather strange—yes, it's a sort of a strange incident that happened in the city of Florence, in Italy; this will be the subject of our play. And this, as you can very well see, is the set. Now for tonight, it represents Florence. But on another occasion, we might use the very same set to represent Rome, or Pisa, or any other city—and that's what we call "the magic of the theatre." It really is. Now, this doorway here—this represents the house of a scholar of law, a learned man—and this road here we call the Road of Love; and they say that if you stumble along the Road of Love, you will never rise again. Then, further along in the play, you'll be able to see what sort of a father-confessor, clothed in a friar's habit, lives in that church over there. And then here we have the home of a young man whose name is Callimaco, and he's just returned to Florence after having lived for many, many years in the city of Paris; and he's generally considered by his neighbors to be a very fine fellow. And you see, there was a certain very clever young woman who was very greatly loved by this same young man, and because of this she was the victim of a bizarre and cruel trick, as you will very soon see. It was very cruel and very bizarre, but it's my sincere wish all the same that you, too, could somehow be tricked in a similar fashion—

And so we have before us—a lover; a pedant; and a corrupt friar; —and then, in the second scene, a scheming parasite. These make up our evening's entertainment. ———

And if this frivolous material seems unworthy of a writer and a man who would like to be taken seriously, who would like to be considered to be a person who might just possibly have something important to offer to the world—you may say he wrote this pitiful and silly little play simply to make his dull, unhappy days pass a bit more pleasantly. He has no other recourse, no choice, you see, because all other doors have been repeatedly slammed

11

AROUSE

INTRO-DUCE CHARACTERS

WARN

Audience Reaction—Score Analysis: text scored by director R.H. O'Neill for audience reaction.

Text: *The Mandrake* by Niccolo Machiavelli. Translated by Wallace Shawn. International Creative Management, Inc. 1978. Reprinted by permission.

MANDRAKE by Machiavelli ACT I, sc. 1, ii PROLOGUE O'Neill				
CUE NUMBER	CHARACTERS	MISE EN SCENE	ACTION	OBJECTIVE
BEAT I	(costumes, props)	(set, sound & lights)	(active character initiating action)	(what I want audience to feel)
①	none	house lights dark on stage	to reveal dullness of world without art	quiet expectations
②	narrator majestic page boy outfit, plumed red cap, tunic, tights, slippers; gold half mask on stick	fade up Pachelbal's Canon to swelling intensity fade up all stage lights to brilliance	NARRATOR SUMMONS AUDIENCE appears u.c., top of stairs, x's d.c. toward audience	to intrigue with this mysterious character
③		③ lower Canon	to entice	to fascinate
④		④	to stimulate	to humor
⑤		⑤	to glorify	" "
⑥		⑥	to punctuate	" "
⑦		⑦	to rally	to engage interest
⑧		⑧	to spook (shakes open hands at audience)	to excite
⑨	Choreograph movement of narrator	⑨	to fathom	to compel with story
⑩		⑩ slide of Florence	to demonstrate Florence	" "
⑪		⑪	to demonstrate Italy	" "
⑫	Same costume and props	⑫	to hail topic	" "
⑬		⑬	to exhibit set	to fascinate with spectacle
⑭		⑭	to transport	" "
⑮		⑮ Music and lights remain same	to rapture	" "
⑯		⑯ slide of Colosseum	to transport to Rome	" "
⑰		⑰ slide of Tower of Pisa	to transport to Pisa	" "
⑱		⑱	to imagine	to hypnotize
⑲		⑲	to hail	to electrify
⑳		⑳	to reinforce	to hypnotize

Problem

You have formed a fairly clear idea of what you want the cast to do, but cannot predict the likely audience reaction on opening night.

Solution

When you score the text, organize a separate sheet or column in your prompt book for "Audience Reaction." Imagine what you think the audience should feel (sadness, delight, shock, disbelief, mystery, surprise, distress, awe) and how you might direct a particular moment or segment to get that reaction. (Suggestion: Remember to score the text in pencil and make changes as necessary.)

You need to be cautioned against working for emotional end results from the audience at the expense of the script's truth and the performer's believability. The performers and directors must be truthful to the play, its message, language, and tenor. Note how the score for the objective fits the text in the scene breakdown for *The Mandrake* on page 285.

Beware that performance work for pleasing an audience can cause problems. You don't want to pander to an audience. If an audience and play do not mesh, change your audience—or change your play. There are many instances where an excellent production is dampened by its inappropriateness for a particular audience. *No Exit*, Jean Paul Sartre's play about three dead misfits trapped in one room (a "living hell"), should not be performed for members of a retirement community expecting *Mame!*

Reaction to the Theater Space

Even with an appropriate play you will need to familiarize yourself with staging conditions in the theater. Get to know that theater as soon as you can gain access to the house. If the opportunity exists, attend a performance, or at least visit the empty theater while scoring the text. This method of pre-planning prevents large-scale errors by providing information about space, sightlines, acoustics, and so forth. If working in a new space, you should feel uncomfortable about planning movement and sound without making an effort to study the size of the stage.

Overfamiliarity with the space can also present difficulties. Many directors sit enthusiastically close to the stage, prompt book in hand, coaching actors, intensely involved with production ideas. You should begin to consider how the *audience* is responding to the actors within that space as early as those first few rehearsals. Move about frequently in the audience space, watching the rehearsal from as many visual (and aural) points as possible. You may be surprised at how different a production looks from the back or side of the house. You may find changes essential for the entire audience (not just the last rows) to understand the action. Consider these changes:

- adjust upstage gestures hidden from the audience on one side
- move actors into different positions so they can be seen and heard from all angles
- bring some of the more important actions into a downstage or center-stage position
- change the position of stage furniture or other hindrances to effective movement
- effect costume and/or color changes based on how they will "carry" to the back of the house
- make small props, important to the action, more visible

EXERCISES

1. Come to the theater one day when there is no rehearsal. Approach the building, lobby, and other public areas, and look at them as objectively as possible. Make notes.
2. If possible, attend another director's production in your theater. Approach the situation as a member of the audience might, noticing areas of the physical plant, as well as the handling of the important elements of staging.

The Danger of Self-Involvement

The best performing artists—musicians, actors, dancers—often retain a coach to keep them in training, tuned and sharp, and to prevent acquiring harmful idiosyncracies or sloppy techniques. Directors rarely do that. Becoming self-involved, they do not perceive bad habits beginning to overtake their good work. You *can* compensate for this lack of training center, or individual mentor-on-call, by keeping an open mind about the real effectiveness of your own direction, and paying attention to others' reaction to the production.

Do not depend entirely on the responses of the "in" group: cast, crew, and others formally involved with the work. While experienced and competent themselves, the cast, designers, and technicians can fall into the same trap directors do. They lose sight of the immediate impression because of overfamiliarity with the production. They may also react in a subjective manner, such as the assistant stage manager laughing at the comedic antics of a roommate prancing around in a Restoration costume. But the detached audience may not find the scene humorous.

When directors are learning together in a workshop situation, they may have difficulty retaining objectivity toward each other's efforts. Having participated in scene study, discussions, and analyses under the instructor's guidance, they develop into a "sympathetic audience" for each other's works. On the positive side, a supportive atmosphere develops directors' confidence to try interesting and original ideas without fear of rejection. Every effort should be made to observe classmates' work as an audience of strangers might.

Problem

Your actors are having trouble with a scene that involves playing directly to the audience.

Solution

Since an audience is built into the choices, invite a selective audience, one or two persons, to rehearsals—once the lines are learned. The "audience" will function like another character, onstage, and the actors will experience the stage as extending into the auditorium rather than splitting off from it.

Problem

Deep into the rehearsal schedule, some of the freshness of your first reaction has begun to stale, and you cannot decide how humorous or moving certain scenes are. The actors are not implementing any new ideas, and your rehearsals feel boring.

Solution

Do not pressure the cast or yourself into extra rehearsals or complex reworkings of scenes.
1. Instead, consider making one change that would significantly affect every aspect of the production. See what shift in a particularly "flat" scene might enliven it and produce consequences throughout the rest of the play.
2. Use the observations from detached viewers to assist you in identifying needed adjustments.

THE OBJECTIVE AUDIENCE

You can test audience response by bringing in objective groups to rehearsals well in advance of the final dress rehearsal—before it is too late to make changes. For example, when directing in a campus theater, directors can bring in nontheater students, staff, or colleagues. Put on a scene or two, or the entire play if time permits; watch and listen to the audience reaction. Annotate in your prompt book where the difficult moments seem to occur.

An early-audience method can alert you to both bad and good elements of the presentation. Obviously, if the audience laughs during a tragic scene that scene may need some redirecting. If you can, try a few different types of audience groups because reactions may vary. In such cases there may be no real "fault" in the direction itself. The scene may be successful with some audiences and just not with others. Traditionally, a Sunday matinee audience will not respond like a late-evening audience.

If a whole group is not practical, invite a single, nontheater friend to watch a staged rehearsal. (S)he should note (much as a judge would) any negative observations on the production such as unclear actions, words, or scenes. Let those comments assist you in diagnosing difficulties. Or, ask a theater expert, with different strengths from your own, to evaluate the production. If you coach actors brilliantly, have a designer or a playwright come in. Use observers who can judge your weak areas. (A word of caution: Don't allow these "critics" to speak directly to your cast. Filter their comments and present those ideas to the cast yourself. *You* know how to deal with your actors, strangers don't.)

Although the early-audience method will encourage you to reassess your work, your first experience of outsiders' responses will probably bring tension. You may not understand why a play seemingly successful in rehearsal fails in actual performance. Observe actors closely during this preview performance. In their excitement, actors may lose focus, forgetting their scene motivations and objectives. Other problems may simply address something as obvious as a costume or prop change.

Problem

Your early audience did not react as expected to a preview performance. You sense that the actors' lack of focus on scene objectives is causing audience uncertainty.

Solution

Ask yourself: How much can I expect actors to remember from scene to scene, beat to beat, point to point? How much subtlety in performance can actors project or the audience unconsciously absorb? In the rehearsal following your early-audience preview, concentrate on the opening moments of the most troublesome scenes. The most powerful messages about character's relationships and the story are conveyed to the audience during the first few minutes of a scene, and much subsequent information is evaluated against these initial impressions. Judge the visual and aural impact as well, including stage set, color, lighting, sound, or music.

READING THE AUDIENCE

Be as sensitive to your audience as you are to your actors. *Pressing* audiences for responses that are not forthcoming signals that a directors' work may be unclear or, perhaps, may not be meant for a particular audience. Continual *straining* for responses that are not forthcoming may indicate you have not correctly "read" or prepared your audiences.

Professional theater director Paul Baker says, "For example, directors can write their audience a letter in advance and tell them very seriously why they're doing a very controversial play and what's in there (harsh language for example) and that they'll give them tickets to another play rather than this one if they so desire. Warn the audience so they know in advance that this is going to be that kind of play."

Working in a particular community area or theater for some length of time will teach you what *your* audience expects, reacts to positively, or is willing to try. Regional or repertory theaters attract the same (possibly subscription) audiences most seasons. Even though you may not agree with their response, *blaming* the audience for its reaction is rarely productive. Guest directors with one chance to prove themselves may have to sensitize themselves to audience response.

Individual audiences vary from performance to performance. Affected differently by trends and fashions, some groups respond to the rhythm of a work based on what music they listen to; whether they are urban, suburban, or rural; blue collar or preppie; young, middle aged or elderly; and so forth. Professional performers know the composition of matinee groups: school-age children, first-time theatergoers, ladies' luncheon clubs, rushed commuters.

Make adjustments if you are to play to "unsophisticated" audiences for the full run of the play. Read the audiences beforehand. Clearly, you cannot and *should* not expect the production to shift from performance to performance to respond to audience expectation.

Problem

An audience responds negatively to your play.

Solution

1. Make special efforts during the early run of the show to attend all performances. While watching and notating critiques for performers, scrutinize audience reaction. If a particularly humorous line *never* gets a laugh, the action *leading up* to the "punch" line may be unfocused or "soft." Clarify the action in a coaching session and remember that the audience does not realize a certain action will precipitate a funny line. The right atmosphere should be established for the "unexpected" to occur. Since you cannot rework the *audience* for reaction, strengthen the action(s) provoking the desired response.

2. While some gifted and experienced performers are able to transform any audience, an entire *structured* production cannot be redone.

One director, Paul Baker, described how he responded to negative audience response:

> I have endeavored to change the direction of the production when I felt the production (it wasn't just audience reaction) had missed the playwright's original intent. As a managing director of a professional theatre, I have redirected some plays or asked the director to redirect them, and I've shortened them or eliminated certain scenes because of what we felt about the production after consultation with the playwright. Directors should be aware if there is a negative audience response, especially if they see it coming in early previews.

In a smaller theatre, I quite often delay the opening for a week. In the bigger theatre, it is harder because you're locked into six weeks' performance schedule. I don't think you adjust or curtail a play because of audience reaction; you do it because the production doesn't resemble anything you had envisioned when you, the designer, and the playwright first discussed the production.

Nevertheless, few productions have a long enough run to enable a director to make substantial changes in mid-season. A production scheduled for nine performances over three, long weekends should not expect to go into rewrites, redesigns, or changes in basic concept. In most professional/regional theaters, other commitments prevent guest directors from staying long after opening night recognition. "Reading" the audience may have to be left to the resident artistic director, or to an assistant director who has the director's permission to make adjustments for the good of the production as it proceeds.

Paul Baker believes directors have a responsibility to bring a very alive product to the stage, to introduce audiences to new works of bright young writers, to do classics with a fresh interpretation, and to engender innovation.

In theory a theatrical work of art exists in the mind, in a diagram on paper, in discussion among dramatists, scholars, or in rehearsals on acting technique; but in reality theater is intended for the audience.

THE DIRECTOR AS AUDIENCE: FROM ENTRANCE TO EXIT

The director acts like a barometer predicting the ongoing experience of the audience. Be conscious of the first impression the audience receives in *all* areas of the theater. Although you might minimally control the physical plant, observe elements which seem to lie outside your realm of interest. The smaller the performing organization, the more likely you can effect improvements in the physical condition of the theater.

John Bettenbender cautions as follows:

You have to set up priorities when directing. It's hard to take care of all the details, but I find the more I have control of the theatre myself, whether I'm the artistic director or the producer, the better these facets are, because I have to give them my attention. The whole theatre experience, from the time people arrive, is all part of this magic you are trying to create. I directed in a summer theatre in Chicago. The most influential reviewer of the most influential newspaper came on opening night. I had been unhappy with the theatre set-up; all summer I tried, without success, to get them to do something about the inaccessible walkways, dangerous gravel paths, awkward parking and service arrangements. The reviewer liked the play, but she devoted the first two paragraphs of the review to the gravel and the ponds and the steps and everything else that was wrong I had complained about. Then she went on to say that the show was good. A lot of people read the review of the theatre and not of the play. Half the review was written about "the inconveniences to be overcome to see this little gem."

In campus and community theaters, you might find yourself in the position of supervising volunteers simply because there is no one else to do so. Do not regard this chore as unnecessary from the directorial point of view. Negative audience reaction to the physical environment can seriously affect audience reaction to the play itself.

By the time the play starts, the audience may already be predisposed to dislike it. If the lobby is littered with stale cigarette butts or one of the entrance doors is stuck shut, they may not feel this supposedly "special" place is at all special. The theater building and lobby are thresholds into the world of theatrical illusion. The audience experiences *this* space before they see the house, the stage set, and the actors. Audience reaction to the entire environment should reflect your intent for this production.

CONCLUSION

Directing involves shifting images in the mind of the audience. The script develops through these adjusting impressions. Good directors take the audience by the hand, so to speak, and move them along with the players, traveling with the action. The farther the subject matter from your audience's understanding, the more comfortable you should make them with the players. The players' performance allows the audience to experience a parallel organic action so it becomes the potential player.

Audience Reaction—To the Theater: an attractive and well-maintained theater prepares the audience for a special experience.
The Alley Theatre. Photo: Ezra Stoller.

Audience Reaction—To the Lobby: an interesting display sets the mood for theatrical illusion.
McCarter Theatre. Photo: McCarter Theatre.

The "ideal" audience—and in rehearsals the only audience—*you* must judge whether an action has the capacity to arouse the potential "actors" in the audience . . . or not. Is this truly funny? Is this truly moving?

In rehearsal, the director functions as audience in two ways. First, by just sitting back, watching, and making suggestions to the actors to keep the production entertaining. And secondly, by creating a vicarious connection with the actors. As the actors onstage are going through their actions, the audience is essentially acting with them. The audience members are potential actors, because they don't just identify with one character, the hero or the villain, but with all of the characters when they are part of the action. However, most plays are written so that the audience primarily empathizes with the lead's experience. A director must engage the audience in that journey. Joseph Chaikin says:

> In Euripides' *Medea,* the director travels along with the lead, Medea, and takes a certain approximate responsibility for going into the territory that she

has traveled. Frequently the passion of a lead actor is immoderate and spills over in some way into other passions. For example, Medea's killing her children is a product of her passion for Jason which created her giving birth to them. So Medea's journey, in a sense, is a journey into her extremity of passion.

The director takes the audience on the pilgrimage of the protagonist, but theater is a group journey. The audience composes the final jury. While one person can view a painting, a play needs larger numbers of people to confirm its reason for existence. You can't do theater without an audience. No matter how expert the director, theater requires an audience of more than one.

> Where none admire, tis useless to excell; where none are beaux, tis vain to be a belle.
>
> (George, Baron Lyllelton, *Soliloquy on a Beauty in the Country*)

FINAL PROJECTS

1. Choose a scene from a three or four character play. For a class size of about twelve, this leaves you a potential audience, including the instructor, of at least six to eight. Rehearse the scene, and have actors learn their lines in preparation for a "dress rehearsal." When the work seems ready, invite outsiders to view it or videotape it.

   An audience of strangers: The outside audience should *not* see any of the rehearsals, and the director should *not* discuss any problems about the play with them beforehand. You want an audience of "strangers," that has not been involved in the process. Run the scene without stopping, observing carefully the audience reaction to the whole scene and its parts. Afterwards discuss the audience's reaction with them, and/or use what you have observed to further your work.

   Videotaping: Have actors go through a scene on videotape about midway through rehearsals, after they are free from scripts or prompting. Wait a day or two then watch the tape as though you were a stranger viewing it for the first time. If you find that the presentation does not capture what you *thought* you were getting across, make notes and work on the weak spots.

2. Find a director willing to permit you to attend a rehearsal about ten days before opening night. Make notes on problems an *audience* member would observe. What areas need improvement?

Chapter 11

The Director as Administrator
Organizing the Production

The perfect representation of dramatic pieces is a matter requiring great time and practice. It is an immense business—pieces, casts, rehearsals, stage-business, stage-scenery, stage-effect, final performance, and with all this the regulation of a band of people . . . impatient of control.

William B. Wood, 1779–1861,
theater manager, Philadelphia,
Baltimore, and Washington

Although you may not think of yourself as an administrator, much directing work falls into this category. The director functions in any production primarily as *artist*. If you cannot execute the creative requirements of production, you will not generate interesting work. But, artists must also confront practical realities to accomplish their goals. Ted Swindley, director of Stages, a professional theater which he founded seven years ago in Houston, Texas, describes his job as follows.

> My official function is everything. Primarily I'm responsible for the overall artistic design of the theater. I plan the season, have complete control over what we produce: casting, directors, designers. I'm also in charge of the administrative side of the theater. I am very much involved in planning, marketing, publicity, development for a ten play main stage season, a five play young audience's season, and a playwright's festival. Personally, I direct four to five shows a year.

At some point you must administrate to secure the success of your artistic work. Today many directors do not work in generously funded organizations with paid assistants. While commercial theater directors usually have a business manager to supervise administrative concerns, the director may be responsible for other administrative areas: trimming budgets, hiring assistants, writing letters, making phone calls, and attending public-relations events. Directors for small theater companies must also engage in the tasks of *house manager* and *executive producer*.

Most full-time positions for directors require much administrative work over a theater season (*artistic director*), or theater studies (*director of theater*). Responsible to the board of trustees, the artistic director directs some plays but *oversees all* the theater's productions, monies, facilities, and staff. No matter which level of directing you are engaged in, certain areas of administration will be part of your terrain.

As *administrator*, you must examine matters which will strengthen both the production and your position. Tom Markus, a director at Yale University, sees three fundamental concerns:

> 1) logistics, the ability to organize and control space, money, and time; 2) personnel relations, the ability to get people to believe they've had the idea of doing what you want them to do all along; 3) analysis, the ability to imagine what a completed event might be based on an analysis of the text, the people, and logistics. . . .
>
> Administering with artistic sensitivity takes 120% of your effort. Not many people do it very well . . . There's a lot of nonsense about "I'm an *artiste* and I shouldn't have to deal with all of that." Well that's a little like the painter saying, "I'm an *artiste*, and I don't want to worry about the frame of a canvas!"

Administration and your other roles should enhance one another. Learn to use your time productively as actor, interpreter, historian, and so on, to insure artistic success. Heed Benjamin Franklin's sound advice, "Let all things have their places; let each part of your business have its time." This chapter stresses four critical aspects of administration facing directors: theater organization, pre-production planning, publicizing, and public relations.

THEATER ORGANIZATION

To direct well, you should understand the pressures of the theater organization you are working within including: 1) educational theater—university, college, or secondary school; 2) professional theater—commercial or resident; or 3) community theater—amateur, recreational, or semi-professional.

The first theater organization you may be dealing with is *educational theater*, where the major stress is teaching inexperienced actors and technicians. University theater provides the advantages of free space (with directors and staffs on annual salaries), financial security (no pressures to make money at the box office), and time. At some institutions, directors work in well-equipped, up-to-date facilities, with a substantial budget and a year-round faculty of theater experts. However, other campuses run with ill-equipped auditoriums and volunteers.

Time can assist you in organizing volunteers, teaching actors, and instructing student technicians. Cultural events, related reading, informative lectures, background discussions, creatively paced rehearsals, and stimulating travel maximize the quality of each student's contribution.

Problem

You have ten days to rehearse a new, inexperienced actor for a role in a college production.

Solution

Outside rehearsals, arrange to get together with the actor for individual sessions. Work carefully on problems so that the actor will be capable of maintaining pace with the rest of the cast in rehearsals. Create additional time to nurture this player, to soothe nerves, and to minimize stress.

Problem

You have to handle difficult actors over whom you have no authority, since they were selected by your advisor/producer.

Solution

1. Minimize their impact by rehearsing them apart from the group except for nonstop run-throughs where no talking is allowed.
2. Cancel rehearsal on their scenes the first moment they get unruly.
3. Keep close contact with and maintain the trust of the advisor. Have the advisor express support of you to the cast at the outset of an important rehearsal.
4. Deal with difficult actors through the advisor, having the advisor effect your changes in their scenes.
5. Next time, clarify your authority *in writing* before rehearsals begin.

Problem

While you are running a large musical sequence in a rehearsal hall, your supervisor disrupts rehearsal, insults your directing style, and starts to change your blocking.

Solution

1. Stop the rehearsal and call a break. Take your supervisor aside, admit that a serious problem exists, and arrange to meet *privately*. Do not allow the rehearsal to develop into a war; you will only lose, as you are the temporary director. Tell the supervisor that you intend to work cooperatively with the organization but will allow no public insulting. You will not lampoon the organization or the staff but you demand the same treatment. *And you plan to direct the production until the end.* Do not put yourself in an either/or situation where you can be fired or forced to quit. Directors must be able to complete assignments and handle painful personality problems, including attacks and public criticism.
2. Invite your supervisor to lunch or to your house. When you are not in charge, meet on your own turf as opposed to another's office. After you have both cooled off, work out a cooperative solution to the problem in a favorable environment that supports your integrity as a director. If the arrangement involves changing blocking, make sure that *you* give the cast the appropriate adjustments so you don't lose your authority as director.

Although you may not immediately direct in *professional theater*, you should know its pitfall: financial pressure. Long before rehearsals begin, a director may feel coerced to operate out of the main principle of cost control. (S)he may choose one-set plays with small casts and innocuous ideas that please the lowest common denominator. A typical predicament of a director (name withheld) was described as follows:

> Since we were in a financial crunch, I, the artistic director, sought ways of cutting expenses. I didn't hire an outside director for the musical, which I have no business directing. Because I was only too aware of the financial intricacies, I used inhouse lighting and set designers. I made all the compromises to keep the costs down. Not being a musical director, I delegated the casting to our casting director in conjunction with our musical director who cast performers I would not have chosen for this play. But I figured, well, the casting director knows musicals, and the musical director and choreographer have approved . . . The production ended up being entertaining but dreary. I went along with the wrong mix of people, and it was a disaster from my point of view.

An artistic disaster also results from too few rehearsals. Although highly skilled, your colleagues still need time to work with you creatively. When rehearsals last only two weeks, a director may resort to a clever idea to paste on top of a production. Many professional directors are working in a state of commerce, rather than in any kind of state of grace in which people can be exploratory, nonperformance obligated . . . absorbing and touching their feelings.

Look for ways to heighten creativity. Remember, "All life is an experiment. The more experiments you make the better" (Ralph Waldo Emerson). Makeshift furniture, props, and lights can transform cavernous rehearsal halls into inspirational facilities. Insure that actors can perform comfortably in their new environment and beware of poorly equipped playing and backstage areas.

Resident theater boasts good facilities and staff, but often a pressed staff is dependent on grants and subscriptions. Your colleagues are frequently overworked and simultaneously engaged in other creative projects. Problems occur for a guest director when (s)he doesn't know the limits of authority, the other projects involved, and the services *not* available. Assess your place within the pecking order of the permanent artistic establishment.

Community theater requires adaptation to the social structure of the group. Because community theater tends to attract a self-perpetuating clique of loyal devotees, hidden lines of power are rigidly maintained.

Appraise your authority over the group lest you discover too late that the person controlling final artistic decisions has no background in theater, but much clout within the social organization. You might have to do some socializing to get to know the individuals. If members of the board of trustees like parties, you may find yourself working best with them over a cocktail or lunch. Identify how to inspire an already tightly knit group who have refined their talents through much hands-on experience. Remember, you must either create your own organization or adapt to the demands of an existing one.

Tom Markus claims:

> The only way a director today can be successful without being a good organizer is if that director has an extraordinarily good organizer who is his/her aide-de-camp. That is, it's possible if somebody has either a personal secretary or a production stage manager who does all the work for him/her. But, I have never met a director who was good, and wasn't a good organizer.

Creating an Organization

The ideal situation for many directors is creating your own production organization or restructuring an existing one. Hiring is one of a director's most important jobs, although choosing among unknown people can be a perplexing task. A former employer's enthusiasm in a phone call may indicate one candidate's potential for a strong group commitment. Another sign of a person's ability may be the number of shows (s)he has done with one company, how many times a designer has collaborated with a good director, or how long a technician has worked for a specific theater.

Talking to the person helps you evaluate their commitment and industry. Joseph Chaikin recommends:

> In interviews with artists, directors can look for people that turn them on, that inspire their imagination. Such collaborations will excite continual discoveries because these people are so fascinating to work with. Interesting people will charge and be charged by directors in a back and forth process. Both parties may come up with things that neither of them had thought of before.

When interviewing, listen for any evidence of dissatisfaction likely to resurface, impeding collaboration. Ask candidates if they object to signing agreements. If they do, find out why. Written agreements help you avoid vague arrangements by detailing the nature of assignments. When appropriate, incorporate descriptive clauses limiting people from doing two jobs at once. Often underpaid and compelled by their work, theater people may overbook themselves, and then be unavailable for meetings or rehearsals you had planned.

Working with an Existing Organization

When directors work within effective organizations, their tasks can be easier.

> The director must establish the political hierarchy so that everyone knows who can talk to whom, about what. It is important that all the key decisions about people, money, time, and space be made by one central figure—one

who has an overview of the artistic mission. Without a very clear vision of this, there is going to be chaos. The business manager, for example, may try to decide where money should be spent or withheld; and the business manager can have no idea what that decision will mean to the success of the production in rehearsal. No director has time to get into debates about such matters and so the director ought to be the sole person to make all decisions.

(Tom Markus)

An organization's viability is indicated by how much control a director has over a production and how much is under the jurisdiction of others. For example, some producing directors cast the entire season, choose all costumes, stage sets, and props *before* hiring guest directors. Your subordinate relationship to a producer can prove troublesome when (s)he, though well-intentioned, has low standards.

PRE-PRODUCTION PLANNING

Nothing is orderly til man takes hold of it. Everything in creation lies around loose.

(H.W. Beecher)

For every play you direct, administration, related to your own creative work, or *pre-production planning*, will be necessary. Do not ignore the fact that you depend upon some type of administrative structure for producing the play.

To function effectively, you must know how much decision-making power you have over *artistic concerns*—casting, designers, mise en scene, rehearsing; and *administrative choices*—hiring, budget, facility, box office. Authority can be judged by which staff you control and which is accountable to others, such as the producer or the board of directors. Ask yourself, "Who in this organization gets to say No?"

Assessing the Budget

After evaluating the political hierarchy, you need to determine how to make the play work with the financial resources available. Budget affects most aspects of theater direction. The less funding, the fewer items such as raw lumber, new lighting units, and quality fabric you can purchase for design. The production depends largely on donated talent and materials.

Business-oriented supervisors, who do not experience the hardships and traumas occurring at daily rehearsals may reduce the money allocated for technical labor and materials. Other performing-arts events—lectures and concerts—only need a bare stage! Directors and actors end up exhausted, doing many people's jobs.

Restricted budgets affect actors since unpaid actors donate the most time and energy to the production. If the director can give them even a small stipend, (s)he may have more control over their schedules.

Table 11.1: Budget Proposal Example

Proposed Budget: *Play Title*

Item	Pre-Production	Production	Miscellaneous	Totals
1 Theater rental				
2 Rehearsal hall				
3 Office rental				
4 Office supplies/ equipment				
5 Telephone				
6 Postage				
7 Stationery				
8 Royalties				
9 Script fees				
10 Cast salaries				
11 Crew salaries				
12 Office salaries				
13 Director salary				
14 Designer salaries				
15 Custodian salaries				
16 Publicity costs				
17 Set construction				
18 Furniture rental				
19 Equipment rental				
20 Costume costs				
21 Costume cleaning				
22 Make-up/wig purchases				
23 Box-office staff				
24 Ushers				
25 Program printing				
26 Photographer fee				
27 Refreshments				
28 Tickets/box-office supplies				
29 Utilities				
30 Custodial supplies				
31 Flowers/plants/gifts				
32 Lobby decoration				
33 Transportation/gas				
34 Other				
			TOTAL:	

Assess the budget prior to selecting the play. A little theater with a restricted budget and admission by donation may limit you to choosing a short, contemporary play with a small cast. If the institution wants a musical or a Shakespearean production, with spectacular costumes, sets, and a champagne reception to follow, your funding will need to be expanded. Do not dive into a situation where the excellence of the production depends upon the strenuous overwork of all concerned. In so doing, you perpetuate the myth that quality theater appears magically; and that theater workers—gypsies who complain easily because of their excessive egos—can produce results under *any* conditions.

Usually you are presented with a budget before production begins. Examine all items carefully. The organization's definition of a "production budget" sometimes includes areas that you may overlook: program printing, transportation reimbursements, telephone and postage costs, and costume cleaning bills. The production aspect of the budget may be diminished by miscellaneous hidden expenses. When monies are limited, list production priorities in case you have to choose among several requirements. Table 11.1 lists most costs of a production.

Formal and Informal Contracts

In commercial, professional, and Equity-based theaters, budgets are affected by union contracts protected by professional memberships and implemented by lawyers or agents. Directors (especially guest directors) must be careful about negotiations and should seek legal advice. Note the working rules for the Society of Stage Directors.

SSDC Society of Stage Directors and Choreographers

1501 Broadway　31st Fl.　New York, NY 10036　(212) 391-1070

WORKING RULES & GUIDELINES

1. A copy of your contract to direct or choreograph a production must be filed with the SSDC office prior to the commencement of rehearsals. Under no circumstances may you go into rehearsal without a properly signed contract. The fine for failure to file a copy of your contract before the first day of rehearsal is $250 for Broadway productions and $100 for all other productions.

2. The By-Laws of SSDC, as well as the rules and regulations of the Society, provide for disciplinary action against any member who signs a contract agreeing to fees and royalties less than those stipulated in our Broadway, Off-Broadway, LORT, Stock and Dinner Theatre Minimum Basic Agreements.

3. Society members are required to file form contracts for all employment in SSDC jurisdiction for which such form contracts exist. Failure to follow this requirement will result in a penalty of $100 for each production.

4. No member of the Society may work for a producer whose name is on the Unfair List. If in doubt, check with the Society office.

5. Royalty deferrals must have prior approval of the Society, except for an initial four-week period on Broadway and an initial six-week period Off-Broadway (the weeks need not be consecutive). Failure to obtain approval from the Society for a continuation of royalty deferrals subjects the member to a fine of up to $1000.

GUIDELINES WHEN DEALING WITH MANAGEMENT

1. Notify the Society immediately if you are dismissed.

2. Notify the Society immediately when you replace a member of SSDC on a production.

3. Notify the Society immediately if you do not receive fee or royalties due as stated in your contract.

4. The provisions of the Society's Minimum Basic Agreement with the League of New York Theatres and Producers apply to all contracts, whether Broadway, first-class tours, or bus-and-truck tours.

5. Transportation and per diem must be provided for directors and/or choreographers of any assignment for which they must travel.

6. The minimum basic agreements do not limit the right of the director or choreographer to obtain, through negotiation, higher fees and royalties.

7. Advise your agent and/or attorney that clauses which appropriate the creative work of the director or choreographer may no longer appear in any Broadway or Off-Broadway contract. The work of the director or choreographer may not be appropriated by the producer or author.

8. Pension and welfare contributions by the producer in behalf of the director and choreographer are provided for in all of the Society's minimum basic agreements.

9. If you will be negotiating with a producer who is not a member of the League of New York Theatres and Producers (or COST, CORST, Indoor and Outdoor Musical Stock, Dinner and LORT) or with a producer who does not recognize the Society, it is your responsibility to advise the office immediately.[1]

Also consider informal written arrangements with your nonunion cast, crew, and staff, especially if they are volunteers. A good requirement is to at least get a job description or written letter-of-agreement outlining:

1. minimum number of days present and hours work in the theater
2. administrative and organizational responsibilities
3. fees and reimbursements

Observe the following typical agreements:

Remember: Written agreements can put you at a disadvantage if they bind you so rigidly that flexibility is eliminated, or if you are pressured to fulfill difficult obligations. Agreements with some options and loopholes are preferable to contracts which you cannot maneuver for the good of the production.

---

[1]From "Working Rules and Guidelines," Society of Stage Directors and Choreographers, N.Y. Reprinted by permission.

CONTRACT[a]	**AGREEMENT**[b]
Play Title — Theater — Dates	*Play Title* — Theater — Dates
Name_____, Role (or Job)	Name_____, Role (or Job)
$ Salary Amount for Rehearsal dates and Performance dates extra rehearsals to be paid as follows: ($ amount)	See attached Rehearsal and Production Schedules.
Cast and Crew to be present as requested for:	Cast member to be present at: Crew (List rehearsal times)
Photo session — date Tech run-throughs — dates Press conference — date Trustees Reception — date	Missed rehearsals cannot be made up. Two missed rehearsals may be cause for dismissal.
Salary to be issued weekly by check. Pickup Friday after 12 noon in Business Office.	Each cast-member must give at least 10 crew-hours in pre-production. Arrange times with Technical Director.
See attached Rehearsal Schedule. No individual changes possible.	Cast and crew are entitled to 2 free tickets for each performance.
Signature/Director Signature	Signature/Director Signature
date date	date date

[a]for salaried, nonunion cast and crew   [b]for volunteer cast and crew

EXERCISES

Using the informal agreements reproduced above as guides, write up agreements for the cast and staff members of Henrik Ibsen's *A Doll's House* for:

1. a low-budget, non-Equity theater group in a mid-city location;
2. a college production with unpaid graduate students as leading performers and undergraduates as crew, staff, and administration;
3. a regional theater (salaried cast and crew) where ticket taking, publicity, ushering, refreshments are staffed by unpaid volunteers.

Staff

Besides budgetary matters, accurately assess your staff limitations. Evaluate the particular weaknesses of your assistants and the contribu-

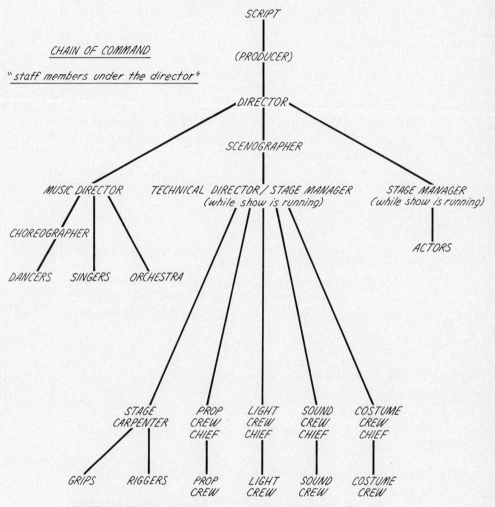

The Production Organization

SCRIPT

CHAIN OF COMMAND

"staff members under the director"

(PRODUCER)

DIRECTOR

SCENOGRAPHER

MUSIC DIRECTOR

TECHNICAL DIRECTOR / STAGE MANAGER
(while show is running)

STAGE MANAGER
(while show is running)

CHOREOGRAPHER

ACTORS

DANCERS   SINGERS   ORCHESTRA

STAGE CARPENTER   PROP CREW CHIEF   LIGHT CREW CHIEF   SOUND CREW CHIEF   COSTUME CREW CHIEF

GRIPS   RIGGERS   PROP CREW   LIGHT CREW   SOUND CREW   COSTUME CREW

Staff: small organizations may combine the duties of various crews; larger ones may subdivide these duties even further.

tions they can reasonably and pleasurably give. For instance, your box office manager may not be able to supervise the house *and* serve refreshments simultaneously.

The production staff has inherent problems of a sensitive nature which directors sometimes misunderstand. Directors, performers, playwrights, designers, and others in creative positions rarely acknowledge the expertise contributed by those in technical and administrative positions. Performers are applauded nightly. Playwrights, designers, and directors are hailed in newspaper reviews, but the staff is taken for granted.

Lack of recognition particularly demoralizes unpaid volunteers, student assistants, interns, apprentices, and part-time clerks earning minimum wage. If they *feel* unappreciated, it is usually because they *are* unappreciated, and they will probably be among the first to show signs of strain.

Establish a good working relationship with crew and staff members before the pressure of rehearsals restricts meeting time. For a fiscally strong, union organization with well-paid crew and staff, one introductory meeting may suffice. However, in college and local theaters be prepared for more staff difficulties and absenteeism as external pressures, such as final exams or social/family obligations, intervene.

Supervising includes almost anything from pulling costumes to lining up ushers for the run of the production; it involves knowing when to step in and when to leave assistants alone. Take a pleasantly supervisory attitude at the beginning of production work so you don't become an intruder after some difficulty has arisen.

Acquire the habit of stopping by occasionally to see how staff work is progressing. In nonunion theaters, you may discover no one is overseeing the less visible departments. However, beware of violating the chain-of-command within the organization and making decisions in areas properly assigned to others. Individual items should be placed under the control of competent staff members under you and the chain of command clarified—as in the following chart prepared by Larry Warner.

Sample: University Theatre Production Administration
Loyola University, New Orleans

I. HOW IT WORKS
   A. *Pre-Season Planning* (during Spring Semester preceding)
     1. Department Faculty elect Director of Theatre
     2. Director of Theatre assembles list of possible play selections from Department Faculty, potential Production Directors, department majors, and his/her own suggestions
     3. Department Faculty and Director of Theatre select the season's productions from this list and select Production Directors and Production Designers (and, if possible at this time, Guest Artists)
     4. Director of Theatre works out production schedule and dates
     5. Director of Theatre plans and puts into operation pre-season activities (including season brochure, securing rights, etc.)
   B. *During Season*
     1. Director of Theatre coordinates the work of all production participants: Publicity, Business Management, Box Office, Technical Director, Production Directors, Designers
     2. Director of Theatre coordinates special events (Alumni Night, President's Night, etc.) with Business Manager and Production Director
     3. Director of Theatre maintains up-to-date accounting of expenses
     4. While each Production Director has artistic autonomy over his/her production,

from casting through closing, the Director of Theatre should maintain contact with each production throughout the season, in his/her capacity as representative of the Department Faculty and Producer

    5. Should disputes arise between members of a production staff, the Director of Theatre will arbitrate between disputants; if disputes cannot be settled by the participants, the Director of Theatre will make final decision on the question; should disputes arise between the Director of Theatre and a Production Director, the Department Faculty will act as arbitor and make a final decision

  C. *After Season*

    1. Director of Theatre reports to the Department Faculty an end-of-season report, containing budget and attendance figures, student and general public reactions and suggestions for the future, etc.

    2. Director of Theatre also acts as resource for his/her successor in questions and advice concerning the future season

II. CHAIN OF COMMAND

  A. The Department Faculty, by virtue of its greater permanence than any other production component, is the final authority in *all* production matters. Concurrently, the Department Faculty is thereby ultimately responsible to the University for all production activities

  B. The Director of Theatre is responsible to the Department Faculty for the general management production activity

  C. The Production Director is responsible to the Director of Theatre for all artistic decisions on the specific production

  D. The Technical Director is responsible to the Production Director

  E. The Production Designer(s) are responsible to the individual Production Director for artistic decisions and to the Technical Director for financial decisions

Problem

You are a guest director in a theater which has volunteer help provided by transcript credit undergraduate students and the social Community Theater Arts Guild; each group claims to be overworked and overlooked in favor of the other.

Solution

Volunteers take on unglamorous theater work for a variety of reasons. When settling disputes or soothing ruffled feelings, remember an organization highly dependent on volunteer aid cannot always obtain ideal personnel.

Two difficulties exist: a *motivation* gap—"serious" students *vs.* "social" adults; and a *generation* gap—"student-age" assistants *vs.* "older" community residents. Meet separately with each group to discuss why problems have arisen, then call a general meeting. Suggest that the Theater Guild visit the university theater to observe their student-interns' involvement and student representatives attend a Guild meeting to appreciate its members' interests.

Time Constraints

Besides personnel and budget, time will limit you. Many productions have to be directed in two or three weeks, and most in less than six weeks.

However, some inexperienced directors create minimal rehearsal schedules rather than exploring the maximum time that would be useful. Time releases you from pressuring colleagues to meet harsh deadlines.

Some directors create extraordinary events because they manage their time and focus on important elements. "When schemes are laid in advance, it is surprising how often the circumstances fit in with them," advises William Osler. The standard scheduling tactic long familiar to daily listmakers is: give "A" priority to tasks which must be accomplished first today; "B" to secondary tasks; and "C" to those which can wait. Base priorities on the long-term benefit you expect from the time and energy invested in the task. Today's deadlines can be crucial steps to a big payoff.

Problem

Your rehearsal schedule for the production is too long.

Solution

1. Reevaluate the time provided for given tasks. For example, coaching sessions can be held on specified weekday afternoons, run-throughs on certain evenings. Contain your work with particular individuals to a specific number of days per week and hours per day.
2. Set definite start and finish times for rehearsals and meetings; then log (and later assess) your use of time.
3. List the purpose of each rehearsal—technical rehearsals, climax scenes, musical aids, and so forth—and examine its importance to the overall impact of the production.
4. Evaluate which company members could complete their necessary assignments in less time.

PUBLICITY

Next to preplanning, generating *publicity* may tax your administrative skills. Since few people realize the demanding nature of excellent publicity, some theaters eagerly assume that directors *want* to do their own publicity. Others resign themselves to tiny audiences. Find out if a "hidden" responsibility to generate audiences exists for you, and familiarize yourself with some basic strategies. Many directors don't choose a script because of its promotability, but as soon as they pick one, they begin thinking about how to promote it.

Besides attracting an opening-night audience, publicity should project a "quality-image" of the theater organization. Promoting a production involves industry, expertise, and a willingness to invest funds, time, and effort. One director discusses this commitment:

I do a great deal of budget projection and allocation, living within certain budgets, tying promotional aspects of a play in with production aspects, so we can promote what it is we're putting on. For example, with our last play, we had cast changes, script changes, personnel problems, design problems. But all the time that we were having those, I knew that our publicity department had to have open access to the people in the rehearsals to promote the show correctly. So when the director would say, "We can't have anybody in today," I would say, "We have a feature that's coming out Thursday, and that feature writer has got to see part of the rehearsal today so they know what the heck they're writing about!"

Some large performing arts organizations support permanent publicity/public relations departments with busy assistants properly wording press releases and whisking programs to the printer on time. Specialized work in visual advertising (posters, brochures, mailers) is jobbed out to graphic artwork companies. Only heavily subsidized professional theaters can afford to pay independent agencies to produce complete publicity campaigns.

Publicity can be well-planned and designed even on a low budget. Press releases must be properly typed and mailed on time, and flyers nicely designed, free of informational errors (even if photocopied at a shopping-mall machine). Similarly, program/playbills (even those produced on a limited budget) can look professional and project a positive image of the production to the audience. Few people know the technical difference between type*setting* (done by a professional printer) and type*writing* (any typewriter). However, most people subconsciously withdraw from advertising that does not look "professional." A director of *Hamlet* might prefer a distinctive advertisement, but even a light-hearted comedy deserves an attractive public announcement.

Free Advertising

Some advertising is linked to public relations. For example, small-budget theater organizations often rely on the good will of local newspapers, radio stations, and Calendars-of-Events for free announcements and descriptions of their upcoming productions. This information is usually sent to the media through *press releases*, typed information with photo included.

Newspapers, radio stations, and other mass-communication organizations are not required to use press releases. The theater has no control over the amount of information taken, the wording, or decision whether or not to print a publicity photo. The theater might send a three-page press release listing the entire cast and crew, some background information on the play, and an interesting scene shot with leading actors engaged in a fencing duel. But the editor may have room on the Entertainment page for only four free sentences to announce the play, performance dates, and a phone number for ordering tickets. These pages may already be filled with *paid* advertising for movies, sports, concerts, fairs, and restaurants. If your theater wants to guarantee space,

COLLEGE THEATRE

Program: a simple design using available illustrations can be effectively produced on a limited budget.
Design: N.M. Boretz. Costume illustration from *French Fashion Plates from the Gazette du Bon Ton* by LePape, Dover Publications, 1979.

you must pay for it. Otherwise, you rely on an editor's goodwill or a slow day in the news.

To insure the press release looks professional to the receiving editor, check it over for stylistic errors, proper wording, and correct spelling of names. Press releases should always be typed, double-spaced, with wide margins on both sides for marking by the receiving editor. The crucial information should be included in the first few sentences. If the theater has a letterhead—printed stationery—use it for press releases.

Should the photograph not look professional, it will not reprint well. Never send instant film or color snapshots to a newspaper. Discuss the photo session with your theater's publicist. If possible, a professional photographer should take scene shots—in full costume for a period piece. During pre-production planning, arrange in advance for per-

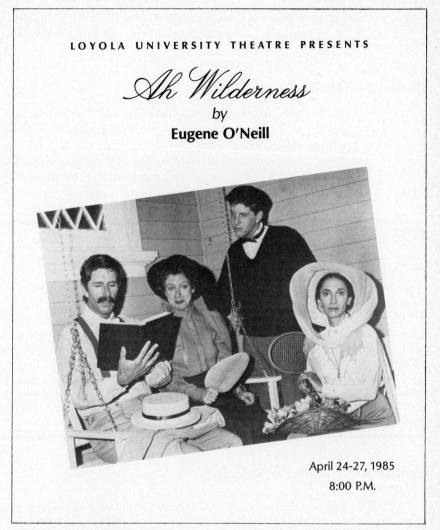

LOYOLA UNIVERSITY THEATRE PRESENTS

Ah Wilderness
by
Eugene O'Neill

April 24-27, 1985
8:00 P.M.

Advertising Announcement: typeset by a professional printer with an eye-catching photograph, a "flyer" reflects the quality of the production.
Design: Loyola University, New Orleans. With David Greenan. Directed by R. H. O'Neill.

formers to come in earlier before a rehearsal for photos to be taken. The photo session should take place in time for developing and choosing film for press releases, so they can be sent two or three weeks prior to opening night. Arrange for the costumer and lighting technician to be ready and available for the photo session. Photos of actors rehearsing in jeans and T-shirts are useless. If the actual costumes are not available, urge the costumer to get as close as possible to the "look" of the play. Newspapers tend to choose action-oriented closeups of two to four actors. Since not every performer can be pictured, choose four representative actors you can costume with flair. If the set is not built, go to a place similar to it, outside the theater, to capture the atmosphere of the play.

Paid Advertising

More easily acquired, paid adverusing will *definitely* be printed or announced. Advertising managers of newspapers and local radio stations provide sound advice. They can also tell you the best days or times for theater advertising and provide technical assistance regarding effective size, length, and information to be included. Sometimes they have discount rates for nonprofit or educational theater.

Problem

Your assistant director did not notice that "advertising" was not budgeted nor student assistants assigned to publicity for your college production. Opening night looms three weeks away, and the campus community is unaware of the upcoming production.

Solution

1. See if a small amount of remaining money can be used for advertising. Photocopy neatly designed flyers—the least costly form of "printed" advertising. When possible, print enough to place in every student and faculty campus mailbox.
2. If the budget cannot absorb the price of a large ad in the campus newspaper, try a few well-worded lines in the classified section, several of which you may be able to place over the three-week period. Recruit student help to set up tables for advance ticket sales in well-trafficked areas on campus.

Public Relations/Socializing

Few of our plays can boast of more wit than I have heard him speak at supper.
(Sir George Etherege, 1635–1691)

Besides publicizing, many directors have social obligations within the theatrical organization. Usually the fund raiser as well as policy maker, an artistic director performs this ongoing duty. Socializing for directors involves public relations for particular projects, productions, or upcoming benefit performances. You may be asked to attend lectures, seminars, receptions, dinners, or cocktail parties sponsored by the Alumni Association, Donor Committee, Friends of the Theater, Faculty Club, Chamber of Commerce, and Flower Society. Success for local theaters sometimes depends upon the goodwill of professional and charitable groups. Their members contribute to the theater, attend special events, and elicit funding from the surrounding community. A socially adept director enhances the theater image and establishes contact with present and future audience members.

CONCLUSION

The Director as Artist has introduced you to the array of roles played by modern directors, with the goal of inspiring serious study and engagement in your directing. Participate fully in your directing training because you are the future of our theater. Through you, the actors, designers, and musicians create their miracles. On every directing project, you initiate the action.

FINAL PROJECTS

BUDGET

1. Analyze the budget (see Assessing the Budget). List at least *three* items *you* might omit. Give a *reason* for each exclusion.
2. Using this budget as a sample guide, decide on priorities for a production of *The Glass Menagerie* by Tennessee Williams for
   • a college theater
   • a community theater
   • a subscription audience regional theater
3. Write an itemized production budget request to the Trustees Committee for a summer-stock production of *The Glass Menagerie*. Include a one-page addendum for advertising, managerial, and administrative expenses.

STAFF

1. Arrange for an in-class staff meeting with volunteers for your production of Arthur Miller's *The Crucible*. Describe what you expect of everyone and ask how they perceive their duties.
2. Make up a *Crucible* master worksheet as well as individual worksheets for crew and staff in a community theater. Include *job descriptions* for each category and/or each staff member. Be sure to consider who needs to be present at rehearsals and who can work outside the rehearsal schedule. Meet with the staff to discuss worksheets.
3. In class, ask classmates to take on specified administrative or technical tasks. Then, as director-supervisor, make appointments to visit them at work and discuss their progress.
4. Meet with your tech and theater maintenance crew. Ask what is going most slowly and see if it is a people problem (Is everyone working efficiently?) or a practical problem (Are they waiting for ordered equipment which has not yet been delivered?). Discuss.

TIME AND PUBLICITY

1. Choose a five-minute scene to direct with a one-week rehearsal schedule and stage the scene in class. Hand in a time-sheet evalua-

tion, citing the length and accomplishments of each rehearsal and where the most time was wasted. Determine what areas of concentration would be most beneficial for the actors in a short rehearsal.

2. Choose another class member on your "publicity staff" to design an advertisement for the scene to be distributed via campus mailboxes as well as to an off-campus mailing list. Discuss the quality and effectiveness of the announcement. Available art materials require only a straight-edge ruler and black, felt-tip pen.

3. Arrange for an outdoor lunchtime performance of the scene.

Glossary

action: what the actor/character is doing.

above: a movement or location toward the rear of the stage away from the audience.

acting area: (a) stage space occupied by actors; (b) unit of stage lighting prepared for lighting (of acting).

aesthetic: appreciating what is beautiful in theater arts onstage.

aesthetic distance: the physical and psychological separation of the spectator from the performance being viewed.

all-over: textile pattern arrangements of design shapes which produce the same visual effect from all viewing angles.

analysis: the examination of the script's parts for the playwright's meaning or philosophy.

antagonist: the character in a play who opposes the actions or desires of the main character or protagonist.

arena staging: theater in the round; the action occurs in the center area of a square or circle with the audience surrounding the acting area on four sides.

Aristotelian play structure: the arrangement of a play's elements into exposition, inciting action, rising action, climax, and resolution.

Aristotelian plot: a mounting sequence of incidents created by a *single* action.

asbestos curtain: "fire curtain" usually located in front of the act curtain.

back lighting: light coming from above and behind actors facing the audience.

backdrop *(drop)***:** large cloth (canvas or muslin) sheet on which designs or scene settings are painted, generally placed upstage.

backing: pieces of scenery placed to prevent the audience from seeing into the backstage areas.

balance: weight, number, or proportion in a composition.

balance *(asymmetrical)***:** dissimilar proportions on either side of the center line of the stage balancing each other.

balance *(symmetrical)***:** two groups placed equally distant from the center to create an exact equal grouping on both sides from an imaginary center.

balcony spotlight: spotlight mounted on the balcony's front or railing to light the stage.

base hue: pure hue from which varying shades of color are derived.

beam: (a) abbreviation for "light beam" or "ceiling beam"; (b) cone of light from an instrument which can direct light into a narrow angle of emission.

beat: a small section or "bit" of a scene usually focusing on one action, topic, or impulse.

below: a position, location, or movement close to the audience and away from the back of the theater.

black out: a sudden interruption of lighting which may frequently be used to punctuate an ending of a scene or act.

blocking: the movement used by the actors to support the action of the script.

body positions: the placement and arrangement of actors' facings.

boom: (a) vertical mounting for lighting instruments; (b) color-changing device attached to spotlight.

border: (a) borderlight—row of lights usually hung above the stage; (b) scenic element or drapery hung above acting area to mask upper stagehouse; (c) textile pattern arrangement with dominant design shapes along one edge.

box set: a traditionally realistic setting with three walls, representing an interior space.

business: (a) the handling of a property or some physical, largely stationary activity, done by the character; (b) the fiscal management of a theater.

cable: two or more electrical conductors (wires) combined in one outer covering of insulating material.

callboard: a bulletin board located backstage on which important notices for company members are posted.

cat walk: a narrow platform that connects the fly gallery on both sides of the stage.

character: a role in a play.

character action: how the character performs the action; the quality of the action.

character analysis: an examination, normally written, of all the possible characteristics and actions for each individual character in a play.

characterization: the distinguishing quality of a role, resulting from *how* the character performs the action.

circumstances: the profession, family, habits, and social conditioning of the characters.

climax: the highest dramatic moment or the turning point of a major conflict from which the rest of the play winds down.

closed auditions: tryouts permitting only performing actors to enter audition areas.

color wheel: a rotating disk

operating manually or by remote control that consists of different-colored gels attached to a spotlight.

comedy: a light, amusing play that typically has a happy ending.

composition: the arrangement of the actors with each other physically in a stage space.

conflict: the clash between the scene's hostile or opposing forces.

conflict of opposing needs: friction reinforcing distinctions between characters, often by pitting the action of each against that of the other.

contrast: emphasis through opposites, such as using differing outlines against each other to create emphasis.

control board: switchboard; control unit with switches for stage lighting.

costume parade: technical rehearsal where actors try on their costumes then test them out onstage under lights.

counter focus: secondary line emphasis, serving as a strengthening element, whereby a small portion of a group looks in a direction other than that of the dominant figure.

counter: the movement by an upstage character when another passes downstage.

counterweight system: a structure for flying scenery by using weights, pulleys, ropes, etc.

covering: an actor's movement downstage of other actors or objects to hide them from the audience.

critique: remarks providing the feedback necessary to assist someone in mastering difficult moments.

cross fading: the simultaneous dissolving of light in one area while light in another is intensified, used in a theater to indicate a change of scene.

cross (*open*): an actor crossing the stage keeping the front of the body in view of the audience.

cue-to-cue rehearsal: the practice where the director only runs sections of the play that cue predetermined technical effects.

cue sheet: chart compiled for an operator to run lighting and sound for a production.

curtain line: (a) last line spoken by an actor as the scene ends; (b) imaginary marking used as reference by designer for stage measurements.

cyclorama: device (e.g., large curtain) to represent unending space or sky; may be simple drapery.

dead hung: lighting or other equipment mounted permanently above stage; difficult to raise or lower.

depth space: the space that downstage actors or objects command in the upstage planes.

depth: the distance from the back wall of the stage to its edge.

designer (*for theater*):   artist who conceptualizes and oversees the visual design for an entire production; most tend to specialize as set, costume, or lighting designers.

diction: the spoken dialogue and literary character.

dimmer: device used for gradual variation in lighting intensity.

direct focus: emphasizing the actor by using actual line; this line can either be one line, created by placing an actor downstage to the one emphasized, or by two lines, created by putting a second figure downstage.

dissolve: the fading of one scene into or out of another; the transition from one sequence into the next.

diversified emphasis: arranging four, five, six, or more characters so that the audience's attention can go from one character to another at various times in the scene.

dock: storage space designed especially for flats, sometimes used for a set storage area.

drama: a largely serious play portraying life and character through dialogue and action.

dramaturg: a person providing consultation about literary or historical aspects of a script or production period.

dress rehearsal: practice, usually the last one before

opening, in which the actors wear costumes and rehearse under performance conditions.

dress stage: spreading out actors or balancing them onstage.

drop: a piece of scenery made of canvas hung in the flies in the "lowered" position or "dropped" into the scene.

duoemphasis: focusing attention on two characters of equal importance, when the spine of the scene is carried by both.

dutchman: a piece of canvas tacked and glued across the crack between the front surface of two flats and painted the color of the set.

electrician (*gaffer*):   in professional theater, a union member who operates or repairs lighting equipment (not the lighting *designer*).

elevator: a section of stage floor mechanically raised and lowered; in large theaters, it may rise as high as two stories.

emotional memory: an actor's recalling inner images from personal events to help reexperience the scene and evoke an emotional response onstage.

emphasis: "leading the eye"; it places special importance on a specific point in a composition and tells the audience where to look, at what to look, and when to look.

encounter scene: a scene about the emotional involvement or conflict between characters.

environmental scene: a scene emphasizing the surroundings and growing organically out of the space.

event scene: a scene about a specific situation.

exit line: the easiest line on which to leave the stage; often describing, explaining, or demonstrating the exit; e.g., "Please go"; "See you soon."

exposition the play's structural unit in which all needed information for the audience to relate to the events of the play is supplied.

externalized performance: acting too broadly for the audience rather than against the scene's opponents.

farce: a ridiculous play dealing with outrageous events and impossible situations; e.g., disguises, chases, "pie" throwing, etc.

fill light: light that fills in shadows to prevent them from appearing black.

flats: scenery painted on canvas and mounted on heavy wood strips, folded like screens or separated to store "flat."

flies *(fly loft):* space above stage where scenery and lights are raised out of audience view.

floor cloth *(ground cloth):* a canvas piece covering the stage used to lessen sound of shoes on the wood floor and decrease the reflection of light.

floor plan *(groundplan):* drawing of stage including settings as seen from above; generally simplified for use by the director, technicians, actors.

focus: the use of line to strengthen emphasis, which directs our vision to particular points within the stage arrangement.

FOH *(front-of-house):* illumination generated from audience-space and aimed at actors on stage (for example, from "balcony-light").

follow spot: a spotlight placed in the front of the house to focus on and "follow" the actor moving about the stage; frequently used in musicals.

form: the silhouette, outline, or shape in a composition.

foul: electrical rigging term for *dangerous* tangling of scenery and lines in fly loft.

fourth wall: the imaginary side of the room toward the audience that theoretically has been removed so that the audience can observe the play.

fresnel: spotlight with special lens which produces soft-edge beam.

funnel: (a) neckline of costume cut high and in one piece with bodice; (b) device used to limit beam spread on spotlights (also called *high hat*).

gelatin: a thin sheet of colored transparent material placed in front of a lighting instrument to add color to the light.

general illumination: light spread over most of stage and not focused on specific areas.

genre: a type of drama, such as tragedy, melodrama, comedy, farce, etc.

give stage: to allow focus to settle on the dominant figure onstage.

grand master: device which controls all other units for lighting operated by switchover dimmer handles.

gridiron: the structural framework over the stage that supports equipment used in flying scenery.

grip: stagehand who moves scenery.

groundplan: a scale drawing indicating all of the walls and objects that occupy floor space onstage.

hand prop: small item used or handled by actors (larger *properties* may be placed onstage but not moved or picked up during scenes).

heads up: a warning alert to signify that an object is either falling or being lowered.

history: actor's story, based on the script, of the character's past life including the time, place, surroundings, circumstances, and relationships of the character.

hold: stop dialogue and actions for laughter or applause.

holding the book: to follow closely the script of the play, prompting actors, crossing out cut lines, adding in any new ones, and writing in all stage action and business.

house lights: lighting in the audience area; usually off or dimmed during performances; on (or "up") while the audience arrives and departs and during intermission.

improvisation: the actor's on-the-spot enactment of a situation by using ad-libbed dialogue and spontaneous actions.

inciting incident: the significant, initial event that starts the conflict moving in a script; it may occasionally occur before the opening of the play.

indirect focus: a roundabout line emphasis using a mazelike effect which eventually gives predominance to one figure.

inner image: the substitution or personal source used by the actor to motivate the action.

inner problem: unsettled question, a source of perplexity or delight that the character is dealing with.

intensity: (a) brightness or dullness of a color hue; (b) power of a light source.

internalized performance: acting with too little energy or inner life and insufficiently responding externally to the conflict.

interpreter: one who brings to realization by performance the meaning of a play.

key sheet: a tabulation of all the stage manager signals for different sound cues, entrance of action, changes in light, etc.

kill: to eliminate a prop, piece of scenery, action, etc.

klieglight: trademark name for theater spotlights manufactured by Kliegl Bros.; "klieg" is commonly used to refer to any theater spotlight.

lash line: soft rope used to tie flats together.

layout: the distribution of electrical equipment for a production specified in the working plans and drawings.

leg *(leg drop)*:   drapery hung in the wings to mask extreme sides of stage and backstage from audience view.

levels: differing heights from the stage floor; also series of platforms onstage; wider than steps and used as performance areas.

light area: the location onstage to be covered by two spotlights hitting from right and left; many interior sets have six light areas.

line: the real or imaginary direction in a composition.

lines: the ropes attached to the top of curtains, flats, etc., that are flown in over the stage set.

"loading a scene":   heightening its emotional level by intensifying conflict.

loading doors: large double doors through which the scenery is brought onto the stage from the outside.

magic "if":   phrase used to create the feeling of truth when you say, "*If* the stage conflict were true, then I would do such and such, then I would behave in this manner."

manager: person responsible for the needs of all production people and actors.

masking: concealing from the view of the audience any part of the action.

mass: the amount of material or the distribution of weight in a composition.

module: dimension chosen by designers or scenographers to serve as a standard measurement for construction; more economic in building, with possibilities for multiple use.

monologue: solitary speech where conflict depends on the warring forces within one actor.

motivation: why a character does something or wants something.

move on: moving toward the center of the stage from either side; *move off* has the opposite meaning.

movement: any change of an actor's place or position onstage.

movement *on*, *before*, and *after* **the line:**   the three possibilities uniting movement and dialogue; normally the movement should come *on* the line.

multiple setting: a variety of sets within one simultaneous setting; several locations coexist on the same stage and the action moves from one part of the stage to the next.

notes: specific informal suggestions directors give to company members.

objective: what the character wants, that drives the action.

objects: "weapons" actors use to implement the verbal battle waged in the scene.

obstacle: what's in the way of the action.

obstacle *(mental)*: an interior unseen block to character action.

obstacle *(physical)*: external block to character action that does not have to be imagined by the actor.

offstage emphasis: an arrangement of actors to focus on an offstage event.

open auditions: tryout where everyone auditioning is invited into the room so the director can call freely upon a range of actors.

open turn: the process of the actor turning out in view of the audience; the opposite of *closed turn.*

operating line *(hauling line)*: heavy rope used to pull arbor (steel frame with counterweights) up and down.

period *(period play)*: historical time period defined by certain dress and fashion decor.

physical action *(physicalization)*: external action that evolves from the character's objective in the scene.

physical traits: movements, patterns, and external appearances such as the costumes, hairdos, make-up, accessories of the characters.

picturization: the meaning suggested through the composition or arrangement of the actors to each other physically in a stage space.

pin rail: a long beam built into the wall of the stage building and running the full depth of the playing part of the stage; pins to the pulley line may be fastened so the end of lines pass through overhead pulleys on the grid and are brought down on the one side of the stage.

pit: the sunken area in front of the stage in which the orchestra plays.

places: an order used by the stage manager or director to summon actors and technicians to their stage areas for a scene to begin.

plane: the depth, height, and width of stage space that a surface dominates, e.g., up right, center, etc.

plasticity: good stage lighting that emphasizes the three-dimensional qualities of performers and stage set.

playing space: the portion of the stage space that is within the sight lines or vision of the audience.

plot: the mechanics of dramatic storytelling.

plug: a piece of scenery placed in the opening of a unit such as a window, door, or archway to create a change in function.

pocket: metal receptacles sunken below the level of the stage floor that contain outlets for electric current from the switchboard.

poles *(character)*: central characteristics of each part necessary to the unfolding of the story.

practical: something used for a functional as opposed to a decorative purpose, such as a window that can be opened and closed.

preblocking: an estimate of where characters enter and move to.

preliminary blocking: gauging the bases and boundaries of movement.

press release: typed, double-spaced, one-page announcement, containing vital information about an upcoming play, to be sent to the media for publicity purposes.

privacy scene: a scene of seclusion, where the solitary individual has an interior focus.

projector *(slide projector)*: device for producing images on a surface or screen.

prompt book: the director's working script including notes about character, lights, sound, blocking, and other plans for the production.

properties *(props)*: all movable objects or set pieces needed for the action of the play. Large objects such as pieces of furniture are called "stage props" and small objects are called "hand props."

proscenium: the wall containing the permanent arch dividing the auditorium from the stage.

proscenium stage: a picture-frame stage with audience in front only.

protagonist: the main active character whose actions and desires propel the spine of the play.

rake: slanting the floor at an angle; the stage floor and the auditorium floor may both be banked upward toward the back.

reinforcement: strengthening emphasis by relating an actor to a scenic unit such as to a doorway or window.

relationship: a character's ties or connection to other people, places, things, and events.

relaxation: absence of unnecessary tension blocking expressive physical action.

repetition: copying figures to strengthen emphasis and add support through form.

research: the investigation of facts to support you in assessing and manifesting the nature of the play.

return:　a flat or piece of drapery placed downstage when the set is narrower than the space ordinarily allowed between the tormentors.

revolving stage:　a turntable or circular disk which pivots at the center; settings may be placed on this turntable to create quick changes of scenery.

rhythm:　a regularly recurring accent or pattern in a play, determined by the nature of the play itself, its genre, its dialogue, characters, place, events, and, above all, its action.

rigging:　the pulley and rope attached to the gridiron and used to fly scenery or a light instrument.

rope line rigging:　a system of rope blocks and pulleys used to fly scenery over the stage set.

rundown sheet:　a listing of each act's scenes and characters to determine the logical development of the action.

scene breakdown:　production plan of the various ingredients onstage.

scenic movement:　the scene's visual and aural environment.

scene tag:　phrase description of a scene's action.

scenographer:　artist and design supervisor who, in consultation with the director, works on both conceptual and practical ideas for production and then oversees the actual work of designers, technicians, and assistants.

schedules:　charts listing equipment, hookups, etc., for lighting plots.

scoop:　(a) floodlight with scoop-shaped aluminum reflector; (b) curved neckline of costume cut low in front and wide on shoulders.

score:　(a) the actor's record of the components (action, objective, obstacle, inner image) of each scene; (b) the director's record or scene breakdown of the various ingredients onstage.

scoring:　the division of the play into units or beats to study its structure.

scrim:　thin fabric which seems opaque when front lighted, and transparent when light is focused on objects behind.

sequence:　a regular recurrence or repetition of a proportional space between figures.

set line:　the outline of the complete set in relation to the stage floor.

set prop:　property used for appearance only; *unlike* a hand or practical prop, it may be nonfunctional.

shape:　the form of an arrangement, largely responsible for the mood or emotional feeling aroused in the spectator.

share:　to create equal dramatic emphasis between two or more characters in a scene.

side lighting: lighting directed at the sides of the performers as they face the house.

sight lines: lines on a ground-plan indicating the audience's view from all areas of the house including the most extreme seats.

single emphasis: focus on one principal actor at a time.

sound: the aural design including live or taped music and sound effects.

space: empty area around a figure which can be used to distinguish it and establish dominance through isolation.

space staging (*open staging*)**:** stage arrangement where the primary design element is lighting.

special: a spotlight aimed so that it covers a special person or area important to the action.

spectacle: the visual aspect of the production designed to appeal to the eye by its signs, proportions, colors.

spine: the through line of action or driving force in a scene, play, or character.

spotlight: all single units that direct a ray of light to a designated area.

stability: using the weight of characters on the down left and down right areas of the stage to tie down the picture to the stage.

stage areas: the various acting locations onstage, composed of planes and levels.

state of mind: emotional state that, like a metal net, supports and contains all the inner images.

steal (*ease, cheat,* or *drop*)**:** inconspicuous movement by an actor into a different position or area.

strike: taking the set apart and offstage after production run ends; also putting away costumes, accessories, and props.

strip light: a row of low-watt bulbs producing a shadowless illumination and used for toning and blending.

strobe light: light designed to flash frequently producing flickering effect.

structured improvisation: exercise aimed at strengthening the scope of the scene's conflict by combining the use of spontaneous ad-libbed actions within the limits of time, place, relationship, circumstance, etc., of a scene.

stylization: the manner of producing a specific production, related to its period, or to a specific vision of the director.

subtext: thoughts and feelings an actor uses to create the character's inner life beneath the lines.

switchboard (*control console*)**:** the source of distribution of all electric current to lighting instruments onstage.

take stage: to claim a more dominant position in relation to another actor; the opposite of *give* or *share stage*.

teaser: first piece of canvas above the stage between the two borders.

technical rehearsal *(tech)***:** any practice involving the use of lights, sounds, stage sets, costumes, or make-up.

technician: craftsperson who executes the set, costume, or lighting plot called for in the design.

tempo: a steady progression, a formula that is repeated or a pattern uniformly built up.

theme: message of the play that evolves through the characters' words and actions.

thickness piece: material attached to the edge of a flat to give it the look of a real wall.

thought: the idea of the play's statement.

three unities: one time, place, and action in a play's structure.

throwaway part: small, shapeless, or incidental role that can be performed in many ways.

thrust stage: a combination of proscenium and arena stage in which the audience is seated on three sides of the stage, and the fourth provides some opportunity for scenic backing.

tormentor light: spotlight mounted offstage from either tormentor.

tormentors: curtains hung at sides of proscenium opening.

tragedy: a serious play which excites pity and terror by a succession of unhappy events, and in which typically, the lead character is by some passion or limitation brought to catastrophe.

trap: a movable section of the stage floor often used for magical or special effects.

unit stage: a playing space made up of steps, ramps, and platforms that remain unchanged for different plays and scenes in a play.

visual line focus: a form of direct focus, where an actor looking at an object attracts others to do likewise.

vomitorium: one of two entrances on the downstage sides of thrust or adapted arena stages in which the actors enter the stage by a ramp or stairs.

winch: machine used for hauling ropes and cables, or lifting very heavy objects.

wing-and-drop setting: an arrangement composed of a backdrop and side flats leading up to it; several wing-and-drop settings can be placed behind the initial one.

work lights: inexpensive onstage lights (not spotlights) used at rehearsals and during scenery set-ups.

Bibliography

GENERAL

Allensworth, Carl with Dorothy Allensworth and Clayton Rawson. *The Complete Play Production Handbook*. New York: Harper & Row, 1982.

Armer, Alan A. *Directing Television and Film*. Belmont, Ca.: Wadsworth, 1986.

Arnott, Peter. *The Theatre in Its Time: An Introduction*. Boston: Little, Brown & Co., 1981.

Artaud, Antonin. *The Theatre and Its Double*. New York: Grove Press, 1958.

Baker, Paul. *Integration of Abilities: Exercises for Creative Growth*. New Orleans: Anchorage Press, 1977.

Balukhaty, S.D., *The Seagull Produced by Stanislavski*. London: Dennis Dobson, 1952.

Barry, Jackson. *Dramatic Structure: The Shaping of Experience*. Berkeley: University of California Press, 1970.

Beckerman, Bernard. *Dynamics of Drama*. New York: Drama Book Specialists, 1970.

Bladel, Roderick. *Walter Kerr: An Analysis of His Criticism*. Metuchen, N.J.: Scarecrow Press, 1976.

Blau, Herbert. *The Impossible Theater*. New York: Collier Books, 1965.

Boleslavski, Richard. *Acting: The First Six Lessons*. New York: Theatre Arts Books, 1933.

Borchardt, Donald A. *Think Tank Theatre*. Lanham, Md.: University Press of America, 1984.

Braun, Edward. *The Director and the Stage*. New York: Holmes & Meier, 1982.

Brockett, Oscar G. *History of the Theatre* (3d ed.). Boston: Allyn and Bacon, 1977.

Brook, Peter. *The Empty Space*. New York: Atheneum, 1968.

Carra, Lawrence. *Controls in Play Directing*. New York: Vantage Press, 1985.

Clurman, Harold. *The Fervent Years: The Group Theatre and the Thirties*. New York: ADA Capo Paperback, 1983.

———. *On Directing*. New York: Macmillan, 1972.

Cohen, Robert. *Acting Power*. Palo Alto, Ca.: Mayfield, 1978.

———. *Theatre*. Palo Alto, Ca.: Mayfield, 1981.

Cohen, Robert and John Harrop. *Creative Play Direction*. Englewood Cliffs, N.J.: Prentice-Hall, 1974.

Cole, David. *The Theatrical Event*. Middletown, Conn.: Wesleyan University Press, 1975.

Cole, Toby and Helen Chinoy (Eds.). *Directors on Directing*. Indianapolis: Bobbs-Merrill, 1963.

Corrigan, Robert W. *The Making of Theatre From Drama to Performance*. Glenview, Ill.: Scott, Foresman & Co., 1981.

Craig, David. *On Singing Onstage*. New York: Schirmer Books, 1978.

Dean, Alexander. *Fundamentals of Play Directing* (4th ed.). Revised by Lawrence Carra. New York: Holt, Rinehart and Winston, 1980.

Dietrich, John E. and Ralph W. Duckwall. *Play Direction* (2d ed.). Englewood Cliffs, N.J.: Prentice-Hall, 1983.

Epstein, Helen. *The Companion She Keeps: Tina Packer Builds a Theater*. Cambridge, Mass.: Plunkett Lane Press, 1985.

Esslin, Martin. *An Anatomy of Drama*. New York: Farrar, Straus, and Giroux, 1979.

Gelb, Arthur and Barbara. *O'Neill*. New York: Harper & Row, 1960.

George, Kathleen. *Rhythm in Drama*. Pittsburgh, Penn.: University of Pittsburgh Press, 1980.

Goodwin, John. *Peter Hall's Diaries*. London: Hamish Hamilton, 1983.

Gorchakov, Nikolai M. *Stanislavski Directs*. New York: Grosset and Dunlap. Translation by Miriam Goldina. Copyright 1954, Funk and Wagnalls 1962, Harper & Row.

Grote, David. *Script Analysis, Reading and Understanding the Playscript for Production*. Belmont, Ca.: Wadsworth Publishing, 1985.

Grotowski, Jerzy. *Towards a Poor Theatre*. New York: Simon & Schuster, 1969.

Guthrie, Sir Tyrone. *A Life in the Theatre*. New York: McGraw-Hill, 1959.

———. *Astonish Us in the Morning*. Detroit: Wayne State University Press, 1977.

———. *In Various Directions*. Westport, Conn.: Greenwood Press, 1979.

Hagen, Uta. *Respect for Acting*. New York: Macmillan, 1973.

Hayman, Ronald. *How to Read a Play*. Great Britain: Eyre Methuen, 1977.

Hethmon, Robert (Ed.). *Strasberg at the Actor's Studio*. New York: Viking Press, 1965.

Hodge, Frances. *Play Directing: Analysis, Communication, and Style*. Englewood Cliffs, N.J.: Prentice-Hall, 1971.

King, Nancy. *Theatre Movement: The Actor and His Space*. New York: DBS Publications, 1972.

Lessac, Arthur. *Body Wisdom: The Use and Training of the Human Body*. New York: DBS Publications, 1981.

Linkletter, Kristen. *Freeing the Natural Voice*. New York: DBS Publications, 1976.

Marker, Lise-Lone and Frederick, J. *Ingmar Bergman: Four Decades in the Theatre*. Cambridge, England: Cambridge University Press, 1982.

Patterson, Michael. *Peter Stein, Germany's Leading Theatre Director*. Cambridge, England: Cambridge University Press, 1981.

Saint-Denis, Michel. *Theatre: The Rediscovery of Style*. New York: Theatre Arts Books, 1976.

Schechner, Richard. *The End of Humanism*. New York:

Performing Arts Journal Publications, 1982.

Shurtleff, Michael. *Audition.* New York: Walker & Company, 1978.

Sievers, W. David, Harry E. Stiver, Jr., and Stanley Rahan. *Directing for the Theatre* (3d ed.). Dubuque, Iowa: William C. Brown, 1974.

Simonson, Lee. *The Stage Is Set.* New York: Theatre Arts Books, 1963.

Spolin, Viola. *Improvisation for the Theatre: A Handbook of Teaching and Directing Technique.* Evanston, Ill.: Northwestern University Press, 1963.

Stanislavski, Konstantin. *An Actor Prepares.* Translated by Elizabeth Reynolds Hapgood. New York: Theatre Arts Books, 1948.

————. *Building a Character.* Translated by Elizabeth Reynolds Hapgood. New York: Theatre Arts Books, 1949.

————. *Creating a Role.* Translated by Elizabeth Reynolds Hapgood. New York: Theatre Arts Books, 1961.

————. *My Life in Art.* Translated by J.J. Robbins. New York: Theatre Arts Books, 1924.

Stransky, Judith with Robert B. Stone. *The Alexander Technique: Joy in the Life of Your Body.* New York: Beaufort Books, 1981.

Styan, J.L. *The Elements of Drama.* Cambridge, England: Cambridge University Press, 1979.

————. *The Dramatic Experience.* Cambridge, England: Cambridge University Press, 1983.

————. *Drama, Stage, and Audience.* London: Cambridge University Press, 1975.

————. *Max Reinhardt.* Cambridge, England: Cambridge University Press, 1982.

Toporkov, Vasily Osipovich. *Stanislavski in Rehearsal.* New York: Theatre Arts Books, 1979.

Tuska, Jon (Ed.). *Close-Up: The Contemporary Director.* Metuchen, N.J.: Scarecrow Press, 1981.

Williams, Raymond. *Drama in Performance.* New York: Basic Books, 1968.

Wills, J. Robert (Ed.). *The Director in a Changing Theatre.* Evanston, Ill.: Northwestern University Press, 1963.

PERIODS OF THEATER HISTORY

Greek and Roman Theater

Arnott, Peter D. *Greek Scenic Conventions in the Fifth Century,* B.C. New York: Oxford University Press, 1962.

Bieber, Margarete. *The History of the Greek and Roman Theatre* (2d ed.). Princeton, N.J.: Princeton University Press, 1961.

Flickinger, Roy C. *The Greek Theatre and Its Drama* (4th ed.). Chicago: University of Chicago Press, 1960.

Hamilton, Edith. *The Greek Way.* New York: W.W. Norton, 1952.

————. *The Roman Way.* New York: W.W. Norton, 1932.

Jaeger, Werner. *Paideia: The*

Ideals of Greek Culture (3 vols.). Trans. by Gilbert Highet. New York: Oxford University Press, 1939-1944.

Kitto, H.D.F. *Greek Tragedy* (2d ed.). London: Methuen, 1950.

Lucas, Frank L. *Senaca and Elizabethan Tragedy*. Cambridge, England: Cambridge University Press, 1922.

Nicoll, Allardyce. *Masks, Mimes, and Miracles*. New York: Harcourt Brace Jovanovich, 1931.

Pickard-Cambridge, A.W. *Dithyramb, Tragedy, and Comedy* (2d ed.). Revised by T.B.L. Webster. Oxford: Clarendon Press, 1968.

————. *The Dramatic Festivals of Athens* (2d ed.). Revised by John Gould and D.M. Lewis. Oxford: Clarendon Press, 1968.

————. *The Theatre of Dionysus in Athens*. Oxford: Clarendon Press, 1946.

Pallottini, Massimo. *The Etruscans* (rev. ed.). Bloomington: University of Indiana Press, 1975.

Segal, Erich. *Roman Laughter: The Comedy of Plautus*. Cambridge, Mass.: Harvard University Press, 1968.

Taplin, Oliver. *Greek Tragedy in Action*. Berkeley: University of California Press, 1978.

Vitruvius. *Ten Books of Architecture*. Translated by Morris H. Morgan. Cambridge, Mass.: Harvard University Press, 1960.

Webster, T.B.L. *Greek Theatre Production* (2d ed.). London: Methuen, 1970.

Medieval Theater

Collier, Richard J. *Poetry and Drama in the York Corpus Christi Play*. New York: Archon, 1978.

Johnston, Alexandra F. and Margaret Rogerson. *Records of Early English Dramas: York*. Toronto: University of Toronto Press, 1979.

Kolve, V.A. *The Play Called Corpus Christi*. Stanford, Ca.: Stanford University Press, 1966.

Nelson, Alan H. *The Medieval Pageants and Plays*. Chicago: University of Chicago Press, 1974.

Southern, Richard. *The Medieval Theatre in the Round*. London: Faber & Faber, 1957.

Wickham, Glynne. *Early English Stages, 1300–1660* (2 vols.). New York: Columbia University Press, 1959–1972.

Commedia dell'Arte and the Italian Renaissance

Bjurstrom, Per. *Giacomo Torelli and Baroque Stage Design*. Stockholm: Almquist and Wiksell, 1961.

Duchartre, Pierre L. *The Italian Comedy: The Improvisation, Scenarios, Lives, Attributes, Portraits and Masks of the Illustrious Characters of the Commedia dell'Arte*. Translated by R.T. Weaver. London: Harrap, 1929.

Hewitt, Barnard (Ed.). *The Renaissance Stage: Documents of Serlio, Sabbattini, and Furttenbach*. Coral Gables, Fla.: University of Miami Press, 1958.

Kernodle, George. *From Art to Theatre: Form and Convention in the Renaissance.* Chicago: University of Chicago Press, 1943.

Lea, Kathleen M. *Italian Popular Comedy: A Study of the Commedia dell'Arte, 1560–1620* (2 vols.). New York: Oxford University Press, 1934.

Nagler, Alois M. *Theatre Festivals of the Medici, 1539–1637.* New Haven, Conn.: Yale University Press, 1968.

Nicoll, Allardyce. *Stuart Masques and the Renaissance Stage.* New York: Harcourt Brace, 1937.

Smith, Winifred. *The Commedia dell'Arte.* New York: Columbia University Press, 1912.

The Shakespearean Theater

(Arden editions of Shakespeare are excellent for footnotes.)

Baldwin, T.W. *The Organization and Personnel of the Shakespearean Company.* Princeton, N.J.: Princeton University Press, 1927.

Beckerman, Bernard. *Shakespeare at the Globe, 1599–1609.* New York: Macmillan, 1962.

Bentley, Gerald E. *The Jacobean and Caroline Stage* (5 vols.). New York: Oxford University Press, 1941–1956.

———. *The Profession of Dramatist in Shakespeare's Time, 1590–1642.* Princeton, N.J.: Princeton University Press, 1971.

———. *Shakespeare: A Biographical Handbook.* New Haven, Conn.: Yale University Press, 1961.

Chambers, E.K. *The Elizabethan Stage* (4 vols.). London: Oxford University Press, 1923.

———. *A Short Life of Shakespeare.* Oxford: Clarendon, 1933.

David, Richard. *Shakespeare in the Theatre.* New York: Cambridge University Press, 1978.

(Granville-Barker, Harley. prefaces to Shakespeare's plays.)

Harbage, Alfred. *Shakespeare's Audience.* New York: Columbia University Press, 1958.

Hodges, C.W. *The Globe Restored* (2d ed.) New York: Oxford University Press, 1968.

(Holinshed, Raphael. Chronicles.)

Nagler, A.M. *Shakespeare's Stage.* New Haven, Conn.: Yale University Press, 1958.

Plays and Players (English theater magazine for reviews of modern and contemporary productions).

Reynolds, George F. *The Staging of Elizabethan Plays at the Red Ball Theatre, 1605–1625.* New York: Modern Language Association, 1940.

"Shakespeare: An Annotated Bibliography." *Shakespeare Quarterly (1924–present). (SQ* was originally called *The Shakespeare Association Bulletin.)* Annual bibliography of writings about Shakespeare.

Shakespeare Survey: An Annual Survey of Shakespearean Study and Production. New York: Macmillan, 1948–present.

Southern, Richard. *The Staging of Plays before Shakespeare.* New York: Theatre Arts Books, 1973.

Speaight, Robert. *Shakespeare on*

the Stage. New York: William
Collins Sons, 1972.
(Variorum collection—a
compilation of Shakespearean
performance.)

Theatre in France and Spain to 1700

Crawford, J.P.W. *Spanish Drama
before Lope de Vega* (rev. ed.).
Philadelphia: University of
Pennsylvania Press, 1937.
Lancaster, H.C. *A History of
French Dramatic Literature in the
Seventeenth Century* (5 vols.).
Baltimore: Johns Hopkins
Press, 1929–1942.
Lawrenson, T.E. *The French Stage
in the XVIIth Century: A Study in
the Advent of the Italian Order.*
Manchester: Manchester
University Press, 1957.
Lough, John. *Paris Theatre
Audiences in the Seventeenth and
Eighteenth Centuries.* New York:
Oxford University Press, 1957.
Turnell, Martin. *The Classical
Moment: Studies in Corneille,
Molière, and Racine.* London: H.
Hamilton, 1947.
Wilson, Margaret. *Spanish Drama
of the Golden Age.* Elmsford,
N.Y.: Pergamon, 1969.

Oriental Theater

Ambrose, Kay. *Classical Dances
and Costumes of India.* London:
A & C Black, 1950.
Ando, Tusuro. *Bunraku, the
Puppet Theatre.* New York:
Walter/Weatherhill, 1970.

Haar, Francis. *Japanese Theatre in
Highlight: A Pictorial
Commentary.* Tokyo: Charles E.
Tuttle, 1952.
Kawatake, Shigetoshi. *An
Illustrated History of Japanese
Theatre Arts.* Tokyo: Foreign
Affairs Association, 1956.
Keene, Donald. *Bunraku: The Art
of the Japanese Puppet Theatre.*
Tokyo: Kodansha
International, 1965.
Pound, Ezra, and Ernest
Fenolloso. *The Classic Noh
Theatre of Japan.* Westport,
Conn.: Greenwood Press, 1970.
Scott, A.C. *The Classical Theatre of
China.* New York: Macmillan,
1957.

English Theater 1642–1800

Boas, Frederick. *An Introduction to
Eighteenth Century Drama,
1700–1780.* New York: Oxford
University Press, 1953.
Cibber, Colley. *An Apology for the
Life of Mr. Colley Cibber.*
London: J. Watts, 1740.
Hotson, Leslie. *The Commonwealth
and Restoration Stage.*
Cambridge, Mass.: Harvard
University Press, 1928.
Krutch, Joseph W. *Comedy and
Conscience after the Restoration.*
New York: Columbia
University Press, 1949.
Nicoll, Allardyce. *History of
English Drama, 1660–1900*
(6 vols.). London: Cambridge
University Press, 1955–1959.
Southern, Richard. *The Georgian
Playhouse.* London: Pleiades
Press, 1948.

Eighteenth-Century European Theater

Bredsdorff, Elias, et al. *An Introduction to Scandinavian Literature from the Earliest Time to Our Day.* Copenhagen: E. Munksgaard, 1951.

Bruford, Walter H. *Theatre, Drama, and Audience in Goethe's Germany.* London: Routledge & Kegan Paul, 1957.

Cook, John A. *Neo-Classic Drama in Spain: Theory and Practice.* Dallas: Southern Methodist University Press, 1959.

Goldoni, Carlo. *Memoirs of Carlo Goldoni.* Translated by John Black. New York: Alfred A. Knopf, 1926.

Gozzi, Carlo. *The Memoirs of Count Carlo Gozzi* (2 vols.). Translated by J.A. Symonds. London: J.C. Nimmo, 1890.

Lancaster, H.C. *French Tragedy in the Reign of Louis XVI and the Early Years of the French Revolution, 1774–1792.* Baltimore: Johns Hopkins Press, 1945.

———. *French Tragedy in the Time of Louis XV and Voltaire, 1715–1774.* Baltimore: Johns Hopkins Press, 1950.

———. *Sunset: A History of Parisian Drama in the Last Years of Louis XIV, 1701–1715.* Baltimore: Johns Hopkins Press, 1945.

Mayor, A. Hyatt. *The Bibiena Family.* New York: H. Bittner, 1945.

Prudhoe, John. *The Theatre of Goethe and Schiller.* Oxford: Basil Blackwell & Mott, 1973.

Slonim, Marc. *Russian Theatre from the Empire to the Soviets.* Cleveland: World Publishing, 1961.

Varneke, B.V. *History of the Russian Theatre: Seventeenth through Nineteenth Century.* Translated by Boris Brasol. New York: Macmillan, 1951.

Nineteenth-Century Theater: European and American

Appleton, William W. *Madame Vestris and the London Stage.* New York: Columbia University Press, 1974.

Hewitt, Barnard. *Theatre U.S.A., 1668–1957.* New York: McGraw-Hill, 1959.

Hughes, Glenn. *A History of the American Theatre.* New York: Samuel French, 1951.

Matthews, Brander and Laurence Hutton. *Actors and Actresses of Great Britain and the United States from the Days of David Garrick to the Present Time* (5 vols.). New York: Cassell, 1886.

———. *French Dramatists of the Nineteenth Century* (5th ed.). New York: Charles Scribner, 1914.

Moody, Richard. *America Takes the Stage: Romanticism in American Drama and Theatre, 1750–1900.* Bloomington: Indiana University Press, 1955.

Quinn, Arthur H. *A History of the American Drama from the Beginning to the Civil War* (2d ed.). New York: Appleton-Century-Crofts, 1943.

Modern Drama to 1940

Antoine, Andre. *Memories of the Theatre Libre.* Translated by Marvin Carlson. Coral Gables, Fla.: University of Miami Press, 1960.

Artaud, Antonin. *The Theatre and Its Double.* Translated by Mary C. Richards. New York: Grove Press, 1959.

Appia, Adolphe. *The Work of Living Art and Man Is the Measure of All Things.* Coral Gables, Fla.: University of Miami Press, 1960.

Bentley, Eric. *The Playwright as Thinker: A Study of Drama in Modern Times.* New York: Reynal & Company, 1946.

Boleslavski, Richard. *Acting: The First Six Lessons.* New York: Theatre Arts Books, 1933.

Brockett, Oscar G. and Robert R. Findlay. *Century of Innovation: A History of European and American Theatre and Drama since 1870.* Englewood Cliffs, N.J.: Prentice-Hall, 1973.

Brustein, Robert. *The Theatre of Revolt.* Boston: Little, Brown & Co., 1964.

Clurman, Harold. *The Fervent Years: The Story of the Group Theatre in the Thirties.* New York: Hill and Wang, 1957.

Cole, Toby (Ed.). *Playwrights on Playwriting: The Meaning and Making of Modern Drama from Ibsen to Ionesco.* New York: Hill and Wang, 1961.

Craig, Edward Gordon. *On the Art of the Theatre* (2d ed.). Boston: Small, Maynard, 1924.

Esslin, Martin. *Brecht: The Man and His Work.* Garden City, N.Y.: Doubleday, 1960.

Gassner, John. *Form and Idea in the Modern Theatre.* New York: Holt, Rinehart and Winston, 1956.

Houghton, Norris. *Moscow Rehearsals: An Account of Methods of Production in the Soviet Theatre.* New York: Harcourt Brace Jovanovich, 1936.

Kirby, Michael. *Futurist Performance.* New York: E.P. Dutton, 1971.

Modern Theater since 1940

Abramson, Doris E. *Negro Playwrights in the American Theatre.* New York: Columbia University Press, 1969.

Addenbrooke, David. *The Royal Shakespeare Company: The Peter Hall Years.* London: William Kimber, 1974.

Barrault, Jean-Louis. *The Theatre of Jean-Louis Barrault.* Translated by J. Chiari. New York: Hill and Wang, 1961.

Bentley, Eric. *In Search of Theatre.* New York: Alfred A. Knopf, 1953.

Bordman, Gerald. *American Musical Theatre.* New York: Oxford University Press, 1978.

Gassner, John and Edward Quinn. *The Reader's Encyclopedia of World Drama.* New York: T.Y. Crowell, 1973.

Grotowski, Jerzy. *Towards a Poor Theatre.* New York: Simon & Schuster, 1968.

Houghton, Norris. *Return*

Engagement: A Postscript to "Moscow Rehearsals." New York: Holt, Rinehart and Winston, 1962.

Innes, Christopher. *Modern German Drama: A Study in Form.* New York: Cambridge University Press, 1979.

Kerensky, Oleg. *The New British Drama: Fourteen Playwrights since Osborne and Pinter.* New York: Taplinger, 1979.

Kerr, Walter. *Journey to the Center of the Theatre.* New York: Knopf, 1978.

Little, Stuart. *Enter Joseph Papp: In Search of a New American Theatre.* New York: Coward, McCann & Geoghegan, 1974.

Patterson, Michael. *German Theatre Today.* London: Pitman Publishing, 1976.

Schechner, Richard. *Environmental Theatre.* New York: Hawthorne Books, 1973.

Styan, J.L. *The Dark Comedy: The Development of Modern Comic Tragedy.* Cambridge, England: Cambridge University Press, 1962.

CONTEMPORARY PERIODICALS AND NEWSPAPERS

American Theatre
London Literary Supplement
Modern Drama
The New York Times
Performing Arts Journal
Plays and Players
The Drama Review (TDR)
Shakespeare Quarterly
Theater
Theatre Crafts
Theatre in Poland
Theatre Journal
Theatre Quarterly
Variety
The Village Voice

Index

Note: Page numbers in italics indicate illustrative material.